The International Relations Dictionary

THE INTERNATIONAL RELATIONS DICTIONARY

Third Edition

Jack C. Plano
Roy Olton
Western Michigan University

ABC-CLIO
Santa Barbara, California
Oxford, England

JX
1226
P55
1982

Copyright © 1982 by Jack C. Plano and Roy Olton

First edition 1969.
Second edition 1979.

Library of Congress Cataloging in Publication Data

Plano, Jack C.
    The international relations dictionary.

    (Clio dictionaries in political science)
    Includes index.
    1. International relations—Dictionaries.   I. Olton,
Roy, 1922–   II. Title.   III. Series.
JX1226.P55   1982   327'.03   82–3996
                                        AACR2

ISBN: 0–87436–332–2
ISBN: 0–87436–336–5 (pbk.)
10 9 8 7 6 5 4 3 2 1

ABC-Clio, Inc.
2040 Alameda Padre Serra, Box 4397
Santa Barbara, California 93103

Clio Press Ltd.
Woodside House, Hinksey Hill
Oxford, OX1 5BE, England

Manufactured in the United States of America

Clio Dictionaries in Political Science

SERIES STATEMENT

Language precision is the primary tool of every scientific discipline. That aphorism serves as the guideline for this series of political dictionaries. Although each book in the series relates to a specific topical or regional area in the discipline of political science, entries in the dictionaries also emphasize history, geography, economics, sociology, philosophy, and religion.

This dictionary series incorporates special features designed to help the reader overcome any language barriers that may impede a full understanding of the subject matter. For example, the concepts included in each volume were selected to complement the subject matter found in existing texts and other books. All but one volume utilize a subject matter chapter arrangement that is most useful for classroom and study purposes.

Entries in all volumes include an up-to-date definition plus a paragraph of *significance* in which the authors discuss and analyze the term's historical and current relevance. Most entries are also cross-referenced providing the reader an opportunity to seek additional information related to the subject of inquiry. A comprehensive index, found in both hard cover and paperback editions, allows the reader to locate major entries and other concepts, events, and institutions discussed within these entries.

The political and social sciences suffer more than most disciplines from semantic confusion. This is attributable, *inter alia,* to the popularization of the language, and to the focus on many diverse foreign political and social systems. This dictionary series is dedicated to overcoming some of this confusion through careful writing of thorough, accurate definitions for the central concepts, institutions, and events that comprise the basic knowledge of each of the subject fields. New titles in the series will be issued periodically, including some in related social science disciplines.

— JACK C. PLANO
Series Editor

vii

CONTENTS

A NOTE ON HOW TO USE THIS BOOK

The International Relations Dictionary is organized so that entries and supplementary data can be located in either of two ways. First, items are arranged alphabetically within subject-matter chapters. Terms relating to regional arrangements like NATO or the Arab League, for example, can be found in the chapter titled "International Organization." When doubtful about which chapter to look up, consult the general index. Page numbers for entries appear in the index in heavy black type; subsidiary concepts discussed within entries can be found in the index identified by page numbers in regular type. For study purposes, numerous entries have also been subsumed under major topical headings in the index, giving the student access to broad classes of related information.

The student can also more fully explore a topic by using the extensive cross-references provided in most entries. These may lead to materials included in the same chapter or may refer him or her to the subject matter of other chapters. Page numbers have been included in all cross-references for the convenience of the reader. A few concepts can be found as entries in more than one chapter, but in each case the definition and significance of the item is related to the subject matter of that chapter in which the entry appears.

The authors have designed the unique format of this book to offer the student a variety of useful application in the quest for information. These include its use as: (1) a *dictionary* and *reference guide* to the language of the international field; (2) a *study guide* for the introductory course in international relations; (3) a supplement to the *textbook* or to a group of paperback monographs adopted for use in international relations courses; (4) a *source of review material* for the political science major enrolled in advanced courses; and (5) a *social science aid* for use in cognate fields in such courses as international economics and military history.

PREFACE TO THE THIRD EDITION

More than a dozen years have passed since *The International Relations Dictionary* emerged to serve as a guide to the rich technical language of international relations. This new edition, like the earlier ones, contains those concepts, theories, facts, and phenomena which the authors believe to be essential to a basic understanding of the international political system.

This book is organized in a format uncommon in dictionaries. Entries are grouped into subject-matter chapters to parallel topics in most current international relations textbooks. In addition to a definition or description, each entry contains a paragraph of *significance* so that the historical roots of a term can be studied. In addition, an extensive cross-reference system is used throughout the book, offering opportunities for the reader to seek additional information. The comprehensive index and the Guide to Countries also facilitate its use as a reference work.

In the world of scholarship, precise language is truly the first scientific tool. The authors believe that the ability to communicate in common in a technical language is fundamental to an understanding of any scholarly field of study. The orientation of this book reflects the classroom experiences of its authors and their belief that emphasis should be placed on learning the basics in every introductory course. The basics in the field of international relations include those concepts, theories, and facts that contribute most to an understanding of how our international political system functions.

The entries included in this book have been systematically selected and organized to complement the subject matter typically found in leading textbooks and in course materials. Thus, the instructor or student can use the *Dictionary* as a teaching/learning supplement to a text or as a tool for unifying courses developed around individual readings. The authors have tried to incorporate relevant data accurately, but we would appreciate it if readers alert us to any sins of omission or commission. However, please note that the authors have been discriminating rather than exhaustive; we selected only those terms which we consider to be most pertinent to an understanding of the international relations field.

The authors wish to express our appreciation to the many students who over the years have challenged and excited our interest in the field of international relations. We hope that the excitement and interest have been contagious. *The International Relations Dictionary* grew out of our recognition of the need for it, made obvious by these classroom interactions. We extend our appreciation to the Clio Books staff, with special thanks to: Bonnie M. Simrell, Editor-in-Chief; John Wagner, Assistant Editor; Lloyd W. Garrison, Reviewer; Cecelia A. Albert, Assistant Editor; and Judith Brown and Michelle Fisher, Marketing Services. Finally, we wish to thank Dr. Robert W. Kaufman, Director of the University Center for Environmental Affairs, Western Michigan University, who facilitated the transfer of copyright.

— JACK C. PLANO
— ROY OLTON
Western Michigan University

GUIDE TO COUNTRIES

The International Relations Dictionary

1. Nature and Role of Foreign Policy

Balance of Power A concept that describes how states deal with the problems of national security in a context of shifting alliances and alignments. The balance system is produced by the clustering of related individual national interests in opposition to those of other states. The system originates when revisionist states threaten the security of the status quo powers. The balance-of-power concept in the relations of states can be expressed in terms of a power equation. The factors (states) on each side of the equation may be in a situation of approximate equilibrium, or one side may possess a temporary preponderance of power over the other. Because states are sovereign and seek to maximize their individual national interests, the balance of power is normally in a condition of flux. A state may also pursue a conscious balance-of-power policy as Britain did during the nineteenth century. Britain viewed her interests as best served by playing a role of "balancer" to maintain an equilibrium of power on the Continent, shifting her weight to the weaker side when the equilibrium was threatened. *See also* NEUTRALISM, p. p. 36; POWER, p. 17; REVISIONIST POLICY, p. 19; STATUS QUO POLICY, p. 20.

Significance The balance-of-power phenomenon pervades international politics and is the central feature in the power struggle. It is the net effect, or result, produced by a state system in which the independent sovereign members are free to join, or to refrain from joining, alliances and alignments as each seeks to maximize its security and to advance its national interests. The balance of power is not the conscious expression of a general

3

interest in an abstraction, such as peace, since peace may or may not serve individual national interests, depending on the time, place, and situation. The balance of power has no central organization to guide it, and the combinations of states that comprise the balance are usually characterized by shifting membership, brief duration, and limited objectives. A multiple balance of power prevailed from the seventeenth to the mid-twentieth century. It was dominated by shifting combinations of at least five great powers which tended to insure flexibility, limited objectives, and the continued existence of the participants. A simple or bipolar balance emerged after World War II, however, dominated by the Soviet Union and the United States. Such a configuration of the balance is inherently dangerous since it reduces flexibility, polarizes interests around issues that divide the superpowers, and minimizes opportunities for realignment. The fraying of Cold War alliances and the development of polycentrism on both sides of the power equation, however, seem to have brought a return to a multiple-balance configuration. The international balance-of-power mechanism, whether simple or complex, is likely to prevail unless or until worldwide political power is reorganized on a basis other than that of a decentralized system of independent sovereign states.

Bipolarity   A rigid balance-of-power system in which decisive power is polarized into two rival power centers. Bipolarity is the converse of polycentrism, which is the development of a number of power centers, allowing greater flexibility for keeping the balance system in equilibrium. The bipolar model tends to evolve when, for the sake of security needs or ideological or political dependence, states are forced to commit themselves to one side and join together within the power configuration dominated by either of the two great powers. *See also* BALANCE OF POWER, p. 3; POLYCENTRISM, p. 16.

Significance   Rigid bipolarity characterized the balance-of-power system that emerged after World War II. Two superpowers, the United States and the Soviet Union, dominated the rival military, political, economic, and social camps—the "Free World" and the Communist bloc. The monopoly of nuclear weapons held by each superpower within its camp forced all others into a position of dependence for security, and polarized the determination of questions of peace and war. Neutral states were under constant pressure from both sides to submit to superpower hegemony through alliances for protection against the allegedly aggressive designs of the rival bloc. Since the 1960s, the rigidity of the bipolar model has tended to be moderated by the impact of growing polycentrism. Contributing to the breakup of the power polarization have been such factors as the revival of political and economic nationalism, the proliferation of nuclear weapons, the weakening of hegemonic control with the realization that nuclear weapons cannot be used without risking self-destruction, and growing ideological divisions within each camp.

Capability Analysis The systematic evaluation by a state of its military, political, diplomatic, and economic abilities to achieve its national interest objectives. Before undertaking a planned initiative, decision makers analyze the capability or power potentiality of their state within the framework of the international system and relative to states directly affected. All of the major elements of state power—both tangible and intangible—may be involved in determining the feasibility of a policy. An analysis of tangible factors may include geography (relative size, location, topography, and climate), population (size, age and sex composition, and manpower reserves), natural resources (the availability of raw materials), economic strength (agricultural and industrial output), administrative organization (the nature and effectiveness of governmental machinery), and military power (the relative size, organization, equipment, training, and reserves of the armed forces). Intangible factors, always more difficult to assess than the tangible because they cannot be measured accurately, might include such considerations as national character and morale, the quality of diplomacy, relationships among the leaders of various states, and the reaction levels of states. *See also* ELEMENTS OF NATIONAL POWER, p. 169; FOREIGN POLICY, p. 7; POWER, p. 17.

Significance An effective capability analysis must involve a realistic appraisal of a state's ability to accomplish a specific objective vis à vis other states within the context of the international milieu. Capability never exists in a general or absolute sense; it is always relative to the interactions and the capabilities of other states, and to time. France's Maginot Line fortifications, for example, would have provided an impregnable defense in 1914, but in 1940 they constituted a dangerous anachronism that encouraged an erroneous analysis of French capabilities and contributed to the defeat of the French army.

Decision Makers   Those individuals in each state who exercise the powers of making and implementing foreign policy decisions. Official decision makers may be influenced—sometimes decisively—by private individuals and groups that serve as consultants or function as unofficial members of the nation's "establishment." Opinion elites and the general public may also affect foreign policy actions by setting limits on the decision makers through support for some policies and rejection of others. In most states, the chief of government—whether his title is president, prime minister, premier, or chairman—plays the key role in the decision process. In others, the highest decision maker may be the leader of the single party that controls power, as in many communist states, or the dictator or oligarchs who hold no official position but control the decision process, as in some Fascist states. Others who function as high-ranking decision makers in most states include the minister of foreign affairs, sometimes called secretary of state, and the bureaucracy that functions under his direction in the state's foreign office. Other ministries, particularly defense, and high military officers contribute to decision making. In many democratic states, key legislators of the majority party or coalition also play a role in making foreign policy decisions, and in some—such as the United States—leaders of the opposition party or parties may also participate in the process. *See also* FOREIGN OFFICE, p. 7; PUBLIC OPINION, p. 78.

Significance   In international politics, although states are the actors, it is human beings in their role of decision makers who act and react to the stimuli of the international environment. It is individuals, not abstract entities called states, who define and interpret the concept of national interest, that plan strategies, that perceive issues, that make decisions to act, and that evaluate actions undertaken. As a result, psychological factors are crucial in the decision process, since individuals tend to act and react differently to the same kinds of stimuli. Changes in governmental personnel, consequently, may result in new approaches to foreign policy problems. In those states where officials holding the formal powers to make decisions are not the actual decision makers, however, changes in governments or officials may not influence policy decisions. In addition, all decision makers are conditioned and limited in their actions by the domestic and international environment related to specific decisions or to the process of making them.

Foreign Office   An executive agency charged with the formulation and implementation of foreign policy. Other names for the foreign office include foreign ministry, ministry of foreign affairs, and department of state. Foreign offices are presided over by a foreign secretary, foreign minister, or secretary of state. In large states, foreign offices tend to be organized on both geographical and functional lines. *See also* BRITAIN: FOREIGN SECRETARY, p. 410; DECISION MAKERS, p. 6; FRANCE: MINISTER OF FOREIGN AFFAIRS, p. 434; SECRETARY OF STATE, p. 402.

Significance   The foreign office of any state is the vehicle through which the bulk of relations with other countries is conducted. It is in the foreign office that reports from diplomats in the field are received, collated, and evaluated as the raw materials of foreign policy. It is also in the foreign office that policy instructions are drafted and dispatched to the diplomat in the field. Once relatively small operations, foreign offices in the major states have become huge bureaucratic institutions employing thousands of persons at home and abroad. Formerly, foreign office personnel were amateurs recruited haphazardly. The complexity, diversity, and volume of interstate relations in the modern world, however, require increasingly higher degrees of education, selectivity, training, and professionalism.

Foreign Policy   A strategy or planned course of action developed by the decision makers of a state vis à vis other states or international entities, aimed at achieving specific goals defined in terms of national interest. A specific foreign policy carried on by a state may be the result of an initiative by that state or may be a reaction to initiatives undertaken by other states. Foreign policy involves a dynamic process of applying relatively fixed interpretations of national interest to the highly fluctuating situational factors of the international environment in order to develop a course of action, followed by efforts to achieve diplomatic implementation of the policy guidelines. Major steps in the foreign policy process include: (1) translating national interest considerations into specific goals and objectives; (2) determining the international and domestic situational factors related to the policy goals; (3) analyzing the state's capabilities for achieving the desired results; (4) developing a plan or strategy for using the state's capabilities to deal with the variables in pursuit of the goals; (5) undertaking the requisite actions; and (6) periodically reviewing and evaluating progress made toward the achievement of the desired results. The process seldom proceeds logically and chronologically; often several steps in the process may be carried on simultaneously, and fundamental issues may be reopened when conditions change or setbacks occur. Because the international situation is in constant flux, the policy process is continuous.

Significance   Foreign policy, although it cannot be wholly separated from domestic policy, has assumed a major role in the decision processes carried on by most states. In general, the more powerful states devote far greater efforts and resources to the development and implementation of foreign policy than the medium-sized or small powers. Although often used in a generic sense to encompass all foreign programs carried on by a state, the term "foreign policy" can be applied more precisely to describe a single situation and the actions of a state to accomplish a limited objective. A state, consequently, must pursue numerous policies, identify many goals, map out various strategies, evaluate different kinds of capabilities, and initiate and evaluate specific decisions and actions. A semblance of coordination must be maintained among policies so that all planning and actions fall within the broad framework of national interest guidelines. Most such activities are carried on within a state's foreign ministry by a foreign secretary or secretary of state through a bureaucracy divided into regional and country units. Foreign policy actions are difficult to evaluate because (1) short-range advantages or disadvantages must be weighed in relation to long-range consequences; (2) their impact on other nations is difficult to evaluate; (3) most policies result in a mixture of successes and failures that are hard to disentangle.

Foreign Policy Objectives   The ends which foreign policy is designed to achieve. Foreign policy objectives are concrete formulations derived by relating the national interest to the prevailing international situation and to the power available to the state. The objectives are selected by decision makers seeking to change (revisionist policy) or to preserve (status quo policy) a particular state of affairs in the international environment. *See also* CAPABILITY ANALYSIS, p. 5; NATIONAL INTEREST, p. 9; SITUATIONAL FACTORS, p. 20.

Significance   Foreign policy objectives are produced from an analysis of ends and means. Logically, the ends sought should determine the means selected for their achievement. Where several courses of action are feasible, the one that will most clearly advance the national interest should be adopted. The reverse situation sometimes prevails, however, and the means available may determine what objective a state ought to seek, just as events sometimes seem to outrun policy. Although concrete foreign policy objectives vary from state to state, they tend to involve such abstract goals as self-preservation, security, national well-being, national prestige, the protection and advancement of ideology, and the pursuit of power.

National Interest   The fundamental objective and ultimate determinant that guides the decision makers of a state in making foreign policy. The national interest of a state is typically a highly generalized conception of those elements that constitute the state's most vital needs. These include self-preservation, independence, territorial integrity, military security, and economic well-being. Because no single *interest* dominates the policymaking functions of a government, the concept might more accurately be referred to in the plural, as *national interests*. When a state bases its foreign policy solely on the bedrock of national interest with little or no concern for universal moral principles, it can be described as pursuing a realistic, in contradistinction to an idealistic, policy. *See also* FOREIGN POLICY, p. 7.

Significance   Each of the more than 160 nations in the contemporary state system interacts with other members as it develops policies and carries on diplomatic actions in pursuit of its subjectively defined national interest. When their interests are harmonious, states often act in concert to solve mutual problems; when their interests conflict, however, competition, rivalry, tension, fear, and ultimately war may result. Techniques developed in the state system to reconcile conflicts of national interest include diplomacy, peaceful settlement, international law, regional organizations, and global institutions, such as the United Nations and its agencies. The key problem of foreign policy making and diplomacy is that of translating the relatively vague and general interests of a nation into concrete, precise objectives and means. Although decision makers must deal with many variables in the international milieu, the concept of national interest usually remains the most constant factor and serves as a guidepost for decision makers in the policy process.

National Style   The characteristic behavior patterns of a state as it attempts to deal with its foreign policy problems. National style can be described as a function of ideological values, common historical experiences, traditions, and precedents. Thus, in established countries, a change in regime is not likely to result in a drastically altered approach to international problems. The effort can be made, however, consciously and explicitly to alter the national style. Under the constitution of the Fifth French Republic, for example, the personalized executive leadership of President Charles de Gaulle weakened legislative dominance in French national life. In the developing countries, by definition, national styles are being created and evolving.

Significance   Ascertaining the national style of another country may prove helpful as a guide in the conduct of relations with that country. That a country has a characteristic style, however, is no guarantee that it will always act in a predictable fashion. Situational factors related to a specific problem may be similar over time but are never exactly the same. Nevertheless, in the diplomatic arena, where the variables are not subject to scientific controls, no guide to action and reaction should be overlooked.

Nonaligned Movement   A large group of nations (95 in 1981) that actively refuses to be politically or militarily associated with either the West or the Soviet bloc. The nonaligned movement had its roots in Bandung, Indonesia, where leaders of twenty-five Asian and African countries met in 1955 and proclaimed themselves to be a third force in world affairs. Marshal Josip Broz Tito of Yugoslavia and Prime Minister Pandit Jawaharlal Nehru of India emerged as the leaders of the new movement. At its first formal Conference of Nonaligned Countries held in Belgrade in 1961, the participants adopted a definition of nonalignment which states that a nonaligned country must "1) pursue an independent policy based on peaceful coexistence; 2) not participate in any multilateral military alliance . . . ; 3) support liberation and independence movements; and 4) not participate in bilateral military alliances with the Great Powers." *See also* THIRD WORLD, p. 21.

Significance   The nonaligned movement received its impetus from the desire of many Third World nations to remain aloof from East-West conflicts; the movement is now a formal organization. In its early days, the nonaligned movement also had the practical advantage of placing participants in a position to bargain for assistance from both sides in the Cold War. Six nonaligned summit conferences have been held: Belgrade (1961); Cairo (1964); Lusaka (1970); Algiers (1973); Colombo (1976); and Havana (1979). Many developing nations of the Third World have refused to participate in the Conferences of the Nonaligned Countries, some because they are involved in military alliances with great powers and others because they find little value in taking a neutral posture. By agreement reached in Belgrade in 1961, Conferences of Nonaligned Countries will be held every three years.

North-South Relations   The continuing political, economic, and social relationship between the industrialized, developed countries (the "North") and, largely poor, developing countries (the "South"). The term *North-South relations* is used to describe this relationship because most of the rich, developed countries are located geographically north of the Third and Fourth World countries. Countries of the South are mainly African, Asian, and Latin American, whereas countries of the North are European, North American, Japanese, and Oceanic. The North develops joint policies and approaches through organizations such as the twenty-four-member Organization for Economic Cooperation and Development (OECD). The South for its part coordinates policies and develops a common approach largely through the workings of the Group of Seventy-Seven (G77), which functions as a caucus for the approximately 120 nations of the South. In the United Nations General Assembly and other principal organs, the long-standing East-West Cold War conflict gave way in the 1970s and 1980s to a continuing North-South dialogue as a result of the growing political power of the developing states. *See also* INTERNATIONAL DEVELOPMENT ASSOCIATION (IDA), p. 134; NEW INTERNATIONAL ECONOMIC ORDER (NIEO), p. 140; UNITED NATIONS CONFERENCE ON TRADE AND DEVELOPMENT (UNCTAD), p. 153.

Significance   The North has been mainly concerned with keeping countries of the South free from Soviet influence and open to trade and investment by private companies, mostly multinationals. The South has been primarily concerned about achieving economic development and modernization, ending colonialism and neo-colonialism, and protecting human rights, especially by ending racial discrimination. In foreign aid to the South, the North has preferred to offer technical assistance and infrastructure aid, leaving actual development in the hands of private capital, especially those of multinational corporations. The South, on the other hand, prefers grants and low-interest loans, increased trade, and higher prices for their raw materials as means for obtaining the capital to produce economic growth. To improve their position vis à vis the North, countries of the South have campaigned over the years for programs that would better meet their economic needs. These campaigns have included: (1) the Special United Nations Fund for Economic Development (SUNFED) proposal in the United Nations to set up a huge capital fund from which the South could receive grants or obtain low interest loans; (2) the establishment of the United Nations Conference on Trade and Development (UNCTAD) to increase the South's export trade with the North so as to earn more capital for development; (3) the creation of the International Development Association (IDA) as an affiliate of the World Bank, to grant soft loans (no interest charged and fifty years to repay); and (4) the creation of a New International Economic Order (NIEO), which would replace the existing world economic system with a new one in which the nations of the South would receive fairer treatment and higher prices for their commodities. These and other campaigns aimed at improving the South's opportunities to develop and modernize have generally failed because of the refusal of the North to participate or, in some cases, giving only half-hearted support. In the case of SUNFED, for example, after a campaign of many years the South finally had the votes to secure a two-thirds majority in the General Assembly. Using this power, the South created a SUNFED-type United Nations Capital Development Fund (UNCDF) to disburse grants and loans of capital, but the North declined to contribute to the new fund. This case demonstrates that, in North-South relations, the South has achieved the ability through sheer numbers to garner the votes, but it lacks the ability to compel the North to honor the decisions of the voting majority and to give full support to them.

Patterns of Power   The ways in which individual states organize and use their power to maximize their security and achieve their national interests in competition with other states.

The patterns of power involve the characteristic responses available to the state in an international system in which the power of other states represents an actual or potential threat. The patterns include: (1) unilateralism—dependence on one's own power; (2) alliances—the power configuration of group against group; (3) collective security—a universalized power system of "one for all, and all for one"; and (4) world government—a cooperative federal structure, or a world empire dominated by one government. *See also* CAPABILITY ANALYSIS, p. 5; PATTERNS OF POWER, pp. 12–16; POWER, p. 17.

Significance The patterns of power offer options to decision makers who must cope with a state system that acknowledges sovereignty as its central feature. Sovereignty involves the power of the state to make final decisions, and a state system so organized implies that the use of power is spread among the states and, consequently, each state may constitute a threat to every other state. Each, therefore, must use its power to meet potential threats by pursuing policies through one or more of the available patterns. The choice will hinge on the state's formulation of its national interest, its perception of the interests of other states, and its assessment of its own power compared to the power of other states in a specific time, place, and situation. The choice for the patterns of unilateralism or alliances implies a decision to operate within the state system as it exists. The choice for collective security or a form of world government implies a decision to seek security by changing the nature of the state system, since these patterns require the diminution or elimination of individual state sovereignty.

Patterns of Power: Alliances A configuration of power wherein the state seeks security and the opportunity to advance its national interests by linking its power with that of one or more states with similar interests. The alliance pattern implies a decision by a state to alter or maintain a local, regional, or global power equilibrium. Such action is usually followed by the other side's also seeking alliance partners. Thus the alliance pattern presents the typical appearance of bloc versus bloc. The pattern is most often established by formal treaties of alliance, but less formal understandings or ententes are also possible. *See also* ALLIANCE, p. 158.

Significance The pattern of alliances is currently the most widely used technique by which states augment their individual national powers in the interest of national security. Some critics, like Woodrow Wilson, have argued that the balancing of power by means of military alliances is counterproductive in that it actually encourages war and is ultimately antithetical to security. This is often explained in terms of a security-insecurity paradox: when one state increases its security with an alliance, the security of the other side is weakened, thereby leading to efforts to strengthen it. Thus a cyclical heightening of tensions is instituted; now, in the nuclear age it is common to speak of this pattern as the "balance of terror." However, the alliance pattern continues to be followed in spite of its limitations, because of: (1) the limitations of unilateralism in an increasingly technological era; (2) the failure of the state system to establish the conditions essential for the operation of either a universal collective security system or a cooperative system of world government; and (3) the dangers inherent in any single state attempting to dominate the world by force.

Patterns of Power: Collective Security   A power system in which each state of the world would guarantee the security and independence of every other state. The key to the collective security pattern is universality of participation and obligation. Under these conditions, an aggressor nation would have to expect to face the united oppositon of the entire community. This fundamental assumption was written into the Covenant of the League of Nations and the Charter of the United Nations, the only two efforts thus far to create functioning systems of collective security. The term *collective security* sometimes is used inaccurately to describe regional or bloc security arrangements. Such groupings as NATO, the Warsaw Pact, and the Rio Pact are often referred to as regional collective security arrangements; not only are they permitted by the United Nations Charter, they are available for use at the direction of the United Nations. The concept of regional collective security arrangements is a contradiction in terms since it does not fulfill the requirement of universality. These organizations are examples of the pattern of alliances and not the pattern of collective security. *See also* COLLECTIVE SECURITY, p. 301.

Significance   Actually, collective security is only a theoretical pattern of power. As an idea, it has excited the attention of statesmen and scholars since World War I, but in fact such a security system has never operated. The League of Nations system never fulfilled the requirement of universality; even the great powers were not all under the same obligation at the same time. The United Nations system has not yet been able to establish great-power unanimity on the exact nature of the status quo to be maintained by the system. As a result, the ideal of collective security is given lip service, while reliance for security continues to be placed on self-help and balance-of-power alliances.

Patterns of Power: Unilateralism   A policy whereby a state depends completely on its own resources for security and the advancement of its national interest. Unilateralism can take a variety of forms: (1) Isolationism or neo-isolationism implies a decision not to participate in or to severely limit participation in international relations. (2) Neutrality involves giving up, by unilateral act or by treaty, the option of military participation in international affairs unless attacked. (3) States that participate actively in international politics but which rely on their own wits and strength are also engaged in unilateralism. (4) Nonalignment describes the current disinclination, mainly among the developing countries, to commit themselves exclusively to the interests of one great power.

Significance   Unilateralism, once the most common pattern of power, has become increasingly difficult to pursue. Historically, it has been most successful for states well-placed geographically but hard to reach with existing methods of transportation, communication, and military technology. Britain, Japan, and the United States are classic examples of states that benefited from this techno-geographical situation for a long time. States in continental Europe do not enjoy the same advantage, but formerly they entered into alliances only on a temporary and emergency basis, because the military technology available then allowed sufficient time to make arrangements after a threat arose or even after a war had begun. The industrial, scientific, and technological revolutions, however, have made unilateralism less attractive for maximizing security and advancing the national interest. The motorization of land and sea travel and the development of the airplane and the rocket have made states more readily accessible to one another; distance no longer offers protection. Also, science has increased the economic cost and the destructiveness of arms and warfare so much that most states are increasingly hard-pressed to undertake their own defense unaided. For these reasons, reliance on unilateralism has declined, and states are increasingly dependent on regional security through alliances.

Patterns of Power: World Government   The concentration in a single supranational authority of a monopoly of force and the power to make policies binding on individual states and their citizens. World government requires the surrender of sovereignty as it is now exercised by nation-states. It is theoretically possible to create such a superstate either through military conquest or by cooperative effort. The ancient Roman Empire is the closest historical example of a successful effort at world government by conquest. Later attempts at world conquest by Napoleon and by Adolf Hitler fell far short of the Roman experience. No effort has ever been made to establish a world government by peaceful international cooperation. *See also* WORLD GOVERNMENT, p. 363.

Significance   The world government pattern would solve the international power problem by eliminating the international sovereign state system. In the atomic age, any effort to create a world government by coercive power would be likely to trigger mutual annihilation. The only other alternative is a form of world federation. The suggestion that the United Nations be converted into a world government indicates lack of understanding of the nature of that organization. The United Nations is a confederation in which certain limited powers have been conferred on the central body. Sovereignty, however, continues to reside in each individual member. In a federation, sovereignty resides in the collectivity and each individual unit is subordinate to the authority of the whole. Because states in the international community do not agree on fundamental values, the states of the world are not willing to contemplate such a surrender of sovereignty. The writing of a world constitution is not the answer. Constitutions do not create mutual trust, they are its product. It is arguable, however, that a world government might evolve out of wider regional agreements, perhaps based on the model of the European Community. Cooperative government at the world level, however, is impossible until advocates of diverse ideologies are able to agree on a definition of the common good, and until international cooperation transcends national loyalty.

Polycentrism   An international balance-of-power situation characterized by a number of power centers. Polycentrism, or a flexible balance, is reminiscent of the nineteenth century in that it is composed of a number of active participants. It has replaced the post-World War II bipolar balance controlled by the Soviet

Union and the United States. *See also* BIPOLARITY, p. 4; TITOISM, p. 49.

Significance The return to polycentrism has meant the breakdown of United States and Soviet domination of international politics within a bipolar system of rival alliances. Causal factors have included: (1) the nuclear "balance of terror" between the United States and the Soviet Union, which has reduced the credibility of their promises to defend their allies; (2) intra-alliance differences, such as those between France and the United States, over the nature of the status quo; (3) economic prosperity in Eastern and Western Europe with a consequent lessening of economic dependence on the Soviet Union and the United States; (4) the resurgence of nationalism in old and new countries alike; and (5) the emergence of a large number of new states, whose leaders see their national interests in economic, social, and political modernization rather than in terms of Cold War rivalry. Polycentrism means that an increasing number of states are able to make independent decisions that affect the level of tension in the world.

Power Influence and control exercised by one nation over others. Power is both the means used and the goal sought by states in political, military, economic, and social competition with each other. Although not every state action is motivated by power considerations, those directly related to enhancing or defending the national interest are always deeply involved in power politics. The exercise and pursuit of power is carried on by decision makers who use the governmental machinery of the state to develop and implement foreign policy. Political power, therefore, involves a psychological relationship between elites who exercise it, and those who are influenced or controlled by it. The exercise of power takes many forms including persuasion, ideological and psychological warfare, economic coercion, moral suasion, cultural imperialism, legally recognized measures short of war, and, ultimately, war. *See also* CAPABILITY ANALYSIS, p. 5; ELEMENTS OF NATIONAL POWER, p. 169.

Significance The exercise of political power has been the central feature of the state system since the emergence of the concept of sovereignty. Major states have always exercised and sought power more frequently and more effectively than smaller states, with the success for each policy dependent upon the relative capabilities of the state. As one state seeks more power, however, those nations threatened or attacked by its policies react by building up their own power. The power of states that act most aggressively, therefore, tends to be brought under control by the development of countervailing power on the part of those threatened, resulting in the evolution of a balance of power. In addition, there are institutional restraints on the exercise of power in the state system: international law, world opinion, disarmament and arms control agreements, and collective security arrangements such as the United Nations system.

Realist-Idealist Dichotomy   Alternative approaches of decision makers in forming foreign policy. The realist approach to policymaking is fundamentally empirical and pragmatic, whereas the idealist approach is based on abstract traditional foreign policy principles involving international norms, legal codes, and moral-ethical values. The realist school starts with the assumption that the key factor prevalent in all international relationships is power. The wise and efficient use of power by a state in pursuit of its national interest is, therefore, the main ingredient of a successful foreign policy. The idealist, on the other hand, believes that foreign policies based on moral principles are more effective because they promote unity and cooperation among states rather than competition and conflict. Moral power, according to the idealist, is more effective than physical power because it is more durable. It involves not force and coercion but winning over the minds and allegiances of people to accept principles that ought to govern state conduct. *See also* FOREIGN POLICY, p. 7; FOURTEEN POINTS, p. 73; MACHIAVELLIAN DIPLOMACY, p. 239.

Significance   The realist-idealist dichotomy relates particularly to the debates over the "best" approach to foreign policymaking in the United States. Many realists regard the United States as the leading, if not the only, state in the world misled by popular attitudes and moral self-righteousness into adopting idealistic guidelines to govern the making of foreign policy decisions. The result, according to the realists, is the inability of the United States to compete effectively with other states that base their policies on the hard realities of national self-interest. Idealists tend to reject the power-centered realist approach as a pseudoscientific Machiavellianism likely to produce only minor, short-lived gains for the nation. For the idealists, the most successful policies have been based on principles and moral values, and have won support from millions of peoples of different nations. Examples of successful idealist approaches include the Fourteen Points enunciated by Woodrow Wilson, the Atlantic Charter proclaimed by Franklin Roosevelt and Winston Churchill, and the United Nations Charter. In practice, most policies are a mixture of realism and idealism, in which the realist approach specifies the means for achieving goals and the idealist approach justifies and wins support for the policies adopted.

Revisionist Policy   Any foreign policy by which a state seeks to alter the existing international territorial, ideological, or power distribution to its advantage. A revisionist policy is basically expansionist and acquisitive in nature; hence a state will be likely to pursue such a policy if its decision makers are dissatisfied with the status quo and believe that the state has the ability to achieve its objectives. *See also* BALANCE OF POWER, p. 3; STATUS QUO POLICY, p. 20.

Significance   A revisionist policy is pursued, typically, by a "have not" or "unsatiated" state that seeks to improve its relative international position by undertaking strategic initiatives. Although it uses various nonbelligerent offensive tactics in seeking its objectives, ultimately a revisionist state may commit acts of aggression or declare war in its effort to change the status quo. Revisionism by its very nature tends to produce defensive policies in status quo states. The power alignments that result from revisionist-status quo divisions among states encourage the formation of alliances and counteralliances and the emergence of a balance-of-power system. Revisionist states tend to view diplomacy, treaties, international law, and international organizations as means for gaining advantages in the power struggle rather than for ameliorating conflicts and resolving issues. Nazi Germany, for example, revised its power and territorial status during the 1930s by rearming in violation of the Versailles treaty, by carrying out numerous acts of duplicity, by threatening war, by exerting political pressures on weak governments, and by winning diplomatic victories such as the Munich Agreement of 1938. When these tactics were no longer successful, Adolf Hitler took his nation into war against the status quo bloc.

Situational Factors   The international and national variables considered by decision makers when making foreign policy. Situational factors include: (1) the general international setting or environment, including the attitudes, actions, and national interest considerations of policy officials in other states; (2) the relative power or capability of the state as calculated by its decision makers; and (3) the specific actions and reactions undertaken by other states related to the policy decision and its execution. *See also* CAPABILITY ANALYSIS, p. 5; FOREIGN POLICY, p. 7.

Significance   Analysis of situational factors that influence decisions is a crucial stage in the foreign policy process. Although no policymaker is capable of recognizing or analyzing all such factors that may impinge upon the decision process, identifying and understanding the more crucial ones and their relationship to the means and objectives of the state increase the chances for success. Still, because situational factors remain largely imponderables, incomplete and incapable of precise measurement, the foreign policy process is more of an art than a science. The judgments of decision makers consequently must often be based on fragmentary knowledge and subjective evaluation of available data.

Status Quo Policy   Any foreign policy aimed at maintaining the existing international territorial, ideological, or power distribution. A status quo policy is basically conservative and defensive in nature; hence, a state will pursue such a policy if it enjoys an advantageous position in world politics and seeks stability rather than change, so as to maximize its existing advantages. *See also* REVISIONIST POLICY, p. 19.

Significance   A defensive status quo policy is pursued, typically, by a "satiated" or "have" state or bloc in direct opposition to an offensive or revisionist policy carried on by a "have not" or expansionist state or bloc. The power alignments that emerge out of status quo-revisionist divisions among states encourage the formation of alliances and counteralliances and the development of a balance-of-power system. Status quo states tend to react to the initiatives of revisionist states, avoid open conflict or escalation of military actions, emphasize orderly diplomatic procedures, and seek to achieve negotiated agreements that will leave them in possession of whatever advantages they enjoyed prior to the emergence of the rival bloc. International law as a conservative force in world affairs is frequently invoked by status quo states to defend existing rights. In the contemporary world, more than forty states are allied militarily with the United States to defend the status quo by deterring aggression or other forms of violent, revolutionary change initiated by revisionist states. The Soviets, for instance, define the status quo in the world in terms of indigenous revolutionary change toward the Marxist-inspired historical victory of communism. Unlike most status quo-revisionist configurations, each side in the great power rivalry regards the other as an imperialist threat to its subjectively defined status quo interests.

Third World   The economically underdeveloped and developing countries. The Third World differs from the First World (the United States and its industrialized allies and partners) and the Second World (the Soviet Union and its East European adherents). The United Nations now identifies a Fourth World composed of those countries with an exceptionally small annual per capita income.

Significance   Almost one hundred countries, containing the majority of the world's population, have achieved independent status since World War II. Most are poor, weak, and inexperienced. Typically, they produce primary and semifinished products and their population growth impedes economic progress (measured by living standards in already developed countries). With a majority in the General Assembly of the United Nations, these countries—organized as a caucusing bloc called the Group of Seventy-Seven (G77)—increasingly control the agenda to focus attention on their concerns and demands. First organized as nonaligned states in the Cold War, these countries continue to meet from time to time but concerted action is difficult to achieve given the size of the group and the diversity and complexity of the interests involved. Cuba hosted the Nonaligned Conference of 1979. Most but not all Third World countries participate in the Nonaligned Movement.

2. Nationalism, Imperialism, and Colonialism

Apartheid (Apartness) The Republic of South Africa's official policy of racial segregation established through openly discriminatory legislation. The policy is designed to perpetuate continued control of the state by the European (white) minority. South Africa's population of about 28 million is approximately 70 percent African (black), 20 percent European (white), 10 percent Colored (mixed), and 3 percent Asian. South Africa is an economically developed country that produces about one-third of Africa's total income with only about 4 percent of the land and 6 percent of the population.

Significance The harshness of white rule has led to violence that threatens to become a blood bath at any time. External opposition led by the Afro-Asian nations raises the specter of foreign intervention and keeps the South African situation a live issue at the United Nations. Although *apartheid* stands condemned by world opinion, the economy continues to grow. All efforts to produce meaningful economic sanctions have failed thus far. Growing internal and external frustrations threaten regional and perhaps world peace.

Charismatic Leadership Leadership characterized by a mystical or spiritual messianic quality that elicits widespread emotional popular support often bordering on reverence. Charismatic leadership tends to merge with the spirit of nationalism and to become identified with, or symbolic of, the state itself. The charismatic leader, particularly in newly emergent

23

nations, appears to his followers to be the personification of truth, one who is beyond the fears and ambitions of ordinary mortals, and is the chosen instrument for the realization of the nation's destiny. In this sense qualities of charismatic leadership were found in such dominant personalities as Jawaharlal Nehru of India, Mao Tse-tung of China, Sukarno of Indonesia, Nkrumah of Ghana, Nasser of Egypt, and Kenyatta of Kenya. *See also* NATIONALISM, p. 33.

Significance   Charismatic leadership is a phenomenon often associated with nation building and the growth of national consciousness. It is particularly observable in the transitional societies of developing countries still characterized by illiteracy, poverty, and the absence of a tradition of institutionalized representative government. In such situations, this type of leadership may be benevolent and paternalistic. As rising expectations put increased demands on the regime, however, the temptation to resort to the authoritarian imposition of values and solutions to problems may prove irresistible, and a highly personalized dictatorship may result. When the ruler turns to increasingly oppressive measures or loses his symbolic character as the leader of the revolution, *coups d'etat* may follow, as in the cases of Ghana and Indonesia.

Chauvinism   Extravagant, demonstrative superpatriotism. Chauvinism implies uncritical devotion to the state, extreme jealousy of its honor, and an exaggerated sense of its glory. The term is derived from the name of Nicolas Chauvin, a Napoleonic soldier who was notorious for his unrestrained devotion to his leader and the Empire. Chauvinism can be described as an extreme form of nationalism that holds that the state can do no wrong. *See also* NATIONALISM, p. 33.

Significance   Chauvinism is particularly dangerous in an age of total war and nuclear destruction. Superpatriotism, by its excessive concern with and glorification of one nation-state, tends to become myopic. It can unnecessarily intensify international problems by failing to take account of the rights and interests of other states, or by riding roughshod over them. Chauvinism may also involve an unrealistic fear for the security of the state, particularly in a time of profound international ideological cleavage. A state preparing for war—as in the case of

Nazi Germany in the 1930s—may use chauvinism to unite the people and to secure the sacrifices needed to gird the nation for battle.

Colonialism   The rule of an area and its people by an external sovereignty pursuing a policy of imperialism. Historically, two broad types of colonialism can be identified: (1) that which involved the transplanting of emigrants from the mother country to form a new political entity at a distant location; and (2) that which involved the imposition of rule over the technologically less-developed indigenous peoples of Asia and Africa. In either case, the colony was established to advance the military security, economic advantage, and international prestige of the imperial power. *See also* DEPENDENT TERRITORY: COLONY, p. 26; IMPERIALISM, p. 29.

Significance   Opposition to the superior-inferior relationship and the racialism inherent in colonialism gave rise to a nationalism among dependent peoples of Asia and Africa that proved to be an irresistible force in world politics after World War II. The war demonstrated that white, Western imperialists possessed no inherent invincibility: witness the early victories of the Japanese forces. Many of the colonial powers in Asia were exhausted by the war to such a point that they granted independence either voluntarily or as a result of violence. Independence movements were encouraged by principles enunciated in the Declaration Regarding Non-Self-Governing Territories of the United Nations Charter that served to legitimate their aspirations for nationhood. By 1960, the emergence of new nations had doubled the membership of the United Nations, which strengthened the assault on colonialism. In that year, the Assembly adopted the historic Declaration on the Granting of Independence to Colonial Countries and Peoples and, in the following year, established a special Committee on Decolonization to implement its principles. The wave of independence movements that had started in Asia swept over Africa in the late 1950s and in the 1960s, adding over thirty new nations to the state system. The Portuguese territories of Angola, Mozambique, and Portuguese Guinea, along with the League of Nations-mandated territory of South-West Africa, were some major objectives of United Nations decolonization efforts. With a numerical majority in the General Assembly, the former colonial states have directed the focus of United Nations attention to the problems of political, social, and economic development. The concept of neo-colonialism, however, symbolizes their ambivalence in seeking assistance from their former colonial masters while at the same time rejecting any real or imagined interference in their internal affairs. Yet the transformation of over one billion people and numerous colonial territories to independence and statehood that has occurred is one of the most remarkable phenomena of the post-World War II period. But the emergence of national independence has often meant that majority groups have willingly or unwillingly forced minority groups to accept the sovereignty of the new state. The aspirations of minority national groups remain one of the most intractable problems in the search for international peace and stability in the Middle East (Palestinians), in Southeast Asia (Cambodians), and in many of the new states of Africa.

Dependent Territory: Colony   A noncontiguous territorial possession of a sovereign state. Colonies have been established by settlement, cession, and conquest, and their acquisition marks the successful pursuit of a policy of imperialism. Early in the twentieth century, much of Asia and almost all of the continent of Africa had been carved up into colonies by Britain, France, Belgium, Germany, Italy, Spain, Portugal, and the Netherlands. Colonies differ from other dependent territories—such as protectorates, spheres of influence, and leaseholds—in that the imperial power possesses full sovereignty over a colony. *See also* COLONIALISM, p. 25; IMPERIALISM, p. 29.

Significance   Colonies served the imperial powers as markets for manufacturers, sources of raw materials and investment opportunities, strategic locations and sources of manpower for national defense, and as symbols of prestige and great-power status. In the process of holding and administering their colonies, however, the metropolitan powers brought dependent peoples literacy, education, an ability to compare their conditions with other societies of the world, and nationalism, which created increasing dissatisfaction with continued subordinate status. Since World War II almost all colonies have become independent states either by peaceful negotiation with the imperial power, by force, or by some combination of the two.

Dependent Territory: Leasehold   An area used by a foreign state under a lease agreement with the territorial sovereign. Leaseholds may be of short or long duration, and the extent of authority exercised by the lessee is established by specific agreement in each instance. Such lease agreements have been concluded freely or under various degrees of duress. By the leasehold technique, for example, major European powers acquired economic rights in China during the nineteenth century.

Significance   As concessions to a foreign power, leaseholds are sources of tension and conflict in this age of rampant nationalism. Illustrations of leaseholds include the British lease of Kowloon (opposite Hong Kong), and the American leases of Guantánamo Bay (in Cuba) and, until 1979, the Panama Canal Zone. To nationalists, leaseholds restrict the free exercise of territorial sovereignty and thereby imply an unacceptable superior-inferior relationship.

Dependent Territory: Protectorate   A relationship between a strong state and a semisovereign state, or an area or people not recognized as a state. Protectorates have been established voluntarily and by force, normally either to thwart the interests of third states, or to provide for the administration of law and order in territory over which no responsible government exists. The term "protectorate" also applies to the country under protection. The extent to which the alien government exercises sovereign powers in the protectorate is controlled by treaty between the parties.

Significance   The protectorate is a device whereby a powerful state can exercise various degrees of control in another area without actually annexing it. Usually the protector at least exercises control over foreign affairs and national defense. In the late nineteenth and early twentieth centuries, for example, France established protectorates over Tunisia and portions of Morocco, Britain entered into a similar agreement with Egypt, Japan with Korea, and the United States with Cuba. To provide for the establishment of law and order, Britain created protectorates in the territories adjacent to her colonies in Gambia and Sierra Leone. Protectorates are rapidly disappearing in an age when nationalism makes people unwilling to accept a subservient status.

Dependent Territory: Sphere of Influence An area dominated by the national interests of a foreign power. In a sphere of influence, the foreign power does not possess sovereignty but imposes on the area an international servitude that restricts the free exercise of local territorial sovereignty. Such servitudes may be positive, as when the dominant state is granted a monopoly of commercial exploitation, or negative, as when the weaker state is required to refrain from fortifying a common border.

Significance Spheres of influence, created with or without the voluntary agreements of the territorial sovereign, have usually been conceded by third states on a *quid pro quo* basis. This has amounted to recognition of the paramountcy of one state in a region, and agreement not to interfere with its pursuit of national interest in that portion of the territory of the weaker state. Spheres of influence may be established and recognized formally, as in a treaty. Thus Britain and Russia in the entente of 1907 agreed to recognize each other's sphere of influence in the southeastern and northern portions of Persia (Iran). During the nineteenth century, Britain, France, Germany, Japan, and Russia created spheres of influence in China. The term *sphere of influence* is also used more loosely and informally to describe the area over which the hegemonic power of one state has been or could be extended, as in the cases of the United States in the Caribbean area, China in Southeast Asia, and the Soviet Union in Eastern Europe.

Ethnocentrism The belief that one's own group and culture is superior to all others. Ethnocentrism is a universal social phenomenon that distinguishes "we" from "they." The phenomenon emphasizes the differences between societies, their values, and the states that symbolize those values. The values of the "we" group are the standards by which "they" are evaluated, and since "they" are different, "they" are, by definition, inferior. *See also* NATIONALISM, p. 33; XENOPHOBIA, p. 37.

Significance Ethnocentrism is not nationalism; but nationalism is the dominant and potentially most dangerous form of ethnocentrism in the modern world. Ethnocentrism ascribes to the national values a monopoly of truth, beauty, morality, and justice, and assumes the universal validity of the national values. It thus neglects the fact that people and nations are the products of different circumstances and historical experiences, and that by beginning with a different set of premises they may with equal logic arrive at a different set of values or "self-evident truths." Because of different historical experiences, the word "democracy," for example, may suggest individualism to an American and collectivism to a Soviet citizen. The chief international danger in ethnocentric nationalism, therefore, is in the incapacity to understand the motivations of other states and hence to develop a realistic foreign policy.

Imperialism   A superior-inferior relationship in which an area and its people have been subordinated to the will of a foreign state. Imperialism can be traced through several chronological stages of development in the modern world. The first stage, which dates approximately from the voyages of Columbus to the end of the Seven Years' War in 1763, was a consequence of the emergence of the European nation-state system, the economic philosophy of mercantilism, and, in some cases, religious fanaticism and missionary ardor. During this period, much of the New World of the Western Hemisphere was brought under European control by conquest and colonization, and the first imperial forays into Asia were launched by trading companies chartered by European states. In the second stage, from 1763 to about 1870, little imperial expansion occurred because of European preoccupation with the development of liberal nationalism and the Industrial Revolution. The third stage, from 1870 to World War I, saw the last great wave of imperial expansion sweep across Africa and much of the Far East. In this period the industrial states reacted to increasing competition in international trade by seeking to create protected markets and sources of supply. By World War I imperialism had reached its zenith and began slowly to recede. Following World War II, the process of liquidating empires accelerated as the concept fell into disrepute, the economic costs of imperialism increased, and a wave of nationalism enveloped Asia and Africa. The motives for imperialism have varied over time and with the nations involved, but major arguments have included: (1) economic necessity—markets, raw materials, gold, "trade follows the flag"; (2) national security—strategic location, materials, manpower; (3) prestige—"manifest destiny," a "place in the sun," "the sun never sets on the British Empire"; and (4) humanitarianism—missionary activity, the "white man's burden," civilizing mission. *See also* COLONIALISM, p. 25; COMMUNIST THEORY: IMPERIALISM AND COLONIALISM, p. 56; IMPERIALISM, p. 29.

Significance   Imperialism spread the ideas, ideals, and material civilization of the Western world to all parts of the globe. The imperialists took much out of their territories, but they left behind improvements and attitudes about such things as education, health, law, and government that are associated today with nation building and the revolution of rising expectations. Currently, the term *imperialism* is an emotion-laden concept used in a wide variety of circumstances and therefore difficult to define and apply. Since World War II it has become a term of opprobrium and abuse used indiscriminately by the United States, the Soviet Union, and the People's Republic of China, by new regimes against former imperial masters, and by some of the developing nations in resentment against their economic dependence on the industrialized states. In any international political relationship, some states are more powerful and domineering than others and able to exert more influence in economic, political, military, and cultural affairs. That one is stronger than another does not *ipso facto* create an imperial-subordinate relationship unless the stronger, through its coercive power, establishes its rule over the weaker against its will. Because the term *imperialism* has been used loosely to describe a bewildering variety of dissimilar motivations, policies, and situations by propagandists and ideologues, it has lost much of its descriptive utility in political analysis.

Imperialism: Cultural   Imposing an alien ideology or civilization on an unwilling society. Cultural imperialism as a calculated policy by which a government imposes its values on others should be distinguished from the increasing spread of alien cultural influences resulting from trade, travel, and communication. National leaders who resent or fear foreign influences may brand them as cultural imperialism, but in doing so they are using the term as a propaganda device and not as an objective tool of analysis (unless the intent of the foreign government can be demonstrated).

Significance   Cultural imperialism may provide for an effective and long-lasting form of domination in that much of the original culture is destroyed and in time will cease to exist as an alternative. Since language is a fundamental vehicle for the expression of a culture and its "self-evident truths," it has been a primary weapon of cultural imperialism. When a subject people is forced to learn a new language to secure employment or education, for example, it gradually and subconsciously accepts the ideas and values expressed in the new tongue. At the same time, its dependence on the original language as a carrier of its own culture diminishes, and such attributes of the culture as can be expressed only in the original language are changed or disappear. If, however, the recipients welcome certain foreign values, as in the cases of Japan in the nineteenth century or Kemal Ataturk in Turkey after World War I, or as many of the peoples who are experiencing the revolution of rising expectations are doing, cultural imperialism is not involved.

Imperialism: Economic   Involvement of one country in the economy of another to such a degree that the sovereignty of the latter is impaired. Economic imperialism may result from a conscious policy or from the capital flow of private foreign investment. Through its state-trading practices, the Soviet Union dominated the economies of its East European partners after World War II. Indirect control is illustrated by the "dollar diplomacy" of the United States in the Caribbean area earlier in the century. That a relationship exists between economics and imperialism has been evident since the days of mercantilism. The first well-developed modern theory was formulated by the British economist John Hobson in 1902, in his book *Imperialism*. Hobson explained imperialism in terms of the search for new markets and capital investment opportunities. Hobson's ideas also influenced V. I. Lenin in developing his communist theory of capitalist imperialism. In his *Imperialism: The Highest Stage of Capitalism* (1917) Lenin presented imperialism as the result of the "monopoly stage of capitalism." He asserted that excess capital accumulated in the home country because of underconsumption. The competitive search for new markets and investment opportunities, he concluded, led to imperialism and to imperialist wars that would hasten the inevitable downfall of capitalism. *See also* COMMUNIST DOCTRINE; LENINISM, p. 44; COMMUNIST THEORY: IMPERIALISM AND COLONIALISM, p. 56; DOLLAR DIPLOMACY, p. 381.

Significance   Economic imperialism implies a more subtle form of relationship than exists in traditional imperialism since the former does not involve actual political rule. The results may be similar, however, since the more economically dependent the weaker state is, the more difficult it may be to resist political demands by the stronger power. Yet, where the rights of expropriation and expulsion exist, the charge of economic imperalism is more difficult to sustain. The developing countries require large amounts of investment capital from foreign sources. Because of their former colonial status, they are extremely fearful of any semblance of foreign economic control or exploitation. In many instances they have sought to avoid the "strings" attached to bilateral grants and loans and any consequent derogation of sovereignty by seeking economic assistance through international financial agencies, particularly through agencies of the United Nations.

Irredentism   The desire of the people of a state to annex those contiguous territories of another country that are inhabited largely by linguistic or cultural minorities of the first state. Irredentism is a term of Italian origin and comes from the expression, *Italia irredenta*, meaning "Italy unredeemed" or Italians not liberated from foreign control. After the creation of the Kingdom of Italy, the slogan was widely used by nationalists working for the annexation of bordering Italian-speaking communities, particularly those under Austrian rule in Trentino and the Tyrol. *See also* NATIONAL SELF-DETERMINATION, p. 35.

Significance   Irredentism is an aspect of nationalism closely related to self-determination and is a source of international tension and conflict. It can occur wherever a political boundary does not coincide with linguistic or ethnic boundaries. Even with the best of intentions, boundaries in areas of mixed populations are difficult to draw with a precision that satisfies all parties concerned. Irredentism can also be used as a rationalization for territorial aggrandizement. Illustrations of irredentas include Alsace and Lorraine for France after 1870 and the Sudetenland of Czechoslovakia for Germany after the Treaty of Versailles. In the contemporary world, the Bonn government's concept of German reunification implies that East Germany and those former German territories annexed by Poland and the Soviet Union are irredentas. Irredentism among the new states of Africa will remain a potential source of conflict for years to come because the former imperial powers mapped their boundary lines with little reference to the linguistic, cultural, or communal integrity of African peoples.

Nation   A social group that shares a common ideology, common institutions and customs, and a sense of homogeneity. *Nation* is difficult to define so as to differentiate nations from other groups exhibiting some of the same characteristics, such as religious sects. In the *nation*, however, there is a strong group sense of belonging associated with a particular territory considered to be peculiarly its own. A nation may comprise part of a state, be coterminous with a state, or extend beyond the borders of a single state. *See also* NATIONALISM, p. 33; STATE, p. 286.

Significance   The concept of the nation emphasizes the people and their one-ness; this aspect is also implied in such derivative terms as nationality and nationalism. In common parlance the words *country, state,* and *nation* are often used synonymously, but they do not mean exactly the same thing. *Country* has geographical connotations, *state* expresses the legal organization of a society, but the term *nation* involves a sociocultural perception of the group. The hyphenated term *nation-state* aptly describes a socially and culturally homogeneous group possessing the legal organization to participate in international politics.

Nationalism   The spirit of belonging together, or the popular will that seeks to preserve the identity of a group by institutionalizing it in the form of a state. Nationalism can be intensified by common racial, linguistic, historical, and religious ties. It is usually associated with a particular territory. The concept may also be thought of as a function of the ability of a particular group to communicate among themselves more effectively than with outsiders. However the phenomenon of nationalism may be explained, its essential characteristic is an active sense of the uniqueness of the group vis à vis the rest of the world. Nationalism developed first in Western Europe through the consolidation of individual feudal units into kingdoms. It was not until the French Revolution and the wars of Napoleon, however, that nationalism came to be identified with the common man. *See also* CHARISMATIC LEADERSHIP, p. 23; CHAUVINISM, p. 24; ETHNOCENTRISM, p. 28; IMPERIALISM, p. 29; IRREDENTISM, p. 32; NATIONAL SELF-DETERMINATION, p. 35; XENOPHOBIA, p. 37.

Significance   Nationalism as a mass emotion is the most powerful political force operative in the world. It makes the state the ultimate focus of the individual's loyalty. This loyalty is exercised and kept alive by the manipulation of a variety of symbols—national heroes, national uniforms, national pledges of allegiance, and national holidays (holy days). As a mass social phenomenon, nationalism can promote solidarity and a sense of belonging. It can also engender hostility, divisiveness, tension, and war between rival nationalist groups or states. Since World War II, nationalism, originally a European concept, energized millions of dependent peoples in Asia and Africa in their transformation to independence. In the older states, the revitalization of nationalism has weakened the Western alliance and produced schisms within the once monolithic Communist bloc.

Nationalism: Integral   An intolerant, ethnocentric form of nationalism that glorifies the state as the highest focus of individual loyalties. Integral, or totalitarian, nationalism aggressively concentrates on the security of the state, the augmentation of its power at the expense of other states, and the pursuit of national policies motivated by narrow self-interest. Liberal nationalism began to give way to integral nationalism by the end of the nineteenth century under the impact of industrial, trade, imperial, and military rivalries and as a result of increasing popular pressures for the state to protect economic and social interests against foreign competition. Integral nationalism is best typified by the Fascist totalitarianism of the 1930s and 1940s. Various manifestations of the same phenomenon are also observable in the ideological rivalries and national power struggles of the post-World War II period. *See also* FASCISM, p. 69.

Significance   The emphasis of integral nationalism begins where that of liberal nationalism left off. Liberal nationalism was concerned with the creation of the nation-state. Integral nationalism projects the state as a whole into the international arena in competition with the interests and policies of other states. Whereas the state was once considered the servant of the people, under integral nationalism increasing degrees of conformity and orthodoxy are demanded from people in the name of the preservation of the state and the fulfillment of an ideological, often messianic, national purpose.

Nationalism: Liberal   The aspirations of a group to achieve statehood and establish government based on popular sovereignty. Liberal nationalism is philosophically connected through the American and French Revolutions with the decline of absolute monarchy as a legitimate form of government. It is closely associated with the democratic concepts of self-determination, individualism, constitutionalism, natural rights, and popular sovereignty. *See also* DEMOCRACY, p. 61; NATIONAL SELF-DETERMINATION, p. 35.

Significance   Liberal nationalism emphasizes freedom from foreign domination, self-rule, and middle-class democracy. Following the popularization of these principles, the Spanish empire disintegrated, Italy and Germany were unified as national states, and ultimately, monarchy survived only where it adopted the constitutional form. The state was regarded as the servant of the people; and the frequency of war, it was hoped, would decline since it would not serve the best interests of the new sovereigns. The principles of liberal nationalism have also inspired the elites of the national independence movements in the 1950s and 1960s.

National Self-Determination   The doctrine that postulates the right of a group of people who consider themselves separate and distinct from others to determine for themselves the state in which they will live and the form of government it will have. National self-determination is closely linked with the concept of liberal nationalism and is implicit in the American Declaration of Independence and the French Declaration of the Rights of Man and Citizen. It is the vehicle by which national groups seek to insure their identity by institutionalizing it in the form of an independent sovereign state. The name most frequently associated with national self-determination is that of Woodrow Wilson. The doctrine is found in his 1918 peace aims, the famous Fourteen Points. In the 1919 peace settlements it was instrumental in establishing the independence of Albania, Austria, Czechoslovakia, Estonia, Finland, Hungary, Latvia, Lithuania, Poland, Romania, and Yugoslavia. It also figured in the creation of the mandates system and its successor, the trusteeship system. The principle of self-determination has also been associated with the technique of the plebiscite as a basis for solving problems relating to boundaries and territorial sovereignty, as in the Kashmir dispute between India and Pakistan. *See also* NATIONALISM, p. 33; PLEBISCITE, p. 243.

Significance   National self-determination is frequently asserted as a right by national minorities and has often served as a rationalization for rebellion and secession when demands for separate government have not been met. As an expression of nationalism, the doctrine contributed to the vast increase in the number of states since the start of the nineteenth century, particularly since World War II. Combined with nationalism and carried to its ultimate conclusion, it is also an invitation to ongoing political fragmentation. It has already progressed to the point that the word *mini-state* has entered the vocabulary of international relations. International law, however, recognizes no such absolute right. Consequently, national self-determination is more a political than a legal phenomenon and succeeds or fails on the basis of internal and external power considerations.

Neutralism   An attitude or policy of independence and nonalignment in the Cold War power struggle. Neutralism describes the political position of states that have decided not to commit themselves to an alliance with either the United States or the Soviet Union, and, hence, not to be included in either the Eastern or Western bloc. Neutralism implies determination to maintain freedom to maneuver according to the dictates of national interest and, therefore, should not be considered a new phenomenon in international politics. Neutralism also should not be confused with the legal concept of neutrality, which implies a policy of impartiality toward belligerents in a war. *See also* NEUTRALITY, p. 280.

Significance   The policy of neutralism or noncommitment, coupled with the great increase in the number of states, has helped to undermine rigid bipolarity and to restore freedom of action in the international balance of power. By pursuing an independent course, the nonaligned countries are free to define their own national interests and to devote primary attention to the pressing problems of modernization and national integration. The neutralists are thus in a position to take aid from any source and, to some extent, to force the Eastern and Western blocs to compete for their support. The impact of neutralism has been particularly evident in the General Assembly, where the

Afro-Asian countries are now in the majority. They have forced the older states to abandon much of their preoccupation with East-West relations and to concentrate increasing attention on the economic and social concerns of the new majority.

Xenophobia   Fear or distrust of foreigners and of the policies and objectives of other states. Xenophobia is related to the mass emotions of ethnocentrism and nationalism in that they all involve a relationship between an in-group and outsiders that creates distinctions favorable to the former. Xenophobia involves perceptions of other people not as individuals but as stereotypes of something feared or hated. See also NATIONALISM, p. 33.

Significance   Xenophobia may be manifested in attitudes of superiority to outsiders, but usually is a cloak for feelings of suspicion and resentment. It is particularly observable among people who have suffered from real or imagined exploitations by the peoples of other countries. China, for example, stereotyped all foreigners as barbarians and for centuries refused to deal with them as equals. China was later subjected to humiliating treatment by European powers, and Chinese xenophobia took the form of intense anti-Westernism. Such feelings of mixed pride and inadequacy can be exploited for a variety of purposes. Foreigners are made scapegoats for the difficulties faced by newly independent countries, and frustrations are thus channeled away from rather than against the domestic regime. In much of the developing world, for example, xenophobic propaganda charges of "neo-colonialism" are aimed at freeing a country from what may or may not be exploitative foreign economic interests. Xenophobia can also occur between segments of the population of a single country, as in the antipathy against the large Chinese populations found in many countries of Southeast Asia.

Zionism   Originally an international effort to create a Jewish national homeland in Palestine. The First Zionist Congress met under the leadership of Theodor Herzl in 1897. For many years, Zionism remained a minority Jewish view. The majority (assimilationists) were satisfied with citizenship in the countries of their birth, especially in Western Europe and the

Americas. After Adolf Hitler's murder of millions of Jews during World War II, Zionism received new support. The creation of the state of Israel in 1948 fulfilled the Zionist dream of a Jewish state. Today, Zionists promote political, economic, financial, and military support for Israel, and the immigration and resettlement of Jews in Israel.

Significance Zionist groups are particularly active in countries like the United States that have large Jewish populations. Zionists encourage American Jews to pressure political parties and the government to ensure continued foreign policy support for Israel. Zionists also operate to counter the demands of Arab interests in the continuing Arab-Israeli conflict, and on such issues as recognition of the state of Israel, refugees, disputed territories, and the status of the city of Jerusalem. Zionism as a political force includes many non-Jews as well as Jews.

3. Ideology and Communication

Atlantic Charter   The joint declaration issued by President Franklin Roosevelt and Prime Minister Winston Churchill in August, 1941, following their historic meeting aboard a ship in the mid-Atlantic. The Atlantic Charter proclaimed the principles that were to guide the two countries in their search for a just peace and a stable world after the destruction of the Nazi regime. These included: (1) the Four Freedoms—freedom from fear and want, and freedom of speech and religion; (2) the application of the principle of self-determination in all territorial changes; (3) the right of all peoples to choose the form of government under which they live; (4) equal access to the trade and raw materials essential to prosperity, and economic collaboration among all nations; (5) peace with security for all states; (6) freedom of the seas; and (7) renunciation of the use of force, establishment of a permanent system of general security, and disarmament of all nations that threaten the peace. *See also* PROPAGANDA, p. 76; PSYCHOLOGICAL WARFARE, p. 186.

Significance   The Atlantic Charter, like the Fourteen Points enunciated by Woodrow Wilson during World War I, was a major propaganda instrument aimed at sparking mass support for the Allied cause in World War II. It was aimed in particular at overcoming isolationist sentiment in the United States since the Charter was proclaimed four months before the Japanese attack on Pearl Harbor and the American entry into the war. Charter principles, especially the Four Freedoms, gained broad support as war aims, but their influence became even greater in the postwar period. Many of the principles of the Atlantic Charter have been implemented. The principle of self-determination, for example, served to legitimate the aspirations of millions of colonial peoples for independence and statehood. The "permanent system of general security" took shape in the form of the United Nations, and economic collaboration has been fostered on an unprecedented scale. The Atlantic Charter continues to be invoked by those who pursue idealistic approaches to foreign policy issues.

Brainwashing   A psychological technique for reorienting the individual's thinking so that it will conform to a predetermined mode. The term *brainwashing* is derived from the Chinese colloquialism of *hsi nao* (wash-brain) and corresponds to the communist goal of "thought reform." Brainwashing is carried out by obtaining a confession of wrongdoing, which is followed by a process of re-education. The means used to effect brainwashing upon an individual include combining extremely harsh and lenient treatment, interspersed with physical and psychological punishments and rewards designed to break traditional patterns of thought and institute new ones. *See also* PSYCHOLOGICAL WARFARE, p. 186.

Significance   The technique of brainwashing was used on a massive scale by the Chinese Communists to inculcate new thought patterns in the masses in the years following the 1949 victory of the Communists in the Civil War. During the Korean conflict, the Chinese attempted—successfully in some cases—to brainwash American prisoners of war. Some prisoners renounced their allegiance to the United States, confessed to having committed war crimes such as waging germ warfare, and voluntarily chose exile in China to repatriation. Brainwashing as a technique for reshaping the individual's values and changing his allegiance remains largely an unknown factor, although psychological warfare experts believe it can be used more effectively to change ideological values than to change national allegiances.

Capitalism   An economic theory and system based on the principles of laissez-faire free enterprise. Capitalist theory calls for private ownership of property and the means of production, a competitive profit-incentive system, individual initiative, an absence of governmental restraints on ownership, production, and trade, and a market economy that provides order to the system by means of the law of supply and demand. The theory also assumes the free movement of labor and capital and free trade domestically and in foreign markets, which should result in an international division of labor and national specialization. Although some forms of capitalism have always existed in human society, the sophisticated theories underlying modern capitalism were initially developed by the classical economists, beginning with Adam Smith's publication of *Wealth of Nations* in 1776. *See also* FREE TRADE, p. 127; KEYNESIANISM, p. 136; MERCANTILISM, p. 139.

Significance In the late eighteenth and nineteenth centuries, the new doctrine and practice of capitalism together with the democratic concepts of political liberalism began to replace the established order of mercantilism and monarchy. Mercantilism's stringent governmental controls over internal and foreign economic activity and trade gave way progressively to an individual- and freedom-centered system of entrepreneurship and free trade. The resulting burst of economic activity helped to produce the Industrial Revolution. The twentieth century has witnessed the fruition of capitalism and, in turn, its substantial modification. In some states the change took the form of an expanding role for government in economic affairs; private ownership and initiative were combined with governmental promotion and regulation in a new "mixed economy." In others, capitalism has been replaced by socialism or communism based on rigid state control and operation of the economy and trade. In the contemporary world, some observers believe that the basic nature of individualistic, free enterprise capitalism has been perverted in some democratic states by a warfare economy and the vast power linkage between giant industrial corporations and the government. In the Soviet Union and the communist states of Eastern Europe, reforms have reduced governmental planning and central control of the economy and have encouraged a profit motive for individual industries and their workers. On the ideological level, it has proved difficult to gain acceptance of the concepts of capitalism in many underdeveloped states where private initiative, savings, and mass consumer markets barely exist.

Communism An ideology that calls for the elimination of capitalist institutions and the establishment of a collectivist society in which land and capital are socially owned and in which class conflict and the coercive power of the state no longer exist. Although numerous political philosophers since Plato's time have developed theories embracing diverse forms of communism, modern communist doctrines were first postulated in the nineteenth century by socialists and other reformers, such as François Fourier, Robert Owen, and Claude Saint-Simon. Dismissing this group as well as church communalists as "Utopians," Karl Marx and Friedrich Engels fashioned a doctrine of "scientific socialism" that has become the basis for the contemporary ideology of communism. Numerous communist theoreticians and political leaders since the mid-nineteenth century have interpreted, modified, and added to these theories. The most important contributors to communist ideology have been Vladimir Ilyich Lenin, Josef Stalin, Leon Trotsky, Mao Tse-tung, and Josip Broz Tito, with Lenin's contributions recognized by communists as the most formidable. Marxism-Leninism espouses a philosophy of history that shows an inevitable progression from capitalism to socialism as a result of the internal contradictions inherent in the nature of capitalism. According to communist doctrine, these will produce intensifying class warfare and imperial and colonial rivalry culminating in the overthrow of the bourgeoisie by a proletarian revolution. A socialist program carried out under a "dictatorship of the proletariat" will then end class warfare, eliminate the need for the state, and move the society into the final, classless, stateless stage of pure communism. *See also* COMMUNIST DOCTRINE, pp. 43–49; COMMUNIST THEORY, p. 50–59.

Significance   From the publication of the *Communist Manifesto* of 1848 up to World War I, Marxian communism served only as a topic of intellectual debate and a rallying doctrine for unsuccessful agitators in many countries. The Russian military and social collapse in 1917 provided the historical opportunity for the Bolshevik Revolution and for Communists to "build socialism in one country." In the period from 1945 to 1949, following World War II, occupation by the Red Army brought communist regimes to power in Eastern European countries and North Korea, while indigenous communist forces won power by their own efforts in Yugoslavia and Mainland China. The communist world, considered to be a monolithic entity by many Western observers during the 1950s, was rent by a major Sino-Soviet schism in the 1960s and a growing independence of communist states in Eastern Europe based on the Yugoslav model of Titoism or national communism. The major doctrinal split among communist theoreticians and strategists since 1917 has been the issue of whether communism and nationalism are complementary doctrines or whether the ideal of "proletarian internationalism" and the promotion of world revolution should take precedence over national political and economic development. The new generation of technocrats and bureaucrats in the Soviet Union and in the communist states of Eastern Europe has increasingly assumed leadership roles and has become absorbed in achieving economic growth and material improvement for their peoples. In the mid-1960s the Chinese Communists, caught up in an internal power struggle between party ideologues and the "managers," undertook a "Cultural Revolution" under the direction of Mao Tse-tung, to restore the purity of the revolution and its ideological goals. Chinese leaders castigated the Soviet and Eastern European Communists as "reactionaries." Rhetoric aside, the schism between the Chinese and Soviet camps involves a struggle for leadership of a communist world that is rapidly disintegrating under the impact of growing nationalism and polycentrism. Traditional Marxism-Leninism, with its central theme of an inescapable apocalyptic revolution in the mature capitalist states, has been replaced largely by a new emphasis on proving communism to be a superior social system in practice. Communist revolutionary efforts are currently directed toward capturing control of nationalist movements in the developing nations and promoting "wars of national liberation" among the frustrated masses of Asia, Africa, and Latin America.

Communist Doctrine: Khrushchevism   Contributions to Marxist-Leninist theory and applications of communist doctrine in the Soviet Union made by Nikita S. Khrushchev. Khrushchevism was developed from 1956, when Khrushchev emerged as the dominant leader in the post-Stalin power struggle, to 1963, when he was deposed from power by a party faction headed by Leonid I. Brezhnev and Aleksei N. Kosygin. Khrushchev began his rise to power when he replaced Josef Stalin as First Secretary of the Communist Party after the latter's death in 1953. He consolidated his control in 1958 when he removed Nikolai A. Bulganin as Chairman of the Council of Ministers and assumed that post also. Khrushchev's main contributions to communist doctrine include: (1) repudiation of Stalin's "cult of the individual" and the restoration of the "true" Marxist-Leninist approach of collective leadership; (2) enunciation of the doctrine and policy of "peaceful coexistence" between communist and capitalist states while calling for "wars of national liberation" in the underdeveloped world; (3) denunciation of Stalinist totalitarianism and the institution of less tyrannical policies within the Soviet state; (4) establishment for the first time in any communist country of a specific timetable (within twenty years) for a socialist state to complete the historical transition to pure communism; (5) a declaration that although classes and the state will wither away the Communist party will remain as a directing force in the future society; and (6) development of the tactical position that communism would defeat capitalism in peaceful competition in the world by proving itself to be a superior social and productive system. *See also* PEACEFUL COEXISTENCE, p. 184; SOVIET UNION: CULT OF THE INDIVIDUAL, p. 459; WARS OF NATIONAL LIBERATION, p. 200.

Significance The contributions of Khrushchevism to communist doctrine and practices were largely a product of the internal and external factors that confronted Soviet leaders in the post-Stalin era. Because the strains resulting from dictatorial repression threatened the stability of Soviet and Eastern European societies, for example, Khrushchev denounced the Stalinist period of terror even though he had been an accomplice in it. In time, he too moved toward one-man rule and was denounced by his successors for developing a "cult of personality." In the foreign affairs arena, Khrushchev recognized that the nuclear weapons revolution made a major war between the East and the West an unthinkable anachronism. Unstable political and economic conditions in the nations of Asia, Africa, and Latin America, on the other hand, presented communism with a ready opportunity for gains that Khrushchev cultivated by offering a socialist "short-cut" to development and modernization. Although Khrushchevism offered no major theoretical contributions to Marxism-Leninism, the interpretation and application of communist theory by Soviet leaders during the Khrushchev period resulted in a number of new emphases that had the effect of revising earlier communist policies and of creating a major schism in the communist world between Soviet and Chinese factions.

Communist Doctrine: Leninism The theoretical interpretations and practical applications of Marxist doctrine contributed to the ideology of communism by the Russian revolutionary leader Vladimir Ilyich Lenin. The main contributions of Leninism include: (1) the theory that imperialism, the highest stage of monopoly capitalism, results from the contradictions of capitalism that force trusts and cartels to seek abroad for outlets for surplus capital and production and to bring world sources of raw materials under their control; (2) the theory that imperialist competition between capitalist states generates war; (3) the theory that revolution can take place in a precapitalist colonial society no matter how primitive; (4) a redefinition of the Marxist conception of revolution to include such non-Marxist opportunities as a national disaster that the ruling class cannot handle or general public discontent with the government; and (5) the utilization of the Communist party, guided by a small dedicated elite, to lead the revolution and to serve as the instrument for implementing Marx's "dictatorship of the proletariat." A prolific author, Lenin's main ideas are found in his works: *What Is to Be Done?* (1902), *Imperialism: The Highest Stage of Capitalism* (1917), and *State and Revolution* (1918).

Significance　　Leninist contributions in theory and practice to the doctrines of Marx were so substantial that communists have since called their basic ideological framework Marxism-Leninism. As a theoretician, Lenin foresaw the contemporary revolution of self-determination that has swept Asia and Africa, and he predicted the struggles in the underdeveloped lands that Nikita Khrushchev referred to as "wars of national liberation." As a revolutionary practitioner, Lenin conducted a continuous revolution and rejected all appeals from Communists and others for gradualism and revisionism. His most important contribution, however, was probably as a practical political leader. He rallied the Russian people after the disasters of World War I and the Civil War, initiated the political, economic, and social reorganization of the nation, and charted a course for socialism that has made the Soviet Union a superpower in the latter half of the twentieth century.

Communist Doctrine: Maoism　　Interpretations of Marxism-Leninism, and the policies developed and actions taken by the Chinese Communist party under the leadership of Chairman Mao Tse-tung. Maoism's theoretical base was popularized by the aphorisms included in the widely distributed *Quotations From Chairman Mao Tse-tung*. Mao's main theoretical contributions include: (1) a theory for fighting guerrilla war in agrarian colonial and semicolonial countries with the active support of the peasants; (2) a definition of democratic centralism in the Chinese context to mean that the people should enjoy a measure of freedom and democracy while at the same time submitting themselves to "socialist discipline"; (3) a definition of Marx's "dictatorship of the proletariat" in the Chinese situation as "a people's democratic dictatorship, led by the working class and based on the worker-peasant alliance"; (4) a theory that recognizes contradictions within the people's socialist system as well as between it and the capitalist enemy; (5) rejection of Soviet doctrinal appeals for "peaceful coexistence" in favor of "permanent revolution" throughout the world against the remaining bastions of capitalism; and (6) rejection of the primacy of economic development and material betterment in favor of maintaining the purity of the revolution and the creation of the "new Chinese man" and a new society freed of all contradictions. *See also* CHINA (PRC): CULTURAL REVOLUTION, p. 422; CHINA (PRC): MAOISM, p. 422.

Significance   Maoism evolved as a peculiarly Chinese interpretation and application of the principles of Marxism-Leninism by that nation's communist leaders during Mao's thirty-five years as undisputed head of the Chinese Communist party. The central events of the long struggle for power that shaped the nature of Maoism include the early Civil War period from 1928 to 1934, the "Long March" of 1934–35, the struggle against the Japanese and the alliance with Chiang Kai-shek from 1937 to 1945, the resumption of the Civil War in 1946, and the victory of the Communists in 1949. Maoist policy developments since 1949 that relate to communist theory include: (1) the brief "hundred flowers" campaign for free discussion in the mid-1950s; (2) the "Great Leap Forward" development program and the establishment of communes in 1958; (3) the struggle with the Soviet Union for leadership of world communism and the resulting schism in the international movement during the early 1960s; (4) the explosive "Cultural Revolution" struggle that began in 1967 between the technocrats on the one hand and the ideologues led by Mao on the other; and (5) the emergence of a period of détente in the 1970s between China and the West, leading to China's admission into the United Nations and its recognition by the United States and other Western countries. Although most Maoist principles can be traced to Marx, Engels, Lenin, and Trotsky, Chinese leaders have claimed that interpretations, adaptations, and applications of Marxist-Leninist doctrines undertaken under Chairman Mao's direction add up to an original contribution.

Communist Doctrine: Marxism   The body of economic, political, and social theories developed by Karl Marx and his collaborator Friedrich Engels in the nineteenth century. Marxism offers a comprehensive "scientific" philosophy of history that explains mankind's development dialectically as a series of class struggles which have produced new social orders. Marx viewed capitalism as a system suffering from irremediable internal contradictions with an intensifying class struggle that would culminate in a revolution carried out by the proletariat against the bourgeoisie. A period of "dictatorship of the proletariat" would follow in which capitalists would be stripped of their wealth and power, land and the means of production nationalized, and class distinctions abolished. According to Marx the state would then "wither away," a final stage of pure communism would be ushered in, and man would live in a perfect classless, stateless society of spontaneous cooperation in which each individual would contribute according to his ability and receive according to his needs. Marx's ideas were developed in *The Communist Manifesto* of 1848 and in his principal work, *Das Kapital*, of which the first volume was published in 1867. *See also* COMMUNIST THEORY, pp. 50–59.

Significance   Marxism has had a profound impact on twentieth century history through the development of communist and socialist parties that espouse its doctrines and provide an open or covert force that challenges established orders. The success of the Marxist-inspired Russian Revolution of 1917 and the coming to power of communist regimes in Eastern Europe, China, North Korea, Cuba, and Vietnam split the world into rival ideological and military camps and affected the international relations of all states. Leaders of communist states have flexibly interpreted and pragmatically applied Marxism, but none has renounced or repudiated the doctrine. Although the Soviet Union and several other communist states claim to have completed the establishment of socialism and are proceeding to move into the final stage of pure communism, little evidence exists to support this assertion. In the Soviet Union, for example, a new class of technocrats and bureaucrats has arisen and the machinery of the state, far from "withering away," has remained a pervasive force, though more humane than under the Stalinist dictatorship. In the contemporary ideological struggle, the main target of communist propaganda has shifted from the advanced industrial states to the poor, underdeveloped nations. The thrust of the appeal has also been diverted from the Marxist-inspired dogmas of historical development and capitalist contradictions to promises of a shortcut to economic and social modernization through a temporary communist dictatorship.

Communist Doctrine: Stalinism   The theoretical interpretations and practical applications of Marxist doctrine contributed by Josef Stalin, who dominated the party and governmental machinery in the Soviet Union from the mid-1920s until his death in 1953. The main contributions of Stalinism were in the methods of organizing the Soviet people for achieving industrialization, improving agriculture, defense of the nation against the Nazi attack, and the reconstruction of the war-devastated nation. Stalin demonstrated that, in addition to the Marxist and Leninist prescriptions for the victory of communism, military occupation by a communist great power, as demonstrated in Eastern Europe after World War II, could also accomplish the goal if international circumstances were favorable. In the area of theory, Stalin contributed little to communist doctrine, limiting himself to redefining Marxism-Leninism to apply it to the domestic and international milieu of his day. Stalin predicted in his last published work in 1952, for example, that instead of war between the socialist camp and the capitalist states, Lenin's theory that war may occur between capitalist nations as a result of their imperialistic rivalry was still applicable. He asserted that it could conceivably be applied to predict war between such close allies as the United States and Britain.

Significance   Stalinism, as a result of the program of de-Stalinization carried on by his successors to power, has been denounced for fostering a "cult of personality," dictatorial rule by one man, personal infallibility, establishment of a totalitarian state, and the liquidation of suspected opponents through purges and secret police methods. Concepts developed and applied by Stalin in the Soviet Union that have had an impact on communist doctrine include his idea of "socialism in one country," Five Year Plans for fostering economic development, the collectivization of agriculture, and the writing of the Soviet Constitution of 1936. Despite the denunciation of Stalinism, many of the theoretical and practical applications of communist theories carried out over the thirty-year period of Stalin's rule remain basic to the contemporary doctrine of communism.

Communist Doctrine: Titoism   The theory and practice of national communism espoused by Josip Broz Tito, communist leader of Yugoslavia. Titoism emerged as a new doctrine in 1948 when President Tito rejected the monolithic approach to world communism forcefully pushed by Josef Stalin, under which national communist parties were expected to accept the direction and control of the Communist party of the Soviet Union. For Tito, nationalism and communism are complementary doctrines that should be fused into a new movement that permits each communist state to retain full political independence and to choose its own "road to socialism."

Significance   Titoism initially had the impact of shattering the unity of the Eastern European Communist bloc that had been forged under Soviet hegemony. Since 1948 Yugoslavia has pursued a policy of nonalignment in foreign affairs, has traded with and accepted aid from both East and West, and has developed its economy and political system pragmatically, free from external ideological or political controls. Although Stalin attempted to break the Titoist revolt, Nikita Khrushchev denounced Stalinism and reached a rapprochement with Tito in 1955. This rapprochement was continued through the 1970s and into the 1980s by Khrushchev's successors, Leonid Brezhnev and Aleksei Kosygin. The main impact of Titoism, however, has been its general acceptance by most of the communist world, leading to a growing emphasis on the separate development of national communism according to the needs and conditions of each communist state. As a result, polycentrism—the establishment of numerous and relatively independent centers of power—has flourished within the once-monolithic communist camp.

Communist Doctrine: Trotskyism   The theories of Leon Trotsky, a leading communist revolutionary, who challenged Josef Stalin for the leadership of the Soviet Union after Lenin's death in 1924. After the Bolshevik Revolution of 1917 and the Civil War period, Trotsky argued for using the communist base in Russia for the achievement of world revolution. Stalin, on the other hand, called for building socialism in one country to give communism a sound base, impregnable to capitalist counter-revolution. Stalin won the power struggle in the late 1920s, ousted Trotsky from the Communist party of the Soviet Union, and exiled him. Trotsky continued his opposition to Stalin and Stalinism in exile; he was assassinated in Mexico in 1940. Trotskyism as an ideology called for unity and common effort among the proletariat of all countries to establish a world communist commonwealth. Trotsky believed that the Russian Revolution failed because it had created a bureaucratic ruling class that exploited the workers and betrayed their interests.

Significance Trotskyism became a synonym for deviationism and revisionism, two of the major sins against communist orthodoxy. Although Trotsky was a brilliant Marxist theoretician and author, as well as a military tactician who had saved the Bolshevik Revolution by forging the Red Army into a first-class fighting force, he was outmaneuvered in the post-Lenin power struggle by Stalin who held the crucial post of Secretary General of the party. Trotskyism continues to find support in several countries among Communist party members who reject the idea of national communism and proclaim the Trotskyite goal of communist cosmopolitanism. A policy similar to Trotsky's ideal of uniting all Communists in a common world revolutionary campaign was advocated by the leaders of Communist China in the 1950s and 1960s.

Communist Theory: Class Struggle The conflict between the proletariat and bourgeoisie that, under capitalism, results from the increasing impoverishment of the workers and a polarization engendered by a growing class consciousness. For Marx, the class struggle emerged out of the basic contradictions identified by the dialectical process as inherent in capitalism as well as in primitive, slave, and feudal social systems. It is, in other words, what communists perceive to be the means by which the transition from capitalism to socialism will occur. Although many revolutionaries antedating Marx had based their doctrines on the class struggle theme, Marx was the first to accord it the central role in a philosophy of historical evolution.

Significance The communist doctrine of class struggle assumes that there are only two social classes in capitalist society, that the two have contradictory interests, and that each will become implacably hostile toward the other. To encourage these developments, communist agitators in many countries have endeavored to develop a militant class consciousness among the proletariat. Critics of communism reject the idea that class struggle is predetermined and inescapable; they point out that in the United States, for example, the great majority of people consider themselves to be "middle class." Marx's predictions that the workers' lives would grow increasingly harsh and that poverty and unemployment would increase, leading to a sharpening of class interests, have not been borne out in the experience of modern industrial societies.

Communist Theory: Communism   The final stage of the dialectical process in which the "new communist man" lives in a classless, stateless society, accepts a new and higher morality, and spontaneously cooperates with his fellow man. Marx anticipated that pure communism would follow the transitional stage of proletarian dictatorship because the proletarian state would simply "wither away" as the classless society was achieved. Communism would constitute man's final and highest stage of social development since the energizing force of class conflict would no longer exist, nor would there be a need for further evolutionary progress. According to Marx, the production and distribution of material wealth under communism would change from a socialist basis of "from each according to his ability, to each according to his work" to a system based on the communist principle of "from each according to his ability, to each according to his needs."

Significance   The ultimate objective of pure communism linked Marx with Mikhail Bakunin and the philosophical anarchists of his day, who also considered the state an instrument of oppression and sought its elimination. Communist theorists and national leaders, while never repudiating the ideal of pure communism, have often rationalized it as a distant objective that cannot be achieved as long as hostile capitalist states threaten the socialist states. In the early 1960s, however, Premier Nikita Khrushchev announced to the representatives of eighty-one communist parties convened in Moscow that the Soviet Union was completing the building of socialism and would be the vanguard in the movement to communism. The communist vision of building a pure society—a veritable heaven on earth—has attracted intellectuals, moralists, and others to the cause. Many, however, have been disillusioned by the harsh discipline, rigid thought control, and police state methods practiced by the Communists.

Communist Theory: Contradictions of Capitalism
The fundamental irreconcilable conflicts inherent in the nature of capitalism that, according to communist dogma, are instrumental in bringing about its collapse. For Marx, the contradictions of capitalism start at the production stage when the worker receives only a small portion of the value of the article produced in the form of wages, with the rest in the form of surplus value or profits kept by the capitalist. The result is a lack of enough purchasing power to buy the goods that are produced. This underconsumption, according to Marx, produces increasingly severe economic depressions within nations, an increasing impoverishment of the working class, growing unemployment, a class struggle, and, ultimately, the victory of socialism.

Significance   Communists believe that the theory of the contradictions of capitalism demonstrates that capitalism contains the seeds of its own destruction and will fall, not from attack by outside forces, but because of its own self-generated weaknesses and conflicts. Increasingly severe economic slumps culminating in the Great Depression of the 1930s appeared to Communists to be the denouement of the Marx-predicted apocalypse of capitalism. Critics of communist dogma, however, point out that economic slumps have become less serious since the 1930s, that through trade unions and other means workers have been able to win a bigger slice of the economic pie, and that governmental fiscal and monetary policies permit adjustments within each nation's economy to avoid the pitfalls that Marx predicted. The applications of Keynesian economic doctrines and the development of mass consumer credit are viewed by some observers as the key ingredients in modifying and strengthening the capitalist system.

Communist Theory: Democratic Centralism   The doctrinally sanctioned method for making and implementing decisions within communist parties. Democratic centralism, as developed by Lenin, calls for democratic participation through free discussion and deliberation by all Communist party members in the development of party policies. Once decisions have been made, however, further dissent and debate are no longer

tolerated, and well-disciplined party members are expected to lend their full support to the execution of policies by the centrally directed party organization. In other words, diversity during the formative stages of policy development must give way to monolithic unity in support of the party elite in implementing policy.

Significance The working principle of democratic centralism was developed by Lenin to fuse the practical and psychological advantages of rank and file participation with the need for ideological unity and bureaucratic efficiency stemming from central control. For Lenin, the approach was necessary to provide the internal cohesion and efficiency needed both in waging the struggle to achieve power and in implementing the socialist program after the revolution had succeeded. The principle of democratic centralism was abandoned under the dictatorial rule of Josef Stalin and for almost a quarter of a century decisions were made and enforced by a small oligarchy under Stalin's control. In more recent years there has been a trend in the Soviet Union and in Eastern European communist states toward a restoration of the principle of democratic centralism in the decision processes of the national communist parties. The communist states of Asia, however, have continued to function under the tight control of party elites.

Communist Theory: Dialectical Materialism The concept that explains how the union of opposites produces social development. The dialectic, which Marx borrowed from the philosophy of Hegel, postulates a process by which each idea (*thesis*) produces a contradictory idea (*antithesis*), leading to a conflict out of which a new, higher idea (*synthesis*) emerges. Marx adapted the dialectical method to his materialist outlook and used it to describe the process in which the dominant economic classes in each society engage in struggle and produce new economic systems, culminating ultimately in the creation of a pure, classless, stateless society of communism. Lenin described dialectics as "the study of the contradiction within the very essence of things."

Significance Dialectical materialism is vital to the philosophy of communism because Marxists believe that it constitutes a science of society that reveals the laws of social change. By inverting Hegel's philosophy, ideas for Marx became merely a reflection of material reality rather than the dominant factor in history. Utilizing dialectical materialism as prescribed by Marx, the dedicated Communist accepts the historical inevitability of the transition from capitalism to socialism because all aspects of human society are controlled by material forces that govern individual choice and define man as a socially determined product. Critics reject the dialectical method developed by Marx on the grounds that it is unscientific, rooted in ideological faith, and pretentiously deterministic as a monistic causal interpretation of history.

Communist Theory: Dictatorship of the Proletariat
The transitional stage following a proletarian revolution in which communist power is consolidated, the bourgeoisie eliminated as a class, and socialism established. For Marx, the dictatorship of the proletariat meant that the workers would control the machinery of the state and would use it to reorganize society and convert the means of production from private to public ownership to provide for the transformation of society into its final stage of pure communism. For Lenin and Stalin, the dictatorship was vested in the Communist party and its leaders as representatives of the proletariat. For those two leaders, its primary function was to defend the state and the revolution against a renaissance of the bourgeois class which, they believed, had increased rather than decreased its resistance following the overthrow of its power.

Significance The dictatorship of the proletariat provides the means in communist theory for the realization of the goals of communism. Although Marx believed that the historical transition of society from capitalism to socialism was inevitable, he designated the proletarian class as the means for effecting the transformation. Since communist theory postulates that all states rest on force, and that law is merely the expression of the will of the dominant class, the proletarian class is assigned the role of using the state machinery to carry out its objectives. Critics of communism, however, note that the intended dictatorship *of* the proletariat has, in all communist states, been applied in the form of a dictatorship *over* the proletariat carried on by a single party leader or group of oligarchs. In the Soviet Union the term *proletarian democracy* has been substituted in state and party propaganda for the less appealing *dictatorship of the proletariat.*

Communist Theory: Economic Interpretation of History
The assumption that the basic economic system or "mode of

production" of a society determines its political, moral, legal, cultural, and religious superstructure and provides the motive force that guides the development of society from lower to higher stages. Marx's "materialist conception of history" starts with the proposition that man's basic activity relates to the production and acquisition of his means of subsistence. The system for the organization, ownership, and operation of these productive forces and the distribution of food and material wealth produced by them determines the nature of society, and through class conflict provides the inner motive power for the society's evolution. The three factors of production identified by Marx as most directly related to social change and historical development are labor, raw materials, and the instruments of production.

Significance   Marx's emphasis on the fundamental role of the economic system in societal development and in shaping other human institutions has led observers to characterize him as an economic determinist. Under capitalism, the dialectically inspired contradiction between modern productive techniques and bourgeois ownership leads, according to Marx, to an inescapable conflict in the form of class struggle. Marx and Engels, as well as contemporary Communists, have denied the allegation of determinism, preferring to regard it as an evolutionary historical process rather than a simple cause-and-effect relationship. Nevertheless, Marx and Marxists have always focused on the central theme that economic forces produce class struggle, which will inevitably result in the collapse of capitalism.

Communist Theory: Historical Inevitability   A philosophy of history in which Marx posited the preordained necessity and scientific certainty of the replacement of capitalism by socialism. Historical inevitability, according to Marx, results from the contradictions embedded in a society's mode of production which, under capitalism and preceding primitive, slave, and feudal patterns, has pitted the servile class against the exploiting class, producing an automatic movement from one stage to the next. To an orthodox Marxist, free will and individual initiative are insignificant in the broad sweep of the historical development of mankind.

Significance   The doctrine of the historically inevitable triumph of socialism has given communism a mystical aura with the anticipatory quality of a religious faith. For Marx, the means for achieving socialism may initially be evolutionary and democratic or may require violent revolution by the proletariat against the ruling class but, in the denouement of the historical process, a violent clash between the two classes is unavoidable. The automatic movement of history from one stage to another postulated by Marxist dogma, however, reaches a climax and concludes with the victory of socialism, the ending of class conflict, the withering away of the state, ushering in the final era of communism.

Communist Theory: Imperialism and Colonialism

An assumption that economic contradictions created by the nature of capitalism lead states into policies of overseas imperialism and colonialism. Capitalist imperialism and colonialism have been explained by Communists since Lenin's time as the means for opening new outlets for investments, for finding new markets for the excess production that cannot be sold on the home market because of the impoverishment of the masses, and for securing cheap raw materials for domestic factories. The need to pursue overseas policies of conquest and control grew out of the changing nature of capitalism, which had moved from the early competitive stage to a "monopoly stage" dominated by cartels and trusts. The result, according to Lenin, would be increasing imperialist rivalry leading to major wars among capitalist states.

Significance   The theory that imperialism and colonialism are produced by the contradictions of capitalism can be inferred from Marx's writings, but it was not fully developed as an essential feature of communist dogma until Lenin expounded it in his *Imperialism: The Highest Stage of Capitalism* in 1917. In developing the theory, Lenin borrowed heavily from the views expressed by the English economist J. A. Hobson, who, in his book, *Imperialism* (1902), developed the thesis that Western policies of imperialism and colonialism could be attributed to the propensity of the capitalist system to oversave, thereby creating the need to supplement the underconsuming domestic market by exploiting overseas outlets. Lenin's doctrine altered Marxism by predicting that proletarian revolutions need not occur only in the most advanced industrial nations but could take place in undeveloped societies in Asia and Africa where monopoly capitalism dominated the people. Critics of communist doctrine point out that, since Lenin's time, historical developments have disproved his theory. Lenin's forecast that such upheavals would deny capitalist states raw materials and overseas markets has proved false because the newly independent nations are striving to expand their sales of primary commodities, and trade has flourished. Moreover, the era of imperialism and colonialism has ended with a peaceful transition of most colonial peoples to independence and self-government. Communist victories have occurred not as a result of class struggle but only where communist leaders have inspired or taken over nationalist movements. In addition, the advanced countries have prospered since giving up their overseas possessions. These historical facts, critics assert, negate the Leninist theory of imperialism and colonialism. Supporters of the Leninist theory point out that Third World peoples are undergoing a progressive radicalization and that Western neo-colonialism, carried on by gigantic multinational corporations that control much of the economic activity in the Third World, has replaced the traditional imperialism and colonialism.

Communist Theory: New Communist Man   The belief that an evolution of human nature can be produced by changing man's social environment. The concept of the "new communist man" assumes that man's true nature—kindly, cooperative, and gregarious—has been warped by the competitive, hostility-prone, and conflict-ridden social environment of capitalist society. According to communist theoreticians, when private property is abolished and capitalist institutions are replaced by socialist ones, human potential for virtue will prevail.

Significance   The new communist man in Marxist doctrine will be a product of the sweeping economic and social changes that occur during the transitional period of socialism. The doctrine gives Marxism a religious basis since it postulates that man will in effect be reborn and recast into an earlier uncorrupted form guided by a new and higher set of moral values. This will occur, according to communist theory, in the final historical stage of pure communism when man will live in a classless, stateless, cooperative society free from arbitrary restraint and coercive power. The schism in the world communist movement between Moscow and Peking as well as growing nationalism changed the ideological references about the new communist man to "the new Soviet man" and "the new Chinese man." Critics of communist doctrine assert that there is no evidence that human nature is changing under socialism or that there is less propensity to commit crimes. Soviet penal law, for example, applies formidable penalties for various frequent offenses against public property, and Soviet citizens continue to commit ordinary types of "bourgeois" crimes.

Communist Theory: Revolution   The use of force by the masses to win and hold power in the violent climax to the class struggle anticipated by communist doctrine. Marx believed that in democratic states the proletariat could conceivably take power initially by winning the battle of the ballot box, but he forecast that when the proletariat sought to dislodge the bourgeoisie from its control of economic and political institutions, a counter-revolution would be likely to result. Lenin modified Marxism by postulating that the bourgeoisie would never relinquish its dominant role until its power was smashed by a violent proletarian revolution. In enunciating a policy of peaceful coexistence, Nikita Khrushchev declared in 1961 that communism does not need war to spread its ideals, that its weapon "is its superiority over the old system in social organization, political system, economy, the improvement of the standard of living and spiritual culture." Wars of national liberation fought by the masses in the underdeveloped lands of the world, however, were recognized by Khrushchev (and later by Leonid Brezhnev) as necessary and just.

Significance   Much communist literature in the nineteenth and twentieth centuries has been concerned with the nature of the Marxist-predicted revolution. The central question of debate has been whether the culmination of the class struggle would require a violent overthrow of the established government or could be accomplished peacefully through democratic processes. Most communist theorists have recognized violent revolution as the legitimate and necessary means for achieving socialism, but none has advocated war by communist states against capitalist states as a proper or useful strategy. Communist leaders from V. I. Lenin to Leonid Brezhnev have expounded the idea that "revolution cannot be exported," that it must "result from indigenous conditions," and that the internal situation within societies must, in the Marxist sense, be "ripe for revolution." Soviet leaders, however, have justified support for revolutionary groups in other states on the ground that, when advanced capitalist states export counterrevolution to prevent the natural outcome of the class struggle, Communists are duty bound to provide support for the "progressive" forces involved in the struggle.

Communist Theory: Socialist Program   The basic changes to be undertaken, following a communist revolution, that would transform society from capitalism to socialism and prepare the way for transition into the final classless, stateless stage of pure communism. The main objectives of the socialist program set forth by Marx in the *Communist Manifesto* of 1848 include: (1) abolition of all private ownership of land; (2) a sharply progressive income tax; (3) abrogation of all inheritance rights; (4) state control of all banking and credit; (5) state ownership and operation of all communication and transport; (6) collectivization of agriculture and creation of industrial armies; (7) equal obligation for all to work; (8) abolition of child labor; and (9) free education for all children in public schools. The socialist program, according to communist theorists, is to be implemented during the period of transition under the dictatorship of the proletariat.

Significance   The socialist program offered by Marx resembles a party platform aimed at gaining support for a set of governmental policy proposals. Although communist states have generally implemented most of the planks in the program, some are also partly or wholly embodied in governmental programs carried on in capitalist states. Marx and other early communist leaders believed that such economic and social reforms could never be carried out in advanced industrialized countries because of the intractable opposition of the bourgeoisie to any changes that might threaten their dominant role. The socialist program in the Soviet Union has in recent years been substantially altered and supplemented as a result of increased dependence on sales taxes rather than income levies, by the evolution of a new class of technocrats and bureaucrats, and by the application of economic reforms that establish a profit motive and the semblance of a market economy.

Communist Theory: Surplus Value   The Marxian postulate that the price of any product includes not only the "socially necessary" labor cost of production but also a "surplus value" that takes the form of profit for the capitalist. For Marx, the theory of surplus value meant that the worker who contributes all the value to a product is cheated out of his just compensation while the capitalist profits by exploiting another's labor. The surplus-value concept was developed by Marx by combining the classical labor theory of value expounded by John Locke, Adam Smith, and David Ricardo with the mercantilist doctrine of subsistence wages. The first propounded the idea that all value is based on mixing one's labor with the raw materials of the earth, and the second articulates the philosophy that workers should be paid extremely low wages to provide them with an incentive to work by making their lives a struggle for sustenance.

Significance　The theory of surplus value developed by Marx constitutes the starting point in communist doctrine for explaining the contradictions of capitalism. The natural tendency for capitalists to try to expand surplus value or profits, according to Marx and Lenin, creates an increasing impoverishment of the workers, underconsumption, and surplus production that results in economic depressions, imperialism, and colonialism. A class struggle between the exploited and exploiters follows as a necessary consequence. Defenders of capitalism, however, assert that profits reward entrepreneurial ability and are essential to the creation of risk capital and the encouragement of investment. Moreover, critics of communism point out that the economic well-being of workers in capitalist states has improved more rapidly than that of workers in communist states, where surplus value goes to the state.

Consensus of Values　Mutual attitudes, beliefs, and aspirations among human beings. When a consensus of values exists, political action may be both motivated by and directed toward the achievement of common goals. When a group possesses a high level of value consensus, it is often described as a "community." *See also* POLITICAL COMMUNITY, p. 331; VALUES, p. 83.

Significance　The degree of value consensus helps to determine the actual or potential level of political, economic, and social integration and the degree of stability within a social group. When rival social groups within a state are unable to agree on basic policy matters, for example, revolution or civil war may erupt. Among nations, the creation of international institutions and the development of international law can proceed only as rapidly as a consensus of values evolves, and disagreement on basics may result in international conflict. On the regional level, a growing consensus among Western Europeans encouraged by functional integration programs has helped to develop a European community consciousness that may produce a future federal union in the region.

Cultural Exchange International programs carried on by states or by private groups to foster intercultural appreciation of artistic and scientific achievements and understanding of political, economic, and social institutions. Cultural exchange programs are often instruments of foreign policy employed by states to strengthen relations with friendly nations and to contribute to a relaxation of tension between peoples of potentially hostile countries. *See also* CULTURAL EXCHANGE, p. 378.

Significance Major governmental efforts to influence foreign peoples through cultural exchange activities date back at least to the period of the French Revolution. Since World War II, cultural exchange programs have been directed more toward achieving national interest objectives than toward improving international understanding. During the Cold War period such programs have been carried on by both East and West. The United States, for example, has fostered two-way exchanges of students and professors under the Fulbright Act of 1946, a broad leadership exchange program under the Smith-Mundt Act of 1948, diverse overseas cultural programs financed under the surplus agricultural disposal program of Public Law 480, exchange tours of artists, musical groups, authors, poets, and other cultural leaders, and has sent thousands of Peace Corps volunteers to the underdeveloped countries. The Soviet Union has sponsored Youth Festivals, sent its top performing and creative artists abroad, established a Friendship of Nations University in Moscow for the youth of the underdeveloped countries, and has sent diverse educational and scientific groups on special cultural missions. Both sides have tried to convey the image of a highly cultured society that foreign peoples might well emulate in their own development. In addition to those programs motivated by foreign policy objectives, the United Nations Educational, Scientific, and Cultural Organization (UNESCO) has encouraged and sponsored national and international programs aimed at improving cultural cooperation and international understanding.

Democracy An ideology constructed around the liberal values of individual freedom, equality, human dignity and brotherhood, limited government, the rule of law, and the democratic political process. Although numerous political philosophers since Aristotle have contributed to the ideology of democracy, the foundations for modern democratic doctrines were fashioned by eighteenth and nineteenth century liberals, who transformed it from a theoretical formulation into a working system of government. Major contributors to democratic theory during this period include James Harrington, John Locke, Jean Jacques Rousseau, Thomas Jefferson, Thomas Paine, Jeremy Bentham, James Mill, John Stuart Mill, and Alexis de Tocqueville. The twentieth century has seen the further transformation of democratic doctrines from their earlier legal forms and principles to a full-blown ideology that postulates concepts for the "best" society rooted in individual freedom, social concern, and human dignity. During the twentieth century, democracy, which since the latter part of the eighteenth century had been associated with the economic freedoms of laissez-faire capitalism, was reoriented toward the assumption of responsibility by a democratic government to deal with some of the economic and social maladjustments arising out of the Industrial Revolution. Individual theorists whose writings support a positive governmental role include L. T. Hobhouse, John Dewey, and Joseph Schumpeter. Democratic theory, however, remains a loose-knit congeries of theories, concepts, and practices, diversely interpreted and pragmatically applied, rejecting alike dogma and the belief that the social good can be objectively or scientifically determined. It presupposes that the individual can make social policy judgments and that a free society provides the best environment for constructing social institutions and ordering human relations. Political democracy, with its emphases on constitutionalism, sovereignty vested in the people, the accountability of public officials, civil liberty guarantees, the rule of law, and majority rule, remains the core of the ideology. Even these fundamental concepts, however, find diverse application among democratic states, and few contemporary theorists have sought to expand them. See also DEMOCRATIC THEORY, pp. 63–68.

Significance   Since the American and French Revolutions the democratic ideology has been pitted competitively against many rival political systems. Among these have been monarchy and the divine right of kings, aristocracy and oligarchy, fascism and the creed of the omnipotent state, and communism and its dogmatic creed of violence. Though often rejected after being tried by societies that misunderstood its principles, abused its freedoms, or sought quick and easy solutions to their problems, democracy nevertheless has remained an attractive ideal for intellectuals and the masses. It has prospered most in the Atlantic community, in the English-speaking Commonwealth countries, and in the Western European environment that nurtured it through its Graeco-Roman and Judaeo-Christian roots and refined it through almost two centuries of speculative theorizing and pragmatic trial and error. Its particular effectiveness in these regions may also relate to the special conditions that encourage its development including considerable degrees of social cohesion and consensus of basic values, a stable economic base, and educated and responsible peoples. In the contemporary world, the major ideological contest has pitted the concepts of the democratic society against those proclaimed in communist theory. The battleground for this competition consists of approximately one hundred twenty Third World nations, many of them newly emergent from a century or more of colonialism.

Democratic Theory: Accountability A fundamental tenet of democratic theory that establishes the ultimate responsibility of all public officials to the people. Accountability is maintained through elections, constitutional controls, initiative, referendum, and recall, public opinion surveys and polls, the activities of political parties, public meetings, freedoms of assembly, petition, speech, and press, and roll-call voting in legislative bodies.

Significance All democratic systems accept the principle of accountability, but the institutions and procedures for implementation vary from country to country. In practice, the main lines of accountability run from the lowest bureaucratic levels up to the ministerial or cabinet levels, thence to the chief executive and legislative body, and finally, through elections, to the voters. The lines of authority, consequently, run in the opposite direction. A responsible political party system enhances the ability of the people to keep government accountable in policy matters as well as in decision making and administrative areas. A working system of accountability distinguishes democratic systems of government from those based on absolutism and from those "guided" or "façade" democratic systems that use the forms and institutions of democracy but in fact exercise authoritarian powers over the people. As a rule, political systems that incorporate the highest levels of accountability and responsibility to the people—such as the British system—can be regarded as the most democratic.

Democratic Theory: Civil Liberties   Guarantees that, in a democratic system, the individual's freedom will not be arbitrarily curtailed by government. Civil liberties are usually incorporated in a bill of rights or constitution that enumerates specific limitations on the authority of public officials. Major rights typically protected include freedoms of assembly, association, press, religion, speech, property, and due process and fair trial for those accused of crime. In the modern era, democratic governments have increasingly assumed a positive role in offering protection for the civil rights of individuals and groups from arbitrary interference by others in the society.

Significance   Protection of the individual's civil liberties and freedom to dissent is a key ingredient of the democratic creed. No right, however, can be absolute; all rights are limited by the need for protecting and advancing the legitimate interests of society. In a democracy, interference with the individual's freedom must not be arbitrary but reasonable and just, meeting the requirements of due process and the rule of law. The main problem in any democratic system is that of establishing an equilibrium between freedom and authority. If freedom is abused on a mass scale resulting in deprivations of the rights of individuals and groups by others, the consensus that permits free expression and dissent may break down and give way to anarchy or authoritarian control over the society. A viable democratic society provides for as great a measure of individual freedom as is consistent with the requirements of an orderly democratic society.

Democratic Theory: Constitutionalism   The basic concept that democratic government is limited in the scope of its authority, permitting government officials to exercise only those powers and perform those functions permitted by law. The major limitations of constitutionalism are incorporated in the fundamental charter or contract, whether written or unwritten, which is given formal or tacit approval by the people of the state.

Significance   The principle of constitutionalism applied to a working system of government provides one of the basic attributes that distinguishes a democratic system from those based on a form of absolutism. In a state in which many fundamental constitutional principles remain largely unwritten, as in Britain, the government is limited by custom, tradition, and what the people are willing to accept in the way of political innovation and policy development through the many facets of the political process. In the United States and many other democratic countries, a written constitution serves as a contract between the people and the government. Through the process of judicial review, laws and governmental actions that exceed constitutional limitations can be struck down by the courts, thus buttressing the principle of limited government and supplementing the role of the people in controlling their government through elections and other political techniques. Yet, the limitations on government in modern democratic states have proved to be extremely flexible, permitting governments through public acquiescence in broad interpretations of fundamental laws to become regulatory and service institutions.

Democratic Theory: Individualism   The concept underlying democratic systems of government that holds that the chief purpose of government is to foster the well-being of the individual and to permit each person to realize his or her full capabilities. The doctrine of individualism posits that government has an obligation to respect and to protect each person's rights and to safeguard them from trespass by other individuals or groups.

Significance   Historically, the democratic doctrine of individualism has been based on the ideas that the people exercise supreme political power, that government authority is limited, and that each individual possesses certain inalienable natural rights. Economic individualism emerged in the Western state system during the eighteenth century, when the individual-centered doctrines and practices of laissez-faire capitalism began to replace the state-oriented systems of mercantilism. The American and French Revolutions that occurred in the latter part of the eighteenth century complemented the new economic liberalism by building working political systems based on the importance of the individual. The American Declaration of Independence and the French Declaration of the Rights of Man and Citizen, for example, placed their main emphasis on providing freedom for the individual to enjoy in full measure the exercise of natural rights endowed from birth. The main ideological conflict in the contemporary world pits the democratic concept of individualism against the collectivist theories expounded in socialist and communist doctrine.

Democratic Theory: Majority Rule   The principle that decisions in a democracy should be made by the greater number of citizens in any political unit. Although the majority possesses the right and the power to govern, democratic theory also demands that minority rights be protected and that the minority be permitted to criticize and offer alternatives to the policies of the majority and seek, through the electoral process, to become the majority.

Significance   The principle of majority rule has been accepted by most democratic theorists as the *sine qua non* of the doctrines and practices of democracy. If the majority does not rule, power must then be exercised by an elite group selected on the basis of wealth, status, ability, or other criteria. Typically, if the majority will does not prevail, the governing system takes the form of absolutism or authoritarian control. Although rule by the majority is facilitated in a working two-party system—as in Britain—coalition governments based on groups of parties that join to form a majority and establish a government are most common in democratic states. Some democratic theorists reject majority rule in favor of government by consensus or by a concurrent majority which offers minority groups a veto over major policies. Antidemocratic theorists regard majority rule as "mobocracy" or government by the untrained, unfit, and emotionally unstable masses. The application of the principle of majority rule to a working system of government, however, tends to encourage stability through widespread participation of citizens in public affairs.

Democratic Theory: Natural Law   The concept of an unchanging, universally applicable set of laws governing human relationships that provides a moral standard by which to judge the actions of men and governments. The principle of *jus naturale* incorporated in democratic theory limits the powers of government, establishes the concept of natural justice, and propounds the idea of equality of all mankind in a universal society governed by the law of nature.

Significance   The theory of natural law was first expounded by early Greek philosophers, then postulated as the main guidepost in the development of a universal society by the Stoics, later modified by the Romans and by Church philosophers during the Middle Ages, and finally brought to flower as the central theme in the eighteenth century natural rights doctrine underlying the ideology of democracy. In the latter case, the concept's transformation from "law" to "rights" reflected the new emphases on individualism, popular sovereignty, and limited government that were embodied in the American Declaration of Independence and the French Declaration of the Rights of Man and Citizen. For the first time, working systems of government based on the democratic principles that recognized the natural and inalienable rights of citizens were established and flourished. The concept of natural law has also been influential in the development of legal, moral, ethical, and religious systems, but its main function has been to serve as a standard for individual and governmental conduct and to limit the powers exercised by the state over the individual. The ambiguous nature of the natural law concept, however, has made it subject to conflicting interpretations and to challenge by those who reject it as a subjective metaphysical idea. Positivist legal scholars, for example, have challenged the validity of the concept of natural law with their doctrine that law constitutes the sovereign will of the state and therefore can only be promulgated by government.

Democratic Theory: Popular Sovereignty   The basic democratic principle that the people are the ultimate source of all legitimate political authority. The concept of popular sovereignty was enunciated in the eighteenth century natural rights philosophy that served as the intellectual base for modern democratic theory. The doctrine of popular sovereignty holds that the people of a political unit or society possess supreme authority, that they establish government and delegate powers to public officials through a social contract or constitution, and that the government so created remains accountable to the people who retain the supreme authority.

Significance   The theory of popular sovereignty seeks to explain the origins and location of power in democratic societies. It has also served as a justification for revolution against established civil authority when government has deprived the people of their rights. This doctrine was expounded by the American and French revolutionaries in 1776 and 1789. Although political power is ordinarily exercised indirectly by the people through representative institutions, under the doctrine of popular sovereignty the people retain the right to alter, abolish, and create new forms of government. In the final analysis popular sovereignty expounds the idea of government by consent—an idea alien to any form of authoritarian or absolutist system. In the contemporary ideological struggle, the idea that government in democratic states can be changed in free elections and basic laws altered or abolished by the action of the people has served as a major propaganda weapon for the West.

Democratic Theory: Rule of Law   A fundamental principle of democratic government that proclaims the supremacy of law, establishing limits for public officials in the exercise of their powers. The concept of the rule of law buttresses the doctrine of limited government by protecting the rights of individuals from arbitrary interference by officials.

Significance   The rule of law in a democratic system contrasts sharply with the unlimited personal power and authority of rulers in an authoritarian state. Under the rule of law, all individuals are equal before the law and none can be convicted of crime except through procedures guaranteed to insure due process, fair trial, and punishment provided by law. In recent years, however, protest movements that encourage mass violations of "unjust laws" as a means for attacking the established rules, particularly in civil rights and Selective Service areas, have seriously challenged the rule of law in the United States and several other democratic countries. Many protestors view the law as a device used by "the establishment" to enhance and protect its own interests while those of minority groups remain unrecognized and unprotected. The rule of law can flourish in a democratic state only when a general consensus of values prevails among diverse groups that unjust laws and practices will be challenged through legitimate channels of the political process.

Eurocommunism   The special role, policies, and programs of national Communist parties in Western European democratic countries. Eurocommunism evolved in the 1960s and 1970s as the monolithic control by the Soviet Union over European Communist parties ended. Eurocommunism implies a renunciation of revolution as a means of gaining political power. In addition, communist leaders in Western Europe tend to espouse nationalism, good government free from corruption, administrative efficiency, and effectiveness in fighting economic problems such as inflation and unemployment. They also tend to accept the role of the Catholic Church and many of them are active members. Occasionally, communist leaders of Western Europe have criticized Russian and East European leaders and policies, an action unknown before the advent of Eurocommunism. *See also* COMMUNISM, p. 41.

Significance Eurocommunism is a new ideological approach aimed at winning over the voters of Western Europe. Communist leaders and their organizations in Western Europe have sought to accomplish this goal by rejecting violence and offering a viable alternative to the center, right-wing, and other left-wing parties. As a result, Communist parties in Western Europe have garnered about 12 percent of the total West European vote in recent years, and approximately 15 percent of the total vote cast in the direct elections to the ten-nation European Parliament. Western observers view the development of Eurocommunism as a mixed blessing, providing on the one hand a moderating force that impinges on Moscow's policies, and on the other an attractive electoral choice that could in time lead to Communist parties joining government coalitions in several states. The impact of such an event on NATO, for instance, could be substantial.

Fascism   The ideology of the extreme right which fosters an authoritarian society based on rule by an elite headed by a supreme leader or dictator. Fascists usually win power in a state through a *coup d'etat* or during a turbulent revolutionary period when real or imaginary fears of communism lead large numbers of people to accept a radical transformation of democratic institutions to meet the problem of governmental instability. Fascism is often based on an exaggerated adulation of the nation, rejecting individualism and democratic concepts of limited government in favor of a system in which a disciplined people gives its full loyalty to an organic, monolithic state. Dissent is eliminated and unity is fostered by secret police terror, by extensive propaganda programs, by the curtailment of civil liberties, and by a single party monopoly of power. An aura of xenophobia and militarism often pervades a fascist state. Under fascism, private ownership of land and capital is retained, but all private businesses and organizations are regimented and directed by the state in pursuit of national objectives. *See also* FASCIST THEORY, pp. 70–72.

Significance   Modern fascism emerged out of the social, economic, and political crises of the interwar period of the 1920s and 1930s. The prototype of the fascist state was forged by Benito Mussolini in the years following his coming to power in Italy in 1922 in the wake of an anticommunist reaction to the Bolshevik Revolution in Russia. Fascist regimes were established subsequently by Adolf Hitler and the Nazi party in Germany, by Francisco Franco and the Falangist party in Spain, by Juan Peron and his Peronista party in Argentina, and in several Eastern European countries during the 1930s and 1940s. Although fascism as an ideology came into general disrepute following the defeat of the Axis Powers during World War II, neo-fascism has made gains in many of the new underdeveloped countries of the world, where military juntas have seized power following the breakdown of fledgling democratic institutions. Fascist systems face serious problems of succession since the stability of the regime is often based on the glorification of the supreme leader, a charismatic personality who dominates the nation by capturing the emotional support of its people. Fascism as an ideology contemptuously rejects the democratic political process based on freedom, fair elections, and accountability, but its most active hostility is directed against Communists and left-wing Socialists.

Fascist Theory: Anti-Communism   The belief and widely applied propaganda technique of fascism that holds that only a united totalitarian state headed by a supreme leader (dictator) can master the threat posed by the conspiratorial tactics of communism. The anti-communism of fascism exploits the fear of communism prevalent in all classes in the advanced states, using it both to win and to hold power. Political enemies are often disposed of by a fascist regime by labeling them "Communists" or agents of international communism. Fascist theory promises to defeat communism by establishing a "true" socialism that eliminates class struggle by reconciling the interests of all groups in common support for and service to the nation.

Significance   Fascism, possessing no extensive or coherent body of theory, has gained adherents and has won power mainly by offering unity and stability to societies during times of crisis when communist-inspired revolutions—real or imagined—have threatened the established order. Germany in the early 1930s, for example, was beset with mass frustrations growing out of economic malaise, severe unemployment, and social disintegration. Adolf Hitler and the Nazi party, by promising to save the country from communism, gained the financial backing of wealthy industrialists and the voting support of a substantial portion of the middle and working classes to win power in 1933. In recent years military cliques in many underdeveloped countries have seized power through *coups d'etat,* establishing fascist-type regimes with the support of local power elites to protect the nation from actual or alleged communist threats.

Fascist Theory: Elitism   The principle that state power should be exercised by a single hierarchically structured party headed by a supreme leader or small group of oligarchs. Fascist elitism rejects democratic processes, constitutional limitations on state power, and pluralism in favor of an organic state in which every group and individual plays a role assigned by the governing elite. Opposition to rule by the elite party group is not tolerated, and the power of the state is used to destroy all resistance to the regime.

Significance   Rule by a highly centralized nationalistically inspired elite group is one of the most common characteristics of fascism. In Germany during the 1930s, for example, Adolf Hitler and the Nazi party ruthlessly liquidated all opposition parties and individuals through the establishment of a totalitarian dictatorship. Similar tactics were pursued by Benito Mussolini's Fascist party in Italy, by Francisco Franco's Falangist party in Spain, and by the Peronista party in Argentina. Although fascist elites have usually sought support from the masses through propaganda, nationalistic fervor, and military ventures, they have looked with contempt upon any meaningful role for the "average man" in the political process. Some scholars regard Plato as the first fascist theorist because of the elitist doctrines woven into the fabric of his ideal state.

Fascist Theory: Militarism   The emphasis placed by Fascists on military organization and discipline to strengthen the single national party and to provide order and security for the state. Under fascism militaristic values are inculcated in the young at school and in youth organizations, military heroes are revered, and spectacular ceremonies and parades extolling the virtues of the soldier are used to cultivate an honored role for the military as the defenders of the nation and to encourage acceptance of a well-disciplined social order.

Significance   Most fascist dictatorships have come to power and have maintained their rule with the active support of the military. Adolf Hitler and Benito Mussolini, for example, donned uniforms and became the commanders-in-chief of their nations' armed forces, thus dominating the military rather than permitting it to dominate them. Francisco Franco of Spain and Juan Peron of Argentina also functioned as military as well as civilian chiefs of their states. In the contemporary world, rightwing, fascist-type takeovers of power in many underdeveloped countries of Asia, Africa, and Latin America have brought military cliques into power as a result of mass frustration stemming from the failure of democracy to produce the expected bounty of economic development.

Fascist Theory: Statism   The concept that sovereignty is vested not in the people but in the national state, and that all individuals and associations exist only to enhance the power, the prestige, and the well-being of the state. The fascist concept of statism repudiates individualism and exalts the nation as an organic body headed by one supreme leader and nurtured by unity, force, and discipline. Under this doctrine, the state creates worthy individuals who realize their destiny only by contributing to the glory of the state.

Significance   The fascist concept of statism is a modern adaptation of earlier forms of autocratic rule in which the individual offered complete obedience to the ruler, who personified the state. Nationalism, militarism, and, in some fascist states, racism have been used to inculcate values that exist and assume importance because the state decrees them. In a fascist state, no other loyalty than that to the state is permitted. The entire ideology of fascism in pre-World War II Italy and Germany was dominated by the dogmas of individual subjection to and immersion in the mystical entity of the nation.

Fascist Theory: Totalitarianism   Authoritarian control by the state over individuals and organizations so that all activity is harmonized with the policies and goals of the regime. Fascist totalitarian tactics include using secret police and terrorist operations, eliminating dissent, denying civil rights, and carrying on an all-pervasive propaganda program through state-controlled media of communication. A single political party inspired by the ideology of fascism monopolizes power and uses the machinery of the state to carry out its objectives.

Significance Fascist systems of government vary in the extent of totalitarian control each system extends over the people of its state. Each tends to be pragmatic in the amount of autocratic control that its leaders believe to be necessary or expedient to impose. For Fascists, totalitarianism is aimed at uniting the people in a highly integrated nation so that the public interest always takes precedence over private interests. Of the fascist states, Germany achieved the highest level of totalitarian control during the 1930s and 1940s under the leadership of Adolf Hitler and the Nazi party.

Fourteen Points An instrument of psychological warfare composed of idealistic principles which President Woodrow Wilson enunciated in 1918 as a rationale for winning World War I and for maintaining the peace to follow. In his Fourteen Points Wilson called for open diplomacy, freedom of the seas, disarmament, removal of economic barriers, international supervision of colonies, peaceful change based on self-determination, and the creation of an association of nations that would guarantee the political independence and territorial integrity of great and small states alike. *See also* LEAGUE OF NATIONS, p. 322; PROPAGANDA, p. 76; PSYCHOLOGICAL WARFARE, p. 186.

Significance The Fourteen Points illustrates the powerful impact that an idealistic program can have on the thinking and actions of millions of human beings. The proposal served as a useful propaganda instrument in the last phase of World War I by helping to bolster sagging Allied morale and to weaken German resolve. By winning over the mass European publics, Wilson was able to apply direct pressure to force the other Allied leaders—David Lloyd George, Georges Clemenceau, and Vittorio Orlando—to compromise at the Versailles Peace Conference on their designs for territorial aggrandizement and more punitive terms for Germany. Wilson's demands for a general association of nations received such widespread support that almost all countries joined the new League of Nations. His call for "open covenants, openly arrived at" encouraged the development of conference diplomacy, and his demands for applying the principle of self-determination led to the holding of numerous plebiscites. The principles proclaimed in the Fourteen

Points continue to influence the conduct of international affairs and are widely used in ideological and propaganda efforts.

Ideological Warfare   A type of conflict between rival value systems or "ways of life" that involve efforts to gain mass conversions. Ideological warfare involves the utilization of propaganda, cultural programs, educational, artistic, and scientific exchange projects, foreign aid, and other activities aimed at winning or maintaining allegiance. The major ideological confrontations in the contemporary world are between the communist and "free world" states, and between Soviet and Chinese communism. See also IDEOLOGY, p. 74; PROPAGANDA, p. 76; PSYCHOLOGICAL WARFARE, p. 186; PUBLIC OPINION, p. 78.

Significance   Ideological warfare has become a major factor affecting international relations in the twentieth century. It is both a unifying force pulling together people of diverse national backgrounds in a common cause, and a disintegrative force that tends to pit "true believers" against each other in holy war fired by fanatical zeal. Each side in the contemporary ideological struggles has tried to convince uncommitted millions of the strength of its position, the superiority of its social system, and the rightness of its cause as opposed to the warlike, imperialistic, decadent, and cruel nature of the rival system. The deep-rooted hatred inculcated in the minds of the people for the ideology of the other camp makes tolerance and compromise elusive. Consequently, ideological warfare increases the possibilities of an eventual open military clash between the supporters of the rival systems.

Ideology   The articulation of basic political, economic, and social values as a body of ideas that serves as the basis for an ideal social system or "way of life." An ideology is concerned with the nature of the political system, the exercise of power, the role of the individual, the nature of the economic and social system, and the objectives of society. As a fundamental belief system, an ideology not only incorporates a society's basic values but itself becomes the major value to be defended and, in many cases, spread to other societies. See also IDEOLOGICAL WARFARE, p. 74; PROPAGANDA, p. 76.

Significance   An ideology is a dynamic force in the power equation since the unity and vitality it creates can be directed against other states or groups. A set of ideas can win over human minds without using organized power, but ideologies are seldom spread without ideological warfare campaigns supported by organized power. Typically, ideological convictions are closely intertwined with religious or nationalistic sentiments, and each tends to identify with and support the other. In Vietnam, for example, the Vietcong successfully related communism to local issues, nationalism, and good organization to develop their challenge to the Saigon regime. Historically, ideology has constituted a divisive force in international and national affairs when coterminous rival systems and their adherents have sought to achieve victory over others.

Iron Curtain   A phrase coined by Winston Churchill in 1946 to describe the Soviet policy of isolating the communist states of Eastern Europe from Western Europe. The term *Iron Curtain* described the barrier established by the communist nations under Soviet direction, the secrecy and censorship imposed within the region, and the absence of communication with the West. *See also* COLD WAR, p. 164.

Significance   The Iron Curtain was rigidly maintained for an extremely tense decade during the Cold War. Although a relaxation occurred following Josef Stalin's death in 1953, some of the harsh controls were restored as a result of the abortive Hungarian uprising of 1956. In the late 1950s, however, a progressive moderation in the policy of isolation began. By the late 1970s, the Iron Curtain had been lifted to the point where several million Western tourists visited Eastern Europe each year, numerous educational and cultural exchanges were going on, diplomatic and consular relations had been restored to near normalcy, and restrictions on communication and travel generally had been relaxed. Many of the communist states, however, retained travel restrictions that deprived their citizens of equal access to the West. In addition, in the early 1980s Soviet involvement in Afghanistan and the Western response to it signaled that the era of détente might be ending.

Mass Media   The technical apparatus for communicating with millions of people. The mass media include radio, television, newspapers, magazines, books, motion pictures, and official publications. *See also* PROPAGANDA, p. 76; PUBLIC OPINION, p. 78.

Significance   Scientific and technical improvements in mass communication have made the world a battleground in the war of ideas. Within democratic states, the mass media play a vital role in helping to inform and interest the citizenry in public affairs. In dictatorial or oligarchic states, the governing elite monopolizes the mass media to control the thinking and the actions of their people so as to establish legitimacy, eliminate opposition, create unity, and channel the energies of their people toward state-determined objectives. In the international arena, many states employ various technical means of communication for spreading propaganda and waging ideological warfare in their efforts to gain support for their policies and programs while trying to discredit their rivals. The mass media are also effective when directed at national opinion elites. These elites help to shape the attitudes of the mass publics. Some studies of the role of the mass media also indicate that they are more useful in reinforcing rather than creating or destroying mass views.

National Front   Alliance with non-communist groups, used by a communist party to achieve its goals. The national-front approach is often used in underdeveloped countries where the Communists team up with nationalist elements in independence movements or undertake leftist-inspired revolutions against indigenous elites. *See also* WARS OF NATIONAL LIBERATION, p. 200.

Significance   The national-front approach dates back to the era of the 1930s when the Communists pursued a policy of encouraging the formation of anti-Fascist "popular front" party coalitions in the democratic states of Europe. In recent years, Communists have made extensive use of the national-front tactic in joining with anticolonial, anti-Western groups and parties in many nations of Asia and Africa. The National Liberation Front (NLF) of South Vietnam, for example, included non-communist nationalist elements as well as members of the Communist party of South Vietnam. After a national front has achieved its objectives, typically, the coalition dissolves and competition for power between the communist and non-communist elements of the front is resumed.

Propaganda   Any form of communication aimed at implanting data, ideas, or images in human minds to influence the thinking, emotions, or actions of individuals or groups. The objectives of propaganda include: (1) to win or strengthen friendly support; (2) to shape or alter attitudes and perceptions of ideas or events; (3) to weaken or undermine unfriendly foreign governments or their policies and programs; and (4) to counteract the unfriendly propaganda of other countries or groups. To be effective, propaganda must be relevant, credible to the recipients, repeated often, simple, consistent, interesting, identifiable with a local or national situation, and disguised so as not to be recognizable as propaganda by those at whom it is aimed. Propaganda may take the form of an appeal to the idealism of the recipients, it may be factual but distorted through careful selection, or it may be based on outright falsehoods. Propaganda activities are instruments of psychological warfare aimed at influencing the actions of human beings in ways that are compatible with the national-interest objectives of the purveying state. See also IDEOLOGICAL WARFARE, p. 74; PSYCHOLOGICAL WARFARE, p. 186; PUBLIC OPINION, p. 78.

Significance   Technological developments in the science of communication through the mass media and refinements in the art of psychological persuasion have given added impetus to the use of propaganda to pursue national objectives. Since the term *propaganda* often connotes an evil intent to deceive, state leaders commonly dismiss the communications efforts of other governments as nothing more than "propaganda" while at the same time they present their official publications, news reports, and analyses as the unvarnished truth based on "straight news" and objective analysis. Once a government acquires a domestic or foreign reputation for having a "credibility gap" in its communications to various publics, its effectiveness in using propaganda to support its policies or programs is seriously weakened. Although most countries devote some efforts to international propaganda activities, the United States and the Soviet Union carry on the most intensive and extensive operations. The United States, for example, operates a vast network—radio and television broadcasting (Voice of America), information centers, reading rooms, book and pamphlet distribution, and exhibits and displays of various kinds—under the United States International Communication Agency (ICA) programs. In addition, the United States government secretly provided much of the funds needed to carry on Radio Free Europe and Radio Liberation operations over a period of years.

Public Opinion Views and attitudes on domestic or foreign actions and issues held by the people of a nation, community, or group. Public opinion often fluctuates in response to independent or controlled stimuli in the political and social environment. It may in turn have a considerable impact on the environment by giving direction to the decision makers or by influencing or controlling their actions. In a totalitarian state, public opinion is shaped, manipulated, and controlled by the ruling elite using the mass media, censorship, elimination of opposition, rigged elections, and nationalistic propaganda. In a democracy, no single public opinion prevails; there are, rather, many publics in a pluralistic society holding diverse views on a variety of subjects. Public opinion can be identified and measured with varying degrees of accuracy through elections, plebiscites, the initiative, referendum, and recall procedures, pressure group activities, polls, public demonstrations, and by elected officials who secure the views of constituents by various means of inquiry. *See also* IDEOLOGICAL WARFARE, p. 74; MASS MEDIA, p. 75; PROPAGANDA, p. 76.

Significance Public opinion is a crucial element in the field of international affairs, both in the development of domestic support for foreign policies and in the efforts to influence publics in other states. No major foreign program carried on by a democratic or totalitarian state is likely to succeed unless a major proportion of its people give their active or, minimally, their passive support to it. In addition, world opinion, consisting of the diverse views of many governments and peoples, can be developed into a powerful restraining force on state action in the General Assembly of the United Nations. Prestige, an element and objective of state power, is closely related to the views held by publics in both friendly and unfriendly countries. Some efforts to influence public opinion are directed at mass publics, whereas others are aimed more selectively at opinion elites. Although many studies have been carried on to gain a better understanding of the nature, role, and measurement of public opinion, it remains a vague, yet powerful, component of the political process because people act not necessarily on the basis of what is true but on what they believe to be true.

Public Opinion: Mass Public The general public as it relates to the making of governmental decisions. The mass public, far from being a cohesive unity with common attitudes, prejudices, and views, consists of many publics holding diverse, often conflicting, opinions. The views of the mass public on specific issues may be expressed or divulged in various ways, but they are usually most effectively presented in democratic states through the electoral process or in polls. Mass opinion goes through three stages in the process of influencing governmental actions: formulation, expression, and direct effect upon or embodiment in policy decisions.

Significance   The role of mass public opinion in influencing the policymaking process is typically more effective in domestic matters than in foreign affairs. Still, no political leader— certainly not in a democratic state—can ignore the attitudes of the general public if these are clearly and actively hostile toward the means or objectives of a long-range foreign policy program. Although foreign policy initiatives do not normally emerge from mass views, the latter often set the limits for policy experimentation. A leading example of a situation in which the views of the mass public played a decisive role in controlling policy leaders was the restraining force of American isolationist and neutral sentiment on the efforts of the Roosevelt administration to expand its aid to the Allies from 1939 to 1941 prior to Pearl Harbor. Mass opinion also contributed substantially to the resignation of President Richard M. Nixon in 1974, the first resignation of a President in American history.

Public Opinion: Opinion Elites   Leadership elements influential in developing and shaping public opinion as a force in the political process. Opinion elites that influence foreign policy decisions include business, professional, educational, labor, farm, religious, patriotic, and other interest-group leaders and persons active in upper-echelon political, administrative, and communications areas. Opinion elites compete in seeking to interest and influence both official decision makers and the mass public on contemporary issues of concern to the elites.

Significance   The influence of opinion elites on the political process depends mainly on the interest and receptivity of the mass public to the issues and on the degree of intra- and inter-elite competition. The countervailing theory of pressure politics, for example, postulates that a semblance of equilibrium will be maintained among elites and the interest groups they represent since they tend to line up on different sides of major issues and reduce each other's power to influence foreign policy decisions. Although students of the policy process tend to agree that opinion elites play a part in making most foreign policy decisions, their exact role and the degree to which they can influence governmental actions by shaping public opinion remains vague.

Radio Free Europe   The militantly anti-communist private organization that broadcasts programs to the peoples of Eastern Europe. Radio Free Europe is staffed largely by refugees who fled from Eastern Europe during the period of its communization following World War II. Its efforts are supplemented by a second private and equally anti-communist broadcasting group, Radio Liberation.

Significance   Although the major portion of funds for supporting Radio Free Europe comes from private contributions in the United States, some observers believe that the Central Intelligence Agency has lent it substantial official support through indirect and undercover financing. Its policies and propaganda, however, have not always been in harmony with the objectives of the United States government. It has been charged, for example, with fomenting the Hungarian uprising of 1956 by leading Hungarians to believe that American military power and the United Nations would back them if they rose in revolt against their communist leaders. Its efforts have also weakened the United States policy in the 1960s of trying to "build bridges" to Eastern Europe by expanded trade, cultural exchanges, and normalization of diplomatic and consular relations. Supporters of Radio Free Europe claim that its news broadcasts are accurate and honest, that its programs are aimed at inspiring the peoples of Eastern Europe with nationalist pride, and that its policies and broadcasts seek to achieve a "peaceful liberation." Congressional investigations in the 1970s confirmed that the CIA was linked to Radio Free Europe and to Radio Liberation by secretly providing much of their financial support.

Social Cohesion   The degree of unity within a national society. Social cohesion depends upon the relationships among economic, social, and religious groups, the extent to which basic values are shared, common nationalistic and ideological impulses, and the nature of social organization. *See also* CONSENSUS OF VALUES, p. 60.

Significance   Social cohesion helps to stabilize a national group or political community when challenged by external enemies or internal problems. Traditional societies have tended to be the most stable (prior to their exposure to external influences) because their members generally accept the rigid stratification of social classes and rule by a small, powerful elite as their unchanging way of life. The traditional society is village oriented, daily actions are guided by long-accepted customs and traditions, and religion and conservative values provide the guidelines for almost all human actions. The social fabric of such societies, however, loses its resiliency and stability when outside forces bring change and aspirations for a new, better life to the people. A transitional society is characterized by disunity and instability as some members reject the old values and grope for new ones to replace them in the drive to achieve modernization. A "revolution of rising expectations" has swept over most of the centuries-old traditional societies, producing internal unrest and conflict on an unprecedented scale during the transitional stage. Modern democratic, industrially advanced societies, on the other hand, enjoy a high degree of stability and social cohesion as a result of a widely shared consensus of values which permits and encourages diversity in a pluralistic society. Authoritarian societies, both those oriented toward the right (fascist) and toward the left (communist), build social cohesion through such techniques as one-party systems, strict discipline, widespread propaganda, nationalism, and ideological dedication. In each type of society—traditional, transitional, democratic, and authoritarian—social cohesion depends on the extent to which the masses of people accept and are motivated by the basic values of that society.

Socialism   An ideology that rejects individualism, private ownership, and private profits in favor of a system based on economic collectivism, governmental, societal, or industrial-group ownership of the means of production and distribution of goods, and social responsibility. The doctrines of socialism have varied from those which espouse democratic values to those that call for forms of absolutism and dictatorship. Advocates of socialism have included utopians, Christians and other religious groups, political parties, welfare statists, leaders of developing countries, esoteric sects and societies, communists, and anarchists. Major differences among groups professing the ideology have involved the means for winning power and instituting socialism (democratic or revolutionary) and the nature of the socialist system to be established (state-controlled, syndicalist, or merely "cooperative"). In strategy, socialists fall into either of two categories: democratic socialists, who strive to use the political machinery of the state to achieve their goals by democratically winning power and peacefully modifying the existing system; or Marxian socialists, who believe that their objectives can only be achieved through violence and the destruction of existing capitalist and democratic institutions. Socialists are also divided, in terms of objectives, between those who wish to establish a centrally organized system using the power of the state and the syndicalists, who aim for a decentralized system with groups of workers owning and controlling all industries.

Significance   Various socialist doctrines were developed in Europe during the nineteenth century by reform groups, political parties, and intellectuals who were appalled by the suffering of the masses resulting from the factory system ushered in by the Industrial Revolution and from the early abuses of the capitalist system. In the twentieth century, limited systems of democratic socialism have been established in some of the advanced industrial democratic states, such as Sweden and Britain, in the form of extensive welfare state programs and some governmental ownership of basic industries and services. Social democratic parties espousing socialist programs also constitute powerful political forces in many continental European states. The Soviet Union and the communist countries of Eastern Europe regard themselves as socialist systems in transition toward a final stage of pure communism. In addition, the leaders of many developing countries describe their diverse techniques of governmental planning and direction of the drive to achieve economic development as socialist systems. Although socialism is often attacked in democratic countries as a system that stifles initiative and encourages inefficiency, many of its supporters regard it as a viable alternative to capitalism and communism.

Stereotype   A generalized, fixed mental picture or image of a group or society based on limited experience, hearsay, or emotion. A stereotype as a generalization may either accurately or inaccurately describe the characteristics of a group or of its individual members. Stereotypes are often created as a result of predispositions or expectations dominating perception. They exist because of man's limited knowledge of the facts in any situation, and because each person's ability to perceive reality is limited by his or her preconceptions and prejudices.

Significance　　Stereotypes affect the policy process in the field of foreign affairs because individual decision makers, opinion elites, and the general public may be unaware that the mental images they hold of other governments or peoples are inaccurate or biased. Governments also may seek to gain public support for their policies by creating a false public image of another nation that tends to support their decisions or programs. By stereotyping a nationality or an ideological group—that, for example, all Communists are aggression-minded, or that "the Chinese" are cunning and treacherous—serious errors of judgment in policy development and hostile people-to-people relations may result. Policies based on stereotyped images tend to reinforce the "pictures in our minds" because they evoke reactions from the stereotyped nation or group that tend to confirm the images.

Values　　Normative standards or goals that an individual, a group, a society, or a nation professes and strives to achieve. Values serve as guideposts for what men consider to be just and desirable—the kind of society that *ought* to exist. A society's values tend to become embodied within the broad framework of an ideology and are articulated in the form of an ideal or preferred "way of life" for that society and for others as well. Values may also relate to power, prestige, and the pursuit of status by a state. *See also* CONSENSUS OF VALUES, p. 60; SOCIAL COHESION, p. 80.

Significance　　The unity and strength of a society or group depends to a considerable extent on the degree of consensus of values that exists. Values tend to become more numerous and diffused within a pluralistic society of a democratic state, although certain basic standards concerning the nature of the political, economic, and social system remain fundamental to its harmony. Authoritarian societies, on the other hand, attempt to foster a limited, highly integrated set of values directly related to the domestic and foreign goals of the nation. Value conflict within or between societies has been a major contributing factor to internal revolutions and civil wars and to struggles between nations. A conflict over fundamental values between the Hindu and Muslim communities, for example, led in 1947 to the partitioning of British India into two independent states—India and Pakistan. The major conflict over values in the contemporary world involves the ideological struggle between those embodied in the concepts of democracy and those postulated by communism.

4. Geography and Population

Boundaries   The limits within which a state exercises territorial jurisdiction. Boundaries, as delimitations of jurisdiction, relate not only to a specific portion of the earth's surface but to territorial waters, airspace, and subsurface resources as well. Boundaries may be fixed by negotiation, arbitration, adjudication, plebiscite, allocation by an international body such as the United Nations, and cession through purchase or war. Various types of, and reasons for, particular boundaries include: (1) natural separators, as in the case of rivers and mountains; (2) cultural differences, such as the communal distinctions that served as the basis for drawing the boundaries between India and Pakistan; (3) historical and political considerations, as in the case of many of the new African states, whose boundaries were originally drawn by European colonial powers; and (4) those established by military equilibrium, as between Israel and her Arab neighbors, or between North and South Korea. *See also* ODER-NEISSE LINE, p. 100.

Significance   Boundaries are symbols of national independence and power and are also traditional sources of international tension and conflict. Current illustrations of boundaries involving international tensions and conflict are those between East and West Germany, the Soviet Union and Iran, the Soviet Union and the People's Republic of China, the People's Republic of China and India, between Israel and Syria, Jordan and Egypt, and among Somalia, Ethiopia, and Kenya. The significance of national boundaries in terms of national defense varies with the level of military technology involved. Boundaries involving ter-

85

rain features like mountains, rivers, swamps, or deserts may be important considerations in conventional warfare, of more limited significance when air operations are considered, and almost irrelevant in terms of nuclear missiles.

Buffer States   Weak states, located between or on the borders of strong states, that serve the security interests of the latter. Buffer states often exist only at the sufferance of their more powerful neighbors, who desire a "crush zone" between themselves and their rivals.

Significance   Serving, as they do, the economic and military interests of their dominant neighbors, buffer states have contributed to the maintenance of local and general power balances by reducing the chances of direct confrontation and conflict. Thus for many years Afghanistan, Tibet, and Persia served British interests as buffers between India and Russia. Since World War I, the states of Central Europe have frequently been regarded as a zone of buffer states guarding Western Europe from the Soviet Union, or vice versa.

Demographic Cycle   The series of changes in births and deaths that affect the size and composition of a society as it experiences technological change. The demographic cycle proceeds in three stages: from a preindustrial base of relative population stability, through a transitional stage of population explosion, to a final stage in which the rate of population growth slows down, stabilizes, and, in some countries, declines. *See also* DEMOGRAPHIC CYCLE, pp. 87–88.

Significance   Historically the various stages in the demographic cycle have been causally related to levels of economic development. The experience of the countries in which the Industrial Revolution began has been that, although industrialization made it possible to sustain larger populations at higher standards of living, improved economic well-being ultimately resulted in low birth rates. This experience accounts for much of the emphasis that is being placed on economic—particularly industrial—development by the countries presently in the midst of the population explosion. These burgeoning populations and the revolutions of rising expectations in societies around the world are also matters of increasing concern to industrialized countries, regional organizations, and agencies of the United Nations. Historical observation of the functioning of the demographic cycle allows world statesmen to forecast the consequences of current demographic trends. Whether national and international policies can be developed to relate populations to their environment is perhaps the major long-range problem facing the world today.

Demographic Cycle: Stage One   The preindustrial demographic pattern, characterized by high birth and death rates. In stage one, life expectancy is low (approximately thirty years), infant mortality is high, and population increase is steady but slow. This preindustrial population pattern typified the Western societies in the period before the Industrial Revolution and the traditional societies of Asia, Africa, and Latin America prior to the 1930s.

Significance   Stage-one societies experienced a slow rate of population growth for several reasons. The living standard was low, the economy was geared to subsistence agriculture, and nutritional standards were poor. Resistance to disease was low and modern medicine and public-sanitation facilities and standards were unknown. Large families were desirable because of the work children could contribute to the family, because having many children was a form of social security for aged parents, and because disease could be expected to kill off a number of children before they reached maturity. Such societies were also characterized by their early marriage age, the inferior status of women, and a low level of literacy. Stage-one societies have virtually disappeared in the contemporary world; these societies have moved into the second demographic stage as a result of their own as well as international efforts.

Demographic Cycle: Stage Two   The demographic pattern characterized by a population explosion. In stage two, the birth rate remains high, but the death rate declines sharply, resulting in rapid population growth. To begin with, a dramatic decrease in infant mortality results in more young adults, who in turn produce additional children, so that the natural rate of increase also rises. Since longevity has not yet increased substantially, the society tends to be biologically young. However, the same technology that makes industrialization possible eventually brings about an additional population increase by reducing the death rate still further, through improved medicine and sanitation.

Significance   The population explosion, or the second stage of the demographic cycle, when coupled with the revolution of rising expectations, presents serious national and international problems. Not only are the people in these countries demanding more out of life than they did previously, but there are also *more people* in these countries to demand better living standards at an *increasing rate* of improvement. Since their expectation curve is rising faster than their achievement curve, the distance between the two lines increases and may be described as a frustration gap. Thus rising populations and expectations are straining the resources and ingenuity of governments, many of which are relatively young and inexperienced. Some of the resulting problems and frustrations involve: (1) increasing internal tensions, disorders, and frequency of *coups d'etat*; (2) increasing irresponsible international actions designed to divert the masses, if only temporarily, from domestic problems; and (3) growing pressure on developed countries to provide vast amounts of development assistance in ways that will not offend self-conscious young nationalisms. Meanwhile, the gap between the developed and the developing countries is growing wider, increasing the international ferment. Because the size of the active population relative to the total population initially decreases, the burdens on the work force to produce higher living standards are substantially greater than at either of the other two stages of the demographic cycle. In addition, the large proportion of unemployed young people in such societies increases the level of tension and the propensity for revolution.

Demographic Cycle: Stage Three   The demographic pattern characterized by the declining rate of natural increase in the population. In contrast to the preceding stage, in which the birth rate remained high while the death rate fell sharply, in the third stage the death rate continues to fall, but more gradually, while the birth rate declines rapidly. The result is a marked increase in the average age of the population. The decline in the birth rate is usually ascribed to a complex of changes in social attitudes and institutions that make large families less desirable, particularly for economic reasons. Stage three of the demographic cycle is associated with such industrialized societies as the Soviet Union, the United States, Japan, and those of Europe.

Significance   The industrial countries of stage three of the demographic cycle are characterized by high standards of living, which entail increased costs for luxuries, education, and child-rearing, and soaring public expenditures for welfare state programs. In such countries, the costs for young dependents can still be considered an investment in the future, but the costs for old dependents are increasing and represent a social debt. Again, countries in the third stage have a larger portion of their societies in the active working population (ages fifteen to sixty-five) than countries in either of the first two stages. Yet, in spite of high labor productivity, technological developments — particularly automation—threaten large-scale unemployment, increased tensions, and social dislocations that tax the creative capabilities of social and governmental leaders. A continued trend of declining birth rates could also have a serious impact on power relationships if the industrialized countries were to experience an actual population decline at the very time when the populations of most of the countries of the world are growing rapidly and competing with increasing vigor for a larger share of world resources.

Geographic Power Factors: Climate   The effect of weather conditions on national power. The climatic conditions of a state are determined mainly by its characteristic wind, precipitation, and temperature pattern. Historically, the greatest national power developments have taken place in those regions marked by temperate climate conditions. Adverse climatic conditions are not impossible to overcome, but extremes of heat and cold demand a greater expenditure of human energy and resources to sustain life than is the case in regions of moderate climate.

Significance   Climate is probably the most important of the geographic power factors because of its direct effect on man's ability to grow food and perform work. The effects of climate can be altered in some degree, but usually at the expense of increased production costs. Within limits, arid lands can be irrigated, and seawater can be desalinated to overcome insufficient rainfall. Advanced technology can improve working conditions in the colder regions of the world. New strains of seeds and food animals capable of withstanding greater extremes of temperature are being developed. Disease control, improved nutrition, new technological skills, and development capital are enhancing human energy in tropical countries where the climate was once considered too enervating to increase productivity much beyond the subsistence level. The most favorable climates for human activity are those of the temperate zones, which range between twenty and sixty degrees north and south of the equator. Approximately 85 percent of the world's land area, 75 percent of the habitable land, and about 90 percent of the population are located north of the equator, a situation that helps to explain why the North Temperate Zone continues to dominate the international political stage.

Geographic Power Factors: Location   The relationship between physical position on the globe and national power. The location of a state is related to national power through climate, access to and from the sea, control over river, sea, and land transportation routes, and the availability of natural resources. The presence or absence of powerful neighbors is also a function of location.

Significance   Location is a factor in the national power equation in both geographic and strategic terms. Historically, the states that have had the greatest impact on human affairs have been located in the Northern Hemisphere, particularly in its temperate zone. The strategic connection between location and foreign policy has been obvious from ancient times, and more recently has given rise to geopolitics as a field of study. Attention has often been drawn, for example, to a connection between the absence of obstacles to invasion across the northern European plain from the Rhine to the Urals, and the militarism of German and Russian regimes. Water barriers, on the other hand, have made Britain, Japan, and the United States relatively secure from invasion during most of their history. The security and consequently the foreign policies of Canada and Latin America continue to be affected by their proximity to the United States and their distance from other centers of world power, as do those of the states of Eastern Europe in relation to the Soviet Union. Switzerland's traditional neutrality is perhaps the classic illustration of the impact of location on domestic and foreign policy. Location, however, does not grant power but can facilitate its acquisition and use. The contribution of location to national power can also be changed by developments elsewhere in the national power spectrum. Changes in the locations of markets and in the commodities traded, for example, have altered trade routes, and the development of air travel has increased the importance of locations previously less accessible by land or water.

Geographic Power Factors: Raw Materials   The resources of water and soil, their products, and the minerals of the subsoil in relation to national power. Access to raw materials is essential to the standard of living and the security of the state, and dependence upon them relates to the technological developments that create demands for them either at home or abroad. Iron and coal have long been the basis for industrialization, but increasing technological sophistication is creating new demands for other materials, such as uranium as an energy source, titanium for jet engines, and germanium for transistors. The advanced technologies of such fields as space exploration, medicine, and warfare depend on high levels of industrialization requiring a wide diversity of raw materials. The developing countries that are seeking ways to sustain growing populations at improved standards of living are adding to the pressures on diminishing supplies of world resources.

Significance   National power and well-being are directly dependent on the possession and availability of, and capacity to use, raw materials. The uneven distribution of raw materials around the world is a prime reason for international trade and the development of transportation facilities. The need for secure sources of supply has also been both an historic cause of imperialism and war and a reason for the drive to liberalize trade policies that has occurred since World War II. The increasing demand for and shrinking of raw materials occasioned by advancing industrialization and the population explosion is also speeding the search for new supplies, new uses, and the development of substitutes. One approach has been to develop synthetics from raw materials available in relatively large quantities, such as the petrochemical derivatives of petroleum. Although total reserves of raw materials are diminishing, the available supply of many on the world market exceeds demand, resulting in price instability and worsening terms of trade for the supplying countries.

Geographic Power Factors: Size   The effect on the power equation of the relationship between the surface areas of states. Enormous variations in size exist among the more than 160 states of the world, ranging from the Soviet Union with approximately 8.6 million square miles to the Vatican with 108.7 acres. China, Canada, and the United States range from 3.6 to 3.8 million square miles. Brazil, Australia, India, and Argentina each have over 1 million square miles. There are fifty-four states in the range from 100,000 to 1,000,000 square miles, thirty from 40,000 to 100,000, thirty from 3000 to 40,000, and over thirty with less than 3000 square miles.

Significance   Size alone does not guarantee national power, which also depends on such things as population, natural resources, technological level, social cohesion, and leadership. Size is, however, related to the state's ability to develop its power. A greater diversity and quantity of raw materials are likely to be found in large states than in small ones, increasing the opportunities of supporting a growing population. At current technological levels, on the other hand, raw materials from local sources may be inaccessible or unusable, and not all of a state's territory may be capable of supporting life. Human ingenuity may in some degree be able to overcome deficiencies in size; but given the same ingenuity, the larger the country the greater the power advantage it is likely to be capable of enjoying.

Geographic Power Factors: Topography   The effect on national power of the physical features of a state. Topography includes such elements as altitude, river systems, mountain ranges, plains, and marshlands. Such other factors as size, location, raw materials, and climate, when considered together with topography, constitute the geographic element of national power.

Significance   Topography affects both the social and political life of a state and its relations with other states. Altitude, for example, and the direction of slopes in relation to sun and wind are determinants of the kind of agriculture that can be practiced. Mountains, plains, and river systems are related to the concentration of population. Historically, cultural differences have been long-lasting in regions where topographic features have impeded communication. The configuration of the land in terms of the ease or difficulty of ingress and egress has helped to determine the stability of political boundaries as well. Topography is thus an inescapable power factor; but its importance in a given place and time is determined by its relationship to other elements of power, such as the level of technology applicable in the same situation. The relative importance of topography is demonstrated by the differing impact of mountain ranges or defenses in depth across wide plains on conventional military ground operations as compared with aerial or rocket warfare. Modern communications, on the other hand, can overcome virtually any topographic obstacle.

Geopolitics   An approach to foreign policy that attempts to explain and predict political behavior and military capabilities in terms of man's physical environment. Geopolitics, therefore, involves varying degrees of historical determinism based on geography. Friedrich Ratzel (1724–1804) compared the state to a living organism that must expand or die. His disciple Rudolf Kjellen (1864–1922) carried on this process of anthropomorphism, by which the state became more than a legal concept. He developed a body of "laws" on the state as a "geographic organism in space," and gave them the name "geopolitics" in his book *The State as a Form of Life* (1916). Much geopolitical theorizing, although presented in terms of scientific analysis, contains large elements of propaganda. The reputation of geopolitics has suffered because geopoliticians like Karl Haushofer (1869–1946) have frequently been the advocates of particular political ideologies or national policies, which they have sought to explain or justify in terms of geographical causation. The term "geopolitics" may also be used to describe political geography considered in terms of the structure of the world and its component states, or to refer to those aspects of foreign policy planning that must take into account various geographic factors. *See also* GEOPOLITICS, pp. 94–96.

Significance   Political events always occur in a geographic setting, and geographic factors may influence the course of events, but it is always man and not geography that makes political events. Geography is a complex of such factors as size, location, climate, and topography. In addition, geography is an important element, but not the only element, of national power; its importance is relative to such considerations as economics, technology, manpower, and morale. Indeed, an evaluation of all of these elements, considered together as the national power equation, is meaningful only in relation to the power equations of other states considered in the context of some specific time, place, and situation. Geographic facts are persistent concerns of the foreign policy practitioner, but they are not absolutely constant. Open borders facilitate contact but they do not make conflict inevitable. The polar icecap means one thing in terms of sea power, and another in terms of air power. Thus geographic theories, like such monistic causal interpretations of history as economic determinism, are unsatisfactory as complete explanations of human behavior. They are, nevertheless, useful approaches to more widely ranging study of the complexities of international politics.

Geopolitics: Haushofer *Geopolitik*   The German branch of geopolitics developed by Karl Haushofer (1869–1946), army general, geographer, geologist, historian, and Far Eastern traveler. The *geopolitik* of General Haushofer began with the heartland theory of Mackinder, and with Friedrich Ratzel's and Rudolf Kjellen's concepts of space and of the organic state. He and his disciples at the Institute of Geopolitics in Munich used these ideas to explain German defeat in World War I and to plan future German conquests. As a major general in the German army, Haushofer no doubt viewed Adolf Hitler and the Nazi party as upstarts to be used for the realization of Germany's destiny. Hitler, on the other hand, used the Haushofer *geopolitik*, particularly ideas like *lebensraum* (living-space), to suit his own purpose. In line with the heartland theory, Haushofer and his army followers advocated a German-Russian-Japanese bloc, with Germany destined to emerge as the dominant partner. Haushofer also saw that German power would be dissipated in the vastness of Russia should Hitler go through with his plan to invade the Soviet Union. When he tried to dissuade Hitler from this course, he fell from favor, was imprisoned in the concentration camp at Dachau in 1944, released after Germany's defeat in 1945, and committed suicide within a year.

Significance   The Haushofer *geopolitik* was a pseudoscientific conglomeration of geographical metaphysics, economics, anthropology, and racism. It was important, however, because it was accepted by many Germans caught in the psychological doldrums of their World War I defeat. The major precepts of the Haushofer *geopolitik* include the ideas that: (1) the military objectives of the state require policies of economic self-sufficiency; (2)

the German master race is destined to bring peace to the world through domination, and thus other states must acquiesce in granting Germany her required *lebensraum*; (3) German rule must be extended first to all territory German by language, race, or economic interest, and then to the entire world; (4) German domination of the Afro-Eurasian island could be accomplished by overcoming sea power through long land marches, which would make her economically and militarily secure, and would provide the base for complete world domination; and (5) all territorial boundaries are useful starting points for war and are subject to change according to the dictates of German national interest. All geopolitical study has suffered to some extent from the disrepute thrust upon it by the Haushofer *geopolitik* as a rationalism for German territorial expansion.

Geopolitics: Heartland Theory   The theory that the state that could control the human and physical resources of the Eurasian landmass between Germany and Central Siberia would be in a position to control the world. The heartland theory was developed by the British geographer Sir Halford J. Mackinder (1869–1947) in his paper "The Geographical Pivot of History" (1904) and in his best-known work, *Democratic Ideals and Reality–A Study in the Politics of Reconstruction* (1919). The heartland theory emerged from Mackinder's detailed study of the global relationship between land and sea power.

Significance   Mackinder postulated the dominating influence of certain geographic "realities" on the course of world politics. His realities included: (1) a "world island" (Europe, Asia, and Africa) surrounding the Eurasian "heartland" or "pivot area," which is inaccessible from the sea; (2) its coastlands, called the "inner" or "marginal crescent," made up of maritime powers; and (3) insular power bases composed of North and South America and Australia, called the "insular"or "outer crescent." Based on his assumption of the growing ascendancy of land power over sea power, Mackinder warned statesmen that "who rules East Europe commands the Heartland; who rules the Heartland commands the World Island; who rules the World Island commands the World." Mackinder advocated policies aimed at creating an equilibrium of power between the land and sea powers so that no single country would be in a position to dominate the pivot area. By the time of World War II he had refined his theory so that it also took account of the development of air power and the growing national power of the United States, located outside the world island. In 1919 Mackinder warned of the consequences should Germany ever control Russia, and in 1943 of the consequences should Russia control Germany. Mackinder's analyses could also be used in the contemporary world to explain the rationale of the United States policy of containment, or the consequences of a close union of the Soviet Union and China.

Geopolitics: Rimland Theory   The theory that emphasizes the rimlands of Europe, the Middle East, Africa, South Asia, and the Far East as the keys to the security of the United States. The rimland theory was developed by the American geographer and geopolitician Nicholas J. Spykman (1893–1943). In his book *The Geography of Peace* (1944), Spykman developed his theory around the concept of the rimlands, which corresponded to the inner crescent of Mackinder, modified and renamed. It was Spykman's thesis that domination of any of these areas by a hostile power threatened the security of the United States because from such a position the encirclement of the New World became a possibility. Spykman's revision of Mackinder's famous dictum became "who controls the Rimland rules Eurasia; who rules Eurasia controls the destinies of the world."

Significance   In developing the rimland theory, Spykman was concerned that the United States should recognize: (1) the ultimate responsibility of each state for its own security; (2) the importance of a world balance of power; and (3) the necessity of using United States power to stabilize such a balance. His analysis of the security needs of the United States took into account these worldwide factors: (1) geographic—location, size, topography; (2) economic—agricultural and industrial resources, the people, industrial production; and (3) political—national morale, political stability, social integration. Thus Spykman was not a geographic monist, but he stressed geography as the "most fundamentally conditioning factor of foreign policy."

Geopolitics: Sea Power Theory   The theory that posits naval power as the key to world power. Sea power as the basis for a geopolitical theory was first developed by an American naval officer, Admiral Alfred Thayer Mahan (1840–1914), through his perception that the seas of the world connected landmasses rather than separated them. The acquisition and defense of overseas empires, therefore, was dependent upon the ability to control the sea. Central features of Mahan's work include: (1) a scholarly analysis of British naval history that explained Britain's role as a world power; (2) a dedication to the idea of an American world mission to be carried out through overseas expansion; and (3) a rationalization of imperialism on the assumption that countries cannot stand still spatially, but must expand or decline.

Significance The application of the sea power theory to the United States was based on Admiral Mahan's view that the American geographic position was analogous to that of Britain. Mahan argued that European land powers with strong neighbors could not challenge the maritime supremacy of Britain or the United States because of the necessity of supporting large land forces. He concluded that British naval supremacy was not permanent and that the United States could establish its supremacy in the Caribbean and the Pacific. Mahan's book *The Influence of Sea Power upon History 1660–1783* (1890) was read by a generation of expansionists, particularly in the United States and Germany. Mahan's thinking remains relevant in that states with worldwide interests must be capable of projecting and using their power effectively at great distances from their homeland.

Green Revolution A dramatic change in agricultural production begun in the 1960s through development of new high-yielding wheat and rice seeds and the application of large quantities of water and fertilizer. Led by Nobel Prize-winning geneticist, Norman E. Borlaug, who pioneered in the experiments that led to the new seeds, the Green Revolution was aimed at providing the food needed to break the famine cycles of Third World countries, especially those of Asia and Africa. *See also* POPULATION CONTROL, p. 101.

Significance Early successes of the Green Revolution led to a doubling and even tripling of food production in many countries of Asia and Africa during the 1960s. In the 1970s and 1980s, however, the high cost of energy needed to make fertilizer and to pump water has led to a great decrease in production. In addition, drought in many regions has added to these production losses. By the early 1980s, African harvests were lagging by 7 percent behind the explosion in population, and studies showed that the average monthly per capita food shortage in developing countries was almost 4 pounds and this figure would be likely to rise to about 9 pounds per person each month by 1990. Scientists around the world are attempting to launch a second Green Revolution which would be more attuned to an energy-short world. They are attempting, for example, to develop new seeds that could produce two annual harvests instead of one, and to find grasses and other plants that could be planted with wheat and rice to provide them with the necessary nitrogen. The second Green Revolution efforts are part of the global race to develop the means to support a population explosion of massive proportions.

Malthusianism   The theory that postulates that population increases geometrically (2, 4, 8, 16, 32, . . .) while the means of subsistence increase only arithmetically (2, 4, 6, 8, 10, . . .). Malthusianism, therefore, asserts that improvement in the standard of living is not possible and that a livable ratio between population and food supply can be maintained only through the corrective intervention of recurring war, pestilence, disease, and famine. Named for its formulator, the economist Thomas Malthus (1776–1834), Malthusianism went out of vogue when the Industrial Revolution made it possible for the countries of Western Europe to have both a rising standard of living and a substantial increase in population. *See also* DEMOGRAPHIC CYCLE, p. 86; GREEN REVOLUTION, p. 97.

Significance   In the contemporary world, Malthusianism is frequently called Neo-Malthusianism because the old concept is being applied to a new environment. The terms symbolize growing concern with the worldwide worsening relationship between population and food supply. In the industrialized countries, standards of living continue to rise. However, in many of the developing countries, which contain most of the world's population, the standard of living is barely holding its own, and many food exporters have become net importers. The result is a gap between rich and poor societies that is progressively widening. Neo-Malthusians warn that, unless the population explosion is brought under a measure of control, natural resources used less wastefully, and food production increased substantially, mankind's future may well be one of recurring disasters as Malthus had predicted.

Migration   Population movements from one state or region to another. "Immigration" is the movement viewed from the receiving state, while population movements out of a country are called "emigration." The record of human migration is as old as recorded history, but perhaps the greatest wave involved the emigration of over 25 million people from Europe between the 1870s and World War I. In Asia during the same period, Chinese emigration averaged 70,000 to 80,000 annually, although civil war in central China caused this figure to go above 200,000 in 1926 and 1927. Most Chinese migrants have gone to the countries of Southeast Asia, where their communal culture has created problems of national integration. Heavy migration declined after World War I and by the 1930s had virtually stopped. The greatest single migration after World War II involved well over one million Jews from all over the world, mainly Europe, North Africa, and the Middle East, who flocked to the new state of Israel. The term "migration" indicates voluntary displacement from one country to another and does not refer to populations forcibly removed or transferred by treaty. *See also* OVERSEAS CHINESE, p. 101; REFUGEE, p. 188.

Significance   Migration has had advantages and disadvantages for both sending and receiving states. For the country of origin, the migration of its citizens has relieved some social pressures, such as peasant poverty; emigrant remittances have been economically helpful; and the departure of numbers of malcontents or national minorities has aided political stability. The disadvantages of emigration involve the loss of the energies and potential skills of young and vigorous migrants, the economic loss of those already trained, and a loss of military manpower. For the receiving country, immigrants provided necessary skills and manpower, filled up empty lands, and speeded economic development. On the other hand, immigrants created problems of assimilation, caused increasing pressure on job markets, and frequently complicated political relations between sending and receiving countries. Since policies of unrestricted immigration were generally ended after World War I, migration is no more than a theoretical answer to the problems of overcrowding in some countries. Calculations on the basis of comparative population density indicate that such countries as Australia, Canada, Brazil, the Soviet Union, and the United States have room for a large number of immigrants. Space, however, is not the problem. Although some immigration does take place, ethnocentrism, nationalism, fear of economic competition, and other psychological and social prejudices cause immigration policies to be highly selective. Migration, nevertheless, is offered—along with birth control and expansion of food and other resources—as a potential means for reducing some of the pressures resulting from the population explosion.

Oder-Neisse Line   The *de facto* boundary established between East Germany and Poland at the end of World War II. The Oder-Neisse line is named for the two rivers that form the boundary from the Baltic Sea south to the border of Czechoslovakia. Representatives of the Allied Powers met at Potsdam in 1945 to consider, *inter alia*, a provisional German settlement and procedures for drawing up final peace treaties. They agreed that northern East Prussia was to be annexed "in principle" by the Soviet Union, and that, pending a final boundary determination, southern East Prussia and German territory east of the river line were to be "under the administration of the Polish State." The Allies also agreed to an "orderly and humane" transfer of resident ethnic Germans out of Poland, Czechoslovakia, and Hungary. The Oder-Neisse boundary line was recognized by both sides for the first time in the Helsinki Accord of 1975, by which the East and the West accepted the post-World War II status quo in Europe. *See also* BOUNDARIES, p. 85; HELSINKI ACCORD, p. 211.

Significance   World War II ended in 1945 but the Oder-Neisse line remains an issue in East-West relations in general and in German-Polish relations in particular. The Cold War resulted in the *de facto* division of Germany into the Federal Republic (West Germany) and the Democratic Republic (East Germany). No final peace treaty has been negotiated, German territory east of the Oder and Neisse rivers has been annexed by the Soviet Union and Poland, and approximately 10 million Germans were forced to migrate to East Germany, whence most of them ultimately fled to the Federal Republic. Although the Helsinki Accord does not constitute binding international law because it was a diplomatic agreement, not a treaty, it nevertheless shows that the long-standing campaign of West Germany for German reunification may be ending. Diplomatic recognition of East Germany by all Western countries, including the United States, and East Germany's admission into the United Nations, indicate that the Oder-Neisse line may remain a key boundary for the foreseeable future.

Overseas Chinese   People of Chinese ancestry and culture living outside the borders of mainland China and Formosa. Overseas Chinese living in the countries of Southeast Asia exceed 16 million and represent a major problem of cultural assimilation.

Significance   The overseas Chinese are distinct among the minorities of Southeast Asia because of their numbers, their tendency to live in segregated communities, their economic drive, and their cultural and political ties to Peking and Taipei. These qualities often alienate them from local populations, threaten political stability, and hamper the process of nation building. Ethnic minorities are found in all of the countries of the area, but the Chinese minority represents a special problem in Vietnam, Indonesia, Thailand, Burma, and Malaysia, where their rejection of assimilation and their economic strength make them a significant political force.

Population Control   Adjustments in population size resulting from national policies and from individual birth control practices. Government measures, historically, have involved efforts to influence the quantity and the quality of population by various techniques. These include: (1) encouraging or discouraging immigration and emigration; (2) fostering or discouraging large families; and (3) carrying out a policy of mass extermination, as in the case of Nazi Germany. The availability of improved contraceptive methods, especially in Western societies, has made family size increasingly a matter of individual choice. *See also* DEMOGRAPHIC CYCLE, p. 86; MALTHUSIANISM, p. 98.

Significance   The problem of population control is particularly acute in the developing countries and transitional societies of the Third World in the second stage of the demographic cycle. Their societies are attempting to change from a preindustrial to an industrial orientation while simultaneously experiencing a population explosion. Characteristics related to the size and condition of population include: (1) death rates falling faster than birth rates; (2) a large number of young people; and (3) a relatively small work force under pressure to produce rapid improvements in economic conditions. Governments in such countries are cross-pressured to preserve old values and to foster new ones while population growth consumes the added increments of economic development. The sheer magnitude of the problem is forcing traditionally hostile attitudes toward population control fostered by many of the world's religions to give way to policies and programs designed to reduce the birth rate. These include efforts to: (1) eliminate illiteracy as a barrier to the communication of new values; (2) improve health and sanitation so that large families will not need to be produced so as to insure the survival of some children; (3) emphasize the economic advantages of smaller families; and (4) provide information and resources to encourage widespread birth control practices. Governments interested in developing birth control programs are receiving assistance from public and private sources in the developed countries. Modern science continues to facilitate birth control by developing increasingly simple and effective methods involving oral contraceptives ("the pill") and economical intra-uterine devices (the IUD, or "loop"). The problem, however, continues to take the form of a race between the development of disastrous population pressures on scarce resources and the rate at which food production can be expanded and social values changed.

5. International Economics

Autarky   National economic self-sufficiency. Since such a policy lessens dependence on other states, a state may adopt a policy of autarky in anticipation of war or to correct a serious deficit in its balance of payments. A government that adopts a policy of autarky will, typically, curtail imports, encourage the development of substitutes and synthetics to replace imports, and subsidize production for the domestic market. *See also* STOCKPILING, p. 194.

Significance   By adopting a policy of autarky, a state substitutes national economic, political, or military considerations for the free interplay of supply and demand in the international marketplace. Germany during the 1930s, for example, placed major emphasis on developing a self-sufficiency based on synthetics and stockpiling that would make the nation blockade-proof when war came. The autarky plan failed during World War II mainly because of the insufficiency of oil and food reserves. Since World War II, the United States has followed a policy of stockpiling large quantities of commodities essential to a major war effort.

Balance of Payments   The net balance between the total income and expenditures of a nation, both public and private, in its trade and financial transactions with the rest of the world. The balance of payments for a nation resembles an accounting sheet for a private business in reflecting credits (earnings) and debits (spendings). Since a nation's accounts must balance, a surplus or

103

deficit on current account must be offset, for example, by using reserves or by short-term borrowing. Included in the accounting are such credit categories as exports, foreign tourist spending, profits from investments, and shipping and banking income. Debits include imports, tourist spending abroad, foreign investments, interest payments on loans, and payments for services. *See also* BALANCE OF TRADE, p. 104.

Significance   A nation's balance of payments is an indicator that shows its economic strength or weakness in the international economy. If, for example, a country runs up a sizable deficit in its transactions with the rest of the world, steps must be taken to correct the imbalance. A temporary disequilibrium may not be serious and can usually be carried through short-term borrowing to balance the accounts. A long-term, or fundamental, disequilibrium, on the other hand, reflects a basic weakness in the nation, and government action to correct the deficit would be in order. Corrective policies may include higher tariffs, export controls, quotas, exchange control, currency depreciation, austerity programs, export subsidies, or other actions designed to reduce imports, increase export earnings, or both. States generally strive to maintain a "favorable," or surplus, balance so that reserves of foreign currencies and gold can be built up to carry them over future payments crises. Surpluses for some states, however, tend to produce deficits for others. Because corrective actions may substantially reduce international trade, the International Monetary Fund (IMF) was established to provide loans to tide nations over temporary payments crises. The United States has had a deficit in its balance of payments for most years since World War II, resulting in an accumulation of huge dollar balances as international reserves by other countries. These are often referred to as "Eurodollars" and "petrodollars," reflecting the weak trade position of the United States vis à vis some European countries, and the importation of huge quantities of oil annually from OPEC countries during the 1970s and 1980s.

Balance of Trade   A nation's annual net trade surplus or deficit, based on the difference in the values of its total imports and exports. The balance of trade is to be distinguished from the balance of payments; the trade balance is only one part of the many debits and credits that comprise a nation's balance of payments. In a carryover from the days of mercantilism, a

surplus of exports over imports is often called a "favorable"—
and imports over exports an "unfavorable"—balance of trade.
See also BALANCE OF PAYMENTS, p. 103.

Significance   The balance of trade comprises the major part of
a nation's balance of payments. A heavy surplus of merchandise
exports over imports, for example, will enable a state to pay for
activities such as foreign aid and military actions abroad,
whereas a substantial trade deficit will often force a nation to cut
back in these or other international programs. In an effort to
secure a favorable trade balance, a nation's leaders may subsidize
exports, depreciate the currency, raise tariffs and other impediments to imports, join other countries in an OPEC-type cartel
arrangement, or undertake other actions aimed at expanding
sales and income from abroad, or cut back on foreign purchases.

Barter   An arrangement between governments for the exchange of goods. Under a barter agreement, quantities of goods
are exchanged at an agreed ratio without any monetary transactions. Barter arrangements typically are entered into by nations
to overcome foreign exchange problems that hinder trade between them. *See also* BILATERAL TRADE, p. 106.

Significance   Barter agreements to foster trade became commonplace during the Great Depression of the 1930s and during
World War II, when normal trade practices suffered from monetary restrictions imposed by exchange control, blocked accounts,
and competitive depreciations. Since World War II, the communist countries have made wide use of barter arrangements to
open up trade with many developing countries. Soviet foreign
aid, for example, usually takes the form of trade credits that are
paid off in commodities over a period of years by the recipient
country according to the terms provided by a barter agreement.
Barter systems are advantageous not only in promoting trade
but for avoiding balance of payments problems as well. The
main disadvantage of barter is that it promotes bilateral rather
than multilateral trade. State-trading countries are more likely
to utilize barter in their trade since the government holds a
monopoly over all foreign commercial transactions. Barter arrangements are of limited use in systems based on private enterprise because individual firms are unlikely to exchange their
products for foreign goods rather than for foreign exchange.

Bilateral Trade   An understanding between two states to foster cooperation in trade and related economic matters. A bilateral economic agreement may take the form of a clearing arrangement in which payments for imports and exports are paid through a single central bank account, or of a payments agreement that includes all financial transactions between the two countries. In its simplest form, a bilateral agreement may provide for a barter arrangement whereby two countries exchange goods in specified amounts with no payments in foreign exchange. The most common use of economic bilateralism is in trade agreements providing for a mutual reduction in tariffs or other trade barriers. *See also* BARTER, p. 105.

Significance   Bilateral agreements have played a major role in promoting trade between nations during periods of economic nationalism. They have proved useful in overcoming restrictive national policies that involve exchange control, tariffs, and quotas, and they have also been used to direct trade to achieve political objectives. They tend, however, to be preferential arrangements that by their very nature discriminate against other nations and frequently evoke retaliation. The inclusion of most-favored-nation treatment in bilateral agreements—as in those concluded under the Reciprocal Trade Agreements Program and within the framework of GATT—eliminates their discriminatory impact. In this way they may contribute to the growth of a freer multilateral trading system rather than encourage trade discrimination. Communist states utilize bilateral agreements in granting foreign aid to developing countries. They extend long-term credits for technical assistance, capital goods, and military equipment, which are paid for by the receiving state in shipments of commodities over a long period of years.

Boycott   Refusal to buy products from a particular country or group of countries. A boycott may be government-sponsored or may be initiated by private groups which seek to influence consumers against making purchases of goods from the boycotted nation. *See also* EMBARGO, p. 120.

Significance   A boycott is an instrument of trade policy that may be motivated by economic, political, security, or ideological factors. The general American boycott of Japanese imports before World War II was directed mainly at protecting American jobs and industries from low-wage competition. Although such purchases were not prohibited by law, the private boycott substantially reduced imports from Japan and served to worsen political relations between the two nations. Efforts by American patriotic groups to promote a general boycott of goods made in communist countries have had little impact on foreign trade. Government purchasing policies, such as those promoted by the "Buy American" Act, may constitute a partial but indirect boycott of foreign suppliers. In the 1980s, heavy Japanese exports into the United States have created public outcry for protection of domestic industries and jobs, especially in the automobile industry.

Capital   That factor of production—along with land and labor—which is expressed in terms of money and producer goods. The application of capital to the expansion of productive capacities depends upon profits, the amount of profits saved, and the extent to which savings are channeled into investments in the form of capital goods. Advanced capitalist states encourage capital formation through security markets, extensive banking systems, and governmental fiscal and monetary policies. Communist state planning directs a large portion of national income into capital goods development. Sources of capital for underdeveloped states include local savings, private investment from abroad, trade, and foreign aid. Capital provides such essential elements in the economic equation as buildings, machines, tools, supplies, power, and transportation facilities.

Significance   The accumulation of capital is the key ingredient in promoting economic growth in the advanced states and economic development in the underdeveloped countries. Actual capital investment, however, depends upon the size of the market and the demand for goods. Modern economic theories and practices provide for government to encourage transfers from savings into investments when the nation suffers from a dearth of capital or when economic stagnation threatens. In the underdeveloped world, capital accumulation through foreign trade, its major source, is seriously jeopardized by deteriorating terms of trade, protectionism in advanced states, and the development of synthetic substitutes to replace primary commodities. Private investment in underdeveloped states has failed to measure up to expectations because investors in the advanced states fear expropriation and are attracted by vast opportunities for safe investment in industrialized countries. Moreover, most foreign aid programs have focused on technical assistance and infrastructure development and have provided only meager amounts of capital. International institutions—such as the World Bank Group and the African, Asian, and Inter-American Development Banks—supply capital mainly on a "hard loan" basis.

Cartel   An agreement among independent businessmen or countries to restrict competition. A cartel agreement is based on a contractual understanding typically involving prices, production, and the division of the market. The term *cartel* originated in Germany during the 1870s (from the Latin *charta*, meaning "contract"). Cartels are employed mainly in mass production industries where exclusiveness is protected by patents or quality differences are minor, and in the energy field, especially in oil and gas. The market for most primary commodities, especially agricultural products, is highly competitive and does not lend itself to cartelization, resulting in deterioration of commodity prices relative to prices of manufactured products. *See also* OR-GANIZATION OF PETROLEUM EXPORTING COUNTRIES (OPEC), p. 142.

Significance   Up to one-half of world trade during the Great Depression of the 1930s was subject to cartel control. Cartelization of the market has diminished since World War II, however, owing to the establishment of antimonopoly legislation in Britain and joint anticartel action by members of the European Community. Although Germany for many years was the center for cartel activity, Japan has become the most active of the industrial countries, with the government not only approving but sponsoring cartels. In the United States, cartels have been illegal since the passage of the Sherman Antitrust Act of 1890, although under the Webb-Pomerene Act of 1918 business associations competing with foreign cartels for world trade are exempted from the provisions of the antitrust laws. OPEC, the most effective governmental cartel, was established in 1961.

Colombo Plan   A regional economic aid program providing multilateral consultative machinery to encourage and to coordinate bilateral assistance programs among its members. The Colombo Plan was established at a Commonwealth Conference at Colombo, Ceylon, in 1950. It provided initially for a $5 billion, six-year development program with capital furnished equally by the developed and developing states. Over twenty-five states have participated in the program, including Commonwealth countries (Australia, Britain, Canada, Ceylon, India, Malaysia, New Zealand, Pakistan, and Singapore), other Asian countries and protectorates (Bhutan, British Borneo, Burma, Cambodia, Indonesia, Japan, South Korea, Laos, Nepal, the Philippines, South Vietnam, and Thailand), and the United States. A Consultative Committee for Economic Development in South and Southeast Asia, with all participating states represented, meets annually to review old programs, plan new ones, and discuss the problems of economic development. A Council for Technical Cooperation functions as a secretariat at the Colombo headquarters to facilitate the exchange of technical experts among members. *See also* COMMONWEALTH OF NATIONS, p. 302; FOREIGN AID, p. 125.

Significance Although started as a Commonwealth program, the Colombo Plan now includes the United States as a major aid giver and most of non-communist Asia as aid recipients. Because administration of all aid programs remains bilateral, each of the donor states retains full control over the size and nature of its contributions. Yet the Consultative Committee serves as a forum in which the developing states can present their case for larger or more appropriate projects. Since 1950, more than $20 billion in loans and grants have been supplied to Asian nations for developmental purposes, and many thousands of persons have received technical training. During the 1970s, loans and grants dispensed under the Colombo Plan averaged over $3 billion annually.

Commodity Agreement An international contract by which signatory states strive to establish an orderly world marketing system for a primary commodity. Commodity agreements are sought mainly by producer states to overcome the destructive competition that emerges from gross overproduction and results in a world "buyers' market." Through a commodity agreement, states establish production controls, regulate exports, establish minimum and maximum world export prices, and provide for reserve stocks of the commodity. States heavily dependent on imports of the commodity may also join in an agreement. The most successful commodity agreement is the Organization of Petroleum Exporting Countries (OPEC) established in 1961. Because oil importing states are not represented in OPEC, the commodity agreement has been converted into a cartel, with controls over production, pricing and marketing. Encouraged by OPEC's success with oil, commodity agreements have been concluded for such products as coffee, olive oil, sugar, wheat, tea, cotton, rubber, tin, and beef. *See also* TERMS OF TRADE, p. 151.

Significance Commodity agreements may be particularly useful when many developing states competing for scarce foreign exchange produce large surpluses of a commodity, saturating the market and driving prices down. Under conditions of free competition, each producer thereupon increases production to make up for the loss caused by lower prices, with the result that prices are driven even lower. Through agreement, states can establish near-monopoly marketing conditions for their producers by rigorously controlling private actions. Major conflicts may arise, however, when the commodities regulated are produced in the advanced as well as in the developing states, resulting in a conflict between world export price levels and domestic prices. The difficulty of reaching agreement on production and marketing quotas among primary producing states, some of which depend almost entirely on the commodity for their foreign exchange earnings, can be illustrated by the years of intensive but fruitless negotiations to conclude a cocoa agreement. OPEC's successes, however, continue to encourage other primary commodity exporting states to follow OPEC's lead, but most raw materials and foodstuffs suffer from a weak demand in the world market compared to the strong demand for oil.

Convertibility The free interchange of a national currency into units of foreign currency by private individuals or businesses, without control by the government. A convertible currency, therefore, is one that is not regulated in value or amounts exchanged by a national system of exchange control. *See also* EXCHANGE CONTROL, p. 121; FOREIGN EXCHANGE, p. 127.

Significance The convertibility of a currency is most commonly restricted when a government seeks to protect the nation from a serious disequilibrium in its balance of payments, when it maintains an artificially high exchange value for its currency, or when it tries to control currency exchanges to achieve national political or military goals. In developing countries, for example, dollars and other hard currencies are often conserved for use in purchases of capital goods to promote economic growth; the national currency cannot, therefore, be freely exchanged for hard currency to purchase foreign consumer goods. World currencies can be divided into the three basic categories of: (1) the "hard" currencies of the industrialized nations; (2) the "soft" currencies of the developing countries; and (3) the controlled currencies of the communist and state-trading countries. Whereas the currencies in the first group are freely convertible, those in the last two categories may legally be converted into foreign currencies only with governmental approval. This often results in a foreign currency black market with unofficial exchange rates.

Counterpart Funds   Local currencies paid by an aid-receiving country to a donor country for military-, developmental-, or technical-assistance loans. Under grant programs, a recipient country may also be required to establish a special fund of national currency to match the amount provided in foreign exchange. *See also* FOREIGN AID, p. 125.

Significance   Since counterpart funds are not freely convertible into hard currency, they are frequently ploughed back into local infrastructure programs or expended on educational exchange and other noninflationary projects by the aid-giving government. Donor countries carrying on extensive foreign aid programs, such as the United States, hold vast amounts of local currencies in counterpart funds, increasingly giving it a voice in the determination of national policies in recipient countries. In some cases, this situation has given rise to charges of imperialism by groups within the aid-receiving country.

Countervailing Duty   A special assessment levied on imports to offset an advantage or discount provided by a foreign seller or government. A countervailing duty is applied against those products which might provide unfair competition for locally produced articles of commerce as a result of foreign governmental subsidies or other special advantages. The duty levied is in addition to the normal tariff charge. *See also* TARIFF, p. 148.

Significance   Countervailing duties are aimed mainly at nullifying the special market advantage of foreign producers when government subsidies permit them to sell below a normal market price. In the United States, the Secretary of the Treasury has discretionary authority to levy them when he believes that such conditions exist. A countervailing duty is one of many retaliatory weapons used in trade warfare to protect the home market from what is considered to be unfair competition.

Deflation   A decrease in the price level of goods in a nation's economy. Deflation results from a decrease in the supply of money and credit or from the overproduction or underconsumption of consumer goods. Deflation is usually associated with a serious economic decline, whereas inflation typically is a problem during an economic boom. *See also* INFLATION, p. 132.

Significance   Economic tacticians regard deflation as a serious threat to a nation's economy because it tends to foster unemployment, reduce investment, diminish consumption, and generally contribute to economic stagnation. In an economy based on credit, deflation makes debt reduction more difficult and discourages individuals and businesses from incurring new loans. Proponents of a stable monetary policy call for vigorous governmental actions to avoid or correct deflationary swings before they produce serious substantive and psychological damage to the nation's economy. All modern states use monetary and fiscal policies as corrective actions when deflation threatens. In some cases, however, a government may pursue a deliberate deflationary policy to correct inflationary dangers or to make exports more attractive to correct a balance of payments disequilibrium. Deflation problems have not existed in the West since the Great Depression of the 1930s.

Depression   The business cycle period of economic stagnation. A depression is characterized by business retrenchment, weakened purchasing power, mass unemployment, deflation, and a substantially reduced gross national product. In a complex modern economy, the failure of one segment to perform adequately may trigger depressive events in other sectors, leading to a general economic malaise. Historically, depressions in capitalist countries have followed periods of peak expansion in the nation's productive facilities and overexpansions of credit, resulting in a boom-bust cycle. The interdependence of the international economy leads almost inevitably to the spread of a depression beyond a state's boundaries. *See also* DEFLATION, p. 112.

Significance   Economic depressions have always had serious consequences in terms of economic dislocation and social and political unrest. The world depression of the 1930s helped to usher in a period of economic nationalism, dictatorship, and war on a scale previously unknown. At a time of competitive ideological struggle, a major depression in the West could have equally serious consequences by making communism appear more attractive. Classical economic theory held that depressions were a natural phenomenon that would be overcome by self-correcting economic forces inherent in the capitalist system. Today, economic theory and practice are used in governmental fiscal and monetary policies to prevent the nation's economy from sliding into a depression. Government actions during a period of recession, for example, discourage savings, stimulate investment and purchasing, reduce taxes, provide employment, and give a psychological lift so that the slide into a full depression can be avoided. Leading trading nations work out common international monetary and investment policies to help stabilize the world economy when a depression threatens. Utilizing such policies, serious economic recessions in the post-World War II period have been arrested and reversed before a major depression could materialize.

Devaluation   A reduction in the exchange value of a nation's monetary unit. Devaluation is usually a deliberate policy undertaken by a state to depreciate the value of its national currency in terms of gold or other national currencies. *See also* FLEXIBLE EXCHANGE RATES, p. 124.

Significance   Devaluation is often used as an instrument of trade policy by a nation suffering from a serious deficit in its balance of payments. By devaluing its national currency, a state lowers the prices for its products in world markets and stimulates its export trade. At the same time, imports become more costly to its own consumers, resulting in a reduction in the state's import trade. Thus, a state may use devaluation to correct a fundamental disequilibrium in its balance of payments. If other states follow this lead and devalue their currencies, however, all will be back pretty much on the same level of currency relationship as before the first devaluation was undertaken. During the Great Depression of the 1930s, for example, the international monetary system was in disarray as a result of successive competitive rounds of depreciations as many states sought to solve their domestic economic problems by capturing a larger share of the world market. To regain international monetary stability, the International Monetary Fund (IMF) was established after World War II to regulate currency values and to permit members to draw foreign exchange to tide them over periods of financial hardship. The leading industrial countries have also organized to pool additional monetary resources to fight any threatened devaluation during a financial crisis. While numerous devaluations of national currencies occurred since World War II, the most significant ones have been limited to cases involving necessary adjustments approved by the Fund, and competitive devaluations have been avoided. Since the establishment of a flexible exchange rate system with relatively free floating currencies in 1973, major devaluations have been avoided and exchange rates have been adjusted automatically to market conditions.

Directed Trade   The determination of trade policies by a government in pursuit of a state's economic, political, or security objectives. Directed trade differs from free trade, which permits the supply and demand of the marketplace to determine the flow of trade.

Significance   All states direct their trade, ranging from the moderate intervention of liberal democratic states to the totally controlled systems of the communist and state-trading nations. A state may direct its trade in order to bolster its system of alliances, to strengthen its colonial ties, to expand its political influence, to spread its ideology, or to maximize its economic gain. Techniques for directing trade include preferential agreements, boycotts and embargoes, barter, currency regulations, tariffs and quotas, special credits, price manipulation, and bilateral trade agreements. Since World War II, most nations have joined in collective efforts through United Nations agencies to encourage freer trade by the establishment of a multilateral trade and payments system.

Dumping   Sales of goods in foreign markets at net unit prices lower than those charged domestic consumers. Dumping may involve below-cost sales as a means of reducing large inventories or of trying to drive competitive firms out of the market. State-trading countries may use it as an economic weapon in pursuit of political or ideological objectives.

Significance   The technique of dumping has been an international trade practice since the nineteenth century, when trusts and cartels used it to fight for markets. Dumping constitutes a threat to an orderly market system. Although consumers may benefit initially from dumping, ultimately, if competitive firms are driven from the market by the practice, the consumer will pay higher prices for the product. State policy has often supported dumping with export bounties during times of weakness in domestic economies, especially during the Great Depression of the 1930s. The Soviet Union has occasionally disrupted orderly marketing by dumping large quantities of primary commodities received in payment of foreign aid, such as tin and cotton, at below world market prices. Many nations have established special tariff provisions to protect domestic producers against dumping by foreign companies.

Economic Growth   The increase in a nation's gross national product. Economic growth rates may be measured on an absolute basis in contemporary currency values or may be adjusted to take into account population changes and inflationary or deflationary factors. Economists regard an annual growth rate of 5 percent as satisfactory for most nations. Some have substantially exceeded this rate, but most do not achieve it. Although many developing countries have been able to increase gross national income at a high rate, when the figure is adjusted for population growth the net per capita rate seldom exceeds 1 percent except for the major oil exporting countries. Some have suffered per capita income losses despite sizable gains in national income. *See also* GROSS NATIONAL PRODUCT, p. 130.

Significance   Competition among states—especially those having different economic, political, and social systems—is keen as each strives to achieve a higher rate of economic growth than its rivals. As a rule, poorer underdeveloped states can, in two senses, achieve higher percentages of annual increase than the more advanced: the former have labor and resource surpluses; and, since their base is much smaller, minor increments are reflected in high rates of increase. Both sides in the capitalist-communist ideological struggle have claimed superiority for their system in promoting economic growth, but, because of the different means for attaching value to goods and services, it is difficult to compare the economic growth and the rate of growth in two nations like the United States and the Soviet Union. The uncommitted nations of the world will undoubtedly move toward the adoption of that system which gives the greatest promise for achieving rapid economic growth. Economic growth is a crucial element in the power equation because it provides the basic support for future foreign and domestic programs.

Economic Integration: Customs Union   An agreement among states that provides for free trade among members and for a common external tariff on imports from outside the union. A customs union arrangement usually provides for the central collection of import duties and their division among the members of the union according to a formula. The common external tariff rates are typically based on an average of pre-union rates. *See also* BENELUX, p. 297.

Significance   A customs union encourages an expansion of trade among its members by elimination of barriers to trade, specialization in production, and creation of a favorable climate of public opinion supporting intra-union trade. Progress toward further economic unity, involving free movement of capital and labor and the establishment of common fiscal and monetary policies, may be encouraged by the customs union. A customs union may also be a forerunner of political union, as in the cases of Germany and of Austria-Hungary in the nineteenth century. The Benelux Customs Union (Belgium, Netherlands, and Luxembourg) and the European Economic Community (originally Benelux, France, Germany, and Italy) have functioned as economic unions since 1948 and 1958, respectively. Many nations have also established customs unions with their dependent territories, as, for example, in the United States arrangement with Puerto Rico.

Economic Integration: Economic Union   The integration by two or more states of their economies through development of common economic policies. An economic union establishes a common market and a common external tariff, provides for the free movement of labor and capital, harmonizes taxes and subsidies that affect trade within the region, and aims for a general consonance of fiscal and monetary policies. Political institutions for joint economic decision making are essential to an economic union. The European Economic Community (EEC), for example, functions as an economic union through its joint political organs. Other levels of economic integration include free trade areas and customs unions. *See also* EUROPEAN ECONOMIC COMMUNITY, p. 312.

Significance   An economic union provides for the highest level of economic integration short of that which results from full political union. Although it contains features similar to those of a free trade area and a customs union, an economic union differs mainly in the extent to which the members' domestic fiscal and monetary policies are harmonized. The level of integration in an economic union is not fixed but may broaden as the development of community consensus supports additional fields of cooperation. The objective of economic union is to encourage a broader market, greater specialization, and generally higher standards of living through the increased competition that results when the mantle of government protectionism is withdrawn.

Economic Integration: Free Trade Area   A region consisting of two or more states in which tariffs and other barriers to trade have been eliminated. A free trade area is more than a preferential system that retains tariffs but provides for more favorable rates for members. It does not, however, go as far as a customs union that, in addition to establishing a free trade area, provides for a common external tariff applicable to nonmembers. In a free trade area agreement, members retain full freedom to develop their individual trade policies with the rest of the world. Examples of free trade areas include the European Free Trade Association (EFTA) and the Latin American Free Trade Association (LAFTA). *See also* EUROPEAN FREE TRADE ASSOCIATION, p. 313; LATIN AMERICAN FREE TRADE ASSOCIATION, p. 321.

Significance   A free trade area arrangement aims at maximizing trade among its members while leaving its trade relations with other states unchanged. As with all preferential systems, however, "outside" nations tend to view the system as discriminatory because their exports to the free trade area become more expensive and less competitive when compared with those of the "inside" members. EFTA was the first multilateral free trade area to succeed in achieving its basic objective of removing all industrial tariffs among its members.

Economic Integration: Preferential Trade Arrangement   An agreement among several states to grant each other favorable trade treatment. Members of a preferential system mutually reduce their tariff or other trade barriers to an agreed level. The difference between the tariff levels for members and those applied by each member to other states is referred to as the "margin of preference." A preferential system may be multilateral (for example, the Commonwealth of Nations system of preferences) or bilateral (as in the case of the United States-Philippines economic agreement). Any trade agreement between two or more nations that reduces barriers to trade but does not incorporate the most-favored-nation clause to apply those reductions to nonsignatory states is preferential in nature. *See also* COMMONWEALTH OF NATIONS, p. 302; IMPERIAL PREFERENCES, p. 131.

Significance   A preferential trade arrangement may evoke retaliation from other states or trading blocs and lead to a trade war because it tends to discriminate against all trading partners not party to the agreement. Under its rules for trade conduct the GATT group, for example, prohibits the creation of any new preferential systems or increases in the margin of preference by existing systems. The main objective of states in establishing preferential trade arrangements is to encourage more extensive trade with some of their trading partners while continuing to maintain their general levels of protection vis à vis other states. Political and security objectives may also figure prominently in a decision to establish a preferential system. One of the most persistent demands for preferential trade treatment comes from the underdeveloped countries in their efforts to secure lower tariff rates for primary commodities without reciprocity. Free trade areas, customs unions, and economic unions are widely used contemporary types of preferential arrangements.

Economic Nationalism   Governmental direction and control of external economic matters. A policy of economic nationalism aims at achieving a state's economic, political, or security objectives by protecting the domestic market, increasing trade opportunities abroad, or both. Economic nationalism is the opposite of a free trade system, in which economic actions are liberated from governmental regulations and controls. Policies of economic nationalism may range from partial manipulation of a basically free economy by government, to the all-embracing control of economic policy and practice and its direction toward the achievement of national objectives, typical of state-trading countries and of most nations at war. Techniques of economic nationalism include: (1) directed trade; (2) tariffs and quotas; (3) barter arrangements; (4) exchange controls; (5) currency manipulation; (6) export subsidies and controls; (7) embargoes and boycotts; (8) preferential trading systems; (9) expropriation and nationalization; and (10) dumping. *See also* AUTARKY, p. 103.

Significance   Economic nationalism became common state policy during the First and Second World Wars and during the interwar period of the 1920s and 1930s. During the 1930s, for example, most states tried to escape the mass unemployment and general economic stagnation brought on by the worldwide depression through discriminatory and restrictive external economic policies. Some, such as Germany and Italy, sought to develop their war-making potentials through economic policies of autarky (national self-sufficiency) and by directing trade toward the enhancement of national power. Policies of economic nationalism tend to incite retaliatory actions by aggrieved states, often negating initial advantages produced by the policies. The result is a cumulative buildup of restrictions that reduces trade, investment, and other international economic activities and depresses general economic well-being. Post-World War II efforts have been aimed at preventing a resurgence of economic nationalism by constructing a multilateral trading and payments system through collective actions undertaken by international institutions, such as GATT and the IMF.

Embargo   A government edict prohibiting citizens from trading with one or several countries. The embargo may apply only to certain types of products, or it may be a total prohibition of trade. *See also* BOYCOTT, p. 106; ECONOMIC NATIONALISM, p. 119.

Significance   An embargo is a weapon of national economic policy levied for the achievement of strategic or political objectives. Partial embargoes, such as the American prohibition of trade in strategic goods with communist countries, may be aimed at weakening the military capabilities of potential enemies. The total embargo forbidding Americans from shipping any kind of material or product to Communist China, North Korea, Vietnam, and Cuba was directed at weakening these regimes economically, militarily, and politically. American efforts to pressure allied nations to reduce or eliminate their trade with communist countries by threatening the withholding of foreign aid have generally been unsuccessful. A trade embargo may be circumvented through illegal trade or by channeling it through a third country for transhipment to the embargoed nation. The embargoed nation may also increase its trade in prohibited articles with third countries and develop its own industries to overcome the impact of the embargo. The withholding of most-favored-nation treatment from the Soviet Union by the United States also constitutes a form of partial embargo. In addition, in 1979 the United States levied an embargo on the shipment of certain farm products to the Soviet Union as a result of the latter's attack on Afghanistan, although the Reagan Administration removed it in 1981.

Escape Clause   A provision, inserted in a trade agreement, that permits a party to terminate or alter a tariff concession. An escape clause can be invoked only after a specified period of notice has elapsed. In the United States, tariff concessions may be withdrawn if imports substantially threaten or injure a domestic producer. The United States Tariff Commission has established "peril points" at which, when imports reach such levels, the President and Congress are informed of the danger to American producers. The President may then invoke the escape-clause provision in the agreement to reduce the threat of injury. *See also* RECIPROCAL TRADE AGREEMENTS ACT, p. 402; TARIFF, p. 148; UNITED STATES INTERNATIONAL TRADE COMMISSION, p. 405.

Significance The escape-clause and peril-point provisions were introduced by the United States as amendments to the Reciprocal Trade Agreements Act in 1951, and were continued in subsequent trade acts. Other states have—usually reluctantly—accepted the escape-clause provisions when entering into a trade agreement with the United States. The President has invoked them to restore higher tariff rates on a number of occasions, usually to offer protection demanded by powerful domestic pressure groups. Insistence on inclusion of an escape clause in a trade agreement weakens the hand of the negotiator because it implies a lack of sincerity in achieving a maximal expansion of trade.

Exchange Control Government regulation of the exchange of national and foreign currencies. Exchange control substitutes arbitrary decisions of administrative officials for free market forces in the buying and selling of currencies. Control is usually directed toward the objectives of maintaining an arbitrary exchange ratio between the national and foreign currencies, and of permitting exchanges of national into foreign currencies only when national interest considerations are satisfied. Exchange control may range from full regulation over all monetary transactions to a limited supervision over certain types of activities to correct temporary monetary difficulties. *See also* CONVERTIBILITY, p. 110; ECONOMIC NATIONALISM, p. 119; FLEXIBLE EXCHANGE RATES, p. 124.

Significance Exchange control is a technique of economic nationalism. Main objectives are the correction of a serious balance of payments problem or the withholding of scarce foreign exchange from unnecessary imports in favor of capital projects to produce economic growth. In industrialized states, currency exchange has often been regulated to check exports, as used, for example, in many European states to prevent capital flight to the United States during the 1930s when war threatened. Exchange control is most extensive when a nation is at war and all foreign economic activities must be directed toward the achievement of victory. Although Western European states maintained exchange control for some years after World War II, their rebuilding of substantial dollar and gold reserves brought about the elimination or moderation of control. Communist and other state-trading countries, however, maintain full control over currency exchange, and most of the developing nations use it to conserve foreign exchange for economic development projects. A flexible exchange rate system emerged in the 1970s when the United States curtailed the Gold Exchange Standard system and ended fixed convertibility between gold and the dollar. Since that action, currencies of the industrial countries have been permitted to "float" freely with their exchange values determined by market conditions.

Export Control   Governmental restrictions on the sales of certain materials, commodities, products, or weapons in foreign trade. Certain types of weapons, for example, may be excluded from foreign sales through export controls. States possessing nuclear weapons generally prohibit the export of nuclear devices, weapon-grade uranium or plutonium, and technical information. In the economic area, states may restrict the export of certain materials or products that are in short supply within the country, usually for the duration of the shortage. For many years, the United States sought to weaken communist states through the Battle Act (Mutual Defense Assistance Control Act of 1951) which prohibited trade in strategic materials with "any nation threatening the security of the United States." Under the Export Administration Act of 1979, the United States has extended controls over the export of strategic goods and technology having both civil and military uses. Export controls that limit or prohibit shipments going out of a state supplement exchange controls that limit or prohibit imports of certain products, especially in state-trading countries. *See also* EXCHANGE CONTROL, p. 121.

Significance   Export controls are one of the major means by which nations try to safeguard their national security and economic interests in the field of trade. Advocates of free trade reject most export controls as unnecessary encumbrances on the free flow of goods; they advocate eliminating controls in economic areas in favor of free market conditions, and keeping them to a minimum in the security field. In the United States, export control powers vested in the President by Congress are very extensive. In the early 1980s, articles of commerce subject to presidential control included: nuclear materials, crime control and detection equipment, computers, aircraft, large tractors, and petroleum equipment. In addition, the President was empowered to forbid all exports to North Korea, Vietnam, Kampuchea, and Cuba except for a few innocuous educational, gift, and travel materials. United States experience with the Battle Act over a period of years indicates that, although the policy had some early successes, in time most American allies freely sold their economic and strategic products to communist states. As a result, American businessmen brought pressure on Congress to alter the Act to permit them to compete with Western Europe and Japan in the East European and Asian markets.

Export-Import Bank   A United States government corporation that makes direct loans to foreign and domestic businessmen to promote international trade, and to provide financing for social and economic infrastructure projects in developing states. Chartered in 1934, the Export-Import Bank's operations are governed by a five-member bipartisan board appointed by the President with Senate approval. Loans to foreign companies must be guaranteed by their governments, a requirement that has led to governmental control of or involvement in most development projects financed by the Bank. The loans generally cover purchases in the United States of capital equipment necessary to supplement local labor and materials for the projects. The loans must be repaid in dollars. *See also* FOREIGN AID, p. 125.

Significance   The Export-Import Bank was originally established to extend credit to private American exporters in order to encourage foreign trade, especially with the Soviet Union and Latin America. In more recent years, its lending policies have been aimed mainly at helping developing states. Since 1934, the Bank has made loans totaling over $9 billion, with loans extended to Latin America, Europe, Asia, Africa, and Oceania. Substantial profits earned by the Bank have gone into reserves against future losses and to the United States government as dividends. Loans from the Bank have aided developing states in the construction of dams, irrigation projects, canals, roads, processing plants, mines, and manufacturing industries.

Expropriation   Government seizure of foreign-owned property and transfer of ownership to the state. Although recognized as a rightful exercise of sovereign power, under international law expropriation can be neither retaliatory nor discriminatory and is conditional upon payment of prompt and fair compensation. In addition, the United States stipulates that expropriated property be taken only for a public purpose and in accordance with due process of law. Expropriation is a form of nationalization, although the latter term refers more broadly to the purchase or expropriation of either foreign- or domestically-owned private property. A declaration of war leads to the expropriation of all properties owned by enemy aliens.

Significance The threat of expropriation has undermined the flow of capital from capital-surplus states to the developing states. Prompt compensation may be beyond the capabilities of expropriating states, and "fair payment" for properties is a matter of controversy and protracted negotiations. One of the first acts undertaken by a communist government after taking power is often the expropriation of foreign-owned property and the nationalization of privately owned basic industries. Retaliation by a state for the expropriation of property owned by its nationals may take the form of diplomatic protest, severance of diplomatic relations, economic reprisal, or military sanctions. Expropriation of over $1 billion of American-owned assets by the Castro regime in Cuba led to the severance of diplomatic relations. Some supporters of economic development through increased flow of private capital have called for massive government insurance programs in the capital-surplus states to encourage private investment abroad by guaranteeing it against expropriation. The United States is currently involved in over a hundred cases of expropriation of property owned by American nationals in foreign countries.

Flexible Exchange Rates An international monetary system in which the value of each national currency is determined by the free interplay of market forces. A flexible exchange rate system means that the values of national currencies change regularly as a result of the impact of supply and demand for each currency. Flexible exchange rates were instituted in 1973 by the Western bloc of nations headed by the United States. The fixed rate exchange system, in which all leading currencies were tied to the dollar with their exchange values set by agreement through the International Monetary Fund, prevailed until 1972. Because the dollar was tied to gold at the fixed rate of $35 per ounce, all other currencies in that system were tied to gold through their relationship with the dollar. When in 1972 the United States was unable to meet the demands of foreigners to turn their dollars into gold, the system collapsed. A temporary "adjustable peg" exchange rate system replaced the gold exchange standard system, but by 1973 a flexible exchange rate system was operational. *See also* EXCHANGE CONTROL, p. 121; FOREIGN EXCHANGE, p. 127; GOLD STANDARD, p. 129.

Significance   Flexible exchange rates have helped to construct a stable international monetary-value system since 1973 because national currency values are realistically set by supply/demand market forces rather than by governmental fiat. The system has helped countries in their balance of payments adjustments by giving early indications of a weakening or strengthening of national currency values. Exchange rates have tended therefore to be reliable indicators of the general economic condition of each nation. The system survived the period of the 1970s in which tremendous increases in world oil prices occurred, and in which a great expansion in trade and international liquidity with high inflation rates challenged its survival. At times the system has been weakened by great market turbulence—sometimes occasioned by the actions of powerful speculators—and by heavy unemployment and other adverse economic conditions in leading industrial countries. Nevertheless, the flexible exchange rate system has prevailed and is likely to survive all but a cataclysmic world depression or a period of severe economic nationalism, such as occurred in the 1930s.

Foreign Aid   Economic, social, or military assistance rendered to a country by another government or international institution. Foreign aid is offered bilaterally, by regional organizations, and by global agencies under the United Nations system. Economic aid includes such categories as technical assistance, capital grants, development loans, surplus food disposal, public guarantees for private investments, and trade credits. Military aid involves transfers of military hardware, advisory groups, defense support (i.e., paying for civilian projects to make up for money the aid-receiving country has spent on its own defense), and payments to support friendly military establishments. Objectives of foreign aid include supporting allies, rebuilding war-shattered economies, promoting economic development, gaining ideological support, obtaining strategic materials, and rescuing nations from economic collapse or natural disaster. Major economic and military *bilateral* programs of aid are carried on by the United States, the Soviet Union, Communist China, France, Germany, Japan, the Scandinavian countries, and Britain. *Regional* programs of economic aid include those carried on through the Alliance for Progress, the Colombo Plan, the European Development Fund of the EEC, the Organization for Economic Cooperation and Development, and by the African, Asian, and Inter-American Development Banks. *Global* programs carried on under United Nations auspices include the United Nations Development Program, the International Monetary Fund, the World Bank Group (IBRD, IFC, and IDA) and other specialized agencies, the United Nations Conference on Trade and Development, and special autonomous bodies like the United Nations Industrial Development Organization and the United Nations Institute for Training and Research. (*For specific institutions and programs, see* Index).

Significance   The first large-scale foreign aid program was that of United States aid to its allies during and following World War I, of which more than $14 billion in principal and interest remains unpaid. During World War II, a Lend-Lease program was carried on by the Allies that provided for mutual military and economic aid. The post-war period saw the development of several American aid programs, including the Marshall Plan to foster the rebuilding of Western Europe, the Truman Doctrine to provide military and economic assistance to states threatened by communist aggression, and the Mutual Security Program to strengthen the Defenses of the North Atlantic Treaty Organization (NATO) in Western Europe. American aid to underdeveloped countries started with the Point IV program of technical assistance in 1949 and was expanded to include development grants and loans and military aid during the 1950s and 1960s. Soviet aid programs for underdeveloped countries were begun in the mid-1950s in the form of credits to foster bilateral trade. Other industrialized countries of Western and Eastern Europe, and Japan, inaugurated major aid programs to the developing states in the 1960s. All aid-giving nations utilize bilateral, regional, and global channels, although key decisions concerning most economic and military assistance are made unilaterally by the donor country. Most donor countries prefer to give technical assistance and infrastructure development aid because they believe that the capital for industrial development should come from *private* sources, typically multinational corporations. Recipient countries, however, are most earnest in their quest for capital aid in the form of grants or low-interest, long-term loans because they want to maintain control over their development programs and their nation's economic future. Financing for specific capital development projects by Western nations usually takes the form of loans supplied by the World Bank Group or by the African, Asian, or Inter-American Development Banks.

Foreign Exchange   The buying and selling of national currencies. Foreign exchange is necessary to make purchases of foreign goods or to settle accounts. The price or exchange ratio for national currencies is determined by supply and demand in the international money market or by an arbitrary fixing of the rate of exchange through a national system of exchange control. *See also* CONVERTIBILITY, p. 110; EXCHANGE CONTROL, p. 121; FLEXIBLE EXCHANGE RATES, p. 124.

Significance   A businessman wishing to purchase foreign goods must convert his domestic money into foreign currency. When heavy spending abroad jeopardizes the value of a nation's currency, the government may take action. Exchanges may be made subject to approval by government officials (exchange control), foreign products may be made less desirable by altering the exchange ratio between the two currencies (currency depreciation), or tariffs and other trade barriers may be raised to reduce foreign imports. Such governmental protectionist actions, however, usually result in retaliatory measures by affected countries. To avoid resorting to restrictive devices, major countries of the West have entered into "pooling" arrangements whereby currency values on the international market may be protected by large-scale counter-trend buying and selling of major currencies by the pool to maintain exchange stability.

Free Trade   The flow of trade based on supply and demand, free from governmental regulations, controls, and promotional activities. Free trade was espoused by Adam Smith in his *Wealth of Nations* (1776) to foster an international division of labor based on national specialization in production that would raise productivity and standards of living in all countries. The absolute advantage posited by Adam Smith was later modified by David Ricardo's theory of comparative advantage. The latter recognized that many countries would not have an absolute advantage in the production of any goods and should, therefore, specialize in those products which each would be able to produce most efficiently, and trade these for its other needs. Under capitalism, a laissez-faire, or hands-off, policy by government in domestic and foreign trade matters permits the forces of the marketplace to determine economic actions. *See also* DIRECTED TRADE, p. 114; MERCANTILISM, p. 139.

Significance   Free trade was developed in theory and practice as a reaction to enterprise-stifling policies of mercantilism. Relatively free trade flourished in many countries during the nineteenth and early twentieth centuries, but after World War I most countries instituted protectionist policies. The main thrust of international economic relations since World War II has involved a collective effort to tear down the trade barriers erected during the period of economic nationalism in the 1920s and 1930s. Although free trade may be unassailable in theory, practical political and military considerations and the attraction of short-run economic gain have tended to override it in the councils of governments. The trend since 1945, however, has been toward freer trade among most nations and toward free trade among members of the common markets established by regional groups.

General Agreement on Tariffs and Trade (GATT)   An international organization that promotes trade among its members by serving as a forum for negotiating agreements to reduce tariffs and other barriers. GATT first met at Geneva in 1947 to function as an interim arrangement until the proposed International Trade Organization (ITO) could be established as a specialized agency of the United Nations to provide for orderly world trade. When the United States rejected ITO, GATT—which, unlike ITO, is based on executive agreements rather than on a treaty and, consequently, did not have to be approved by the Senate—was developed as the main instrument to encourage freer trade. GATT's membership has increased from the original 23 participants to 83 full and 23 associate members, which together carry on more than four-fifths of world trade. In 1971, GATT approved a General System of Preferences (GSP) which authorizes the developed countries to give preferential tariff treatment to developing countries. In 1976, the United States joined many other countries of Europe and Asia by adopting the GSP approach, resulting in the lowering of hundreds of tariff rates for the imports of developing countries. GATT's current functions include: (1) negotiating the reduction of tariffs and other impediments to trade; (2) developing new trade policies; (3) adjusting trade disputes; and (4) establishing rules to govern the trade policies of its members. Members negotiate bilaterally and multilaterally at periodic meetings. The most-favored-nation clause incorporated in all agreements concluded at GATT sessions insures that trade concessions will be applicable to every member. Its nondiscrimination rule prohibits members from using quantitative restrictions, quotas, export subsidies, special taxes, or other devices to circumvent the concessions granted. *See also* MOST-FAVORED-NATION CLAUSE, p. 140; TARIFF, p. 148.

Significance   GATT's members over the years since 1947 have successfully negotiated substantial reductions in trade barriers. GATT's slow but steady progress was capped by the successful conclusion of the Tokyo Round negotiations in 1979 that reciprocally reduced tariffs by an average of 33 percent, chiefly for the industrial countries. Most developing countries, however, boycotted the signing because GATT had not met their demands, such as liberalizing tariff rates on primary commodities and processed goods. Numerous disputes among members have also been resolved, and major trade wars have been avoided. A comprehensive set of rules to guide members in their trade relations has been approved, and nontariff barriers have been kept in check. GATT's basic objective of building a liberal trading system, however, has been weakened because its membership includes only two-thirds of the world's 160 trading nations. Many developing states still regard GATT as the "rich man's club" and have not opted for membership; Cuba and Czechoslovakia are the only communist members, although Poland and Yugoslavia maintain loose affiliations. GATT faces two major unresolved issues: trade relations between communist and non-communist states, and demands of the developing countries that a new international economic order be created and that a fairer trading system be a central part of that new order.

Gold Standard   An international monetary system that uses gold as the common standard of value. Under a gold standard system, each nation's currency is backed by gold, each has a value measured in gold, and each can be freely converted into gold or any national currency operating within the system.

Deficits and surpluses in the balance of payments are settled by gold flows from one country to another. Under a modified gold exchange standard, central banks buy and sell national currencies backed by gold at a fixed price. *See also* INTERNATIONAL MONETARY FUND, p. 135.

Significance   The gold standard was established as the basic international monetary system from the middle of the nineteenth century to 1914, was restored briefly from 1925 to 1931, and from 1958 to 1972 has functioned in a gold exchange standard form. In 1972, the Nixon Administration was forced to cut the tie between gold and the dollar at a fixed rate of exchange because of the excessive number of dollars in the world that constituted claims against a dwindling supply of American gold. Although the gold standard had the advantage of insuring free convertibility of all currencies in a truly multilateral payments system, the limited supply of gold made it difficult to build adequate reserves during periods of increasing trade. Flows of gold in and out of countries produced unwanted deflations and inflations since the value of a national currency was based on the quantity of gold held by the nation. When governments established national goals of price stability, full employment, and rapid economic growth, the automatic adjusting mechanism of the gold standard system became incompatible and was replaced by "managed" paper currencies. The gold exchange standard system that existed until 1972 was weakened by a world gold shortage, by perennial American balance of payments deficits, and by the rapid conversion of dollar balances into gold by several countries, especially France. In 1967, however, the Group of Ten—the leading industrial powers—agreed to bolster the world monetary system by creating "paper gold" in the form of Special Drawing Rights (SDRs) for all members of the IMF. Through the additional credits thus made available, the major trading nations have attempted to "manage" the international monetary supply in somewhat the same way that governments through their central banks manage their domestic currencies. The price of gold which had remained fixed at $35 an ounce for many years has soared in world markets as a result of heavy inflation affecting most currencies.

Gross National Product (GNP)   The gross value of goods and services produced by a nation's economy. The GNP is expressed in terms of the total market value of all consumer and capital goods and services produced over a specific time period, usually one year. *See also* ECONOMIC GROWTH, p. 115.

Significance   The GNP, when carefully computed to avoid duplication in adding value at different stages of production, serves as a useful indicator of economic growth. It can be used as an analytical tool to compare the performance of a nation's economy with those of preceding years or of other countries. It is often used to compare economic progress between different economic and social systems, such as in capitalist and communist states. In comparing economic growth rates, however, the GNP should be adjusted to constant currency values to avoid distortion by inflationary or deflationary price changes, and capital goods figures should be adjusted to exclude that portion of new investment that merely replaces worn-out or discarded productive capacity. To compare standards of living in different countries, population growth factors must also be used to adjust GNP figures to a per capita income basis. In the United States, the GNP has been maintained at a level approximately double that of its closest national competitor, the Soviet Union.

Imperial Preferences   A system by which Britain and other Commonwealth countries reciprocally grant preferential trade treatment to one another. Imperial preferences originated in 1919, when Britain had no general tariff, as an arrangement whereby members of the Empire granted Britain economic preferences in exchange for protection by the British fleet. The system was expanded in 1932 when Britain adopted a general tariff and, in the Ottawa Agreement, granted special treatment for the Dominions to sell their primary commodities in the British market in exchange for continued preference for British manufactures in their markets. To protect infant industry in the Dominions, their tariffs were raised on all entering manufactured goods, but rates which applied to Britain were kept much lower, though still protective. *See also* COMMONWEALTH OF NATIONS, p. 302; PREFERENTIAL TRADE ARRANGEMENT, p. 118.

Significance   The system of imperial or Commonwealth preferences was a key factor in attracting members and developing unity in the multiracial Commonwealth of Nations. Many newly independent states, such as India, Guyana, and Nigeria, were attracted into joining the Commonwealth to retain their sizable market in the British Isles. Imperial preferences, however, were a major stumbling block for Britain in her efforts to achieve membership in the EEC. France had demanded that Britain relinquish such preferential arrangements as a condition of membership, a situation that could have jeopardized the stability of the Commonwealth. Following Britain's entry into the European Community in 1973, special trade arrangements were concluded by the European Community with many Commonwealth countries.

Inflation   An increase in the general price level of goods in a nation's economy. Inflation may result from an increase in money and credit, from the absence of competitive conditions in the marketplace, or from a decrease in the supply of goods available. Inflationary conditions are often created by the actions of government through deficit spending or by ill-timed monetary policies. Whatever may trigger the forces of inflation, economists believe that mass psychological factors are responsible for increasing its impact and scope. For example, fear of continued price increases may stimulate installment buying that may contribute to further inflation. *See also* DEFLATION, p. 112.

Significance   A monetary inflation may constitute a serious threat to a nation's economy. Low-income groups tend to bear the greatest hardship from a serious inflation, with the result that political stability may be threatened. Progress toward the objectives of economic development may be thwarted by a runaway inflationary spiral that eats up savings that could have been channeled into investment. Foreign trade may suffer because the nation's exports may be priced out of the highly competitive world market. Yet, a moderate, controlled inflation of less than 3 percent annually may provide a stimulus to the economy and help in reducing private and public debts. Inflation in the United States, for example, was kept for many years within an average of less than 7 percent annually, one of the lowest in the world. The period of the late 1970s and early 1980s, however, saw annual inflation rates for most countries soar to 15 to 20 percent, including rates in the United States. In some developing countries, rates soared to over 100 percent annually. On the other hand, those countries with the strongest economies—Japan, Germany, and the OPEC group—have maintained strong currencies with low inflation rates.

Infrastructure Development   The economic, political, and social base to support a society's drive to achieve modernization. Infrastructure development involves institutional change to support a national effort to develop such facilities as roads, dams, power plants, and communication, irrigation, and transportation systems. Once the infrastructure base has been created, a nation's economy may—if capital for industrialization is available—move to the stage of self-sustaining economic growth.

Significance   Infrastructure development is an essential forerunner to industrialization and receives a high priority in the modernization plans of the underdeveloped states. Foreign aid programs of advanced Western states, including the United States, have been based on the assumption that building an infrastructure base and developing technical skills in the underdeveloped states would result in the attraction of private investment capital to give impetus to the process of modernization. In many states, surplus labor in agriculture has been taken off the land and organized to undertake construction projects that require a mass effort in the absence of modern machines. Societies in states that have made progress in infrastructure development but lack capital to utilize the base often suffer from a mass frustration that produces social unrest and political instability.

International Bank for Reconstruction and Development (IBRD)   A specialized agency of the United Nations established by the Bretton Woods Agreement of 1944 to help nations recover from World War II and to promote economic development in underdeveloped lands. The World Bank, as it is called, with 141 members in 1982, is headed by a president and a board of governors that meets annually to determine basic policies. Loan decisions are made by sixteen executive directors who meet monthly in Washington, D.C., the Bank's headquarters, to make decisions through a weighted voting system based on the amount of subscribed capital stock each director represents. By 1980, the Bank's total capital amounted to over $35 billion, with United States subscriptions totaling more than one-fifth. The capital stock represents both a guarantee fund to enable the Bank to obtain working funds from private sources in world capital markets (90 percent) and a paid-up contribution to the loan fund by member governments (10 percent). As a result of the establishment of the International Finance Corporation (IFC) in 1956 to help finance private investment and the International Development Association (IDA) as an affiliate of the Bank in 1960 to offer no-interest, long-term loans, the three public lending agencies function jointly as the World Bank Group. Most loans are made to member governments, although they may be made to private firms if repayment is guaranteed by a member. Most loans for major development projects are made by *consortiums* in which various international and national lending agencies join with private banks to finance the projects. *See also* SPECIALIZED AGENCY, p. 355; CAPITAL, p. 107.

Significance   The World Bank's initial role in aiding the recovery of war-devastated areas was replaced in 1949 by a new focus on lending to foster economic development. By 1980, the Bank had granted about 1700 loans totaling almost $50 billion to almost a hundred countries and territories. Terms of the loans have varied, with interest rates running close to those in private capital markets and with payment periods ranging from ten to thirty-five years. Loans have been granted for such projects as irrigation, mining, agriculture, transport and communications, and general industrial development. The Bank has also undertaken a broad technical assistance program to help prepare the ground for useful loans and to help recipients make effective use of the loans once granted. Although the Bank has progressively increased the pace of its lending operations, it is severely limited in its ability to supply the capital needs of developing states. The main drawback is the inability of many prospective loan-receiving states to finance repayment of loans in hard currency since the debt-servicing capacities of developing states are already overstrained.

International Development Association (IDA)   An affiliate of the World Bank. IDA was established in 1960 as a specialized agency of the United Nations to grant "soft loans" to members to promote economic development. By 1980, IDA had 120 members and a subscribed capital of $1 billion. Although it is a separate institution, its management and staff are the same as those of the World Bank (IBRD). Working funds are obtained from contributions made by capital-surplus states and from loans made to IDA by the IBRD. "Soft loans" features of IDA include the low cost of a loan (no interest, but a small annual service charge), a long repayment period (fifty years), and a slow amortization rate (ten-year period of grace, then 1 percent of loan repayable annually for next ten years, and 3 percent repayable annually for next thirty years). *See also* SPECIALIZED AGENCY, p. 355.

Significance   The International Development Association was set up as a result of criticism of the World Bank's conservative lending policies and because of growing American apprehension over the Soviet Union's aid-trade offensive of the late 1950s. The idea of a soft loan affiliate of the Bank was first discussed in the United States Congress, emphasizing the key American role in its creation. By 1980, IDA had extended many credits totaling more than $15 billion to over fifty countries and territories. Support for IDA comes mainly from recipient countries that regard it as the next best thing to capital grants from the United Nations. Whether aid-receiving countries will be able to pay off IDA loans on schedule, once the ten-year grace period expires, will depend upon their progress in economic development and their ability to earn foreign exchange.

International Finance Corporation (IFC)   A specialized agency of the United Nations, established in 1956. The IFC supplements the role of the World Bank (IBRD) in stimulating economic development by making loans to and direct investments in private companies in developing countries. The IFC's over a hundred members (1980) have subscribed to capital stock in the Corporation at the same ratio as their capital investments in the IBRD. Working funds are secured from the sale of securities in world capital markets and from loans made to the IFC by the World Bank. *See also* SPECIALIZED AGENCY, p. 355.

Significance   The International Finance Corporation had, by 1980, made many commitments totaling almost $10 billion to many developing countries. But, given the magnitude of the problem of economic development, the IFC had barely scratched the surface of world capital needs since 1956. Critics charged that the agency has never gained acceptance among either donor or recipient states, as evidenced by its modest funding and lending activities. Its objective of encouraging the private sector of the economy in developing states by meshing capital from both private and public sources has failed to overcome the basic incompatibilities inherent in such a mixture.

International Monetary Fund (IMF)   A specialized agency of the United Nations established by the Bretton Woods Monetary and Financial Conference of 1944 to promote international monetary cooperation. The major objectives of the Fund include: (1) promotion of exchange stability; (2) establishment of a worldwide multilateral payments system; and (3) provision of monetary reserves to help member nations overcome short-run disequilibria in their balance of payments. By 1980, 132 members had joined the Fund and had subscribed to quotas totaling over $35 billion. The two major stabilizing functions performed by the Fund are (a) regulating currency values by controlling exchange rates and (b) providing a pooling arrangement whereby members may purchase foreign currencies with their own domestic currencies to tide them over periods of serious financial hardship. When a member is able to do so, it repurchases its own currency with foreign exchange, thus replenishing the Fund's available resources. Voting power in the IMF is determined by the size of a member's contribution, with the United States casting more than one-fourth of the total. Since 1962, major industrial nations have functioned as the Group of Ten to defend currency values and to promote international liquidity. *See also* GOLD STANDARD, p. 129; SPECIALIZED AGENCY, p. 355.

Significance The International Monetary Fund was established to avoid a return in the post-World War II era to the anarchic financial conditions of the 1930s, with wildly fluctuating exchange rates and competitive depreciations. Major exchange depreciations, with the exception of those of the sterling bloc in 1949 and 1967, have been avoided, and the Fund has generally been successful in promoting stable currency values. The main problems facing the Fund have been the persistent deficit in the American balance of payments, the shortage of international reserves at a time when trade has expanded at a rapid rate, and growing demands for a return to the gold standard system. Because of the limited supply of gold and dollars available as reserves, the Fund has devoted much study to the problem of creating new types of international reserves. IMF decisions are usually reached initially by the Group of Ten, a caucus of the major industrial powers which casts most of the votes in the Fund.

Keynesianism A philosophy and practice of utilizing the machinery of government, through fiscal and monetary policies, to guide and direct a free enterprise economy. Keynesianism, based on the principles and analyses originally propounded by the British economist, John Maynard Keynes, seeks to improve rather than replace capitalism by providing an orderly, predictable pattern of economic activity based on economic indicators used by policymakers. Techniques used by Keynesians to manage a state's economy include government control and direction of such matters as budgeting, spending, tax policy, interest rates, and credit availability. Keynesianism substitutes rational decisions made by state leaders in pursuit of specific social goals for the undirected free interplay of market forces that characterizes a laissez-faire approach. Keynes believed that the key problem of a capitalist system is oversaving, and he prescribed various kinds of governmental action aimed at encouraging the transfer of savings into investment and consumption. Keynes focused on the role of government fiscal policy to correct the imbalance between *potential* output (controlled by supply factors) and *actual* output (controlled by the aggregate demand of consumers, investors, and government). *See also* CAPITALISM, p. 40.

Significance   The "new economics" approach based on Keynesian principles that emerged out of the Great Depression and World War II experiences has been generally adopted as state policy in most of the advanced, industrial states of the world. Political leaders increasingly have made decisions concerning their states' economies on the basis of recommendations offered by economic advisers who accept the Keynesian approach. By managing a nation's economy, Keynesians seek to avoid cyclical movements, unemployment, and inflation, while at the same time encouraging economic growth and general economic well-being. Keynesianism has functioned effectively since World War II to alleviate downturns in the economies of the industrialized countries. However, weakened by large governmental and consumer debt and heavy inflation, it is challenged today by a new approach—monetarism—that emphasizes a free market with government policy focused on controlling the money supply.

Licensing   A trade-control device whereby a government grants permission to certain private individuals and companies to engage in importing or exporting commodities, and regulates their activities by the conditions of the license. Under a trade licensing system, administrative officials determine which companies shall be permitted to engage in certain types of trading activity. Licensed companies must comply with state policy and administrative directives or they may have their licenses suspended, revoked, or not renewed. Licensing systems have been used primarily to allocate import quotas among several companies. Licensing thus seeks to avoid the rush to import characteristic of a global quota system that permits any importer to purchase goods up to the limit of the quota. *See also* ECONOMIC NATIONALISM, p. 119; QUOTA, p. 144.

Significance State licensing of private trading companies is aimed at controlling the direction, nature, and quantities of exports or imports or both. It substitutes the economic, political, or military objectives of state policy for the free interplay of the marketplace. Many states adopted extensive licensing systems during the period of economic nationalism in the 1930s as a means for attempting to improve domestic economic conditions through control over foreign trade. State licensing is also used as a technique for waging economic warfare to limit or proscribe shipments of goods to enemy or potential enemy states. The use of licensing by the industrial nations to control trade flows has been reduced in the post-World War II era.

Marshall Plan A proposal made by Secretary of State George C. Marshall in 1947 that the United States undertake a vast program of economic aid to help rebuild the war-shattered economies of Western Europe. The United States Congress accepted the Plan in 1948 when it established the European Recovery Program (ERP) to provide grants and loans for European nations that agreed to participate. At American urging, the sixteen countries that shared in the program established a regional Organization for European Economic Cooperation (OEEC) to encourage cooperation in reconstruction projects and to draw up a collective inventory of resources and requirements. The Soviet Union and other communist countries of East Europe were invited to join in the program but declined. From 1948 to 1952, the United States provided $15 billion in loans and grants-in-aid under the Marshall Plan program. *See also* FOREIGN AID, p. 125; MARSHALL PLAN, p. 392.

Significance The success of the Marshall Plan, the first major post-World War II aid program, has since encouraged American policymakers and the United States Congress to use foreign aid as a tactic for combating instability and thwarting communist aims in the developing countries. By 1952, the Plan had sparked a general recovery in Europe that saw prewar production levels surpassed in participating countries. American efforts under the Marshall Plan to encourage the integration of European economies to achieve the objective of a single common market for all of Western Europe have come close to fruition with the expansion of the European Community to ten nations, with several others seeking admission. In 1961, the Organization for Economic Cooperation and Development (OECD) replaced the OEEC. The OECD continues to elicit common action on economic matters from its 24 members, which include 17 European countries plus the United States, Canada, Japan, Turkey, Australia, New Zealand, and Iceland. Economic cooperation fostered by the Marshall Plan was supplemented in 1949 by the Atlantic Community's military-security approach to integration embodied in the North Atlantic Treaty and NATO.

Mercantilism   The economic philosophy and practice of government regulation of a nation's economic life to increase state power and security. Mercantilism provided the economic model followed by European states from the sixteenth through the eighteenth centuries. Each state sought to build up its treasury by maintaining a surplus of exports over imports, so that the favorable trade balance would result in inflows of gold and silver. Cottage industries were encouraged by government policies in agriculture and mining since finished goods offered lower shipping costs and higher prices. Colonies were used as sources of cheap raw materials and as markets for expensive manufactured goods. Governmental regulation and control permeated all sectors of each nation's economy. Wages were kept low to add to the profit for the nation's treasury and to stimulate industriousness among the masses who otherwise, it was believed, were too lazy to work.

Significance   The system of mercantilism dominated the international economy until gradually replaced by the individualistic laissez-faire theories of capitalism during the late eighteenth and early nineteenth centuries. Although mercantilist theories were later discredited, they were practical applications of state power during an age of war and plunder when a state's survival depended upon its financial ability to hire and maintain professional armies. Some "neo-mercantilist" practices, such as emphasis on a favorable trade balance and extensive governmental regulations and promotion of the economy, are followed by many states today. Some nations continue to strive to build up their gold reserves, believing, like the mercantilists, that the precious metal will increase state power. Communist states most closely approximate the mercantilist ideal in subordinating economic policies to the political objectives of the state.

Most-Favored-Nation Clause   A provision inserted in a trade agreement that extends tariff concessions agreed to by the signatories to all nations participating in the reciprocal system. The most-favored-nation clause avoids trade discrimination against third states by granting equal treatment to all. Likewise, more favorable tariff arrangements extended to other states by any signatory will automatically apply to the original parties.

Significance   The insertion of the most-favored-nation clause in a trade agreement means that the parties are not attempting to establish a bilateral preferential arrangement that would discriminate against other trading partners. The clause can turn an otherwise discriminatory series of bilateral agreements into an outward-looking program for the general reduction of trade barriers. It has been used since 1934, for example, to rebuild a liberal trading system out of the maze of discriminatory barriers established during the early years of the Great Depression. Both the Reciprocal Trade Agreements Program and the General Agreement on Tariffs and Trade (GATT) provided for the incorporation of the most-favored-nation principle in all trade agreements. In the United States, the President may withhold the application of the clause from trade with nations that discriminate against American exports. This power has been used to withhold most-favored-nation treatment from the Soviet Union, but not from China and several communist states of Eastern Europe.

New International Economic Order (NIEO)   A major campaign fought mainly in the United Nations General Assembly by the less developed countries (LDCs) to liquidate the existing world economy and replace it with a new system more favorable to the interests of the poor countries. NIEO was first proclaimed at the Sixth Special Session of the General Assembly in 1974 when that body adopted a Declaration on the Establishment of a New International Economic Order. Later that same year, the General Assembly followed up its proclamation with approval of the Charter of Economic Rights and Duties of States which spelled out in detail the principles and practices needed to implement NIEO. Operating politically through its Group of Seventy-Seven (a voting caucus of approximately 120 Third World LDCs that meets before official sessions of the General Assembly to decide on a common course of action), the NIEO issue produced a confrontation between the relatively rich, industrialized countries of the First World with the numerous but largely poor and less developed countries of Africa, Asia, and Latin America.

Significance The drive to establish a New International Economic Order is in effect a demand by the developing countries that the international economic system be restructured and a redistribution of the world's wealth be carried out. From the perspective of the Third World, the international economy is rigged against the poorer, developing countries, thus frustrating their desperate efforts to develop and modernize. They believe that prices for their primary commodities and other products have been kept artificially low in world trade channels for many years as a result of colonialism and neo-colonialism. NIEO is one more political effort by the LDCs to achieve economic goals, and the drive appears to have been another failure. Previous efforts to obtain the capital needed for development have included the Special United Nations Fund for Economic Development (SUNFED) proposal, the United Nations Capital Development Fund (UNCDF), the United Nations Conference on Trade and Development (UNCTAD), the creation of the International Development Association (IDA), and efforts to use the International Monetary Fund (IMF) and World Bank to promote developmental goals. In their efforts to finance development, the LDCs have demanded increased foreign aid from rich to poor nations, transfers of technology, a greater share of decision making power in global economic institutions, such as the World Bank and the IMF, higher and more stable prices for raw materials, and improved access to markets in the developed countries. The mission to sell the rich countries on the idea of creating a New International Economic Order took on the aspects of a holy crusade. The developed countries, led by the United States, have either rejected specific proposals or have permitted them to remain in limbo. This is a natural development because the existing economic order obviously benefits the industrialized countries. One of the by-products of the efforts during the 1970s and 1980s to create a new order in the global economy has been the acceptance of a larger role by the United Nations in providing a central "meeting house" where major economic issues can be discussed and debated. Many LDCs, however, frustrated by their unsuccessful efforts to change the global economy, have begun to look increasingly toward the Organization of Petroleum Exporting Countries (OPEC) and its cartel policies as a more appropriate means for coping with the economic strength of the First World.

Organization of Petroleum Exporting Countries (OPEC)

A group of thirteen oil exporting countries that established an intergovernmental cartel to regulate production and to agree on oil pricing in the world market. OPEC's membership includes seven Middle East Arab states (Algeria, Iraq, Kuwait, Libya, Qatar, Saudi Arabia, and the United Arab Emirates), two African (Gabon and Nigeria), two Asian (Indonesia and Iran), and two Latin American countries (Ecuador and Venezuela). OPEC was established by treaty in 1961, but it was not until the Middle East War of 1973 that its cartel arrangements became effective. A somewhat more politicized organization—the Organization of Arab Petroleum Exporting Countries (OAPEC)—was established in Beirut in 1968 by Saudi Arabia, Kuwait, and Libya. Other Arab countries that joined the new group include Iraq, Egypt, Syria, Qatar, Dubai, Bahrain, United Arab Emirates, and Algeria. OAPEC planned and carried out a major oil boycott during the 1973 Arab-Israeli War. After the war ended, greatly increased demand for oil in the industrialized countries of the West and in the Third World have led to vastly increased prices for oil and a drain of monetary resources which have gone to OPEC members. *See also* CARTEL, p. 108.

Significance   From 1973 to 1975, OPEC's price-setting mechanism essentially quadrupled world oil prices. These increases were responsible for major rounds of inflation in importing countries, reduced productivity, the threat of a major depression, growing unemployment, and frantic efforts to develop alternative sources of energy. The flow of oil produced a reverse flow of money, creating major balance of payments problems for many countries, including the United States. Third World developing countries have been especially hard hit by the high energy costs, leading many to acquire huge debts and to severely cut back on their modernization programs. The United States and other industrialized countries, with little success, have sought to counter OPEC's cartel pricing by creating an importing countries' organization to develop common policy approaches, and by applying diplomatic and economic pressures on OPEC countries. Other actions that have been undertaken to counteract OPEC's economic power have been the storage of huge quantities of oil underground, the encouragement by governments of the development of alternate energy sources, major conservation programs, and special price and policy inducements to produce more oil within nations so as to reduce dependence on imports. If the OPEC countries were to cut off all oil shipments to the industrial countries, the West would be faced with a disaster of immense proportions, probably leading to a military intervention in the Middle East. Because world oil reserves are rapidly being depleted, vast new energy sources must be developed over the next two decades if a general economic collapse is to be avoided.

Protectionism   The theory and practice of using governmental regulation to control or limit the volume or types of imports entering a state. Protectionism involves the use of tariffs, quotas, licensing, exchange control, and other devices to reduce or eliminate imports, or to increase the cost for the consumer of foreign trade commodities that compete with domestically produced articles of commerce. The degree of protection afforded domestic producers varies from state to state, but every country employs some protective measures.

Significance   Trade protectionism has been used by governments since the earliest development of international commerce, but the extent to which the principle has been applied has varied among states and during different historical epochs. Most democratic countries have witnessed continuing political battles between the advocates of free trade and protectionism. Proponents of governmental protection for domestic producers have argued that: (1) infant industries must be protected until strong enough to compete with mature, efficient foreign producers; (2) developing states, by excluding finished products, may force manufacturing companies to establish branch plants, thus encouraging modernization; (3) natural resources, especially those subject to depletion, should be protected from foreign exploitation; (4) production costs should be equalized between domestic and foreign producers to protect labor in the former from low-wage competition from the latter; (5) protectionist devices can be used in trade negotiations to secure *quid pro quo* (reciprocal) concessions from other states; (6) tariff duties can be a sizable source of income for a poor state; (7) national defense requires that essential industries—steel, machine tools, and shipbuilding, for example—be protected so that they are available for fighting a modern war; and (8) nations suffering from serious disequilibria in their balances of payments may use protectionist devices to correct the deficits and to protect their international currency reserves. Opponents of protectionism argue that it tends to vitiate the international division of labor and specialization encouraged by the forces of the marketplace in a free trade environment. The result is that protectionism defends inefficient producers, raises the price of goods for the consumer, and permits governments to direct trade to achieve national goals at the consumers' expense.

Quota   A quantitative restriction established by a state to control the importation of certain commodities. Variations of the quota system used in different countries provide for: (1) increasing customs duties as larger numbers of items are imported, up to the limit of the quota (customs quota); (2) individual quotas for specific countries (allocated quota); (3) a general limit on imports, applicable to all countries (global quota); (4) individual quotas for specific companies (import licensing); (5) reciprocal arrangements for limiting trade (bilateral quota); and (6) import limits determined by the relationship of the articles to domestic production (mixing quota). *See also* PROTECTIONISM, p. 143.

Significance   Quotas have been used to limit foreign competition in the domestic market, to correct balance of payments deficits, to buttress protective tariff systems, to provide a tool for governmental direction of trade, and to wage economic warfare. A quota is a more effective weapon than a tariff for domestic protection or economic warfare because it provides for an absolute limitation on imports whereas a tariff is a tax which, if the consumer is willing to pay the additional cost for the article, merely increases prices but does not bar goods. Most countries of the world use quota systems to supplement their tariff policies, applying the quotas to protect their least-competitive industries or those having the most political influence. In the advanced, industrial states, this usually means quota protection for farmers and other primary commodity suppliers.

Reciprocity   A *quid pro quo* (something for something) basis for international bargaining on tariff rates. While reciprocity is the basis for negotiating mutual trade concessions, it can also imply retaliation for tariff increases by other nations. Tariff rates may be raised unilaterally, but they are seldom if ever lowered without reciprocal reductions. *See also* TARIFF, p. 148.

Significance   Historically, in the United States, the principle of retaliatory commercial reciprocity was introduced by the McKinley Tariff of 1890, which authorized the President to raise certain tariff rates if other countries placed unreasonable duties on American exports. Reciprocity as a tool for direct bilateral negotiations in lowering tariff barriers came into general application with the inauguration of the American-inspired Reciprocal Trade Agreements Program in 1934. Hundreds of trade agreements based on *quid pro quo* concessions were concluded over the next thirty years, with the inclusion of the most-favored-nation clause in each bilateral agreement broadening the impact of reciprocity to include all other nations involved in the program. Reciprocal reductions in tariffs have been accelerated since 1947 through the multilateral bargaining encouraged by GATT machinery. GATT's "Kennedy Round" negotiations carried on from 1963 to 1967 culminated in the removal of most tariffs as serious impediments to trade among the major trading nations. The underdeveloped countries, however, seek to secure more favorable markets in the advanced countries without a reciprocal lowering of their tariffs as one of the best means for spurring their economic development.

Regional Development Banks   Public lending institutions created by governments to foster regional and subregional economic development. Regional development banks have been established in Europe, Latin America, Africa, and Asia. The European Investment Bank, which began to function in 1958, is an institution of the industrially developed states of the European Economic Community. Its headquarters are located in

Luxembourg and it received an initial capitalization of $1 billion. The membership of the Inter-American Development Bank, operational in 1960, is composed of twenty-one American republics. Headquartered in Washington, D.C., the bank was authorized capitalization of $3.15 billion. The African Development Bank, organized in 1965 with headquarters in Abidjan, Ivory Coast, has a membership that includes most African countries and an authorized capital of $250 million. The Asian Development Bank was organized in 1967 with headquarters at Manila and had an initial capitalization of $1.1 billion. In addition to its Asian and Pacific regional participants, the Bank's members include the United States, Britain, West Germany, Belgium, the Netherlands, Italy, and Switzerland.

Significance The establishment of regional development banks has resulted from the dimensions of the problem of economic development which have led, of necessity, to the pooling of scarce capital resources. Most bilateral and multilateral aid programs have tended to focus on technical assistance and infrastructure development aid with little provided to support industrialization. The primary function of the regional banks will be to fill this need. Membership in the regional banks follows no set pattern: the European Bank is composed exclusively of industrially advanced states; the African bank was organized by the underdeveloped countries of that continent exclusively; the Inter-American bank has only one highly industrialized member (the United States); and participation in the Asian bank is divided between developed and less developed countries. Capital is supplied to the regional development banks by governments as well as from the proceeds of the public sales of bonds. The banks are part of the worldwide movement to attack economic problems through the establishment of functional international organizations. Their effectiveness in contributing to modernization and nation-building in the less developed countries will be tested during the 1980s.

Revolution of Rising Expectations A change in attitude, prevalent among millions in the poor nations of the world, from a fatalistic resignation and acceptance of poverty to an optimism that living conditions can be substantially improved. The revolution of rising expectations is engendered by the improved communications that have brought awareness of better living conditions in the advanced nations and recognition that underdeveloped societies can improve life by altering the environment.

Significance   The revolution of rising expectations has helped to produce an increasingly dangerous "frustration gap" in the form of a gross disparity between expectations and achievements. Visible signs of economic development exist in most countries, leading to the growth of ever greater aspirations for improvement; yet the population explosion tends to negate these advances and keep standards of living depressed. As the gap between the rich and poor societies of the world widens, nationalistic fervor, demands for self-determination, and violent changes of governments have come to typify the poorer states. The Communists ambivalently provide aid to help poor states develop while simultaneously they exploit these frustrations by promoting the overthrow of established governments. The policy of the West has been one of offering economic aid to encourage progress while providing military assistance to governments in the poorer states to combat radical groups trying to achieve social change by violent means.

Smoot-Hawley Tariff Act of 1930   An act that imposed extremely high tariff duties on agricultural and industrial imports to the United States. Passage of the bill in Congress resulted from the political pressures exerted by numerous special-interest groups seeking protection. President Herbert Hoover, petitioned by leading economists to veto the bill, permitted it to become law without his signature although he was personally opposed to it.

Significance   The Smoot-Hawley Tariff imposed the highest rates on imports in American history and helped to "export" the American depression to the rest of the world. Most countries swiftly retaliated by raising their tariffs, severely depressing world trade and deepening the effects of the economic malaise. The high rates established by the act have been progressively whittled down through negotiations and the conclusion of agreements under the Reciprocal Trade Agreements Program since 1934 and the General Agreement on Tariffs (GATT) since 1947. Many of the high Smoot-Hawley rates, however, still apply to those communist and developing countries that are not members of

GATT and do not received most-favored-nation treatment. The tragic results of the Smoot-Hawley Tariff Act emphasize the interdependence of nations in the world economy.

Subsidy   Direct or indirect aid offered by government to private individuals or industries to increase their economic well-being. A direct subsidy may take the form of a sharing of the cost of construction, an export bounty, or governmental purchases of a portion of production at a guaranteed price. An indirect subsidy may involve protection of the home market through quotas, tariffs, or other restrictionist devices that permit higher prices for domestic business and industry by reducing foreign competition.

Significance   Every state has adopted subsidy policies for sectors of the economy; such policies vary in their directness, size, and objectives. Subsidies for particular industries often result from political influence. The most extensive subsidies are those aimed at stabilizing an important domestic industry, such as agriculture in the United States, and those used to encourage exports to correct a deficit balance of payments. Export subsidies are often regarded as an offensive instrument of trade policy by other states, especially when they permit dumping—selling a product abroad for less than in the domestic market. Subsidies that benefit one industry may have a harmful economic impact on others that are in direct or indirect competition with the subsidized products.

Tariff   A tax levied on imports or exports. Tariffs are commonly applied on imports to protect domestic business, agriculture, and labor from foreign competition in the home market. In some countries, the primary objective of a tariff is either to raise revenue or to retaliate against the restrictive trade policies of other nations. A tariff is discriminatory if rates vary on similar products from different countries. Tariffs on imports are paid by domestic businessmen, who pass on the cost to the consumer. In the 1980s, most tariff rates are based on an ad valorem duty (i.e., on a percentage of the value of the imported articles) although some are based on weight, quantity, and fixed duties. Unlike specific duties that remain constant despite price changes, ad valorem tariff rates fluctuate with the price variations on imports, rising during periods of inflation. *See also* FREE TRADE, p. 127; PROTECTIONISM, p. 143.

Significance   Tariffs are almost universally applied to imports, whereas tariffs on exports are seldom used because of their adverse effect on foreign sales. States justify their tariff systems as a means to correct deficits in their balances of payments, to protect infant industry, to equalize costs, to attract investment capital, to improve the terms of trade, to raise revenue, to reduce unemployment, to safeguard national defense industries, to retaliate against the discriminatory trade policies of other states, or to serve as a bargaining tool for obtaining trade concessions. Tariffs, like other restrictionist devices, tend to reduce standards of living in all countries because they limit the flow of trade and reduce the international division of labor and national specialization. The high tariff walls set up during the 1920s and early 1930s have been progressively attacked through almost continuous negotiations over a period of almost fifty years. Numerous trade agreements concluded bilaterally under the Reciprocal Trade Agreements Program initiated in 1934, and through the multilateral negotiations carried on within the GATT organization since 1947, have reduced tariff barriers to their lowest point in years. Tariffs have also been attacked through regional preferential systems, such as the common market arrangements established by the European Economic Community and the European Free Trade Association. The history of international trade, however, demonstrates that low-tariff periods are typically followed by a return to protectionism when national economies are depressed.

Technical Assistance   The teaching of new technological skills. Technical assistance programs of foreign aid are offered by the advanced states to the underdeveloped states to help them progress toward the goal of modernization. The transference of skills ranging from the most rudimentary to the highly complex—from teaching simple farming skills to the operation and maintenance of a modern industrial plant—falls within the scope of technical assistance. Technical assistance programs have sought to develop industrial, managerial, educational, public health, agricultural, mining, and administrative skills. *See also* TECHNOLOGY, p. 150; UNITED NATIONS INSTITUTE FOR TRAINING AND RESEARCH (UNITAR), p. 154.

Significance The transference of technical skills to the peoples of the underdeveloped areas of the world was begun on a small scale during the era of colonialism by missionaries, colonial business enterprises, and philanthropic organizatons. Since World War II, major programs have been carried on through bilateral aid, by regional organizations, and by the United Nations. United Nations technical assistance has been offered mainly through its Expanded Program of Technical Assistance (EPTA) and its Special Fund. These two programs were combined into the United Nations Development Program (UNDP) in 1965 to provide a unified approach to the granting of technical assistance. Regional programs that have offered substantial training in modern skills include the Alliance for Progress, the Colombo Plan, the European Development Fund of the European Economic Community, and the Organization for Economic Cooperation and Development. Western states have generally emphasized technical assistance in their foreign aid programs rather than capital grants, with the expectation that the acquiring of skills and their application to infrastructure development would attract private investment from the capital-surplus states to give impetus to the developmental process.

Technology The application of scientific knowledge and human skills to the solution of problems in the practical or industrial arts. The level of technology depends mainly on research and development (R and D)—that is, the acquiring of new basic knowledge and its application to innovation. The process of modernization in the contemporary world involves the transfer of skills from the technically advanced to the underdeveloped societies. *See also* TECHNICAL ASSISTANCE, p. 149.

Significance Improved technology has produced revolutionary changes in military weaponry, industrial production, communication, transportation, and medicine. These changes have in turn produced such results as the danger of nuclear war, a revolution of rising expectations, a worldwide ideological-propaganda-economic conflict, and the threat of a massive population explosion. Technological advances, in effect, have tended to outstrip man's ability to adapt to or deal with the social consequences of progress. The level of technology used by a nation relative to that of other countries, especially potential enemies, is a major determinant in the evaluation of national power.

Terms of Trade The relationship between the prices a country receives for its exports and the prices it pays for its imports. The terms of trade serve as a means for measuring the trend of a nation's gains or losses from trade compared to a previous base period by determining the barter or exchange value of commodities bought from and sold to other countries. If, on the average, export prices rise or import prices fall, or both occur, the nation's terms of trade have improved; if on average export prices fall or import prices rise, or both, its terms of trade have worsened. *See also* BALANCE OF TRADE, p. 104; COMMODITY AGREEMENT, p. 109.

Significance In general, the terms of trade over the past fifty years have tended to improve for the industrially advanced countries and to worsen for the underdeveloped nations. The trend toward higher prices for manufactures reflects the stronger demand for industrial goods and the price-fixing and market-controlling propensities among the multinational corporations that are the prime suppliers. The trend toward lower prices for primary commodities results from the competition among numerous suppliers, which produces a supply that exceeds demand and depresses world market prices. Primary commodity prices have increased substantially only during those years when the industrial nations have been at war. The developing nations have sought to improve their terms of trade through barter arrangements, by use of tariffs and other trade-control techniques, and by commodity agreements that limit supply and maintain price levels. A shift in a nation's terms of trade may have a significant impact on its balance of payments.

Underdevelopment A condition characterized by economic, social, and political backwardness when measured by the standards of the advanced societies. Typical features of underdevelopment include: (1) low national and per capita income and productivity; (2) high rates of illiteracy; (3) high birth rates with decreasing death rates, leading to a virtual "population explosion"; (4) a heavy dependence upon subsistence-level agriculture; (5) extensive use of child labor and few educational facilities and opportunities; (6) decentralized political institutions; (7) a rigid class structure with a minimum of social mobility; and (8) rudimentary communication and transportation facilities. *See also* ECONOMIC GROWTH, p. 115.

Significance Underdevelopment, the accepted way of life for millions of peoples over the centuries, is under attack within most such societies today. The process of modernization to overcome underdevelopment involves fundamental economic, social, and political changes aimed at replacing economic stagnation with self-sustaining economic growth. The failure of most such states to make substantial headway has produced a dangerous "frustration gap" within societies no longer willing to accept their poverty as a normal and continuing state of affairs. Lack of savings and investment capital, the refusal to undertake basic economic and social changes, and the population surge are the main stumbling blocks to progress. Help to overcome underdevelopment is offered by the advanced states of both East and West and by various regional and global international organizations, but little progress—especially when measured on a per capita basis—has occurred.

United Nations Capital Development Fund (UNCDF)

An organ of the General Assembly established in 1966 "to assist developing countries in the development of their economies by supplementing existing sources of capital assistance by means of grants and loans. . . ." The creation of the Capital Development Fund capped, under a new title, more than a decade of effort by the underdeveloped countries to establish a Special United Nations Fund for Economic Development (SUNFED proposal) to provide them with capital grants and low-interest, long-term loans. The UNCDF is headed by a twenty-four-member executive board elected by the General Assembly and a managing director appointed by the Secretary-General of the United Nations. Funds to support its operations are contributed by governments and by non-governmental organizations, and for several years an annual pledging conference was convened by the Secretary-General to elicit contributions.

Significance The Capital Development Fund idea was advocated for many years by the developing states as their best means for securing the capital needed for modernization, congruent with their concept of national sovereignty. The UNCDF, however, represented more of a voting victory than an economic gain. Potential donor states opposed its creation as an unnecessary proliferation that would tend to disperse rather than increase capital resources available for developmental financing. They also are strongly opposed to the equal voting provisions of the Fund, which are a departure from the weighted voting (in proportion to the size of contributions) system used by the World Bank Group lending institutions. The ideal proclaimed over the years by SUNFED supporters, of obtaining contributions to the Fund from each donor state equal to 1 percent of its gross national product, is likely to serve as no more than a distant goal. Because most industrialized countries refused to contribute to the Fund, it has never functioned as its supporters intended.

United Nations Conference on Trade and Development (UNCTAD)   An organ of the General Assembly established to develop world trade policies. UNCTAD began as a special trade conference attended by 122 states at Geneva in 1964 and was given permanent status by the General Assembly in the same year. The underdeveloped states of the world pushed for its creation as a forum where they could apply pressures on the advanced industrial states to lower their trade barriers to permit expanded trade in primary commodities. Their main objective is to increase foreign exchange earnings to support development programs. UNCTAD with a current membership of almost 160 nations is convened in plenary session every three or four years to serve as a center for harmonizing trade and development policies. A Trade and Development Board initiates policy proposals between UNCTAD sessions, and a secretariat is located at UNCTAD's Geneva headquarters.

Significance   The United Nations Conference on Trade and Development represents a political but not necessarily an economic victory for the underdeveloped states in their efforts to secure capital through increased trade. The industrial states that had resisted UNCTAD's creation as a duplication of GATT's role were consistently out-maneuvered at the initial session in 1964 by the underdeveloped bloc's "caucus of the seventy-seven." Economic gains, however, will depend on whether the advanced states will agree to UNCTAD's objectives of stabilizing commodity prices and extending most-favored-nation treatment to the underdeveloped states without reciprocity.

United Nations Industrial Development Organization (UNIDO)   An agency established by the General Assembly "to promote industrial development . . . and accelerate the industrialization of the developing countries, with particular emphasis on the manufacturing sector." UNIDO began its operations as an "autonomous" organization within the United Nations in 1967. Its responsibilities include intensifying, coordinating, and expediting the efforts of the United Nations in the field of industrial development. An Industrial Development Board, elected by the General Assembly, functions as UNIDO's principal organ and develops principles and policies to guide its program. The Board also supervises activities, creates subsidiary organs when needed, and reports annually to the General Assembly. A secretariat functions at UNIDO's headquarters in Vienna.

Significance   The establishment of the United Nations Industrial Developmental Organization resulted from the emphasis that developing states place on industrialization and the voting power of the developing states' bloc in the General Assembly. This emphasis on industrialization as the best route to modernization has not always been shared by the industrialized states, which fear low-cost competition and loss of markets and investment opportunities. African, Asian, and Latin American states also hold a majority of the seats on the Industrial Development Board, which enables them to apply continual pressures on the advanced-state members to offer greater help to achieve industrialization. UNIDO has sponsored an international symposium on industrial development and conducts a Special Industrial Services (SIS) program to provide practical industrial technical assistance to members that request help. Examples of projects aided by UNIDO include a steel-rolling plant in Jordan, textile manufacturing in the Sudan, and the production of raw materials from sugarcane wastes in Trinidad.

United Nations Institute for Training and Research (UNITAR)   An autonomous agency established by the General Assembly in 1963 to train individuals for work in economic and social development, particularly for technical assistance programs. UNITAR programs include granting fellowships to enable individuals from developing countries to upgrade their skills for national or international services, proviing experts to teach special courses at colleges and universities in these states, and conducting research on subjects related to economic development. Its governing body consists of a Board of Trustees, who serve as individuals rather than as representatives of states. Trustees are appointed by the Secretary-General in consultation with the Presidents of the General Assembly and the Economic and Social Council.

Significance   The United Nations Institute for Training and Research attempts to serve as a bridge between the United Nations and the international academic community. One of UNITAR's unique programs involves special training for young people from Asia, Africa, and Latin America in preparation for careers as foreign service officers or secretariat officials. The voluntary participation of eminent scholars and statesmen as lecturers sponsored by UNITAR has aided the development of diverse academic programs in several countries. In the area of research, projects include studies on strengthening the United Nations capabilities and procedures, development and modernization, and communication and information.

6. War and Military Policy

Accidental War   An unintended armed conflict touched off by incidents caused by human error or by electronic or mechanical failure. Accidental war in the nuclear age relates to the possibility that an all-out nuclear exchange between major powers could be triggered by a misinterpretation of intentions or by the accidental delivery of a weapon of mass destruction. Events that could precipitate a major war, for example, include the inadvertent destruction of a major population center, an error on a radar screen that leads to the belief that an attack is under way, or the actions of a demented military commander who orders a major attack. *See also* "HOT LINE" AGREEMENT, p. 212.

Significance   The danger of accidental war between nuclear states has increased with advances in delivery system technology and with the proliferation of nuclear weapons among other states. The development of intercontinental missiles with nuclear warheads, for example, has greatly increased the danger of accidental destruction of a major city and the consequences of that act. Proliferation of nuclear weapons among additional states may increase the dangers more than proportionally because the newcomers to the nuclear club will not have equal experience or effective security systems to protect against human error and mechanical failure. To reduce the threat of accidental war, the United States and the Soviet Union in 1963 established a "hot line" teletype communication link between Washington and Moscow so that discussions could be initiated immediately during a crisis. In 1966, a similar communication

157

link between Paris and Moscow was established, and in 1967 a "hot line" became operational between London and Moscow. In 1968, the Treaty on the Nonproliferation of Nuclear Weapons was opened for ratification. The danger of war by accident among the nuclear powers is emphasized by congressional reports disclosing that thousands of persons each year are removed from access to nuclear weapons because of drug abuse and physical and mental problems.

Act of Chapultepec   A resolution adopted by American states that an attack against any of them by a hemispheric or nonhemispheric state would be considered an act of aggression against all. The Act of Chapultepec was signed in Mexico City on March 6, 1945, by the representatives of twenty-one American republics. This declaration was the forerunner of the Rio Treaty of Reciprocal Assistance of 1947. It provided for sanctions and regional action if an American or non-American state committed aggression against an American state. *See also* RIO TREATY, p. 190.

Significance   The Act of Chapultepec had the effect of expanding the Monroe Doctrine's unilateral guarantee against intervention in the Americas to a system providing for a collective response to aggression from outside or within the Western Hemisphere. The Act resulted from a United States initiative to insure that the Security Council of the proposed United Nations Organization would not prohibit American states from taking collective action on hemispheric security matters.

Alliance   An agreement by states to support each other militarily in the event of an attack against any member, or to advance their mutual interests. Alliances may be bilateral or multilateral, secret or open, simple or highly organized, of short or long duration, and may be directed at preventing or winning a war. Balance-of-power systems tend to encourage the conclusion of military pacts to offset shifts in the power equation. The United Nations Charter recognizes the right to "collective self defense" in Article 51. *See also* PATTERNS OF POWER: ALLIANCES, p. 13; ARAB LEAGUE, p. 294; BALANCE OF POWER, p. 3; CENTO, p. 301; NATO, p. 326; OAU, p. 328; RIO TREATY, p. 190; WTO, p. 361; WEU, p. 362.

Significance   Many contemporary alliances have been expanded into regional organizations for cooperation in economic, social, administrative, and dispute-settlement as well as military matters. Multifunctional alliance systems include the North Atlantic Treaty Organization (NATO) and the Warsaw Treaty Organization (WTO). Others, such as the Arab League, the Organization of African Unity (OAU), and the Organization of American States (OAS), include some measures of commitment to mutual security but are politically rather than militarily oriented. While alliances may contribute to a sense of security and provide a deterrent to aggression, they may also contribute to international tension and the formation of counteralliances. Alliance rivalries tend to produce arms races, frequent crises, and, on occasion, wars. Alliance systems as a function of the balance-of-power mechanism are likely to exist until an effective universal collective security system is established.

Anzus Pact A tripartite treaty of alliance concluded in 1951, by Australia, New Zealand, and the United States, to safeguard the security of the Pacific area. The treaty, which remains in force indefinitely, provides that an attack upon any of the three signatories would be dangerous to all, and that each should act to meet the common danger according to its constitutional processes. The parties further agreed to increase their defense capabilities by self-help and mutual aid. *See also* ALLIANCE, p. 158; SOUTHEAST ASIA COLLECTIVE DEFENSE TREATY, p. 193.

Significance The ANZUS Pact was designed to overcome Australian and New Zealand objections to a Japanese peace treaty. After the French military defeat in Indo-China in 1954, the United States Secretary of State, John Foster Dulles, sought to widen the treaty and provide for the defense of southern Asia from communism through the creation of the wider Southeast Asia Treaty Organization (SEATO). Although SEATO was dissolved in 1977, ANZUS remains in force. ANZUS has also been supplemented by numerous bilateral pacts between the United States and several Asian nations, including the Philippines, Japan, Taiwan, and South Korea. The ANZUS Pact was also a recognition that the United States had assumed Britain's role in providing security for the two Commonwealth members.

Armistice A temporary cessation of hostilities agreed to by belligerents. Sometimes called a "truce," an armistice may be general in scope or may apply only to specific areas. Under international law, an armistice does not affect the legal status of the war, which may be continued in all respects other than those provided for in the truce agreement.

Significance   An armistice may provide a pause in hostilities to encourage negotiations for peace between belligerents, or provide an opportunity for a third party or an international organization to undertake mediatory activity. In the Arab-Israeli Wars of 1948–1949, 1956, 1967, and 1973, for example, armistice agreements stopped the fighting and, in each case, were followed by vigorous but unsuccessful efforts of the United Nations to work out a permanent peace settlement. A truce agreement may also serve as a means for halting the fighting before one side suffers complete defeat or is forced to surrender unconditionally. In World War I, for example, Germany accepted an armistice agreement so that surrender terms could be considered before her armies collapsed and her homeland was opened to invasion.

Baghdad Pact   An alliance to safeguard peace and security in the Middle East that served as the base for the development of the Central Treaty Organization. The Baghdad Pact was concluded in 1955 by Iraq and Turkey and acceded to by Britain, Pakistan, and Iran in the same year. All members of the Arab League and major Western powers concerned with the maintenance of security in the Middle East were invited to join the Pact, but none did. In 1959 the Baghdad Pact was renamed the Central Treaty Organization (CENTO) following the formal withdrawal of Iraq in the wake of its 1958 revolutionary change of government. In 1979, the Iranian Revolution resulted in the withdrawal of Iran and the collapse of CENTO. *See also* AL-LIANCE, p. 158; CENTO, p. 301.

Significance   The Baghdad Pact was developed under American encouragement and represented the Middle Eastern "northern tier" in a global series of alliances fostered by Secretary of State John Foster Dulles to "contain" Communist expansionism. Although the United States never joined, its representatives participated in CENTO committee sessions and it concluded bilateral security pacts with Iran, Pakistan, and Turkey. The United States also underwrote the Pact by supplying military and defense support aid to the parties. The Soviet Union condemned the Baghdad Pact and its CENTO successor as imperialist instruments with aggressive designs. From the start, the security alliance was weakened by the absence of Arab states in its membership, by the evolving neutralism in Pakistani policies, by Soviet arms shipments to several Arab countries, and by the virtual disappearance of British military power in the Middle East.

Balance of Terror   The equilibrium of power among nuclear states stemming from common fear of annihilation in a nuclear war. The balance of terror between the United States and the Soviet Union rests on the mutual understanding that each side possesses various types of delivery systems armed with massively destructive power that cannot be prevented by defensive actions from wreaking mass destruction upon the other's population centers. The knowledge that a surprise first strike could not destroy the other's protected and widely dispersed retaliatory capability has reinforced the deterrence created by the balance of terror. The balance of terror standoff tends to be strengthened rather than altered by the efforts of both sides to produce deadlier weapons and more dependable delivery systems.

Significance   The vast arsenal of destructive power underlying the balance of terror has eliminated total war as a rational instrument of state policy, but has grossly increased the dangers of accidental war. The early post-World War II balance of terror based on atomic weapons has been buttressed by the development of thermonuclear bombs and warheads thousands of times greater in magnitude than the atomic bomb dropped on Hiroshima. For the first time in history, war has become an unattractive instrument for securing political objectives of the state. A gain in relative power in the arms race no longer confers a significant advantage but represents merely a greater "overkill" capacity that does not upset the balance of terror. The development of a perfect defense against all delivery systems—regarded as an unlikely if not impossible undertaking by most scientists and military experts—would upset the balance of terror and increase the danger of war. The threat of mutual annihilation has not prevented limited wars, such as those fought in Korea and Vietnam, but it has restricted the participants' means and objectives.

Belligerency   The recognition by foreign states that a condition of civil war exists within a state. The determination of the point at which an armed rebellion is accorded the legal status of belligerency is a political, not a legal, question. The effect of such recognition is to confer on the insurgents a *de facto* international status with regard to the rights and duties of legal warfare. Recognition of belligerency also acknowledges that the antigovernment forces have a right to govern those areas of the state which are under their *de facto* control. *See also* INSURGENCY, p. 174.

Significance A determination that a state of belligerency exists within a nation may have profound consequences because it permits the states that recognize its existence to give material, political, and moral support to the forces in rebellion. French recognition of the American belligerency during the War for Independence, for example, provided the legitimacy for supplying the rebelling colonists with aid to help win the struggle. The *de facto* recognition of the National Liberation Front of South Vietnam by several states helped accord it a measure of legitimacy otherwise lacking. Premature recognition of antigovernment forces, however, may be considered an unfriendly act and may lead to a diplomatic rupture, the threat of war, or a declaration of war against the recognizing state.

Bilateral Security Pact A treaty between two nations pledging military support for each other in case of an attack by a third state. Bilateral security pacts may provide for immediate and unconditional assistance in case of an attack upon one of the parties, or they may merely call for consultation between the parties. They also may apply against any third state that attacks either party, or they may be limited in their application to attacks launched by specific states named in the pact. *See also* ALLIANCE, p. 158; JAPANESE-AMERICAN SECURITY TREATY, p. 176.

Significance Most bilateral security pacts are guarantees offered by great power states to stand by weaker states when they are in danger. A powerful state pursuing a foreign policy of defending the status quo may enter into security pacts as a means for justifying an intervention if the security or territorial integrity of any of the weaker states is threatened. In the Middle East, for example, the United States underwrote the Central Treaty Organization (CENTO) security system by entering into bilateral arrangements with Iran, Pakistan, and Turkey during the 1950s. Other American bilateral security pacts were concluded with the Philippines, Japan, Korea, Taiwan, and Spain.

Blockade   A naval action aimed at preventing supplies from reaching an enemy. A blockade may be directed against troops in the field or at denying resources and food to an entire civilian population. A pacific blockade, considered not an act of war but a reprisal for a legal wrong, may be levied by one state on another during peacetime to deny the latter's ships (but not those of other nations) access to the blockaded nation's ports. A land "blockade" to deny transit across a nation's territory may also be established during peacetime. In the case of the Berlin Blockade, for example, ground access across East Germany to the beleaguered city of Berlin was denied to Allied forces, necessitating an airlift. Blockade enforcement under international law permits confiscation of ships and cargoes of belligerent and neutral registry that are seized while in the act of attempting to run the blockade. *See also* MEASURES SHORT OF WAR, p. 181.

Significance   International law forbids "paper blockades" by requiring that a blockade be maintained by a force of sufficient size to make it effective. Neutral ships are not otherwise legally required to respect the blockade. In addition, advance warning must be supplied to neutrals and their ships must be given a reasonable amount of time to leave the blockaded state unmolested. A blockade serves as an effective weapon for fighting modern war because of the extensive economic interdependency of states. Examples of wars in which blockades played important roles in bringing war to an end include the North's blockade of Southern ports during the American Civil War and Britain's blockade of Germany during the First and Second World Wars. During the Vietnam War, a major political controversy arose in the United States over whether the North Vietnamese port of Haiphong should be blockaded to reduce the flow of supplies.

Civil Defense   Government programs to protect civilians, maintain essential services, preserve law and order, and continue support for the nation's war effort in the event of an enemy attack. Civil defense preparatory activities include construction and designation of shelters, stocking of food and medicines, disaster planning, providing for emergency communication and transport facilities, and operating warning and radiation-detection systems. Defense for civilians in the contemporary world involves the development of programs to protect against nuclear, chemical, bacteriological, and radiological weapons of mass destruction as well as conventional weapons.

Significance   Civil defense in the preatomic era mainly involved protecting a nation's major population centers so that they might function as postattack mobilization bases. In the nuclear age, however, development of support for the nation's military effort following a major attack on its cities is no longer the primary objective. Some security analysts now conceive of civil defense as a means to insure the survival of at least a portion of a state's population to facilitate recuperation of the nation after the war. Others regard the civil defense efforts of various nations as useless exercises in self-delusion, believing that there is no practical defense against nuclear war. Although none of the nuclear powers has undertaken a major civilian defense effort—preferring to seek security in the development of weapons to deter an attack—two neutral countries, Sweden and Switzerland, devote sizable portions of their national budgets to civil defense programs. Evidence suggests that the Soviet Union leads the United States currently in civil defense preparations.

Civil War   A war fought between different geographical areas, political divisions, or ideological factions within the same country. Civil war may involve a struggle between an established government and antigovernment forces, or it may develop during an interregnum period between groups contesting for power and legitimacy as the new government. *See also* BELLIGERENCY, p. 161; INSURGENCY, p. 174.

Significance   The outcome of civil wars is seldom decided solely by the struggle for power within a state. Other states are often prone to intervene, particularly when the struggle involves an ideological or religious contest for supremacy that duplicates the rivalry of the international balance-of-power conflict. The defeat of the Loyalist government in Spain during the 1930s, for example, was made possible by the infusion of troops and military equipment supplied to the rebel forces of Francisco Franco by Nazi Germany and Fascist Italy. A civil war is most likely to escalate into a broader conflict when states sympathetic to the rebel cause grant diplomatic recognition and provide open military support. Premature recognition of a rebel government, for example, may be considered an unfriendly act by the established government and may lead to a declaration of war.

Cold War   The extreme state of tension and hostility that developed between the Western powers and the Communist bloc of Eastern Europe after World War II. The Cold War period has been characterized by political maneuvering, diplomatic wrangling, psychological warfare, ideological hostility, economic warfare, a major arms race, peripheral wars, and other power contests falling short of an all-out "hot" war. The origins of the Cold War are found in the conflicts over the partition of Germany, in the reconstruction of a new balance of power at the war's end, in the communization of Eastern European states and their conversion into a Soviet sphere of influence, in the development of an active anticommunist philosophy and policy in the United States, and in the building of alliances and counteralliances that created a pervasive atmosphere of fear and suspicion between the wartime allies. *See also* BIPOLARITY, p. 4.

Significance The Cold War was an inevitable development in the complex postwar period of defeated and divided states, power vacuums, ideological rivalry, massive reconstruction programs, atomic weapons, and the political and power rivalry of two emerging superpowers. Forces unleashed by the early hostility in the Cold War gave it a self-generating impetus that sustained its intensity for fifteen years. During the 1960s, however, the Cold War slowly began to moderate, the Soviet Union eased its "Iron Curtain" restrictions, growing polycentric nationalism in Eastern European states weakened Soviet influence, and intense rivalry within the communist camp between the Soviets and Communist China diverted Soviet concern from the Cold War and ushered in a period of détente. Coterminously, the progressive deterioration of American leadership in the Western camp, a weakening of the bonds of unity within NATO, and a growing American concern with Asian problems helped to erode some of the old bitterness of the Cold War. By the late 1970s, however, an escalating arms race and a bitter human rights conflict threatened to revitalize much of the Cold War antagonism. In the early 1980s, as a result of Soviet aggression in Afghanistan, détente was replaced with a new series of escalations in the arms race, a boycott of the Olympic Games in Moscow, and an increasing spirit of distrust and hostility between the superpowers. The internal crisis in Poland in 1981 and 1982 created an additional international flashpoint.

Contraband War materials which may not be sold to belligerents by neutrals. International law recognizes the right of belligerents to deny shipments of contraband materials to the enemy, but the international community has never been able to agree on exactly what goods are contraband and which are unrelated to the war effort. Goods shipped to a neutral port, if ultimately destined for shipment to the enemy, may be seized as contraband under the doctrine of continuous voyage or ultimate destination. A category of "conditional contraband" consists of goods normally for peacetime consumption but which may be useful for military purposes. *See also* BLOCKADE, p. 163; NEUTRALITY, p. 280.

Significance   Modern war, with its emphasis on breaking civilian morale, has tended to obliterate the difference between contraband and permissible goods shipped by neutrals to belligerents. Most goods, even foodstuffs, are recognized in the contemporary world as significant contributions to a nation's war effort. The right of belligerents to stop and search neutral ships and to seize contraband destined for the enemy conflicts with the general principle of the freedom of the seas. During the First and Second World Wars, for example, relations between neutral nations and belligerents on both sides were frequently embittered as a result of such actions.

Coup d'Etat   A swift decisive seizure of government power by a political or military group from within the existing system. A *coup d'etat* differs from a revolution in that it is not based on a popular uprising and does not necessarily involve a transformation in the established political and social institutions of the society, although revolutionary changes may be instituted after a *coup*. The organizers of a *coup d'etat* usually carry it out by capturing or killing top political and military leaders, by seizing control of key government buildings and public utilities, and by using the mass media of communication to calm the masses and gain their acceptance of the new regime. *See also* REVOLUTION, p. 189.

Significance   Throughout history, the *coup d'etat* has been a frequently used device by factions or subordinate members within a society's power structure to attempt to elevate themselves to top positions of leadership. A counter *coup* engineered by supporters of the ousted leaders or by personal enemies of the new leaders often follows a successful *coup d'etat*. Numerous *coups* have occurred in the developing countries during the 1970s and early 1980s, many involving seizures of power by military cliques from constitutionally elected political leaders.

Growing frustrations over failure to realize economic development goals and the threat of revolution may encourage such *coups* in the few still democratically governed underdeveloped countries. The 1980 military *coup* in Bolivia, for example, was a typical military takeover following an election in which left-wing elements won political power. The Greek military *coup d'etat* of 1967 demonstrated that even Western states with long traditions of democratic government are not immune from *coups d'etat*. Eventually, a new regime that has achieved power by *coup d'etat* must acquire a degree of legitimacy in the eyes of the masses to be secure and govern effectively.

Curfew   An emergency or wartime order restricting the freedom of movement of the civilian population in a danger zone to specified time periods. Curfews are frequently established to proscribe movement during hours of darkness. They are widely used in fighting insurgencies that use guerrilla warfare. *See also* MARTIAL LAW, p. 180.

Significance   Curfews are usually imposed by a local military commander when freedom of movement might jeopardize security. They are considered essential because of the increased vulnerability of utilities, communications facilities, and supply lines during the hours of darkness. Following the outbreak of war with Japan, for example, the President declared the West Coast area of the United States to be a military zone and all enemy aliens and natural-born American citizens of Japanese ancestry were ordered to be in their homes from 8 P.M. to 6 A.M. The validity of this action was upheld by the Supreme Court on the grounds that the threat of a Japanese invasion and the large numbers of persons of Japanese ancestry in the area justified the curfew (*Hirabayashi v. United States*, 320 U.S. 81, [1942]).

Declaration of War   A formal proclamation issued by a nation to announce that a legal state of hostilities exists with another nation. The requirement that a declaration of war precede the commencement of hostilities was established as an international obligation by the 1907 Hague Convention Relative to the Opening of Hostilities, but many of the ratifying states have ignored the obligation, and most of the nearly one hundred new nations created since 1907 have never accepted it. A declaration of war is directed not only at enemy nations, but it also notifies neutral states of the new situation and provides for certain domestic changes, such as the assumption by the government of special emergency powers.

Significance   The legal concept of requiring a declaration of war *before* the opening of hostilities destroys the advantage of surprise attack. Increasingly, as the state system has sought to outlaw war or aggression, states have avoided making formal declarations of war against their enemies, preferring to regard them as defensive operations or police actions. Although war has been quite common since the end of World War II, not one war has been formally declared. The increased incidence of ideologically based internal strife in the form of insurgencies, revolutions, and civil wars has likewise reduced the applicability of formal declaratons since a declaration would accord full rights of belligerency to the antigovernment forces. The revolution in warfare technology has also added urgency in keeping local limited wars from escalating through successive declarations of war to the ultimate stage of a total war of mass destruction. The Korean conflict and the Vietnam War are examples of hostilities carried on by a number of states without any formal declaration of war.

Deterrence   Activities undertaken by a state or group of states to discourage other states from pursuing policies unwanted by the deterring state or states. Deterrence involves a strategy of threatened punishment or denial to convince others that the costs of their anticipated action will outweigh the gains. The means by which states pursue policies of deterrence include increasing their general military capabilities, developing superweapons of mass destruction, concluding alliances, and threatening reprisals. To be effective, a deterrent threat must be fully credible to the parties at which it is directed. *See also* BALANCE OF TERROR, p. 161; MASSIVE RETALIATION, p. 181.

Significance   Both the balance-of-power and collective-security approaches to peace are built around the concept of deterrence. A potential war-maker is threatened by the retaliatory action of the rival military bloc in the balance system, and by the collective police action of the international community in the latter. The development of unprecedented nuclear striking power by the United States and the Soviet Union has created a near perfect system of mutual deterrence because neither side can attack the other without suffering unbearable losses and destruction. The key to nuclear deterrence is found in each side's "hardened" and dispersed delivery systems, providing retaliatory capabilities that could survive a surprise first strike by the other and retaliate massively. The nuclear standoff has been compared to the situation of two scorpions in a bottle, each having the capability of stinging the other to death but certain to be destroyed itself in the fatal embrace. Mutual deterrence, however, may be altered by the development of new offensive or defensive weapons by one side, or by an accidental war caused by human error or technical failure, which could destroy the system's inherent stability along with its participants.

Dunkirk Treaty   A fifty-year security pact concluded by Britain and France in 1947 calling for consultation and joint action against any renewal of German aggression. The Dunkirk Treaty of Alliance and Mutual Assistance provides for continual consultation on economic as well as military matters. *See also* BILATERAL SECURITY PACT, p. 162; WESTERN EUROPEAN UNION (WEU), p. 362.

Significance   The Dunkirk Treaty was based on fears engendered by historic German domination of the European continent. The treaty symbolized the reemergence of France as a great power after the French catastrophe in World War II. In 1948, the Dunkirk Treaty served as a nucleus for the creation of the Brussels Treaty Organization, which expanded the bilateral security guarantee to include Belgium, the Netherlands, and Luxembourg. In 1955, the Brussels Treaty Organization, was renamed the Western European Union (WEU), Germany and Italy were added as members, and the objective of the Pact was changed from deterring German aggression to providing for joint action in the event of an attack by the Soviet Union. WEU in turn led to the expansion of NATO through the admission of West Germany. The Dunkirk Treaty, however, remains in force.

Elements of National Power   The factors that collectively constitute the power-in-being and the power potentiality of a state. Some elements of national power are natural factors not ordinarily subject to human control or alteration, while others are variables that depend on human impulses, organization, and capacities. Major components in the power equation include: (1) the size, location, climate, and topography of the national territory; (2) the natural resources, sources of energy, and foodstuffs that can be produced; (3) the population, its size, density, age and sex composition, and its per capita relationship to national income; (4) the size and efficiency of the industrial plant; (5) the extent and effectiveness of the transportation system and communications media; (6) the educational system, research facilities, and the number and quality of the scientific and technical elite; (7) the size, training, equipment, and spirit of the military forces; (8) the nature and strength of the nation's political, economic, and social system; (9) the quality of its diplomats and diplomacy; (10) the policies and attitudes of the nation's leaders; and (11) the national character and morale of its people.

Significance   No single element of national power is likely to be decisive in determining a country's power potential or the outcome of a struggle with other nations. Most power factors are relative in time and to the strength of rivals, and an assessment of national capabilities that omits consideration of the comparative nature of the elements may be dangerous to the nation's security. In 1940, for example, France was militarily and psychologically prepared to fight a 1914–1918 type of war, but new developments in the technology and tactics of warfare by the German army outmoded the "Maginot Line" thinking of France and led to its defeat. The effectiveness with which national power is employed to achieve a state's objectives depends mainly on how capably the nation's leaders marshal, integrate, and direct the elements of national power in pursuit of its goals. A nation's capabilities also depend on how other states assess its elements in the power equation, and the actions produced by these assessments. In the nuclear age, weapons of mass destruction have given the nuclear states unprecedented power-in-being, but, since their destructive power inhibits their use, other elements may outweigh them in computing national power in specific situations.

Enemy Alien   A citizen of a foreign state living in a state which is at war with his homeland. The regulation of enemy aliens is covered primarily by customary law, which leaves much discretion to governmental officials in the state where they reside, subject to the general requirement of humane treatment. *See also* ALIEN, p. 251.

Significance   When war was declared prior to World War I, enemy aliens were generally permitted to depart for their country or to remain in residence subject to their good behavior and avoidance of any actions that might give aid or comfort to the enemy. During the First and Second World Wars, enemy aliens were subjected to various degrees of control. These included registration, denial of freedom of movement, restriction of occupation, and, in some instances, detention in relocation centers.

Escalation   Increasing the intensity or geographical extent of hostilities in a war. Escalation may involve an increase in the number of troops engaged in a limited war, participation in hostilities by additional countries, an expansion in the area of operations, a resort to the use of deadlier, more powerful weapons, or a change in the goals sought by the military action. The objective underlying escalation of hostilities in a limited war situation may be that of seeking the defeat and surrender of the enemy, or it may be that of meting out increased punishment to force the enemy to negotiate or to cease an activity that was the initial *casus belli* (cause or reason for war). *See also* LIMITED WAR, p. 179; TOTAL WAR, p. 197.

Significance   The escalation of hostilities by one side almost inevitably results in counterescalation by the other side if it is within its capabilities. In Vietnam, for example, the American application of graduated deterrence by a progressive buildup in troop strength, growing intensity of the war effort, extension of the bombing to North Vietnam, and the gradual addition of new bombing targets produced counteractions by the Vietcong and North Vietnamese and increased support for them from the Soviet Union and Communist China. This made further escalations dangerous because they could have resulted in a major nuclear war. In the nuclear age, escalation poses the grave danger that the process of raising the ante in the search for victory may get out of control and result in a total war of mutual annihilation. Since escalation is rationally limited to the employment of "conventional" weapons only, many analysts believe that limited wars in the contemporary world can end only in stalemate and political negotiations.

Fifth Column   A subversive movement to weaken a government's defensive efforts during a civil war or an attack by another nation. The term *fifth column* originated during the Spanish Civil War when the rebel forces of Francisco Franco attacked the Loyalists in Madrid with four columns and proclaimed that a fifth existed within the city to aid their cause. *See also* SABOTAGE, p. 192.

Significance   Fifth-column adherents may be motivated in their support for the antigovernment forces by ideological, ethnic, political, or religious attachments to the cause proclaimed by the rebels. Others may merely be pragmatic in their belief that they are standing with the side that is destined to win the war. The actions of the Quisling group of traitors in Norway during the Nazi attack in 1940 offers an example of the decisive role that a fifth column may play in sabotaging government resistance.

First Strike   The strategy of launching a surprise nuclear attack to destroy or decisively weaken the enemy's capacity to retaliate. The first-strike theory assumes that one side could deliver a paralyzing and devastating blow of such magnitude that it could win a nuclear war before the enemy could recover from the blow. A nation's first-strike capability depends on its arsenal of nuclear warheads and delivery systems, but its employment of a first-strike attack is limited by the potential enemy's second-strike or retaliatory capability. *See also* PREEMPTIVE STRIKE, p. 185.

Significance   A nation's security from attack in the nuclear age may depend on the ability of its retaliatory force to deter a first strike by offering the certainty of massive nuclear retribution. If its capacity to retaliate massively is not credible, a nuclear power may be placed in a dangerously vulnerable position. To avoid destruction of second-strike capability, the United States and the Soviet Union have emplaced intercontinental missiles in silos and other "hardened" sites, have dispersed their delivery systems by arming submarines with multiple warhead missile-launching devices, and have kept some of their nuclear-armed bombers in the air at all times. In addition to protecting their offensive weapons, both countries tried to develop anti-ballistic missile (ABM) systems to avert a first strike by providing a measure of defense against incoming missiles and other delivery systems. Yet, if either side ever comes to believe it has an effective defense system in being, it might be encouraged to risk a first-strike attack against the other.

Guerrilla War   Irregular warfare fought by small bands against an invading army or in rebellion against an established government. Guerrilla war is fought mainly in the rural areas by indigenous elements who know the territory and are often indistinguishable from the rest of the population. The success of a guerrilla movement depends largely on the support accorded to the guerrillas by the local population in supplying food and havens, giving aid by carrying supplies, and refusing to divulge information to the antiguerrilla forces. Many within the movement function as part-time farmers and part-time guerrillas. Because an outside source of supply is often the key to the success of guerrilla war, the cutting of supply lines becomes a main strategy for the antiguerrilla units. Guerrilla war is often one phase of a broad political-economic-social-ideological revolution fought against an established order. *See also* CIVIL WAR, p. 164; INSURGENCY, p. 174; SABOTAGE, p. 192; WARS OF NATIONAL LIBERATION, p. 200.

Significance   Guerrilla war has proved to be an effective means of harrassing an invading army, as, for example, in its widespread use in the Soviet Union against German forces during World War II. In the contemporary world, it is offered by the Communists to the peoples of underdeveloped countries as a basic tactic for undertaking the first phase of a "war of national liberation." Control of the rural areas and the isolation of the cities is regarded as the logical first step toward the victory of the masses over regular army forces using sophisticated weapons. To accomplish this, according to Mao Tse-tung, the leading Communist tactician of guerrilla warfare, the guerrilla must be like a fish, swimming in the friendly sea of the rural population. Guerrillas have been defeated in Malaya and the Philippines, but others are actively fighting government forces in several countries of Latin America and in Southeast Asia. The major test for guerrilla warfare was in Vietnam, where Vietcong guerrillas were pitted against more than a million regular troops of the Republic of Vietnam, the United States, and several allied nations.

Insurgency   A revolt against an established government not reaching the proportions of a full-scale revolution. Under international law, an insurgency is a rebellion not recognized as a "belligerency" or civil war. An insurgency may result in the issuance of proclamations by other states warning their citizens to exercise caution in commercial and travel relations, but it is regarded as primarily a domestic matter by the international community. If the revolt is not quashed in due time by the lawful government, however, other states may accord belligerent status to the rebels. *See also* BELLIGERENCY, p. 161; CIVIL WAR, p. 164; REVOLUTION, p. 189.

Significance   The problem of insurgency has tended during revolutionary epochs to become an international issue disrupting interstate relations between rival ideological groups. Since World War II, insurgency has increasingly been ascribed to communist forces using nationalistic and economic aspirations to challenge the established order in many underdeveloped states. Soviet and Chinese proclamations calling for "wars of national liberation" have produced counterinsurgency policies and programs by Western states, especially the United States. During the 1970s and 1980s, major insurgencies have included the limited war in Vietnam, uprisings in the Portuguese African territories of Angola, Mozambique, and Guinea, a ten-year struggle by insurgents in Rhodesia, and several guerrilla wars waged in Latin American countries.

Intelligence   Information gathered by a government about other states' capabilities and intentions. Military or strategic intelligence is concerned with uncovering the strength and location of land, sea, and air forces, new weapons and weapons development, troop morale and combat qualities, strategic and tactical plans, secret alliances and agreements, and civilian attitudes and morale. Counterintelligence units are active at the same time in trying to ferret out espionage agents carrying on military intelligence activities for other nations. Nonstrategic intelligence efforts are also carried on by most nations to secure pertinent political, diplomatic, economic, and social data to aid governments in pursuit of national interest objectives. Most intelligence is secured openly through careful scrutiny of public documents and private news and data sources, but the more critical strategic information often requires the use of clandestine "cloak-and-dagger" methods. However, "spying" can also be successfully accomplished today from great distances by satellites and planes equipped with special radar and photo equipment operating in friendly or neutral air space. See also CENTRAL INTELLIGENCE AGENCY, p. 369.

Significance Most nations are engaged in widespread intelligence-gathering activities in pursuit of useful data about the activities and plans of friends and allies as well as potential enemies. The United States government, for example, has assigned major intelligence responsibilities to at least nine military and civilian agencies while using many others for supplementary work in the field. Much of the open intelligence work, as well as some covert activity, is carried on by diplomatic representatives and their staffs, particularly by military and other attachés. Revolutionary developments in warfare technology have greatly expanded the need to obtain vital information related to the security of nations. When intelligence agents fail to uncover information concerning a potential enemy's intentions and strategic plans, a decisive defeat may result. In the 1967 Israeli attack on the United Arab Republic, for example, the element of surprise permitted the destruction of many Egyptian aircraft on the ground with a resulting air superiority that proved decisive. A surprise Arab attack on Israel in 1973 also produced some early military successes. An erroneous assessment of a foreign situation—as in the American assumption that the Bay of Pigs assault on Cuba in 1961 would trigger a mass uprising—may also place a nation's vital security interests in danger. In 1979, the failure of the United States intelligence community to predict the Iranian Revolution resulted in the seizure of many embassy personnel as hostages.

Intervention Coercive interference in the affairs of a state by another state or group of states to affect the internal or external policies of that state. Under international law, intervention may be legally justified: (1) if the intervening state has been granted such a right by treaty; (2) if a state violates an agreement for joint policy determination by acting unilaterally; (3) if intervention is necessary to protect a state's citizens; (4) if it is necessary for self-defense; or (5) if a state violates international law. Intervention is also justified by the United Nations Charter when it involves a collective action by the international community against a state that threatens or breaks the peace or commits an act of aggression. *See also* DOLLAR DIPLOMACY, p. 381; INSURGENCY, p. 174; MONROE DOCTRINE, p. 393.

Significance   Historically, most interventions have involved the actions of great powers undertaking reprisals against weaker states to protect the rights of their nationals, to secure payment of debts, to obtain trade concessions, or to protect property. Since World War I, ideological factors have constituted the main basis for interventions as major powers have sought to determine the outcome of rebellions and civil wars in other states. After 1917, for example, the Allied Powers sent troops to Russia in an effort to quash the Bolshevik Revolution. The suppression of the Hungarian Revolution by the Soviet Union in 1956 and the American intervention in the Dominican Republic in 1965 were motivated by fears that important states would be lost to the rival ideological camp. Soviet intervention in Afghanistan in the early 1980s was also motivated by a belief that without intervening the country and its people would reject communism and Soviet hegemony. Politically and ideologically motivated interventions are most likely to occur when a great power's hegemonic role is threatened within its sphere of influence. Intervention by small Third World states in the territory of their neighbors, however, has also become a frequent occurrence.

Japanese-American Security Treaty   A bilateral defense pact that provides for joint consultations if the security of Japan is threatened. The original Japanese-American Security Treaty was signed in 1951, and a revised Mutual Security Treaty was signed in Washington in 1960. Under the Treaty, the United States retains the right to maintain land, sea, and air forces in Japan. These forces may be used: (1) without prior consultation, to maintain peace and security in the Far East; (2) following consultation, to defend Japan against an armed attack. The Treaty specified that military operations conducted from Japanese bases outside Japan "shall be subject to prior consultation with the Government of Japan." *See also* BILATERAL SECURITY PACT, p. 162.

Significance   The Japanese-American Security Treaty, along with Japanese rearmament and the special rights granted to American military units to use Japan as a base, produced political controversy in that nation. In 1960, at the time the Security Treaty was considered for ratification, large-scale rioting forced President Dwight Eisenhower to cancel his planned trip to Japan. Although the Japanese Diet approved the Treaty, periodic outbreaks of demonstrations and violence by left-wing student groups kept the issue of the security arrangement alive. Acceptance by the United States in the 1954 Pact of primary responsibility for the security of Japan was necessitated by the American-inspired Japanese Constitution of 1947 that, in Article 9, provided for a renunciation of war and militarism. The 1960 Security Treaty, however, encouraged Japanese rearmament for defense and sought to encourage cooperation between the two nations toward that objective. Today, Japan has a powerful self-defense force consisting of an army, navy, and air force.

Japanese Constitution: Article Nine   That part of the Constitution adopted in 1947 in which the Japanese "forever renounce war as a sovereign right of the nation and the threat or use of force as means of settling international disputes." Article 9 also provides that, to implement the ideal of permanent peace, "land, sea, and air forces, as well as other war potential will never be maintained." The Japanese Constitution was written under the direct supervision of the American occupation forces commanded by General Douglas MacArthur.

Significance   The Japanese Constitution was approved by General MacArthur before the Cold War developed and prior to the enunciation of the "containment" doctrine by the United States. The United States has since encouraged the Japanese to arm in self-defense. Although the Japanese remain fundamentally antiwar in their national philosophy, they have joined with the United States in a bilateral security pact, established a National Police Reserve, and created a Defense Agency consisting of Ground, Maritime, and Air Self-Defense Forces. Article 9 has been interpreted by successive Japanese governments to prohibit offensive, but not defensive, armaments.

Kellogg-Briand Pact   A general treaty, concluded in 1928 and subsequently ratified by almost all nations, that sought to outlaw war as an instrument of national policy. Officially titled the General Treaty for the Renunciation of War and also known as the Pact of Paris, it was drawn up by United States Secretary of State Frank B. Kellogg and French Foreign Minister Aristide Briand. The two main articles provided, first, that signatories "condemn recourse to war for the solution of international controversies, and renounce it as an instrument of national policy in their relations with one another" and second, "that the settlement or solution of all disputes or conflicts, of whatever nature or of whatever origin . . . shall never be sought except by pacific means." In ratifying the Pact, however, many nations attached a reservation that proscribed only "offensive" military actions, not those of a defense character. The United States, for example, stipulated that the Pact did not impair the right of self-defense, including enforcement of the Monroe Doctrine, nor did it obligate the nation to participate in sanctions against an aggressor. *See also* WAR, p. 198; WAR CRIMES TRIALS, p. 288.

Significance   The Kellogg-Briand Pact represented an attempt to strengthen the League of Nations peacekeeping system in two ways. First, it gave the United States, which had refused to join the League, an opportunity to participate in a general condemnation of war. Second, it was aimed at closing the gap in the League's security system that, under its Covenant, permitted states to go to war under certain circumstances. Because of the reservations attached to the Pact's ratification, however, the intended restraint on state actions was largely nullified. Since states that go to war usually claim self-defense, and since no definitions were provided in the Treaty to distinguish a war of aggression from a war of national defense, the Pact did little to discourage resort to war. Trumped-up border incidents, for example, were used by Japan in its attacks on China in 1931 and 1937, and by Italy in its aggression against Ethiopia in 1935, so that the attacking state could claim self-defense. Violations of the Pact of Paris, however, were among the charges levied against individual Nazi and Japanese war criminals convicted by Allied tribunals at Nuremberg and Tokyo after World War II.

Lend-Lease   A program of mutual assistance carried on among the nations fighting the Axis Powers during World War II. The United States initiated the program in March, 1941, with the passage of the Lend-Lease Act, which canceled the "cash and carry" provisions of the Neutrality Act of 1937. The Lend-Lease Act empowered the President to sell, transfer, exchange, lease, lend, or otherwise dispose of any item related to support of the Allied cause, including weapons, food, raw materials, machine tools, and other strategic goods. Under the act, executive agreements concluded by the President with Allied nations provided for a mutual balancing of accounts for services rendered to encourage a common war effort, and to facilitate postwar settlements. *See also* FOREIGN AID, p. 125.

Significance The Lend-Lease program, undertaken by the United States nine months prior to its entry into World War II, constituted the turning point from neutrality to active American support for the Allies. It proved to be a decisive factor in bolstering morale, in supporting hard-pressed Allies threatened with exhaustion of their economic and military resources, and in cultivating a common cause in the war effort. Under the program, the United States became the "arsenal for democracy," providing more than $50 billion worth of goods and munitions—over $11 billion of them to the Soviet Union—from 1941 to 1945. After the war, controversy over payment of Lend-Lease debts owed to the United States by the Soviet Union became a source of conflict that contributed to the emergence of the Cold War. Almost four decades after the war, most recipient countries continue to make annual installment payments to the United States on their Lend-Lease accounts.

Limited War An armed conflict fought for objectives less than the total destruction of the enemy and his unconditional surrender. Limited war may be restricted with regard to the level of destructive power used, the number of participants, the territory involved, or the substitution of political considerations for military strategy, individually or in any combination. Situations of limited war may include: (1) conflicts between nuclear powers in which neither side employs its weapons of mass destruction nor attacks the population centers of the other; (2) hostilities between small states with no direct intervention by the great powers; (3) conflicts between small states aided directly or indirectly by nuclear powers, fought within a restricted geographical area and without using nuclear or atomic weapons; (4) military actions undertaken by a nuclear power against a small state without interference by other great powers; (5) domestic uprisings against a colonial power or established government in which both sides use conventional weapons and receive logistic or manpower support, or both, from rival nuclear powers; (6) collective actions undertaken by police units of an international organization to prevent territorial conquest or to achieve political goals; and (7) the theoretical possibility of limited nuclear wars in which the great powers employ only tactical atomic weapons against strictly military targets. *See also* TOTAL WAR, p. 197.

Significance The development of nuclear and other weapons of mass destruction by the great powers has forced them to keep war limited in scope and intensity and to work for political settlement as a matter of sheer survival. The limited-war concept in the nuclear era emerged during the Korean conflict of 1950–1953, when neither American nor Communist Chinese forces attacked the main base of the other, in Japan and Manchuria, respectively. In the Vietnam War during the 1960s, the United States, the Soviet Union, and Communist China intervened in attempts to affect the outcome of the struggle; yet each, in varying degrees, exercised restraint to avoid escalation into total war. Neither side in a limited war is likely to be able to win a victory in the traditional sense since efforts by either to employ greater force are balanced by counter-actions from the other. Unless one side is willing to accept defeat, hostilities will escalate to the point where both sides will consider that further applications of greater force might involve a suicidal nuclear exchange. Although many theoretical studies have been made concerning the nature and utility of limited war, nuclear powers have had little experience in fighting such wars.

Martial Law Establishment of military authority over a civilian population in time of war or during an emergency. Under martial law, rule by decree replaces civil laws, and military tribunals supersede civil courts. *See also* COUP D'ETAT, p. 166; MILITARY GOVERNMENT, p. 182.

Significance Military officers exercise vast discretionary power under martial law. To avoid abuse of this power most nations circumscribe its application by the military, permitting only political leaders to decide when, where, and for how long it should be invoked. In the United States, for example, only the President nationally and the governors within their states are empowered to declare a state of martial law. Martial law is commonly applied by military government officials of a victorious state in the occupied territory of the defeated states. In the Third World, military *coups* are typically followed by a declaration of martial law.

Massive Retaliation   The threat of nuclear response to restrain the actions of another state. After the Korean War, the Eisenhower Administration adopted a policy of massive retaliation to cope with the threat of limited, peripheral wars fostered by the Communists. The policy was aimed at preventing such wars by announcing in advance that the United States reserved the right to meet any new peripheral aggression not at the point of outbreak but by a "massive retaliation at places and times" of the nation's own choosing. The concept of massive retaliation underlies American and Soviet contemporary policies of deterrence: both sides accept the premise that neither could destroy the other's retaliatory capability in a surprise first strike and that a massive retaliation would follow. See also BALANCE OF TERROR, p. 161; DETERRENCE, p. 168.

Significance   The Eisenhower administration's policy of massive retaliation, according to Secretary of State John Foster Dulles, brought the United States and the Soviet Union to the brink of nuclear war on several occasions during the 1950s. Each time, according to Dulles, the Soviets backed down. With Soviet development of long-range nuclear striking power, however, the American threat lost its credibility. As a result, the Kennedy and Johnson administrations adopted a policy of building "balanced forces" to meet aggression through a system of "graduated deterrence" which would use only that level of force needed to meet the specific threat or act of aggression. American and Soviet development of hardened missile sites, missile-firing submarines, and other nuclear forces that could survive a surprise attack has established an equilibrium of power based on their mutual ability to retaliate massively.

Measures Short of War   Actions undertaken by one state against another to protect its legal rights or punish a wrongdoer, without a formal declaration of war. Measures short of war may involve such unilateral state actions as: (1) breaking diplomatic relations; (2) retortion (a legal but unfriendly action taken against a state that had acted in an equally unfriendly but legal way); (3) reprisal (undertaking a normally illegal action to retaliate against a state that had perpetrated a wrong); (4) an embargo or boycott; (5) a blockade; or (6) the occupation of foreign territory. *See also* BLOCKADE, p. 163; BOYCOTT, p. 106; EMBARGO, p. 120; REPRISAL, p. 189.

Significance   Measures short of war have been recognized for several centuries under customary international law as legitimate exercises of a state's retaliatory power to redress wrongs committed against it. In the absence of a central world authority to punish wrongdoing and protect rights, each state could only resort to self-help to obtain justice. Yet, the use of measures short of war may deepen international controversies and lead to declarations of war. Under the League of Nations Covenant and the United Nations Charter, members in effect renounced resort to self-help measures short of war to settle their controversies with other states. Each member of the United Nations, for example, has agreed to settle its international disputes peacefully by using traditional settlement procedures, by resort to regional agencies or arrangements, or by submitting the dispute to the Security Council, the General Assembly, or to the International Court of Justice.

Military Government   Military rule imposed upon the civilian population of conquered territory. The authority of military government stems from the military necessities of the invading army and the obligation of civilized treatment of the population of the occupied territory. Although military government cannot compel civilians to take an oath of allegiance, it can demand temporary obedience. A military government may also function in liberated areas within a military theater of operations pending the reestablishment of civil government. *See also* MARTIAL LAW, p. 180.

Significance   The application of military government over the peoples of conquered territory is as old as the history of warfare, but its role has been expanded, which requires more sophisticated methods in the contemporary era. Efforts are made not only to control hostile populations but to win them over politically and ideologically. During and following World War II, for example, the Allies helped the Axis nations to reestablish acceptable political, economic, and social institutions while prodding them into restructuring those not acceptable. Their successes are illustrated by the fact that territories occupied by the Western Allies without exception established governments patterned on the democratic model, whereas most of those occupied by the Soviet Union followed the communist model.

Mobilization   Actions undertaken by a state to place it in a condition of readiness for war. Mobilization may include placing the armed forces on alert, calling up reserves for duty, closing frontiers, expelling or controlling enemy aliens, safeguarding against sabotage, establishing curfews, and invoking emergency powers for management of the nation's economy. *See also* WAR, p. 198.

Significance   Every modern nation has developed mobilization plans and standby arrangements to be implemented when war threatens. Often, mobilization indicates that diplomatic negotiations have broken down and the outbreak of fighting may be imminent. The act of mobilizing a nation's strength will inevitably result in countermobilizations by other states and may in itself incite a potential enemy into taking military action. When Russia began to mobilize her reserves on the eve of World War I, for example, German leaders decided they could no longer await the outcome of negotiations and launched an attack. Conversely, mobilization at a critical time may help to avoid war by calling a potential aggressor's bluff. Mobilization for a nuclear war in the contemporary world can be accomplished in a matter of minutes by placing delivery systems on instant alert.

North Atlantic Treaty   A mutual security treaty, signed April 4, 1949, to provide peace and security in the North Atlantic area through joint defense. The North Atlantic Treaty signatories include twelve original parties (Belgium, Britain, Canada, Denmark, France, Iceland, Italy, Luxembourg, the Netherlands, Norway, Portugal, and United States), and three that subsequently ratified (Greece and Turkey in 1952, West Germany in 1955). To implement treaty provisions, the extensive military-political-administrative structure of the North Atlantic Treaty Organization (NATO) was created. The heart of the Treaty is Article 5, which provides: "The Parties agree that an armed attack against one or more of them in Europe or North America shall be considered an attack against them all; and . . . each of them . . . will assist the Party or Parties so attacked. . . ." Since 1969, Article 13 has permitted any signatory to "cease to be a Party one year after its notice of denunciation. . . ." None, however, has denounced the treaty. *See also* ALLIANCE, p. 158; NATO, p. 326.

Significance   The North Atlantic Treaty serves as the basic military alliance of the West to meet the threat of Soviet military aggression in Western Europe and North America. For the United States, the Treaty represented a departure from the historic American policy of avoiding peacetime military alliances. Although no evidence exists to show that the Soviets planned a military attack on the North Atlantic area, the Treaty was a product of the fear and apprehension prevalent in signatory states that such an attack might come. Although the parties to the Treaty consider it to be a defensive alliance, the Soviet-bloc states of Eastern Europe have viewed it as an offensive threat, especially after West Germany joined NATO. As a counterweight to the Treaty and NATO, the communist states signed the Warsaw Pact in 1955 and established the Warsaw Treaty Organization. The main challenges to the concept of North Atlantic unity embodied in the Treaty have come from within, involving a struggle for leadership between France and the United States, a struggle which led France to drop out of NATO while continuing to honor the North Atlantic Treaty.

Peaceful Coexistence   A reinterpretation of Leninism that rejects the inevitability of a major war between the leading Western and communist states. The communist doctrine of peaceful coexistence was enunciated by Soviet Premier Nikita Khrushchev before the Twentieth Party Congress in 1956. As a basis for Soviet policy, the new doctrine called for both sides to avoid nuclear war and to refrain from exporting revolution or counterrevolution. Competition between states with different social systems, according to Khrushchev, was to continue in all nonmilitary areas until communism proved itself superior and presided at the burial of capitalism. *See also* KHRUSHCHEVISM, p. 43.

Significance   The doctrine of peaceful coexistence was a recognition that the threat of nuclear annihilation required the adoption of a new tactical approach for spreading communism. The doctrine did not espouse pacifism, however, since "just wars" of national liberation fought by indigenous peoples were designated as the means for achieving the goal of communism in the developing areas of the world. The right to "export" aid to revolutionary groups to offset capitalist support that propped up reactionary regimes opposed by the masses became an integral part of the new Soviet dogma. Many of the ideas expounded in the doctrine were reiterations of Lenin's and Stalin's interpretations of Marx, but the emphasis on avoiding a major war with the West was based on a realistic appraisal of the dangers of nuclear war. Although Chinese leaders in the 1950s and 1960s delivered scathing denunciations of the peaceful coexistence doctrine as a rejection of the principles of Marxism-Leninism and a mark of cowardice on the part of Soviet leaders, in the 1970s they adopted their own peaceful coexistence doctrine as a basis for a Chinese-American détente.

Preemptive Strike   A first-strike nuclear attack undertaken on the assumption that an enemy state is planning an imminent nuclear attack. The concept of a preemptive attack was developed by Soviet military tacticians during the 1950s as a defense measure to transform an enemy's planned first strike into a less dangerous counterblow. The preemptive attack would be aimed at seizing the initiative to gain the advantage of surprise while a state's offensive power remained undamaged. Also known as a "spoiling" or "blunting" attack, it would be undertaken only after state leaders received intelligence data clearly indicating that the rival state was preparing a nuclear strike. *See also* FIRST STRIKE, p. 172; PREVENTIVE WAR, p. 186.

Significance   The concept of preemptive attack evolved during a period when considerable time was needed to ready bombers and liquid-fueled rockets, which then comprised the main striking forces for nuclear states. The development of push-button warfare with the emplacement of solid-fuel intercontinental ballistic missiles has meant that a nuclear attack could be launched with such speed that the victim of the attack would be unaware of its preparations. Moreover, the dispersal of nuclear delivery systems and steps taken to protect them from destruction during a surprise attack would permit a devastating retaliatory strike against the preempting state. Military analysts also recognize that a preemptive strike could be triggered by false or misleading intelligence data. During a crisis, for example, precautionary activities undertaken by each side to guard against a surprise attack by the other could be interpreted as preparations for an attack. Developments in nuclear technology have all but eliminated the preemptive attack as a rational, credible instrument of military policy.

Preventive War   A military strategy that calls for an attack by a nation that enjoys a temporary advantage in striking power. The doctrine of preventive war calls for a surprise attack that is dedicated to the destruction of an enemy state that is developing a superior force for a crushing future attack. The theory assumes that the other side in an arms race is determined to undertake a future aggression, that time is on its side, and that an immediate decisive strike could destroy that future threat. *See also* PREEMPTIVE STRIKE, p. 185.

Significance   The concept of preventive war is expounded mainly during a conventional arms race between nations of limited military and economic potentiality. In the Middle East in 1967, for example, an Israeli preventive war launched by a surprise attack destroyed several Arab armies that were arrayed against the state. Israeli leaders determined that superior Arab manpower resources and Soviet military aid would be combined in time to jeopardize the existence of the state of Israel. The possibility of a preventive war undertaken by the United States or the Soviet Union has been all but eliminated by revolutionary developments in nuclear and delivery-systems technology. The retaliatory capabilities of each side would make a preventive war attack suicidal for both.

Psychological Warfare   Political, military, economic, and social activities carried on during war or Cold War periods aimed at influencing thoughts and actions. The major objectives of psychological warfare are to weaken an enemy's or potential enemy's will to fight, to strengthen the resolve of a nation's people or those of its allies, or to achieve diplomatic objectives. Psychological warfare is conducted mainly through propaganda or ideological campaigns based on carefully planned strategies and tactics directed toward the achievement of specific goals. The "weapons" employed include radio, television, films, public rallies, demonstrations, slogans, posters, books, newspapers and magazines, news conferences, and other means for reaching and affecting the thinking and emotions of opinion elites or mass publics. Psychological warfare may also be carried on at a more limited, sophisticated level in an effort to mislead or confuse policymakers or military commanders. *See also* FOURTEEN POINTS, p. 73; IDEOLOGICAL WARFARE, p. 74; PROPAGANDA, p. 76.

Significance Psychological warfare as a technique for replacing or improving the use of military force for accomplishing military or diplomatic objectives is as old as recorded history. Its broader use as an instrument of state-craft in the contemporary world has been facilitated by the technological revolution in mass communication that has made it possible to reach the minds and influence the attitudes of millions in foreign lands. Psychological warfare directed at mass publics seeks to evoke such emotional responses as fear, hatred, horror, or fellowship, often taking the form of building stereotyped images in the minds of recipients. The first well-organized use of modern psychological warfare occurred during World War I and took the form of massive Allied propaganda compaigns, which were remarkably successful in weakening the civilian and military morale of the Central Powers and in winning the support of many neutrals to the Allied cause. The enunciation by President Woodrow Wilson of his "Fourteen Points," for example, provided a major psychological victory for the Allies by boosting their sagging morale and by raising the hopes of the Central Powers for a just peace. In World War II and the Korean War, both sides engaged in extensive psychological programs with varied results. The Allied demand for the unconditional surrender of Germany and Japan, for example, backfired by strengthening their will to resist and prolonging the war. The Vietnam War demonstrated the crucial role of psychological warfare in a guerrilla operation in which neither side was able to destroy the other militarily but each sought to win over the "hearts and minds" of the people. Since 1945, psychological warfare has increasingly taken the form of ideological competition under the assumption that, if the individual's loyalty to a belief system can be won over, the victory will be more lasting and meaningful than winning pieces of territory. Psychological warfare has become a major factor influencing a whole range of foreign policy and diplomatic activities carried on by the major powers, as, for example, in the fields of disarmament negotiations and foreign aid.

Refugee   A person who is expelled, deported, or flees from his country of nationality or residence. Since a refugee has no legal or political rights, his welfare has become a matter of concern and action by international bodies. Refugees may be repatriated to their homeland or resettled and assimilated into other societies when governments agree to accept them. *See also* UNITED NATIONS HIGH COMMISSIONER FOR REFUGEES, p. 349; UNITED NATIONS RELIEF AND WORKS AGENCY, p. 353.

Significance   The tactic in modern war of terrorizing civilian populations, along with the deeply rooted ideological and nationalistic hatreds engendered by revolutions and civil wars, has produced millions of refugees in the twentieth century. Large-scale international action to aid refugees began when the League of Nations created the office of High Commissioner for Refugees in 1921 to provide help for 2 million persons who fled Russia during the Bolshevik Revolution. A notable accomplishment in helping refugees during the interwar period occurred with the introduction of the Nansen passport. This was a certificate issued by a state on recommendation of the High Commissioner that substituted for a regular passport and enabled refugees to travel across national boundaries in Europe. World War II produced additional millions of displaced persons who fled their homelands, were expelled, or were deported as prisoners of war or for forced labor. From 1943 to 1947, the United Nations Relief and Rehabilitation Administration (UNRRA) carried on a massive relief and repatriation program for 8 million refugees. UNRRA was succeeded by the International Refugee Organization (IRO), which, during its years of existence from 1947 to 1952, helped to resettle and repatriate almost 2 million refugees from Africa, Asia, Europe, and the Americas. Since 1952, general responsibility for dealing with refugee problems has been vested in the office of the United Nations High Commissioner for Refugees (UNHCR), which is charged with responsibility for finding permanent solutions through resettlement and assimilation. In addition to UNHCR, a special United Nations Relief and Works Agency (UNRWA) has cared for over a million refugees who fled into neighboring Arab countries as a result of the Arab-Israeli Wars of 1948–49, 1956, 1967, and 1973.

Reparations   Compensation demanded by victor nations from defeated states for wrongs committed by the latter before or during hostilities. Reparations often take the form of capital goods removed from the defeated nation's territory to replace those destroyed during the war, but may also involve monetary payments.

Significance   Reparations constitute both a punishment levied on the defeated states, aimed at reducing their war-making potential for a period of years, and a subsidy for the victor nations to aid in their reconstruction. At the end of World War I, the European allies, led by France, demanded huge reparations from Germany to compensate not only for war damage but also to cover disability pensions. In case of German default in payments, the allies retained the right to send punitive expeditions into Germany. German reparations payments, progressively scaled down, continued until 1931, when the World Depression forced a suspension of most war debt payments. After World War II, the Soviet Union carried out an extensive seizure of goods and industrial equipment in the countries occupied by the Red Army, particularly in Germany and Manchuria. Reparations taken by the Soviet Union from Germany alone amounted to an estimated $28 billion.

Reprisal   A coercive measure short of war, undertaken by one state against another as a means for redressing a wrong or punishing an international delinquency. Reprisals may include a show of force, a boycott, an embargo, a pacific blockade, a freezing of assets, or a seizure of property belonging to the offending state. *See also* MEASURES SHORT OF WAR, p. 181.

Significance   Historically, reprisals have been used primarily by powerful states against weaker ones to exact payment or retribution for illegal acts. Before engaging in reprisal action, a state has an obligation to attempt to secure redress through peaceful settlement of the dispute. Acts of reprisal are forbidden if they injure third parties or if the punishment is excessive when compared to the injury suffered. Reprisals taking the form of military action against an offending state are no longer legally permissible under the peaceful-settlement and collective-security provisions of the United Nations Charter.

Revolution   A basic transformation of the political, economic, or social principles and institutions in a state, resulting from the overthrow of an established governmental order. A revolution typically involves a popular uprising and the use of violence against the governing elite. If successful, the revolutionary leaders take control of the government and may then institute basic reforms in accord with revolutionary goals. A revolution differs from a *coup d'etat* in that the latter involves a seizure of governmental power within the elite group without the support of the masses and with little or no basic political change. *See also* CIVIL WAR, p. 164; COUP D'ETAT, p. 166; INSURGENCY, p. 174; WARS OF NATIONAL LIBERATION, p. 200.

Significance Over several centuries of the state system's history, most revolutions have been motivated by ideological or religious principles. The three that have most dramatically and profoundly affected the international system—the American, French, and Russian Revolutions—were bitter ideological contests fought by protagonists of social change against the established order's vested interests. Because most governments in the contemporary world possess a monopoly of modern weapons, revolutions increasingly are taking the form of guerrilla actions supported by ideological sympathizers from outside the state's borders.

Rio Treaty (Inter-American Treaty of Reciprocal Assistance) A regional defense pact, signed at Rio de Janeiro on September 2, 1947, that provides for a mutual security system to counter acts of aggression committed in the Western Hemisphere. Signatories include twenty-one American republics, although one of these—the Castro government of Cuba—has been excluded from participation in the Inter-American System since 1962. Implementation of treaty provisions is handled by the Meeting of Consultation of Ministers of Foreign Affairs of the Organization of American States (OAS) or, provisionally, by the OAS Council. The Treaty applies to the entire Western Hemisphere, an area stretching from the North Pole to the South Pole, and pertains to indirect aggression that is "not an armed attack," as well as to a direct attack, against an American state. In the case of a direct attack, each signatory agrees to undertake action against the aggressor, although each may determine the nature of its response until collective measures can be agreed upon. In cases of aggression not involving a direct attack, such as the support of revolution in one state by another, the signatories agree only to "consult," but a two-thirds vote of alliance members may invoke compulsory sanctions ranging from diplomatic and economic to military measures. *See also* ALLIANCE, p. 158.

Significance The Rio Treaty climaxed a half-century of efforts to secure a hemispheric arrangement for cooperation in defense matters and served to multilateralize the United States opposition to foreign intervention originally proclaimed in the Monroe Doctrine of 1823. The Rio Treaty was the first general security pact entered into by the United States, and its basic commitment that "an armed attack by any State against an American state shall be considered as an attack against all" became a model for the NATO and SEATO treaties. Internal threats to the security of established Latin American governments tend to be a more pressing problem in the 1980s than the possibility of an attack by an extra-hemispheric power. The Treaty has been invoked against the threat of international communism in the cases of the Castro government of Cuba in 1962 and the Dominican revolution in 1965. Economic sanctions and a collective rupture of diplomatic relations with the Castro government have been instituted against Cuba, and a specially created Inter-American Peace Force provided the means for a collective intervention in the Dominican Republic. The main problem of applying the Rio Treaty to deal with revolutions, civil wars, and subversion within signatory countries is that it is likely to reopen old questions concerning "yankee interventionism," and may stifle social revolutions essential for modernization.

Rules of Warfare Principles and practices set forth in international law to govern the conduct of nations engaged in hostilities. The rules of warfare initially took the form of customary law, but since the latter half of the nineteenth century they have been based on major multilateral international conventions. Major instruments that set forth the "laws of war" and their main fields of application include: (1) the Declaration of Paris of 1856, which limited sea warfare by abolishing privateering and specifying that a blockade had to be effective to be legally binding; (2) the Geneva Convention of 1864 (revised in 1906), which provided for humane treatment for the wounded in the field; (3) the Hague Convention of 1899, which codified many of the accepted practices of land warfare; (4) the Hague Conven-

192 / Sabotage

tion of 1907, which revised the 1899 Convention concerning the rights and duties of belligerents and of neutral states and persons, and proclaimed rules governing such new weapons as dumdum bullets, poisonous gas, and the use of balloons for bombing; (5) the Geneva Conventions of 1929, which provided for decent treatment for prisoners of war and the sick and wounded; (6) the London Protocol of 1936, which limited the use of submarines against merchant ships; and (7) the Geneva Convention of 1949, which updated rules concerning the treatment of prisoners, the sick and wounded, and the protection of civilians. In addition to these and other minor conventions and regional treaties, belligerents in the contemporary world are bound by customary international law and a "law of humanity" forbidding unwarranted cruelty or other actions affronting public morality but not covered by either customary or treaty law. *See also* INTERNATIONAL LAW, p. 266.

Significance   The development of rules of warfare is based on the assumption that it is unlikely that war will be completely abolished and therefore should be made as humane as possible. The thrust of international law limiting conduct during fighting is to establish minimum standards of civilized behavior that will be reciprocally respected and mutually beneficial to all belligerents. The rules of warfare are often violated in the heat of battle, in fierce ideological or nationalistic struggles, in civil wars and revolutions, and in those wars where national survival is believed to be at stake. Modern strategic warfare involves a total effort to break the morale of whole populations through indiscriminate destruction of the enemy's industrial potential and population centers as well as his forces in the field. Yet, states at war make an effort to observe most of the rules; flagrant violations are more publicized than lawful behavior. The outbreak of politically and ideologically motivated guerrilla warfare in many countries during the 1970s and 1980s, however, threatens to destroy the ideal of civilized conduct underlying the historical development of the rules of warfare.

Sabotage   Destruction of military, industrial, communication, and transportation facilities in an enemy's homeland or in enemy-occupied territory, carried on by fifth column elements, guerrillas, or professional agents. Acts of sabotage are aimed at reducing production of military equipment, cutting lines of communication, weakening enemy morale, and forcing the enemy to divert large numbers of troops from the fighting fronts to deal with the saboteurs. The term derives from the *sabot* (wooden shoe) that, during the early part of the Industrial Revolution, French workers threw into the new machines to wreck them so as to avoid unemployment. *See also* FIFTH COLUMN, p. 172; GUERRILLA WAR, p. 173.

Significance Sabotage has become a key factor in fighting modern war. Because wars increasingly have involved ideological conflict, any citizen having a strong attachment to the enemy's philosophy may be a potential saboteur. Efforts to inhibit sabotage in an occupied territory by committing atrocities against the civilian population—as attempted by the Nazis in occupied Europe during World War II—tend to be counterproductive because they inspire greater hatred toward the enemy and encourage others to undertake acts of sabotage. In a guerrilla action, such as the Vietnam War, it becomes extremely difficult to undertake preventive action against potential saboteurs since most of the enemy force functions in that capacity, is widely dispersed throughout the country, and is often indistinguishable from other members of the population. Guerrilla sabotage was combated in Vietnam by such means as clearing the entire population from large tracts of land, requiring fingerprint identification cards of all citizens, and subjecting thousands of potential saboteurs to intensive interrogation.

Southeast Asia Collective Defense Treaty A mutual security pact signed at Manila in 1954 that calls on the signatories to consult and to meet the common danger in accordance with their constitutional processes. The Treaty applies to both external aggression and internal subversion in Southeast Asia and the Southwest Pacific. Parties to the Southeast Asia Collective Defense Treaty are Australia, Britain, France, New Zealand, Pakistan, the Philippines, Thailand, and the United States. To implement the Treaty's guarantees, in 1955 its signatories established the Southeast Asia Treaty Organization (SEATO), which functioned through a council and a secretariat located at SEATO headquarters in Bangkok. In 1977, SEATO was dissolved, but the Treaty remains active. By a special Protocol to the Treaty, the security area covered was extended to include Cambodia, Laos, and South Vietnam, but the Treaty excluded Hong Kong, South

Korea, and Taiwan because the Asian signatories were unwilling to assume responsibility for their defense. *See also* ALLIANCE, p. 158.

Significance   The Southeast Asia Collective Defense Treaty, intended to be the Asian counterpart of the North Atlantic Treaty, was concluded under American leadership as part of a worldwide alliance system to "contain" communism within its existing boundaries. Although all non-communist countries of South and Southeast Asia were invited to join the Pact, only three nations heavily dependent on American aid at the time— Pakistan, the Philippines, and Thailand—opted to do so. In recent years, the same kinds of centrifugal forces that have weakened NATO have devitalized the Southeast Asia Treaty commitment. American assistance to India has caused the disaffection of Pakistan, and French demands for the neutralization of Southeast Asia have contributed to the growing disarray of the alliance. The refusal of Britain, France, and Pakistan to support the American effort in the Vietnam War, and the minimal contributions made by other signatories, have left the main burden of providing security in Asia to the United States.

Stockpiling   The accumulation of reserve supplies of raw materials and finished products for use in event of war, when supply sources might be cut off. Stockpiling may enable a nation to overcome a blockade, control of the seas, or disruption of supply sources. Modern nonnuclear war produces unparalleled demand for critical commodities to feed the factories and foodstuffs to maintain the armed forces, the civilian population, and, often, allies as well. *See also* STRATEGIC MATERIALS, p. 195.

Significance   Stockpiling of critical materials may mean the difference between a military collapse and the capability of fighting a long war. Germany, during the 1930s, stockpiled large quantities of strategic materials in preparation for war to avoid a repetition of the First World War experience, when the Allied blockade helped to produce a German defeat. However, in 1945 shortages of certain critical materials—especially oil and foodstuffs—again contributed to the German military debacle. During the Cold War era, the United States amassed the world's largest stockpile of over seventy-five strategic materials. Stockpiling programs carried on by the advanced nations tend to aid the underdeveloped countries by increasing demand for primary commodities (raw materials and foodstuffs), by raising the prices of their exports, and by providing them with food from over-stocked reserves in the advanced countries, as in the American Food for Peace program. Stockpiling also enhances a nation's ability to carry on economic warfare during peacetime by curb-ing imports or by affecting the flow of trade and market prices through dumping practices.

Strategic Materials   Raw materials and semifinished and finished products essential for fighting a modern war. The avail-ability of strategic materials is a significant component in the determination of national power. The number of materials con-sidered to be strategic has increased rapidly with the technologi-cal revolution in warfare that has occurred since 1940. Some of the most critical strategic materials include foodstuffs, alumi-num, cadmium, copper, magnesium, tin, tungsten, mercury, cobalt, uranium, diamonds, petroleum, antimony, and lead. *See also* STOCKPILING, p. 194.

Significance   Access to strategic materials may prove to be a decisive factor in national power when a nation is engaged in a long war of attrition. To bolster its defensive posture, a country may pursue policies of stockpiling strategic materials, of devel-oping synthetics to reduce or eliminate dependence on such materials, of subsidizing their domestic production during peacetime, of cultivating close political ties with major supplier nations, and of preemptive buying to deny strategic materials to the enemy. The United States has used these approaches and has built up a huge stockpile of strategic materials, developed syn-thetic industrial diamonds, subsidized domestic production of petroleum and uranium, and sought to maintain good relations with Latin American countries that supply many strategic materials.

Terrorism   Activities of state or nonstate actors who use techniques of violence in their efforts to attain political objec-tives. Methods used by terrorists include hijacking of aircraft, taking of hostages, sabotage, bombings, bank robberies, political abductions, and assassinations. Terrorist organizations typically attempt to gain the attention of the media and the public by their deeds. Most terrorist organizations represent extremist political positions, with leftist groups involved in attempts to touch off a revolution or civil war, and rightist groups seeking to protect the established order. Many are idealists who regard themselves as dedicated patriots or as defenders of the people's rights. In the three decades following World War II, many of the national liberation organizations in the existing colonies used terrorist tactics in efforts to advance their independence movements. Many ethnic terrorist groups have also engaged in unconventional as well as orthodox techniques of violence in their efforts to establish a separate state. Some terrorist organizations direct their violence against foreign diplomats, military officials, and corporation executives in the belief that they are fighting to liberate their country from outside domination or neo-colonialism. *See also* SABOTAGE, p. 192.

Significance   The terrorists of today often become the patriotic leaders and national heroes of tomorrow. This fact makes it more difficult for the national and international communities to combat them. The use of terror tactics by groups that seek to achieve political objectives has many historical precedents, but growing dependence on modern transportation facilities and easy access to weapons and explosive devices have encouraged its use in recent years. Yet, the frequency and magnitude of terrorist activity remains small in contrast to the wide publicity received by the terrorists. Often, when a particularly gruesome bombing or murders occur, two or three terrorist organizations may try to claim credit for the atrocities. Some of the best-known non-state groups that have employed terrorism include the Palestine Liberation Organization (PLO) in the Middle East, the Irish Republican Army (IRA) in Ulster, the Tupamaros and Sandinistas in Latin America, and the right- and left-wing death squads that operate in Argentina, Brazil, El Salvador, and other countries in the region. Many governments also use various forms of terrorism in seeking to achieve their political objectives, including air strikes and mass executions and imprisonment. Efforts have been made by the international community to condemn terrorist activities through the United Nations, but the majority of the world's leaders retain sympathy for guerrilla warfare and terrorism used for pursuit of political objectives with which they agree. For those seeking to deal with terrorism, the main problem is whether to adopt a policy of counterviolence against them, or to undertake political compromises that might placate them.

Total War A modern war fought for unrestricted objectives with all means available for marshaling national power. Total war involves: (1) participation of entire populations in the war effort; (2) terrorization of civilian populations to destroy their will to fight; (3) the use of modern weapons offering a vast range of destructive power; (4) participation of most nations in the war, with fighting carried on globally; (5) gross violations of the international rules of warfare; (6) intense mass emotional attachment to nationalist or ideological ideals or goals that transform the war into a moral crusade for both sides; (7) demands for unconditional surrender; and (8) the political, economic, and social reconstruction of the defeated states according to the dictates of the victors. *See also* LIMITED WAR, p. 179.

Significance The twentieth century is truly the century of total war. Participants in World War I believed at the start that it would be another brief limited war, but technical progress in weapons development and the commitment of whole populations turned it into a total war of attrition fought for national survival. World War II was fought for unconditional surrender, sought by almost unlimited means, resulting in the most destructive war in history. The threat of nuclear war in the contemporary world entails the risk of total extermination of belligerents and, conceivably, of the human race.

Unconditional Surrender Termination of hostilities without stipulation of terms. In an unconditional surrender, the vanquished nation places itself fully under the discretionary authority of the victor nation or nations, which may legally impose any terms or conditions considered appropriate. An unconditional surrender would be likely to involve, as a minimum, occupation of the defeated state's territory, punishment of "war criminals," imposition of reparations, and a basic change in political, economic, and social institutions in line with the wishes of the victors.

Significance The promulgation of a policy of unconditional surrender by one or both sides during a war is likely to prolong the hostilities until one side is completely exhausted and its armies routed. The doctrine of unconditional surrender typifies the total-war concept of the twentieth century, which constitutes a significant departure from the limited wars fought for limited objectives during the nineteenth century. In World War II, for example, an Allied policy calling for the unconditional surrender of all Axis Powers was enunciated by President Franklin D. Roosevelt at the Casablanca Conference in 1943. Critics of the policy charged that it was unrealistic in denying the defeated great powers a continuing role in the postwar balance of power, that it helped to prolong the war by giving the Axis states no choice but to fight to the finish, and that it necessitated the dropping of atomic bombs on two Japanese cities.

War   Hostilities between states or within a state or territory undertaken by means of armed force. A state of war exists in the legal sense when two or more states declare officially that a condition of hostilities exists between them. Beyond this, international jurists disagree as to the kinds of conditions, intentions, or actions that constitute war by legal definition. *De facto* war exists, however, whenever one organized group undertakes the use of force against another group. The level of hostilities may range from total war utilizing nuclear, chemical, bacteriological, and radiological weapons of mass destruction, to limited war confined to the use of conventional land, sea, and air forces. The objectives of war may range from the total destruction of a state or group to more limited purposes, such as securing a piece of territory or determining a boundary line. It may be fought by well-organized armies or by guerrilla bands ranging through the countryside. The causes of war are many and complex, but unquestionably include political, ideological, economic, religious, and psychological factors. Under international law, the conduct of the belligerents during a war is governed by the rules of warfare developed through custom and broad multilateral treaties. *See also* ACCIDENTAL WAR, p. 157; BELLIGERENCY, p. 161; CIVIL WAR, p. 164; GUERRILLA WAR, p. 173; INSURGENCY, p. 174; LIMITED WAR, p. 179; PREEMPTIVE STRIKE, p. 185; PREVENTIVE WAR, p. 188; RULES OF WARFARE, p. 191; TOTAL WAR, p. 197; WARS OF NATIONAL LIBERATION, p. 200.

Significance   Historically, international law accepted war as a normal function of sovereign states in pursuit of their national objectives. Modern efforts to restrain nations in their resort to war and to civilize their conduct during hostilities were begun during the nineteenth century through large multilateral conferences. Restraints on the use and techniques of warfare that were embodied in nineteenth century conventions, culminating in those which emerged from the Hague Conferences of 1899 and 1907, helped to build the League of Nations system and eventually contributed to the development of the United Nations. The United Nations was set up to maintain peace through three complementary approaches: peaceful settlement of disputes, collective security against aggression, and building an orderly world through economic, social, and humanitarian programs. Although a world war has been avoided since 1945, major wars have broken out in more than forty cases, ranging from the Korean and Vietnam conflicts to internal revolts in many Third World countries. War among the great powers has become dysfunctional with the development of arsenals of weapons of mass destruction that could result in the annihilation of the attacking states as well as those attacked.

Warsaw Pact   The twenty-year Eastern European Mutual Assistance Treaty established by the Communist bloc in 1955. Members of the Warsaw Pact originally included Albania, Bulgaria, Czechoslovakia, the German Democratic Republic, Hungary, Poland, Romania, and the Soviet Union. The treaty of "friendship, cooperation, and mutual assistance" established a unified military command for the armed forces of the eight members with headquarters in Moscow, and provided that each give immediate aid by all means considered necessary, including the use of armed force, to any signatory attacked in Eastern Europe. *See also* ALLIANCE, p. 158; WARSAW TREATY ORGANIZA-TION, p. 361.

Significance   The Warsaw Pact was a Soviet reaction to the creation of the Western European Union and the decision to permit the rearmament of West Germany and its inclusion in NATO. The Pact has served as the basis for the establishment of the Warsaw Treaty Organization as a military-political structure that functions as a counterweight to NATO. The text of the Warsaw Pact, in fact, nearly duplicates the wording of the action clauses of the North Atlantic Treaty. The Warsaw Pact countries also committed themselves to stand in defense of the gains of socialism. Basically, however, the Warsaw Pact created a political and military structure that merely changed the form but not the substance of Soviet hegemonic policy in Eastern Europe. Since 1962, Albania has not participated in decisions or joint maneuvers carried out under the Warsaw Pact.

Wars of National Liberation   A doctrine expounded by the Communists, calling for anti-Western or anticapitalist uprisings in the developing world. Although Marx and Lenin alluded to national revolutions fought by Communists to win power, the broader contemporary definition was first expounded by Premier Nikita Khrushchev in 1961. Wars of national liberation are insurgencies undertaken against the established order in the colonial territories and in the nations of Asia, Africa, and Latin America. Communists consider them to be "just wars" to liberate the enslaved masses from economic and political bondage imposed by Western-oriented elite groups. Communist Chinese leaders have also expounded the doctrine of national liberation wars, calling for a general uprising by the peasants in all class-dominated societies. *See also* KHRUSHCHEVISM, p. 43.

Significance   The doctrine of wars of national liberation has become the basic tactic of Communists in pushing for their goal of the eventual triumph of communism in all countries. Soviet leaders, recognizing that a nuclear war would be suicidal, have declared that all wars are unthinkable and unjust except for those fought by the masses for their own deliverance. While unwilling to become directly involved in the fighting of such wars, the Soviets have accepted a responsibility for supporting them with arms and other forms of aid. Their view is that, so long as the West "exports counterrevolution," aid must be given to support indigenous revolutions. The Vietnam War, insurgencies in the Portuguese colonies, Ethiopia, and Namibia, and guerrilla actions carried on in several states of Latin America are regarded by the Communists as wars of national liberation.

Yalta Agreement   A World War II executive agreement signed at a summit conference of the Big Three (President Franklin D. Roosevelt, Prime Minister Winston Churchill, and Premier Josef Stalin) held at Yalta in the Russian Crimea in February, 1945, to reach agreement on the occupation of Germany, the future of East Europe, a common strategy for the defeat of Japan, and major issues related to the proposed United Nations Organization. Major war-related decisions included: (1) German surrender must be unconditional; (2) German war criminals should be swiftly brought to justice; (3) reparations should be exacted; (4) liberated countries of Eastern Europe should hold free democratic elections; (5) Polish and Russian borders should be shifted westward to the Oder and Neisse rivers at the expense of Germany; and (6) the Soviet Union would join in the war against Japan within three months after the end of the European war. Decisions concerning the proposed United Nations Organizaton included agreement that: (1) original membership in the new world organization would be open to all states that declared war on the Axis Powers by March 1, 1945; (2) the Soviet Union would receive three memberships in the United Nations (Soviet Union, Ukraine, and Byelorussia) instead of the sixteen demanded by Stalin; (3) a trusteeship system would be set up to replace the League of Nations mandates agreement; and (4) the veto power in the Security Council would not apply to procedural decisions and could not be used by a party to a dispute to block its consideration. *See also* EXECUTIVE AGREEMENT, p. 382.

Significance   The Yalta Agreement helped to reshape the power structure and spheres of influence in East Europe and Asia. Because no general peace treaty was signed at the close of World War II, the Agreement became a basic instrument for attempting to harmonize the policies of the victorious Allied Powers toward the defeated Axis states. The main Anglo-American objective—to prevent Soviet domination and the communization of East European states occupied by the Red Army—failed when the Soviets manipulated the elections to secure communist victories in the 1946–48 postwar period.

7. *Disarmament and Arms Control*

Antarctic Treaty of 1959   An agreement to prevent the militarization of the Antarctic continent and to remove it from Cold War conflicts. Signed in December, 1959, the Antarctic Treaty came into force in June, 1961, following ratification by its twelve signatories—Argentina, Australia, Belgium, Britain, Chile, France, Japan, New Zealand, Norway, South Africa, the Soviet Union, and the United States. The major provisions of the treaty include: (1) the prohibition of all military activity on the Antarctic continent, with each signatory accorded the right to aerial surveillance; (2) the prohibition of nuclear explosions or dumping of radioactive wastes on the continent; (3) the right to inspect each other's installations to safeguard against violations; (4) the nonrecognition of existing territorial claims, and agreement that no new claims may be made; and (5) the responsibility to settle disputes peacefully and to cooperate in scientific investigations on the continent. The provisions apply to all land south of 60 degrees south latitude, and the Treaty is subject to review after thirty years.

Significance   The Antarctic Treaty was the first disarmament agreement concluded by the United States and the Soviet Union during the era of the Cold War. A number of inspections have been carried out by national observer teams under Treaty authorization, but no known violations have occurred. The Treaty set a precedent for territorial disarmament, but efforts to apply its successful formula to the negotiation of additional demilitarizaton agreements between the great powers in the Arctic and other regions have failed. A treaty to prohibit nuclear

203

weapons and nuclear testing on the South American continent, however, was signed in 1967 and has since been ratified by most Latin American states (Treaty of Tlatelolco). Disarmament proponents have hoped that the Antarctic Treaty's provisions for inspection by national teams will help to break the deadlock over American and Soviet proposals for international inspection in the negotiations for general and complete disarmament and in limited arms-control fields.

Arms Control   Measures taken unilaterally or through agreement among states to reduce the danger of war by such means as partial disarmament, security arrangements to avoid nuclear war, and the stabilization of force levels. Arms control measures are aimed at restricting only certain aspects of the arms race, as, for example, prohibiting certain types of weapons, restricting nuclear testing, or demilitarizing geographical area.

Significance   Although the terms are sometimes used interchangeably, arms control differs from disarmament in that its main objective is to stabilize rather than to reduce or eliminate arms. Arms control measures adopted to limit the contemporary arms race include: (1) the Antarctic Treaty of 1959 to demilitarize that continent; (2) the Partial Nuclear Test Ban Treaty of 1963 to prohibit all but underground nuclear tests; (3) the Outer Space Treaty of 1967 to bar weapons from outer space and celestial bodies; (4) the establishment of direct communications links ("hot lines") in the 1960s between Moscow and Washington, Paris, and London; (5)The 1967 Treaty for the Prohibition of Nuclear Weapons in Latin America (Treaty of Tlatelolco), which created a nuclear weapons free zone (NWFZ) in Latin America; (6) the Non-Proliferation Treaty of 1967, which seeks to limit the nuclear club to its existing membership; (7) the Seabed Treaty of 1970 which prohibits emplacement of nuclear weapons in the seabed outside the twelve-mile territorial waters by signatory states; and (8) Strategic Arms Limitation Treaties, referred to as SALT I and SALT II, which are efforts by the Soviet Union and the United States to restrain the arms race.

Atoms for Peace Plan   A proposal presented by President Dwight Eisenhower to the Eighth United Nations General Assembly in 1953 that would provide for cooperation among the nuclear states and other nations in the peaceful development and application of atomic energy. The Atoms for Peace plan called for the establishment of an international agency under the United Nations to promote cooperation in the atomic field, and it urged nuclear states to divert fissionable materials from their weapons stockpiles by contributing them for peaceful research and development projects. *See also* INTERNATIONAL ATOMIC ENERGY AGENCY, p. 317.

Significance   The Atoms for Peace plan was offered by the United States as a dramatic new program that might help to restrain the nuclear arms race and break the disarmament deadlock. Although these objectives remain unrealized, the proposal achieved its limited goal of fostering peaceful development of atomic energy with the creation of the International Atomic Energy Agency (IAEA) in 1957. The Soviets, while accepting the idea of promoting peaceful uses of atomic power, rejected the link between that objective and disarmament established by the Eisenhower proposal.

Baruch Plan   A proposal for atomic control and disarmament submitted by the United States to the United Nations Atomic Energy Commission in 1946. Based on the recommendations of a special Board of Consultants (Acheson-Lilienthal Report), the plan was presented by elder statesman Bernard Baruch as the official proposal by the United States to give up its monopoly of atomic weapons under an international security system. Major points incorporated in the Baruch Plan included: (1) establishing an International Atomic Development Authority to control all phases of the development and use of nuclear energy; (2) granting unlimited inspection powers to the Authority to safeguard against violations; (3) applying stiff penalties for any violations related to the use of fissionable materials for weapons development; (4) terminating the manufacture of atomic weapons and destroying all existing stockpiles after the Authority had established control; and (5) changing the voting system in the Security Council so that the veto power could not be used to prevent the punishment of violators.

Significance   The Baruch Plan for atomic disarmament and control, although rejected by the Soviet Union in 1946, continued to provide many of the essential features offered in subsequent nuclear disarmament proposals by the United States. Russian rejection of the plan was based on a recognition that after its implementation the United States alone would retain the capability for making atomic weapons, that the United States dominated the decision processes in the United Nations, and that it would probably control the Authority as well. Moreover, the Soviets at the time were undertaking a crash program to develop an atomic weapons capability that culminated in their first test explosion of an atomic device in 1949. American-Soviet controversies over specific provisions of the Baruch Plan involved disagreement over timing in implementing inspection and control, over national or international development of atomic energy, and over the powers to be exercised by the inspection and control authorities.

Denuclearization   An agreement to prohibit nuclear weapons in a specific zone, country, or region. The denuclearization of various areas was extensively discussed for more than a decade in the General Assembly, in the disarmament commissions and committees, and in other international and national bodies, but only four nuclear-free zones—Antarctica, the seabed, Latin America, and outer space—have been established by treaty. Discussions in the United Nations concerning denuclearization have included such geographical areas as the Arctic, the Bering Strait, the Adriatic, the Balkans, the Mediterranean, the Indian Ocean region, the Middle East, and Scandinavia, but UN resolutions and formal plans and proposals have dealt chiefly with Africa, Central Europe, and Latin America.

Significance   Denuclearization as a partial disarmament measure aimed at avoiding nuclear war is related to such other arms-control devices as a nonproliferation treaty, a complete ban on nuclear testing, and limitations on the production of weapon-grade fissionable materials. The establishment of nuclear-free zones has been supported in principle by both the United States and the Soviet Union, and by the allies of each. The Soviets have also supported specific proposals advanced by Polish Foreign Minister Adam Rapacki in 1957, and by Premier Wladyslaw Gomulka in 1964, for the control of nuclear weapons in Central Europe. The Rapacki Plan called for denuclearization and simultaneous reduction in conventional forces in East and West Germany, Czechoslovakia, and Poland, while the Gomulka

Plan was aimed at overcoming Western objections to the earlier plan by providing only for the freezing at existing levels of all nuclear weapons in the region. The Western powers have rejected the Polish proposals and other plans on the grounds that security against nuclear war should be sought by agreement on a broader nonproliferation treaty, by resolving critical political issues, and by linking partial measures to general disarmament. States in two regions of the world—Africa and Latin America—have tried to exclude nuclear weapons from their areas by denuclearization treaties. A resolution calling upon all African states to agree to the denuclearization of that continent was adopted by the General Assembly in 1965, but implementation of the resolution's principles—which was left up to the Organization of African Unity (OAU)—has not occurred. The Latin American states, on the other hand, began the implementation of similar Assembly resolutions adopted in 1962 and 1963 at a special conference at Mexico City, in 1967, where a treaty was signed (Treaty of Tlatelolco) to ban all forms of nuclear weapons from the region. Nuclear weapons states, including the United States, the Soviet Union, Britain, France, and China, have ratified a Protocol to the Treaty agreeing not to bring nuclear weapons into the region.

Direct Approach   A strategy for seeking agreement on disarmament that places primary emphasis on negotiations for securing arms reduction rather than on related problem areas. The direct approach is best described by its advocates' maxim: "The way to disarm is to disarm." It differs from the indirect approach, which regards armaments as a reflection of major political disagreements that must be resolved before disarmament can become a feasible objective. *See also* INDIRECT APPROACH, p. 213.

Significance   Advocates of the direct approach to disarmament assume that the arms race itself provides the main source of insecurity among its participants. The solution to bringing the arms race under control, therefore, involves reversing its upward-spiraling tendencies and reducing tensions through specific acts of disarmament. Once substantial confidence-building moves have been reciprocally undertaken, the solution of political issues will be facilitated and a general disarmament agreement may be possible. The United States was the leading adherent of the direct approach to disarmament during the interwar period, but the Soviet Union and India have been its most vocal advocates in the United Nations.

Disengagement   The withdrawal of two potentially hostile military forces from positions of direct confrontation. Almost one hundred disengagement plans for demilitarizing and neutralizing central European areas or states were offered during the late 1950s and early 1960s by Western- and Eastern-bloc statesmen, scholars, and disarmament specialists. Most disengagement proposals have called for the neutralization of West and East Germany and part or all of Czechoslovakia and Poland, the acceptance of post-World War II boundary settlements, and the conclusion of a nonaggression pact between NATO and Warsaw Pact countries. *See also* DENUCLEARIZATION, p. 206.

Significance   Proponents of disengagement of Eastern and Western military forces claim that the establishment of a neutralized zone would reduce the danger of a major war growing out of border incidents or accidents, ameliorate Cold War tensions, and provide a start toward a general disarmament. Western opponents, especially American and German political and military leaders, have argued that disengagement would favor the Soviet bloc since it would weaken NATO defenses in Western Europe by nullifying the defense-in-depth strategy and by removing powerful German units from the NATO defense forces. The Soviet Union has opposed most Western schemes out of a fear that the neutralization of Eastern European states would result in loss of control and influence over them, and because it might weaken the hold of communism in the region. The most celebrated disengagement proposal was that presented before the United Nations General Assembly in 1957 by Adam Rapacki, the Polish Foreign Minister. The Rapacki Plan called for an "atom-free, demilitarized zone composed of East and West Germany, Poland, and Czechoslovakia." Although periodically updated, the Rapacki Plan has consistently been opposed by American leaders because it contained no limitation on conventional forces and made no contribution to the political reunification of Germany. Moreover, the plan would eliminate Germany's central role in the defense of Western Europe. The possibilities for concluding a disengagement agreement are remote, although some popular support for the idea remains.

Enforcement   The establishment of machinery to provide and administer the sanctions required to implement a disarmament agreement. The enforcement function is related to inspection because any detection of a violation raises questions concerning its political and military consequences. Setting up an enforcement system would be likely to raise such questions as: (1) What should be the composition, powers, and procedures of the enforcement agency? (2) What specific actions would constitute violations? (3) What punishment or sanction would be applied against a violator? (4) Should a state placed at a security disadvantage by a violation be entitled to undertake unilateral measures to restore the power balance? (5) Would a veto power apply to the determination of sanctions against a violator? *See also* INSPECTION, p. 213; SANCTIONS, p. 285 and 332.

Significance   A viable disarmament agreement must provide for enforcement action of unquestionable effectiveness during and following the process of disarming. No state could or would be likely to countenance a real or imagined violation that threatened its security without the existence of a dependable system for detecting and punishing violators. Since 1962, Soviet and American proposals for general and complete disarmament have provided for the establishment of an International Disarmament Organization (IDO) to inspect and enforce the disarmament process and a United Nations Police Force functioning under Security Council jurisdiction to guarantee peace in a disarmed world. Concern over the effectiveness of the enforcement function has been a major area of disagreement for negotiators in the various disarmament forums.

General and Complete Disarmament   Proposals to eliminate all armed forces and armaments under a system of international control. The first official consideration of proposals for general and complete disarmament during the United Nations era occurred when Premier Nikita Khrushchev of the Soviet Union placed the question on the agenda of the Fourteenth General Assembly in 1959. In the following year, an initial Soviet proposal calling for complete disarmament in three stages within four years and a British three-stage plan for comprehensive disarmament were transmitted to the Ten-Nation Disarmament Committee for negotiation on specific points. The Russian proposal and a combined British-American plan have since constituted the substance of the Western- and Eastern-bloc proposals for general and complete disarmament. Both plans provide for complete disarmament in three stages, inspection and control functions vested in an International Disarmament Organization (IDO), and enforcement carried on through the Security Council of the United Nations. *See also* ARMS CONTROL, p. 204.

Significance   Since 1959, the subject of general and complete disarmament and specific proposals made by the Western and Eastern blocs have been major items on the agenda of the General Assembly, its First Committee, the United Nations Disarmament Commission, the Ten-Nation Disarmament Committee, the Eighteen-Nation Disarmament Committee, the twenty-six-member Conference of the Committee on Disarmament (1969–1978), and the current forty-member Committee on Disarmament. Although significant areas of consensus have been reached, the signing of a general and complete disarmament treaty is little closer today than it was in 1959. Substantial disagreement between the two sides remains on such questions as timing, force levels, the inspection system, the control body, and the enforcement system. Ultimate agreement to eliminate all armies and weapons systems may have to await such unlikely events as the resolution of major East-West political issues, an end to the worldwide ideological-political-economic struggle for supremacy carried on by the two major blocs, a negotiated conclusion of the Cold War, and the full participation of China and France in the disarmament system. General and complete disarmament must be distinguished from arms control efforts. Whereas numerous arms control treaties have been put into effect, no consensus on general and complete disarmament appears likely in the foreseeable future.

Hague Peace Conferences (1899 and 1907)   Special international conferences called at the initiative of Czar Nicholas of Russia to elicit agreement on arms control and other measures for maintaining peace and making war more humane. The Russian proposal at the first Hague Conference that all participants agree to restrict their armaments to existing levels failed to gain support. A vaguely worded resolution calling upon all states to consider limiting their war budgets for "the welfare of mankind," however, was adopted unanimously. At the second Hague Conference, British efforts to secure agreement on arms limitation were discarded when the chief German delegate threatened to veto any arms control proposal. *See also* HAGUE PEACE CONFERENCES, p. 263.

Significance   The Hague Peace Conferences produced no concrete arms control measures but were an important milestone in the disarmament field since they were the first attempts by the international community to limit arms by general agreement. Considerable accord was achieved in collateral fields, however, with the establishment of a Permanent Court of Arbitration and by extensive codification of the laws of war and neutrality. The fruitless search at the Hague Conferences for means to halt the arms race was followed by the catastrophe of World War I. The conferences and the war contributed to the increased vigor with which statesmen pursued arms control and disarmament goals during the 1920s and 1930s under the League of Nations system.

Helsinki Accord   A major diplomatic agreement, signed in Helsinki in 1975 at the conclusion of the Conference on Security and Cooperation in Europe (CSCE), aimed at providing peace and stability in Europe between the East and the West. Known as the Helsinki Final Act, the agreement was signed by thirty-five participants that included the NATO countries, the Warsaw Pact nations, and thirteen neutral and nonaligned European nations. The Accord was divided into four sections or "baskets." Basket I dealt with questions relating to security in Europe, including basic principles guiding relations among states and specific problems of security including the institution of confidence-building measures. Basket II provided for cooperation in the fields of economics, science and technology, and the environment. Basket III provided for cooperation in promoting humanitarian endeavors, including human rights, culture, education, and the free flow of people, ideas, and information throughout Europe. Sometimes referred to as Basket IV, the Accord also provided for the holding of review conferences in which participating states are called upon "to continue the multilateral process initiated by the Conference." Two review conferences were called, the first at Belgrade (1977–78) and the second in Madrid (1980).

Significance   The Helsinki Accord was a major effort to reduce hostility between East and West by getting all European nations and the United States to accept the post-World War II status quo in Europe, and to promote programs of cooperation and understanding among all European nations. Although the Accord was merely a diplomatic agreement, not a treaty, and therefore does not constitute binding international law, it created certain expectations concerning the conduct of participating states and provided for periodic review conferences to goad them into meeting these expectations. Some beneficial results occurred following the signing of the Final Act. Soviet authorities, for example, permitted increased Jewish emigration after Helsinki. The German Democratic Republic declared an amnesty and released many political prisoners. In the field of environmental protection, participating European states signed a convention aimed at coping with problems of air pollution. However, many actions have also negated the principles of the Helsinki Accord, and, following the Soviet involvement in Afghanistan in 1979, relations between East and West deteriorated.

"Hot Line" Agreement   An American-Soviet Memorandum of Understanding signed at Geneva on June 20, 1963, under which an official teletype communications link was established between Washington and Moscow to permit direct contact between heads of government during a crisis. Similar teletype cable links were established between Paris and Moscow in 1966, and between London and Moscow in 1967. The "hot line" agreement was developed out of a fear that nuclear war might be initiated as a result of misunderstanding, miscalculation, accident, or failure to communicate.

Significance   The Cuban missile crisis of 1962 alerted American and Soviet leaders to the grave danger of a nuclear attack resulting from a communications failure when President John F. Kennedy was forced to use commercial facilities to communicate rapidly with Premier Nikita Khrushchev. The "hot line" arrangement supplements the slower, more cumbersome diplomatic channels of communication, but it is essential at a time of great crisis. During the brief Arab-Israeli War of 1967, for example, the teletype cable arrangement was used to communicate more than twenty messages between American and Soviet leaders so that both sides could make it clear to each other that neither wanted an enlargement of the war. The communications link idea was only one proposal of a number discussed by the

United States and the Soviet Union over the years as means for reducing the danger of nuclear war. Other proposals—to establish ground observation posts, give advance notice of major military movements, and permit aerial observation of each other's military facilities for example—were dismissed by the Soviets or by the United States as instruments for espionage or as attempts to gain an advantage in the arms race.

Indirect Approach   A strategy for seeking agreement on disarmament that places primary emphasis on resolving major political and related issues as necessary antecedents to the development of a consensus on disarmament. Advocates of the indirect approach regard disarmament as a secondary rather than an immediate objective, since in their view armaments are a product of the deep insecurities of the state system fostered by conflicts of national interests. The indirect approach differs from the direct approach, which postulates that the arms race itself is responsible for world tensions and, consequently, must be ameliorated first. *See also* DIRECT APPROACH, p. 207.

Significance   Advocates of the indirect approach to disarmament assume that negotiations for arms limitations will be unproductive until the strained relations among the nations caught up in an arms race have been improved by a new climate of trust and mutual understanding. This might mean, for example, that in the contemporary world the resolution of the most divisive Cold War issues and the establishment of an effective United Nations peacekeeping system should be given a higher diplomatic priority than disarmament talks. Although both the East and the West have agreed that there should be no political preconditions to reaching agreement on disarmament, their failure to resolve key disarmament issues reflects a deep mutual mistrust engendered by the abrasive issues that have divided the two camps since the end of World War II.

Inspection   The establishment of machinery to verify compliance with or to detect violations of a disarmament treaty. In the negotiation of an inspection system, specific questions to be answered would be likely to include: (1) Should inspections be carried on by a national or international body? (2) What should be the extent of access to each country's territory? (3) What forms of inspection should be utilized? (4) How frequently should inspections be conducted? (5) What powers should be exercised by inspection teams? and (6) What constitutes a violation of the disarmament agreement? *See also* ENFORCEMENT, p. 209.

Significance Inspection is a key ingredient of any disarmament agreement because the security of each participant depends on the compliance of all to the terms of the accord. The ultimate failure of the Washington Naval Treaty of 1922 to limit naval armaments, for example, was at least partly the result of the absence of any inspection system as real or imagined violations produced counterviolations. An effective system of *national* inspection of other states' activities was created by the Antarctic Treaty of 1959 to supervise the demilitarization of that continent. Both Eastern and Western disarmament plans since 1946 have included provisions for international inspection. The United States has placed major emphasis on inspection by its insistence that a workable, comprehensive *international* inspection system be set up *before* any disarmament is undertaken, a position that the Soviets assert is guided by American espionage designs. In 1979, United States officials announced that the Soviet Union had agreed to permit ten seismic monitoring stations within its borders to make a comprehensive test ban (CTB) treaty feasible, but on-site inspections to enforce a general and complete disarmament have not been agreed upon. Since 1962, both sides in the disarmament dialogue have proposed the establishment of an International Disarmament Organization (IDO) that would function under United Nations control and have "unrestricted access without veto to all places as necessary for the purposes of effective verification." Each side, however, insists on the fulfillment of different sets of prior conditions essential to the establishment of the IDO. The many proposals for the establishment of an effective international inspection authority made during the history of the state system have failed to overcome the fear, mistrust, and suspicion embodied in the twin concepts of sovereignty and nationalism.

International Disarmament Organization (IDO) A verification and control agency that, since 1962, has been proposed by both American and Soviet disarmament plans to supervise the three-stage process to achieve a general and complete disarmament. The Soviet-proposed IDO would consist of a conference and a control council, and the American version would include a general conference, a control council, and an administrator who would manage the IDO under the direction of the control council. Under both plans, the conference would operate as a general policymaking body and the control council would be charged with carrying out the verification, inspection, and enforcement functions. The IDO would be established upon the entry into force of the disarmament treaty and would function within the framework of the United Nations. *See also* INSPECTION, p. 213.

Significance The International Disarmament Organization under both American and Soviet proposals would wield extensive investigative and control powers. It would supervise the destruction or transfer of weapons in successively broader zones during the three stages of disarmament and would check on weapons retained until completion of general disarmament. Although all parties to the disarmament treaty would be represented on the IDO control council under both plans, the Soviet proposal further insists that its composition "must ensure proper representation of the three principal groups of States existing in the world"—socialist, capitalist, and nonaligned. The American plan, unlike the Soviet, provides that stage-two disarmament could proceed only after "all militarily significant states" (i.e., all nuclear weapons states) adhered to the treaty and participated in the IDO. The proposals for the creation of an IDO as the central control body for administering a disarmament treaty remain the basic positions of the United States and the Soviet Union, although little progress has occurred in the field of general and complete disarmament since 1962.

Non-Proliferation Treaty (NPT)   An international agreement to prohibit the diffusion of nuclear weapons among nonnuclear states. The Treaty on the Non-proliferation of Nuclear Weapons was hammered out during four years of intensive negotiations in the Eighteen Nation Disarmament Committee (ENDC) and in the General Assembly's Political and Security Committee, leading to approval of the draft treaty by the Assembly in June, 1968. Under the terms of the treaty, each nuclear-weapon state agrees "not to transfer . . . assist, encourage, or induce any nonnuclear weapon State to manufacture or otherwise acquire nuclear weapons. . . ." Each nonnuclear state agrees "not to receive . . . manufacture or otherwise acquire nu-

clear weapons. . . ." The eleven-article treaty took effect after its ratification by three nuclear powers (Britain, Soviet Union, and United States) and by forty nonnuclear countries. Today, most nations are signatories to the treaty and accept its terms as a limitation on their freedom of action in the nuclear weapons field. To counter the threat of future "nuclear blackmail," the three nuclear powers offered in a Security Council action to provide "immediate assistance, in accordance with the Charter, to any non-nuclear-weapon State that is the victim of an act or an object of a threat of aggression in which nuclear weapons are used. . . ." *See also* DENUCLEARIZATION, p. 206; PARTIAL TEST-BAN TREATY, p. 218.

Significance   The Treaty on the Non-proliferation of Nuclear Weapons represents a major breakthrough in the effort to control the threat of nuclear war. The long standoff in negotiations over the treaty resulted from conflict over Western efforts to establish a fleet of Polaris missile ships within NATO, based on the Multilateral Force (MLF) proposal. The Soviets took the position that such a system involved nuclear proliferation, fearing in particular a German nuclear capability. When dissension within NATO forced the United States to give up the MLF project, subsequent negotiations with the Soviets led to agreement on the treaty. The major aims of the treaty are to reduce the threat of nuclear war, to encourage progress in the search for nuclear disarmaments, and to contribute to the peaceful development of nuclear energy in all states. Its basic objective—to perpetuate the status quo of five nuclear states—is inherently discriminatory but relates to the security of all states, since each addition to the nuclear club increases the dangers of nuclear war through accident, miscalculation, or escalation. Often called the "nth nation" problem because of the unknown number of potential members of the nuclear club, proliferation has been threatened by the twenty or more nations that may already or will soon have the scientific, technical, and industrial base for building a nuclear weapons capability. Countries that now have a nuclear weapons potential in terms of technology and availability of fissionable materials include India, Pakistan, South Africa, Israel, Brazil, Egypt, Japan, Germany, and Italy. Many others are not far behind. The major obstacle to an effective control system is the refusal of a number of these nonnuclear states to sign and ratify the treaty. In addition to the Treaty on the Non-proliferation of Nuclear Weapons, efforts to limit the spread of nuclear weapons have taken the form of negotiations for a comprehensive ban on all nuclear testing and the establishment of nuclear-free zones and continents.

"Open Sky" Proposal   A plan, submitted by President Dwight Eisenhower to Soviet Premier Nikita Khrushchev at their first summit conference in Geneva in 1955, to reduce the fear of a surprise nuclear attack and to break the deadlock in disarmament negotiations. The "open sky" proposal was developed by a panel of governmental and private experts who met at the United States Marine Base at Quantico, Virginia. It provided for the United States and the Soviet Union to exchange blueprints of their military establishments and to carry on continuous aerial surveillance of each other's territory.

Significance   The "open sky" proposal was a dramatic effort to break the stalemate in nuclear disarmament talks. It offered a first-step plan to overcome Soviet objections to American demands for on-site inspections. Ultimately, the Soviet Union rejected the proposal on the ground that its main purpose was to permit American espionage. American initiation and Soviet rejection of the proposal, however, provided the United States with a propaganda victory that was widely exploited.

Outer Space Treaty   An international convention that restrains the arms race, seeks to elicit cooperation, and establishes rudimentary rules of international law for outer space. The Outer Space Treaty was approved by the General Assembly in 1966 without a dissenting vote and was put into force by eighty-four signatory nations in October, 1967—a decade after the launching of the first Soviet sputnik. Major provisions of the treaty: (1) prohibit placing nuclear or other weapons of mass destruction in orbit or on the moon and other celestial bodies; (2) ban military bases and maneuvers on the moon and other planets; (3) provide that all explorations and uses of outer space be for the benefit and in the interests of all countries; (4) forbid claims of national sovereignty in outer space; and (5) encourage international cooperation in exploring space, in assisting astronauts and space vehicles, and in the exchange of scientific information. *See also* JURISDICTION, p. 269; OUTER SPACE, p. 273.

Significance   The Outer Space Treaty culminated nearly ten years of negotiations and debates in the United Nations and disarmament bodies to conclude an agreement that would limit the military space race and begin the process of internationalizing space. The Treaty embodied principles that had been enunciated in six resolutions adopted by the General Assembly between 1958 and 1963, and those proclaimed in the Assembly's broad 1963 Declaration of Legal Principles Governing the Activities of States in the Exploration and Use of Outer Space. As an arms control measure, the Outer Space Treaty has done little to discourage current or future military uses of space. The Soviet Union, for example, has developed a special rocket for placing nuclear weapons in orbit around the earth, and both the United States and the Soviets are pursuing the development of military reconnaissance vehicles to ferret out information about their adversary's defense system. Since the Treaty makes no provision for inspection, it may have the effect of increasing distrust between the space powers and accelerating the arms race in outer space.

Partial Test Ban Treaty (1963)   A treaty signed at Moscow on August 5, 1963, by representatives of Britain, the Soviet Union, and the United States, which bans nuclear weapons tests in the atmosphere, in outer space, and under water. The Test Ban Treaty permits underground nuclear tests so long as such explosions do not pollute the environment with radioactive debris outside the territorial limits of the state conducting the tests. Article IV of the Treaty establishes the right of each party to withdraw from the Treaty after giving three months' notice if "extraordinary events" jeopardize "the supreme interests of its country." The Treaty entered into force and was registered with the United Nations in October, 1963.

Significance   The Partial Test Ban Treaty of 1963 was the first arms control measure concluded in the nuclear weapons field during the United Nations era. Although most countries have acceded to the Treaty, two critical nuclear powers—France and the People's Republic of China—have not become parties. The partial nature of the Treaty overcame earlier demands for an effective inspection system since the three types of weapons tests outlawed by it are capable of detection with existing scientific devices. Negotiations in the field of nuclear testing have continued, with the objective of concluding a comprehensive ban on all testing, but fear that underground tests could be carried on surreptitiously in the absence of on-site inspection, or that a comprehensive test ban treaty would favor the other side, has prevented agreement. The acceleration of the arms race in the early part of the 1980s with the development of new offensive weapons has reduced the likelihood of a comprehensive ban. Under the existing Treaty, numerous underground tests have been conducted by the United States and the Soviet Union, but no violations have occurred.

Ratio Problem   Issues that arise in disarmament negotiations over the schedule for disarming, the categories of forces, and other factors related to the future power relationships of participants. The ratio problem can be overcome only if all states involved in negotiating a disarmament agreement can be convinced that their security will not be jeopardized by an imbalance in weapons at any stage of the disarming process.

Significance   The ratio problem is typically one of the most difficult facing disarmament negotiators because it involves balancing different categories of forces (e.g., land vs. air and naval, or nuclear vs. conventional) and both arms destroyed and arms retained. The United States and the Soviet Union, for example, have searched unsuccessfully for many years for a formula to determine the numbers and types of forces to be disarmed at specific stages and the ratio of forces remaining. A major difficulty in solving the ratio problem results from the inability of each participant to know the actual size of other nations' troop units and the weapons they possess.

Rush-Bagot Agreement (1817)   A treaty between Britain and the United States to demilitarize the American-Canadian border and the Great Lakes in perpetuity. The Rush-Bagot Agreement was part of the peace settlement for the War of 1812. It permits each country to sail on the Great Lakes only those warships required for patrol duty and customs inspection. It was concluded originally in 1817 as an executive agreement and approved the following year as a treaty.

Significance   The Rush-Bagot Agreement remains to date the oldest and most successful disarmament agreement ever negotiated. It avoided a naval race for supremacy on the Great Lakes and stabilized the boundary between Canada and the United States. The Rush-Bagot Agreement has also encouraged good political, economic, and social relations between those two nations of North America.

Seabed Treaty   A 1971 agreement to ban nuclear weapons and other weapons of mass destruction from the seabed of the world's oceans outside each state's twelve-mile territorial waters. The Seabed Treaty was endorsed in 1970 by the Twenty-fifth General Assembly of the United Nations, and was opened for signature and ratification in 1971. Most of the nations of the world have signed the treaty, including three nuclear powers— the United States, the Soviet Union, and Britain—which have also ratified it. *See also* ARMS CONTROL, p. 204; JURISDICTION: TERRITORIAL WATERS, p. 275.

Significance   The Seabed Treaty supplemented earlier treaties aimed at keeping nuclear weapons out of Antarctica (1959), outer space (1967), and Latin America (1967). The treaty, however, is weakened by not prohibiting emplacement of nuclear weapons within a state's twelve-mile contiguous zone off its coasts. By ratifying the Seabed Treaty, the United States for the first time officially agreed to set aside the traditional three-mile limit and endorsed the twelve-mile limit in an international treaty. Moreover, the treaty was also weakened by the failure of two nuclear weapons states—France and China—to participate in the treaty process or to sign the completed document. Critics also charge that the treaty is not very useful because neither of the superpowers intended to emplace weapons of mass destruction in the seabed. Supporters, however, point out that it is best to legally check a seabed arms race *before* it gets underway. Although the treaty prohibits emplacement of nuclear weapons in the seabed of the world's oceans, submarines and other devices that use the sea but not the seabed are permitted to operate freely under its terms.

Strategic Arms Limitation Talks (SALT)   Negotiations carried on between the United States and the Soviet Union with the objective of reaching agreement on the control of strategic nuclear weapons, delivery systems, and related offensive and defensive weapons systems. SALT negotiations were first undertaken in Helsinki in 1969. The initial objective was to limit or eliminate construction of Anti-Ballistic Missile (ABM) systems which both countries were planning at that time. Subsequent discussion covered the whole range of strategic weapons systems, including a comprehensive nuclear test ban, denuclearization of specific geographical areas, limitation on numbers of certain types of nuclear delivery systems, multiple independently targeted reentry vehicles (MIRVs), limits on the building of ABM sites, and avoidance of the escalation of limited war into a nuclear conflagration. In the first series of talks (SALT I, 1969–1972), agreement was reached to limit the number of ABM defense systems to two in each country. In a second agreement, SALT I also limited the number of missile-delivery systems with nuclear warheads, but agreement could not be reached on the number of nuclear warheads in each missile (MIRVing). SALT II guidelines were worked out at the Nixon-Brezhnev Summit Meeting in Washington in 1973. These called upon the two parties to reach agreement on (1) permanent ceilings on offensive strategic forces; (2) controlling the qualitative factors in their offensive weapons arsenals; and (3) ultimately establishing a mutual reduction of strategic forces. By 1979, a SALT II Treaty including arms control provisions was signed in Vienna by President Jimmy Carter and Soviet President Leonid Brezhnev, and was submitted by Carter to the Senate for its consent to ratification. *See also* UNITED NATIONS DISARMAMENT FORUMS, p. 224.

Significance   The SALT I agreements and the SALT II Treaty were products of a period of détente between the two superpowers. With the Soviet invasion of Afghanistan in 1979, its involvement in Africa and Asia, and its growing position of strength in the overall arms race, détente gave way to new American initiatives. These involved, for example, restoration of export controls for trade with the Soviets, a boycott of the Olympic Games in Moscow in 1980, and a new emphasis on rebuilding a position of American military parity or superiority. As a result of these changes, chances that the Senate would approve ratification of the SALT II Treaty were greatly reduced. Although neither the SALT I agreements nor SALT II Treaty can be regarded as major arms control actions, they do provide for some potentially useful precedents for eventual control of what can only be described as dual systems of Mutual Assured Destruction (MAD). The main objective—to set firm limits on major weapons systems of mass destruction to avoid a runaway arms race—remains unrealized. The hope that, at a minimum, SALT negotiations would slow down the arms race and bring it under at least a small measure of control during the 1980s seems to be dashed by new strains in the relationship between the superpowers.

Treaty for the Prohibition of Nuclear Weapons in Latin America An agreement, also called the Treaty of Tlatelolco, which created a nuclear-weapon-free zone (NWFZ) in Latin America. The Treaty for the Prohibition of Nuclear Weapons in Latin America was signed at Mexico City in 1967. By 1980, the Treaty was signed by twenty-five Latin countries and was ratified and in force for twenty-two of them. Two Protocols are part of the main Treaty. Protocol I is applicable for states having territorial interests in the Americas, and Protocol II includes all nuclear weapons states. All are prevented by the Treaty from injecting nuclear weapons into the region, including a prohibition on foreign powers against bringing nuclear weapons into their bases in Latin America. By 1980, all of the major nuclear powers—the United States, Soviet Union, Britain, France, and China—had accepted Protocol II. The Treaty set up operational machinery to oversee enforcement of its provisions known as OPANAL (Agency for the Prohibition of Nuclear Weapons in Latin America). *See also* DENUCLEARIZATION, p. 206; NON-PROLIFERATION TREATY, p. 215.

Significance The Treaty prohibiting nuclear weapons in Latin America is the first successful effort to denuclearize a geographical region carried out by countries in the region. Although most nations involved in the problem of keeping nuclear weapons out of the region have ratified the Treaty and its Protocols, some key Latin countries with growing nuclear programs—Argentina, Brazil, Chile, and Cuba—have not yet fully accepted the Treaty. Procedures used in creating the denuclearized region may prove useful in other regions, such as Africa, the Pacific, and the Middle East.

Unilateral Disarmament A strategy advocated by some disarmament protagonists to overcome a continued deadlock in negotiations by undertaking one-sided initiatives. Unilateral disarmament schemes are predicated on the assumption that both sides in an arms race would prefer to disarm but that the fear, tension, and mistrust generated by the search for security through increased armaments stymies the quest. By demonstrating peaceful intentions rather than merely talking about them, unilateral disarmament theorists believe, one side could put the arms-race cycle into reverse by evoking reciprocation of its disarmament initiatives.

Significance Advocates of unilateral disarmament range from pacifist groups to scholars and statesmen who view it as a national-interest policy rather than a moral question. The idealists of the former group believe that a conquest induced by one side's unilateral disarmament should be met only by a continuing policy of passive resistance. The realists, on the other hand, believe that if one side undertakes a substantial unilateral initiative that is not reciprocated or is used by the other side to gain an advantage in the arms race, an immediate return to a hard-line policy of weapons building is called for. The latter group views unilateral disarmament merely as a "psychological primer" to encourage bilateral disarmament negotiations by demonstrating good intentions. In the contemporary arms race, the massive array of nuclear and other weapons of mass destruction developed by both sides might invalidate a unilateral initiative since the side undertaking it would retain the power to destroy the other many times over. Although unilateral proposals provide an alternative to arms escalation, they are directed at a highly irrational arms-race environment and have not been accepted as policy approaches by national leaders, whose foremost concern is national security.

United Nations Disarmament Commission A body established by the General Assembly in 1952 for the discussion and negotiation of disarmament issues. The United Nations Disarmament Commission since 1958 includes all members of the United Nations, 157 in 1982. It has been called into plenary session on only two occasions; in 1960 to pressure the Soviets to resume negotiations after their walk-out from Geneva talks over the issue of achieving "parity" in negotiations, and in 1965 to overcome a hiatus in great-power talks resulting from protracted disagreement over the specifics of general and complete disarmament. From 1965 to 1978, the Disarmament Commission remained inactive, but at the Tenth Special Session of the General Assembly called to discuss disarmament issues in 1978, it was reconstituted on the initiative of the nonaligned countries, which insisted that the United Nations maintain a universal forum on disarmament. At that session the General Assembly charged the Disarmament Commission with giving consideration to "the elements of a comprehensive programme for disarmament." In effect, this has meant trying to integrate many of the fragmented disarmament issues and initiatives within the United Nations system. United Nations efforts should be concerned in particular with controlling weapons of mass destruction, establishing zones of peace, reducing military budgets, and engaging in disarmament studies.

Significance   The United Nations Disarmament Commission was expanded into a mass forum for marshaling world opinion to pressure the great powers into making concessions to break stalemates in disarmament negotiations, not as a negotiating arena, per se. Its sessions have proved useful in urging the nuclear states to resume negotiations and in exploring new approaches to break the disarmament deadlock. Since 1978, for example, France and China have participated in the Commission's deliberations. On numerous occasions, the Commission has called for a World Disarmament Conference similar in form to the one held in the 1930s under the League of Nations. Despite its efforts to focus world attention on the dangers of the arms race and the need for disarmament, little heed has been paid to the activities and proposals of the Disarmament Commission.

United Nations Disarmament Forums   Various discussion and negotiating committees and commissions created by the United Nations to try to secure agreement on disarmament and arms control measures. In 1946, the first United Nations disarmament forum, the United Nations Atomic Energy Commission, consisting of the permanent members of the Security Council plus Canada, was established to try to implement the Baruch Plan calling for complete nuclear disarmament. In 1947, the Commission for Conventional Armaments was established by the Security Council to supplement the Atomic Energy Commission's efforts. In 1952, these two Commissions were merged by the General Assembly into the United Nations Disarmament Commission, composed like its two predecessors of the permanent members of the Security Council plus Canada. The Disarmament Commission then created a Five-Power Sub-Committee, consisting of the United States, the Soviet Union, Britain, France, and Canada, which met in private from 1954 to 1957. In 1959, the East-West pattern of representation was established with the setting up of the Ten-Nation Committee on Disarmament, with Bulgaria, Czechoslovakia, Poland, Romania, and the USSR on one side, and Britain, Canada, France, Italy, and the United States on the other. In 1961, the Ten-Nation body was enlarged into an Eighteen-Nation Disarmament Committee (ENDC), which was given responsibility to "undertake negotiations with a view to reaching . . . agreement on general and complete disarmament under effective international control." The East-West membership-parity arrangement was continued in the new forum, with eight additional non-aligned countries added to the membership. In 1969, the ENDC was converted into the Conference of the Committee on Disarmament (CCD) with an expanded Third World membership bringing the new forum to a total of twenty-six. In the same year, strategic arms limitation talks (SALT) between American and Soviet negotiators to limit nuclear weapons were begun and have continued over the years. In 1979, the Tenth Special Session of the General Assembly was devoted to breaking the disarmament logjam. At this session, the CCD was expanded into a new forty-member Committee on Disarmament (CD), and the United Nations Disarmament Commission, inactive since 1965, was reconstituted by action of the nonaligned countries who wanted an active forum that was universal in membership. In addition to these forums, the United Nations has encouraged disarmament and arms control talks in various regions of the world, and the Security Council and General Assembly have continued to explore the possibilities of a breakthrough. *See also* BARUCH PLAN, p. 205; GENERAL AND COMPLETE DISARMAMENT, p. 209.

Significance   During the history of the United Nations, various disarmament forums have met in protracted sessions on literally thousands of occasions. Many of their efforts have focused on the achievement of general and complete disarmament, an objective that continues to elude negotiators despite their professed interest in achieving it. Efforts concentrated on securing more limited arms control objectives have been fairly effective. These include the successful completion of the Antarctic Treaty, the "Hot-Line" Agreement, the Partial Nuclear Test Ban Treaty, the Non-Proliferation Treaty, the Seabed Treaty, the Outer Space Treaty, and the Atoms for Peace Agreement. For many years, progress toward nuclear disarmament was limited by the refusal of two nuclear weapons states—China and France—to participate in negotiations. The nonaligned states have kept disarmament issues alive in the United Nations when the East-West great powers have tried to avoid coming to grips with them. The nonaligned, in almost all disarmament forums, have been primarily responsible for applying pressures on the nuclear powers to continue negotiations in the hope that some of the major disarmament deadlocks can be broken. Increasingly, however, Third World nonaligned countries are caught up in an arms race with their neighbors, increasing the problems of trying to secure a completely disarmed world.

Washington Treaty for the Limitation of Naval Armaments (1922)   An agreement reached at the Washington Naval Conference of 1921–1922 by the leading sea powers to limit the size and construction of their capital ships and to establish an agreed power ratio in twenty years. The Washington Treaty provided: (1) that battleships would be limited thereafter to 35,000 tons with 16-inch guns, and aircraft carriers were to be limited to 27,000 tons; (2) that new construction of vessels in this class was forbidden for ten years; (3) that replacements of capital ships after 1931 should establish by 1942 a ratio of: Britain 5; the United States 5; Japan 3; France 1.67; and Italy 1.67; and (4) that signatories would limit their naval bases and fortifications in the Pacific area. Efforts to reach agreement at the conference to limit other naval craft, such as submarines, cruisers, and destroyers, failed to achieve a consensus. *See also* RATIO PROBLEM, p. 219.

Significance   The Washington Naval Treaty is a rare example of agreement by great powers to an arms-control measure. The Treaty was prompted as a means for avoiding a costly post-World War I naval arms race among the victorious powers. The United States, for example, was committed to a policy of equality in capital ship tonnage with Britain, but, instead of undertaking a highly competitive and expensive building program, the United States sought agreement for adjustments by the Treaty that would ultimately produce parity. The Treaty, however, did not provide for inspection and enforcement, and all signatories were soon engaged in nullifying the spirit, and in some cases, the letter of the agreement by competitive naval building programs in related classes of vessels. The Treaty was scrapped by the 1930s with the resurgence of German military power and the evolution of a new world power balance. The Washington Naval Treaty experience indicates that great-power agreement on arms control measures in a limited field is a tenuous matter that is unlikely to survive when a competitive arms race in other military fields and political conflict threaten the security of its signatories.

World Disarmament Conference   An international meeting of all states concerned with achieving world disarmament to draft a major treaty to accomplish that goal. The first World Disarmament Conference was called by the League of Nations and convened at Geneva from 1932 to 1934 with sixty-one states represented. The calling of a second World Disarmament Conference occurred in 1978 when 149 member states and many NGOs met in a UN Special Session on Disarmament to try to achieve a deadlock breakthrough in critical areas.

Significance   The World Disarmament Conference approach is aimed at breaking existing deadlocks in negotiations by encouraging most or all states to participate, by marshaling world opinion to pressure the great powers into reaching agreement, and by tackling all major problems of disarmament and security simultaneously. The first conference, however, failed to produce any tangible results when the great powers presented diverse proposals that could not be harmonized. The main conflict between French demands for arms superiority over Germany and German insistence on arms equality with France weakened the conference from the start. When Adolf Hitler came to power in 1933 and withdrew Germany from the conference, all hope for reaching agreement faded. The second conference, which was called in 1978 by the United Nations General Assembly, attacked the problems of how to bring the growing arms race in the less developed countries under control and to adopt a Program of Action on Disarmament that would result in major progress by the nuclear states. Specific agreements were sought on a Comprehensive Test Ban, on force reductions in Central Europe, on reducing nuclear weapons and their delivery systems, and on banning chemical and radiological weapons. Both France and the People's Republic of China participated in the 1978 Special Session on Disarmament (SSOD).

8. Diplomacy

Agrément   The formal indication by one country of the acceptability of a diplomat to be sent to it by another. The *agrément* by the intended receiving state is a response to inquiries initiated by the sending state prior to the formal nomination of the diplomat under consideration. The procedure followed by the two states is called *agréation*. See also PERSONA GRATA, p. 242.

Significance   The *agrément* is a useful diplomatic device to facilitate good relations between countries. Since any state can refuse to receive a particular individual, advance inquiries as to whether the person is *persona grata* (acceptable) avoids embarrassment to either state. In the practice of the United States, for example, the Secretary of State seeks the *agrément* from the head of the foreign government. When it is received, the Secretary notifies the President, who then submits the name of his nominee for that post to the Senate for confirmation.

Appeasement   Surrender of a vital interest for a minor *quid pro quo*, or for no reciprocal concession at all. Such an agreement could result from weakness or confusion over which of a nation's interests are vital and which secondary. Appeasement is associated historically with the Munich Conference of 1938, where British Prime Minister Neville Chamberlain and French Premier Edouard Daladier accepted Adolf Hitler's demand for the Sudetenland in Czechoslovakia in return for an empty promise of peace. *See also* NEGOTIATION, p. 240.

229

Significance   The charge of appeasement is often invoked as a term of opprobrium applied to any concession granted to a diplomatic opponent. The development of modern communication techniques, the glare of publicity, and the concept of "open diplomacy" have made genuine negotiation difficult. The general public often fails to appreciate that negotiation involves the search for agreement through compromises, and may view any concession as appeasement. Negotiation viewed mainly as a technique for achieving "diplomatic victory" may seriously limit the diplomat's room for maneuver and may impair the development of a stable world community based on the solution of problems through mutual agreement.

Attaché   A technical specialist attached to a diplomatic mission to perform representational and reporting activities related to his special field. Attachés specialize in political, military, economic, agricultural, informational, labor, civil aviation, petroleum, and cultural fields. Some are recruited and hired by a state's foreign office while others are attached to diplomatic missions from other governmental agencies. *See also* DIPLOMAT, p. 235.

Significance   The data and interpretations acquired through the technical expertise of diplomatic attachés constitute an essential part of the raw material for the formation of foreign policy. Although the use of technical specialists in the form of attachés departs from the diplomatic tradition of employing generalists capable of dealing with broad political and economic issues, technological developments require increasingly specialized knowledge. The expanded use of attachés from diverse fields often creates a problem of distinguishing between the collection of technical data and espionage. Many attachés have been accused of spying and have been expelled by the host country, followed typically by the sending state's retaliatory expulsion of an attaché of equal standing.

Comity   Courtesies extended by one state to another. Comity is based on the concept of the equality of states, and is normally reciprocal. The idea of comity emerged during the monarchical era, when the relations of states involved the relations of personal sovereigns and their agents.

Significance   Practices based on comity are indispensable in promoting and maintaining friendly relations between countries. Comity is involved in such matters as: (1) extradition; (2) execution by local courts of judgments handed down by foreign courts; (3) one state bringing a suit in the courts of another country; and (4) diplomatic immunity as an exemption from local jurisdiction. Customs and traditions based on comity have supplemented the development of international law in regularizing the relations of states.

Conciliation   A peaceful settlement procedure in which the representatives of a group of states establish the facts in a dispute and use them as the basis for recommending a solution. Conciliation, which is often linked with inquiry, can be viewed as group mediation. Commissions of conciliation may be established *ad hoc* and are also included in the peaceful settlement provisions of many bilateral as well as multilateral treaties. Such provisions are included, for example, in the Pact of Bogotá of the Organization of American States (1948) and the Brussels Treaty, signed the same year by Belgium, Britain, France, Luxembourg, and the Netherlands. *See also* PEACEFUL SETTLEMENT, p. 241.

Significance   As a peaceful settlement device, conciliation has several advantageous characteristics. It involves formalized, even quasi-judicial procedures, and its recommendations carry the weight of group opinion. Under the Charter of the United Nations, the Security Council can appoint a conciliation commission or can call on the parties to a dispute to do so. On many occasions, however, the Security Council itself acts as a conciliation body as it attempts to resolve international disputes in fulfillment of its responsibility for the maintenance of international peace and security.

Conference Diplomacy   Large-scale multilateral diplomatic negotiation conducted at international meetings. Historically associated with the establishment of peace after a major war, conference diplomacy dates from the beginning of the Western state system at the Congress of Westphalia (1642–1648), which ended the Thirty Years' War. Used with increased frequency in the nineteenth century, conference diplomacy was institutionalized and systematized on a global scale with the creation of the

League of Nations in 1919. As the successor to the League, the United Nations constitutes a world diplomatic conference in permanent session, theoretically capable of dealing with any international political, legal, social, economic, cultural, or technical problem. Regular conference diplomacy also occurs on a limited topical or geographical basis, as in the case of meetings held by the International Monetary Fund, the North Atlantic Treaty Organization, or the Organization of African Unity. Similarly, *ad hoc* conference diplomacy has been employed by the nonaligned countries since the Bandung Conference of 1955. The knowledge explosion and its attendant technological advances have produced a number and variety of both *ad hoc* and institutionalized conferences, many of them called by specialized agencies of the United Nations. The formal and quasi-parliamentary nature of conference diplomacy involves selection of a chairman, adoption of standard working procedures, the establishment of a committee structure to expedite the work, and a system for reaching decisions. *See also* DIPLOMACY, p. 234; NEGOTIATION, p. 240.

Significance   Conference diplomacy is a form of "open" as opposed to "secret" diplomacy, in the Wilsonian sense of "open covenants openly arrived at." The multilateral nature of conference diplomacy facilitates airing grievances, defining problems, exchanging views, and working cooperatively to find solutions to common problems. As a mechanism for the conduct of international relations, it does not, however, guarantee agreement. The records of both the League and the United Nations are replete with examples of "open disagreements openly arrived at." Nevertheless, the technique of conference diplomacy may encourage the solution of problems when national interests are not irreconcilable by providing a forum for discussion and bargaining.

Consul   Public agents sent abroad to promote the commercial and industrial interests of their state and its citizens and to offer protection to fellow nationals living or traveling in the second state. Consuls do not have diplomatic status but by law, treaty, and usage may enjoy privileges and immunities not accorded to other aliens. Consular duties include services related to shipping and navigation, citizenship, passports and visas, protecting nationals accused of crimes, and opening new markets.

Consulates are established in one or more of the major cities of other states, the choice depending on the volume of business. *See also* EXEQUATUR, p. 236.

Significance Consular activities are the same or similar to those performed by the local sovereign, and no country is legally obligated to permit foreign consuls to operate within its jurisdiction. The consul's role is usually defined bilaterally but may be augmented by use of the most-favored-nation clause in consular or commercial treaties which is aimed at avoiding discriminatory treatment. The flow of international trade, travel, commerce, and shipping is substantially dependent upon the exchange of consular missions.

Conversations A diplomatic exchange of views between governments. Conversations may be undertaken for information only, or may lead to more detailed negotiations. Conversations are a normal diplomatic activity carried on by an ambassador or members of his staff, but they may also take place through the use of specially appointed diplomatic agents.

Significance Conversations are exploratory and do not involve definite commitments. Continued contact, however, by probing and putting out feelers on topics of interest to either or both sides, enables a diplomat to determine when the time is right to launch a specific initiative. Conversations, sometimes called "quiet diplomacy," are carried on continuously at both bilateral and multilateral levels at United Nations headquarters as well as at national capitals and international conferences. All major international agreements are preceded by informal conversations that start the process of developing consensus.

Détente A diplomatic term indicating a situation of lessened strain or tension in the relations between two or more countries. A period of détente may be established by formal treaty or may evolve out of changes in national strategies and tactics over several years. *See also* RAPPROCHEMENT, p. 243.

Significance The concept of détente describes an improved environment that may in time contribute to the amelioration of fundamental points of conflict between states. The Locarno

Treaties of 1925, for example, ushered in an era of relative stability in Europe that helped strengthen the League security system through conclusion of such treaties as the General Act of 1928 and the Kellogg-Briand Pact of Paris of 1928. Beginning in the 1960s, a détente in Soviet-American relations based on the idea of peaceful coexistence started to evolve out of an awareness of the possibility of mutual destruction and because of a growing nationalism among alliance partners within each camp rather than from the conclusion of a major treaty. This détente, however, was jeopardized by the Soviet invasion of Afghanistan in December, 1979. It is a matter of decision makers' judgment as to whether a conciliatory or confrontational style of diplomacy will better serve the national interest in a particular situation.

Diplomacy   The practice of conducting relations between states through official representatives. Diplomacy may involve the entire foreign relations process, policy formulation as well as execution. In this broad sense a nation's diplomacy and foreign policy are the same. In the narrower, more traditional sense, however, diplomacy involves means and mechanisms whereas foreign policy implies ends or objectives. In this more restricted sense, diplomacy includes the operational techniques whereby a state pursues its interests beyond its jurisdiction. Increasing interdependence of states has steadily expanded the number of international meetings and the instances of multilateral conference and parliamentary diplomacy. States deal with one another on such a great number of occasions and topics, however, that the bulk of diplomatic activity remains bilateral and is conducted through the normal diplomatic channels of the foreign ministry and the resident diplomatic mission. Critical issues are sometimes negotiated at the highest level, involving heads of government in summit diplomacy. *See also* CONFERENCE DIPLOMACY, p. 231; NEGOTIATION, p. 240; PEACEFUL SETTLEMENT, p. 241; PARLIAMENTARY DIPLOMACY, p. 241; SUMMIT DIPLOMACY, p. 246.

Significance   The type of diplomacy employed—open or secret, bilateral or multilateral, ministerial or summit—varies with the states, the situation, the political environment, and the interests involved. Diplomacy of every type contributes to an orderly system of international relations and is the most common political technique for the peaceful settlement of international disputes. Diplomacy, though aided by technology, remains an art rather than a science and supplies the indispensable element of personal contact in the relations of states.

Diplomat   An accredited agent of a head of state who serves as the primary medium for the conduct of international relations. Diplomatic titles and order of rank were established by the Congresses of Vienna (1815) and Aix-la-Chapelle (1818) and include: (1) ambassador extraordinary and plenipotentiary, and papal legate and nuncio; (2) envoy extraordinary, minister plenipotentiary, and papal internuncio; (3) minister resident; and (4) *chargé d'affaires*, and *chargé d'affaires ad interim*. Though ambassador is the highest rank a diplomat can hold, both ambassadors and ministers may serve as chiefs of mission, are accredited to the head of the state to which they are sent, and are responsible for the conduct of their official families and staffs. The official quarters occupied by a mission are designated an embassy when headed by an ambassador and legation if headed by a minister. Virtually all diplomatic missions are now embassies headed by ambassadors. A *chargé d'affaires* accredited to the minister of foreign affairs is the diplomat placed in charge of a mission before an ambassador or minister has been appointed or from which the chief of mission has been withdrawn. The senior diplomatic officer temporarily responsible for a mission because of the absence, disability, or death of the ambassador or minister is designated *chargé d'affaires ad interim*. In the practice of the United States, the title diplomatic agent is used for a representative accredited to the foreign minister of a dependent state. Diplomats take precedence from the date of their arrival at a particular capital. The senior ambassador is the dean (or *doyen*) of the diplomatic corps at that capital and on occasion represents the corps with the foreign office. *See also* ATTACHÉ, p. 230; LETTER OF CREDENCE, p. 239; NEGOTIATION, p. 240; PERSONA GRATA, p. 242.

Significance   The diplomat provides the personal link between governments for dealing with a great number of subjects of mutual concern. He serves as eyes and ears for his country by observing and reporting economic, political, military, social, and cultural developments. He represents his country both formally and informally as the official agent of communication and, in his personal conduct, as an example of the people of his country. While endeavoring to remain *persona grata* (acceptable to the host government), the diplomat must stand ready at all times to protect and advance the interests of his own country and its citizens. The basic function of the diplomat, however, is one of continual negotiation in the search for accommodation and agreement.

Diplomatic Privileges and Immunities   Exemptions of a diplomat from national and local civil and criminal jurisdictions of the state to which he is accredited. Diplomatic privileges and immunities include freedom from arrest, trial, civil suit, subpoena, and legal penalty. His dwelling, offices, and archives may not be entered, searched, or appropriated, and his privileges and immunities also normally apply to members of his offical staff and household. Consular officers do not have diplomatic status but, because of their functions, may by law, treaty, and usage enjoy privileges not granted to other aliens. Privileges and immunities enjoyed by United Nations delegates and personnel are governed by an agreement concluded between the organization and the United States as the host country.

Significance   Diplomatic privileges and immunities are exceptions to the general rule of international law that each sovereign state is supreme within its own boundaries and has jurisdiction over all persons and things found within its territory. Without such exemptions, governments would be hampered in their foreign relations if their diplomatic agents could be prevented from enjoying full access to the host governments or were prevented from returning home upon the completion of their duties. In the interest of good relations between countries the granting of privileges and immunities also implies a responsibility for the diplomat to obey the laws and regulations of the host country. If the conduct of a diplomat is unacceptable, his own government may be requested to recall him or to waive his immunity so that he can be subjected to civil or criminal process. The receiving state may also declare a diplomat *persona non grata* and expel him from the country. Improper treatment of a diplomat may, however, lead to a serious rupture in relations between two countries, as in the Iranian-U.S. hostage crisis (1979–1981).

Exequatur   A formal act by which a receiving country recognizes the official status of a newly appointed consular officer and authorizes him to engage in those activities appropriate to his office. In those countries which issue no formal exequatur or similar document, the consul enters upon his duties when the receiving government publicly recognizes his status by announcement in the official gazette or some other formal act. *See also* CONSUL, p. 232.

Significance　　States, although not required by international law to receive foreign consuls, issue exequaturs, which authorize the consul to exercise his jurisdiction within the territory of the receiving state with all the privileges and immunities customarily granted to such officers. The revocation of the exequatur by the receiving government terminates the consular mission for the individual upon whom it was bestowed.

Fait Accompli　　An act by one or several states that creates a new situation vis à vis another state or group. Following a *fait accompli*, the other side no longer shares in the power of decision but finds its options reduced to doing nothing or to reacting to the altered situation. *See also* DIPLOMACY, p. 234.

Significance　　In diplomacy the *fait accompli*, as a one-sided act, is the antithesis of negotiation and is frequently the result of a diplomatic deadlock. At other times, it represents an initiative which brings advantages and can be carried through in the hope that other parties will accept it. One example is Adolf Hitler's remilitarization of the Rhineland (1936) in defiance of the Versailles Treaty. Another is the building of the Berlin Wall which presented the Western allies with a *fait accompli*. The determination to act in this fashion is always risky since the other side is also free to react unilaterally.

Good Offices　　A technique for the peaceful settlement of an international dispute whereby a third party acts as a go-between. The good offices of a third state involve diplomatic efforts to reestablish direct bilateral negotiations between the parties, aimed at bringing about a settlement by the disputants themselves. In the absence of treaty provisions to the contrary, the parties to a dispute are not obligated to accept an offer of good offices, nor is the third state entitled to enlarge a dispute through resentment at having its offer declined. *See also* PEACEFUL SETTLEMENT, p. 241.

Significance   In an international dispute when bilateral diplomacy has become deadlocked, good offices is a peaceful settlement procedure that involves a minimum degree of friendly intervention by a third party. The third state acts as a channel of communication only and does not involve itself in the subject matter of the dispute. United States offers of good offices were refused by the disputants at the outset of both World War I and World War II. Hostilities between the United States and Japan were brought to an end in 1945 through the good offices of Switzerland.

Hegemony   The extension by one state of preponderant influence or control over another state or region. A policy of hegemony may result in a client-state or satellite relationship and the creation of a sphere of influence. *See also* DEPENDENT TERRITORY: SPHERE OF INFLUENCE, p. 28.

Significance   Wide discrepancies in power may produce hegemonic relationships between otherwise sovereign and equal states. The preponderant power of one, even with the best intentions, represents at least a potential threat to the security of another. Hence, no sovereign state can be expected to endure such a relationship indefinitely without trying to change it. Several Eastern European post-World War II satellites, such as Romania and Poland, have increasingly asserted their independence from Soviet domination. In 1968, however, Czechoslovak efforts to liberalize their communist system were forcibly suppressed by a Warsaw Pact armed invasion directed by the Soviet Union. Similar attempts to impose or maintain hegemony occurred in 1979 when China attacked Vietnam and the Soviets invaded Afghanistan.

Inquiry   Formal impartial determination of the facts involved in an international dispute. Inquiry procedure involves the establishment of a fact-finding commission by the parties to the dispute or by an international body. After conducting its investigation, the commission of inquiry issues a report of its findings to the disputants or to the international agency. Unless inquiry is followed by additional peaceful settlement procedures like mediation or conciliation, the parties to the dispute are left free to determine the use to be made of the findings. *See also* PEACEFUL SETTLEMENT, p. 241.

Significance   The rationale for using inquiry is that dispute settlement may be facilitated if the facts in the case can be precisely and impartially determined. Disputants may also be willing to submit to inquiry since this procedure does not involve suggestions from third parties on how to settle the controversy as is the case in mediation and conciliation. Inquiry is provided for in many bilateral treaties and was first institutionalized in the Hague Convention for the Peaceful Settlement of International Disputes (1899). It was also among the peaceful settlement procedures included in the League of Nations Covenant and the Charter of the United Nations. The findings of an *ad hoc* commission of inquiry were instrumental in resolving the Dogger Bank incident (1904), which involved the accidental sinking of British fishing vessels by Russian warships. The League of Nations appointed a commission of inquiry (Lytton Commission) to determine the facts surrounding the Japanese invasion of Manchuria in 1931. Efforts at conciliation based on the facts obtained by the commission, however, failed and Japan withdrew from membership in the League.

Letter of Credence   The formal document by which the head of the sending state introduces his diplomatic representative to the head of the receiving state. The letter of credence attests to the diplomat's representative character, expresses confidence in his ability, outlines his mission and the extent of his powers, and requests that full faith and credit be given to activities undertaken by him on behalf of his government. The letter of credence is usually presented to the chief of state in a formal audience. *See also* DIPLOMAT, p. 235.

Significance   The letter of credence certifies the diplomat's credentials. Through this document the sending country indicates its desire for normal diplomatic relations between the two states. Acceptance of the letter of credence by the receiving chief of state indicates that the diplomat is duly accredited and may enter upon his official duties.

Machiavellian Diplomacy   The pursuit of national objectives by crafty, conspiratorial, and deceitful tactics motivated solely by narrow self-interest. The term derives from the name of Niccolo Machiavelli (1469–1529), the Florentine diplomat and scholar who in his celebrated book *The Prince*, described and advocated unscrupulous tactics to win and hold political power. *See also* DIPLOMACY, p. 234.

Significance   In the absence of absolute standards of diplomatic conduct, the distinction between cleverness and machiavellianism may depend on "whose ox is gored." Diplomacy takes its nature more from the times and the international environment than from the personality of the negotiator or the characteristics of his country. At this juncture in world history, the characteristics of the diplomat resemble those of the scientist, technician, and economist. Covert operations carried on by many states in promoting subversion, revolutions, and *coups d'etat*, however, are not dissimilar from the machiavellian intrigues of the sixteenth century.

Mediation   A peaceful settlement procedure whereby a third party aids the disputants in finding a solution by offering substantive suggestions. Mediation may be requested by the parties to a dispute or volunteered by a third state. In international practice, the disputants are not entitled, even during the course of hostilities, to view an offer of mediation as an unfriendly act, nor are they obligated to accept an unsolicited offer of mediation. *See also* PEACEFUL SETTLEMENT, p. 241.

Significance   Successful mediation involves reducing the tension between the disputants and reconciling their opposing claims. The former requires sensitivity and tact of a high order. The latter requires skill in finding a formula whereby the disputants can retreat from their extreme positions and reach a compromise solution to their problems. President Theodore Roosevelt's effort in arranging the Treaty of Portsmouth to end the Russo-Japanese War in 1905 is a classic illustration of mediation. The direct mediation efforts of Secretary of State Henry Kissinger in the Middle East were described as *shuttle diplomacy* because of his frequent flights between Israel and Egypt.

Negotiation   A diplomatic technique for the peaceful settlement of differences and the advancement of national interests. The objectives of negotiation are accomplished by compromises and accommodations reached through direct personal contact. *See also* APPEASEMENT, p. 229; DIPLOMACY, p. 234.

Significance   The essential nature of negotiation is frequently misunderstood by the general public, especially in times of great international tension, when it becomes difficult to offer any concession to an opponent. Yet, reaching agreement through negotiation implies a willingness on both sides to make mutually acceptable concessions (*quid pro quo*). Ultimatums, threatening speeches, boycotts and walkouts, and resort to force may be a part of diplomacy in the broadest sense, but they are not negotiation. Such actions, nevertheless, are often related to negotiation and may affect its ultimate success or failure. Secondary interests may be sacrificed to secure agreement in negotiations, but primary or vital interests are rarely negotiable. Skillful negotiation involves obtaining agreement at the least cost (while leaving the other side relatively satisfied) to good future relations.

Parliamentary Diplomacy   A form of conference diplomacy that emphasizes the search for agreement through the construction of majorities within continuing international institutions. The term, attributed to United States Secretary of State Dean Rusk, emphasizes similar political processes in the General Assembly and other international organs and in national parliaments. Parliamentary diplomacy calls attention to the maneuvering of the various regional and special-interest groups, which resembles legislative caucusing, pork barreling, and log rolling in national assemblies. *See also* DIPLOMACY, p. 234.

Significance   Parliamentary diplomacy serves to define issues, focus attention, and consolidate points of view, but it does not automatically lead to problem solving at the international level. The participants are the diplomatic representatives of sovereign states, who function as instructed delegates without the freedom exercised by national legislators in decision making. Numerical majorities do not automatically change national interests, but they may create an atmosphere conducive to negotiation. Steamroller majorities as a pressure tactic, however, may solidify disagreement and produce discord instead of harmony.

Peaceful Settlement   The resolution of international disputes without resort to force. Pacific settlement involves the procedural techniques by which conflicts over substantive rights and duties of states can be resolved. The two categories of techniques for the peaceful settlement of international disputes are: (1) legal, which involve the application of international law to the facts of the dispute; and (2) political, which involve diplomatic procedures. Arbitration and adjudication comprise the legal methods of pacific settlement, and the political techniques include diplomatic negotiation, good offices, mediation, inquiry, and conciliation. *See also* ADJUDICATION, p. 249; ARBITRATION, p. 252; CONCILIATION, p. 231; DIPLOMACY, p. 234; GOOD OFFICES, p. 237; INQUIRY, p. 238; INTERNATIONAL LAW, p. 266; MEDIATION, p. 240; NEGOTIATION, p. 240.

Significance   The increasing destructiveness of war, together with its social and economic costs, have been responsible for a profusion of efforts to establish and render obligatory a number of generally acceptable alternatives for the resolution of international disputes. The Hague Peace Conferences of 1899 and 1907 produced the first large-scale multilateral efforts to establish obligatory peaceful settlement procedures. These efforts and procedures have been supplemented in such treaties as the Covenant of the League of Nations, the Statute of the Permanent Court of International Justice, the General Act of Geneva (1928), the Kellogg-Briand Pact (Treaty for the Renunciation of War, 1928), and the Charter of the United Nations. Developments in the field of pacific settlement have been augmented by efforts in related fields such as disarmament, international organizational activity, economic development, and educational and cultural changes. The alternative to pacific settlement is limited war or the increasing possibility of thermonuclear holocaust.

Persona Grata   An expression used to indicate that a particular individual would be, or continues to be, acceptable as an official representative of a foreign state. The concept of *persona grata* implies that a state may also declare a diplomatic representative of another state to be unacceptable (*persona non grata*). *See also* AGRÉMENT, p. 229; DIPLOMATIC PRIVILEGES AND IMMUNITIES, p. 236.

Significance   The discretionary authority of a government to determine if a diplomat is *persona grata* occurs first at the appointment stage through the process of *agréation*, which enables the receiving country to express its willingness or unwillingness to receive him. After a diplomat has been received, he may be declared *persona non grata* if he violates local law, international law, or the canons of proper diplomatic behavior. The receiving state may then request the sending state to recall its diplomat, or, more drastically, may hand him his passport and expel him from the country.

Plebiscite   A vote to determine the will of the entire population of an area on a matter of great public interest. Plebiscites have frequently been used in international relations in connection with territorial cessions. Although a specific treaty of cession may stipulate that a plebiscite must be held, there is no customary rule of international law that requires the approval of the inhabitants before sovereignty over a territory can be legally transferred. *See also* JURISDICTION: CESSION, p. 271; NATIONAL SELF-DETERMINATION, p. 35; PEACEFUL SETTLEMENT, p. 241.

Significance   The practice of holding a plebiscite in connection with the cession of territory, though not generally required in international law, has been followed with increasing frequency since the second half of the nineteenth century. The rationale of the plebiscite in international relations can be traced to the democratic concept of popular sovereignty and the doctrine of the right of national self-determination. Some plebiscites were provided for in the peace treaties of 1919, but the device was not generally applied in the territorial transfers resulting from World War II. Although India and Pakistan agreed in 1949 to resolve the Kashmir issue by plebiscite, the United Nations has been unsuccessful in arranging the conditions for its administration. Other recent examples of plebiscites include those conducted by the United Nations in several former African trust territories when they emerged as independent nations. The United Nations also secured the agreement of Indonesia to the holding of a plebiscite to determine whether the indigenous population of former Dutch New Guinea (West Irian) wished to remain under Indonesian rule. A plebiscite has also been suggested as a way of resolving the long-standing dispute between Britain and Spain on sovereignty over Gibraltar.

Rapprochement   A reconciliation of interests of rival states after a period of estrangement. *Rapprochement*, in diplomatic parlance, implies a policy of attempting to reestablish normal relations. *See also* DÉTENTE, p. 233.

244 / **Recognition *De Facto***

Significance   *Rapprochement* is a common diplomatic term of French origin that describes one of the critical changes that can take place in the relations of states. Following World War II, a *rapprochement* in Franco-German relations has virtually ended more than a century of bitter rivalry.

Recognition *De Facto*   An indefinite and provisional recognition by the government of one state that a particular regime in fact exercises authoritative control over the territory of a second state.

Significance   *De facto* recognition is extended pending evidence of the stability of the new regime, or for a practical consideration such as the maintenance of trade. The legality of the assumption of authority by the regime so recognized is immaterial, and such recognition is not necessarily a precondition for the establishment of *de jure* or formal diplomatic relations.

Recognition *De Jure*   Complete, unqualified recognition of one government by another. Once *de jure* recognition has been granted and trouble arises with the government so recognized, its representative character is not denied nor is recognition withdrawn. Instead, diplomatic relations with the offending government are broken.

Significance   *De jure* recognition always involves the establishment of normal diplomatic relations. Such recognition is termed *express* when it is accomplished by a formal act such as an exchange of notes expressing both desire and readiness to engage in regular diplomatic relations. *De jure* recognition is termed *tacit* when accomplished by an act that implies intention to recognize, such as a consular convention.

Recognition of Governments   An official act, such as an exchange of ambassadors, that acknowledges the existence of a government and indicates readiness to engage in formal relations with it. Recognition of a new state cannot be accomplished without recognizing the government in power. For this reason, confusion often arises concerning recognition of states and recognition of governments. Recognition of a state, once accomplished, continues for the life of the state even when a particular government of that state is not recognized. After the Russian Revolution of 1917, for instance, the United States continued to recognize the Russian state even though it did not recognize the Soviet government until 1933. Recognition of a government is not perpetual and may be granted or withheld with each change of regime. A break in diplomatic relations, however, is not a withdrawal of recognition.

Significance   International lawyers are divided on whether or not recognition of governments is a matter of legal right and duty. The practice of states indicates, however, that recognition is regarded as essentially a unilateral political decision. Although historically the United States granted recognition to new governments that demonstrated effective control, during the Wilson administration the United States made "constitutionality" or "legitimacy" of a new regime the prerequisite for American recognition. In a statement of doctrine associated with his name, Mexican Foreign Minister Don Genaro Estrada in 1930 held that the granting or withholding of recognition for political reasons constituted an improper and insulting intervention in the domestic affairs of another sovereign state since it constituted an external judgment of the legal qualifications of a foreign regime. Opponents of the Estrada Doctrine point out that the purpose of recognition is not the passing of judgment but merely the unavoidable necessity of establishing the essential representative character of a new regime. In 1932, Secretary of State Henry Stimson stated, in reaction to the Japanese conquest of Manchuria, that the United States would not recognize the validity of political changes brought about in violation of international obligations or treaty rights (Stimson Doctrine). The Cold War encouraged the granting and withholding of recognition as a discretionary political technique governed by decision makers' interpretations of the state's national interest, as in the refusal of the United States to recognize the government of the People's Republic of China from 1949 to 1979.

Recognition of States   The process by which a political entity becomes an international person in international law and is accepted by existing states as a new member of the community. Once recognition of statehood has occurred, this status continues regardless of internal organization or changes in government so long as the sovereign character of the state continues.

Significance Recognition is a complex and controversial topic of international law because it permits discretionary application of the principles involved. Failure to recognize either a new state or government tends to isolate it and diminish its prestige by restricting its ability to engage in normal diplomatic and legal relations. One of the moot points of international law is whether recognition is declarative or constitutive. If declarative, the new state or regime has rights and obligations prior to recognition. Recognition would therefore indicate a wish to establish normal diplomatic relations and a desire to establish access to national and international courts where rights and duties in the legal relations of the two parties can be defined and controversies resolved. This view appears to have more authoritative support than the constitutive theory, which holds that, as far as the international community is concerned, recognition creates the state or regime. The latter theory raises questions, such as the number of recognitions required and whether an unrecognized state or regime is free to violate international law. Under the constitutive theory, for example, by ratifying the Treaty of Versailles the signatories were recognizing and thus creating the states of Czechoslovakia and Poland in 1919. Each state is free to apply the declarative or constitutive theory, with the decision in fact usually based on political expedience.

Summit Diplomacy Personal diplomacy by heads of state or government as contrasted with diplomacy at the ambassadorial or ministerial level. Summit diplomacy emerged during the era of absolute monarchy and has continued sporadically. Summit diplomacy has experienced a new vogue associated with the perplexing problems of U.S.-Soviet relations, and "summit conferences" between United States and other leaders have been held on relations with the People's Republic of China and Middle East problems. *See also* DIPLOMACY, p. 234.

Significance Summit diplomacy as a mechanism for the conduct of international relations is highly dramatic but has inherently no greater potential for success than other kinds of diplomacy. Diplomacy at the summit may establish broad areas of agreement, leaving details to be worked out at lower levels, or it may break deadlocks at lower levels. The technique may also be employed to improve the climate of relations between states. In some cases, however, it may be too expeditious, for when heads of state negotiate there is no fall-back authority to which matters may be referred to gain time for reflection. National leaders, moreover, are only rarely experienced diplomats. The drama of negotiations between heads of state or government may also make failure at the summit more spectacular, frustrating, and dangerous. Summit diplomacy is least controversial when it formalizes agreements worked out in advance at lower levels.

Treaty   A formal agreement or contractual obligation among sovereign states which establishes, defines, or modifies their mutual rights and obligations. Treaties are international law and, in the United States, are also domestic law by virtue of the "supreme law of the land" clause (Article VI) of the U.S. Constitution. A treaty and other types of international agreements—act, *aide mémoire*, charter, covenant, convention, *entente*, *modus vivendi*, protocol—may involve such topics as peace, territorial cession, alliance, friendship, commerce, or other matters of international concern. *See also* NEGOTIATION, p. 240; PACTA SUNT SERVANDA, p. 281; REBUS SIC STANTIBUS, p. 284.

Significance   The juridical effect, or binding nature (*pacta sunt servanda*), of a treaty is not dependent upon the name of the instrument. A treaty may be multilateral or bilateral, and of specific or indefinite duration. Treaty making as a process involves negotiation, signature, ratification, exchange of ratifications, publication and proclamation, and execution. Ratification of treaties, an executive act by which the state finally accepts the terms of the agreement, is accomplished for each signatory in accordance with its constitutional processes. International contractual obligations may be terminated after specified conditions have been met, at the end of a stated time period, by mutual consent, by unilateral denunciation as during a state of war between the parties, or, theoretically, when conditions essential to the agreement have changed (*rebus sic stantibus*). Since World War II, the relations of states have been regulated with increasing frequency by multilateral treaties on a variety of topics. Examples include the United Nations Charter, the North Atlantic Treaty, the Warsaw Pact, the Rome Treaties on European integration, the Nuclear Test Ban Treaty, and the Outer Space Treaty.

Treaty Ratification   The act by which a state formally confirms and approves the terms of a treaty. Normally an executive act, ratification is accomplished for each signatory of a treaty in accordance with its constitutional processes. This usually requires the consent of one or more houses of the national legislature. In some countries, legislative participation is *pro forma*, but in others—such as the United States—it is the critical stage in the treaty process. *See also* TREATY POWER, p. 401.

Significance   Internationally, treaties come into force when instruments of ratification have been exchanged, in the case of a bilateral treaty, or deposited with a particular government designated in the treaty, in the case of multilateral treaties. In the latter case it may be stipulated that the treaty will enter into force when ratifications from specific states have been deposited or when a specific number of ratifications have been received, as illustrated in Article 110 of the Charter of the United Nations and Article 11 of the North Atlantic Treaty.

Ultimatum   A formal, final communication from one government to another, requiring the receiving government to comply in some stated fashion with the wishes of the sender or be prepared to take the consequences, ultimately war. An ultimatum indicates that the diplomatic process is but one step short of a breakdown and that one sovereign state is willing to risk the use of force if necessary to impose its will upon another. *See also* NEGOTIATION, p. 240.

Significance   Whether a bluff or in earnest, an ultimatum signifies a serious crisis in international relations. It indicates that one of the parties has decided to abandon negotiation and will seek its objectives by other means. Thus in 1914 Germany sent an ultimatum to Belgium to permit the passage of German troops through Belgium against France, or be treated as an enemy of Germany. Both the League of Nations and the United Nations were designed in part to provide meeting places and techniques whereby settlements might be sought beyond the limits inherent in bilateral diplomacy, free from delivery of ultimatums.

9. *International Law*

Adjudication   A legal technique for settling international disputes by submitting them to determination by an established court. Adjudication differs from arbitration in that the former involves an institutionalized process carried on by a permanent court whereas the latter is an *ad hoc* procedure. The first international court of general competence was the Permanent Court of International Justice (PCIJ), which functioned as part of the League of Nations system from 1920 until the demise of the League in 1946. It was succeeded by the present International Court of Justice (ICJ), one of the principal organs of the United Nations. *See also* INTERNATIONAL COURT OF JUSTICE, p. 265.

Significance   Adjudication has been used sparingly to resolve disputes and has been most effective in settling issues of less than vital importance. Advocates of adjudication assert as an advantage of the technique that there is no international question to which a court could not give a final answer and hence no international dispute need remain unresolved. States, however, are hesitant to accept adjudication because in submitting a case to an international court they must agree in advance to be bound by a decision that might be detrimental to their vital interests. Since the doctrine of sovereignty means that a state cannot be forced into court against its will, defendant states are usually unwilling to submit to adjudication. Adjudication may, however, have the advantage of avoiding the problem of national prestige, since a state that abides by an adverse judgment is thereby regarded as supporting the rule of law rather than submitting to the pressure of another state. Adjudication as a settlement tool has been weakened in the contemporary era by revolutionary developments in technology, by the East-West conflict, and by the emergence of many new states that reject many traditional Western concepts of international law.

Advisory Opinion   A legal opinion rendered by a court in response to a question submitted by an authorized body. The advisory opinion procedure differs from contentious proceedings in that there are no parties before the court as complainant and defendant. *See also* INTERNATIONAL COURT OF JUSTICE, p. 265.

Significance   An advisory opinion informs and clarifies but does not bind the requesting body unless it formally approves the opinion of the court. The United Nations Charter (Article 96) authorizes the General Assembly or the Security Council to request an advisory opinion from the International Court of Justice on any legal question. The General Assembly can also authorize other organs and specialized agencies of the United Nations to request advisory opinions on legal questions arising within the scope of their activities. Under the Headquarters Agreement of 1947, the advisory opinion procedure may also be used in connection with disputes arising between the United States and the United Nations. Although the advisory opinion technique is readily available, it has been used infrequently since 1946.

Aggression   An improper intervention or attack by one country against another. Aggression as a legal phenomenon implies: (1) that there is a common standard of conduct or a system of norms within which international relationships are to be conducted; and (2) that action in violation of the standard warrants condemnation and punishment by the community of states. The literature of international law is replete with efforts to define "aggression" and to distinguish between it and legitimate acts of individual or collective self-defense. Ideological cleavages of the Cold War have aggravated the problem of defining "an act of aggression." With no common international standard, communist parties and countries may laud as justifiable "wars of national liberation" that other countries regard as acts of aggression. A further definitional complication is created by the concept of indirect aggression, which may involve subversion, propaganda, economic penetration, and military aid to insurgents. *See also* INTERNATIONAL LAW COMMISSION, p. 267; WAR CRIMES TRIALS, p. 288.

Significance   The efforts of the state system to develop general agreement on a comprehensive definition of "aggression" that could be applicable to specific actions of states have been unsuccessful but are continuing. In practice, international bodies have determined after the fact that aggression has taken place. The International Military Tribunals at Nuremberg and Tokyo, for example, found some Axis leaders to have been guilty of the crime of waging aggressive war. The Charter of the United Nations calls for the suppression of acts of aggression by members of the international community. The fact of aggression is determined, however, by the votes of a majority of states in the General Assembly or Security Council, as when the latter declared North Korea to be an aggressor in 1950. The International Law Commission has tried for a number of years to establish standard categories of aggression leading to a comprehensive definition. Thus far, however, it has not been able to recommend the draft of a lawmaking treaty to the General Assembly. Agreement is unlikely so long as a number of states challenge the justice of the international status quo.

Alien   A person who is not a citizen or national of the state wherein he or she is located. As a general principle of international law, states possess internal sovereignty and are free to admit or exclude aliens as they choose. States extend to aliens most of the same civil, but not political, rights enjoyed by citizens. These usually include the rights of freedom of speech and religious worship, the right to follow certain professions and licensed occupations, the right of contract and of holding, inheriting, and transmitting real property. International law recognizes distinctions between resident aliens who have established a domicile and transient aliens. Resident aliens may be expected to perform many of the same duties as citizens, such as paying taxes and serving in the armed forces. In the public interest they may be subjected to specific restrictions, such as the obligation to inform the government periodically as to their location and occupation. Aliens may also be expelled, provided the expulsion does not discriminate against the citizens of any particular foreign country.

Significance International law concerning the rights and duties of aliens and the rights and duties of states is undergoing a process of transition because of increased travel and communication. Sharp controversy revolves around discrimination against citizens of specified countries, usually in the form of exclusive immigration policies. As a result of wars and revolutions, large numbers of citizens have acquired alien status as refugees. Other problems relating to aliens involve stateless persons who can claim the protection of no country, and large ethnic groups who are often treated as cultural aliens in their country of residence.

Annexation Acquisition of legal title to territory by announcement of the acquiring state that it has extended its sovereignty over and will exercise jurisdiction in the area.

Significance The extension of sovereignty by annexation may be based on such claims as discovery, occupation, or continuous possession. In 1938 Germany simply announced the annexation of Austria based on an act of the Austrian government converting that country into a state (*Land*) of the German Reich. Annexation may be uncontested by third parties, as in the case of the annexation of Jan Mayen Island by Norway in 1920. The announcement of annexation may also arouse considerable protest and the assertion of counterclaims, as in the case of the legal status of Eastern Greenland in 1933. In this case the rival claims of Denmark and Norway were submitted to the determination of the Permanent Court of International Justice, which held in favor of Denmark.

Arbitration An ancient procedure for the peaceful settlement of disputes. Arbitration has several essential features, which include: (1) a *compromis*, or agreement by the parties as to the issues to be resolved and the details of the procedure to be followed; (2) judges chosen by the parties; (3) a decision based on respect for international law; and (4) prior agreement that the decision will be binding. *See also* ADJUDICATION, p. 249; COMPROMIS, p. 255.

Significance Arbitration, like adjudication, is a legal technique for dispute settlement and is to be distinguished from political methods involving a form of diplomatic negotiation, such as good offices, mediation, inquiry, and conciliation. Arbitration may be arranged *ad hoc*, or may be compulsory if a treaty to that effect exists between the parties. History records many bilateral arbitration treaties on a variety of subjects. The Hague Conference of 1899 institutionalized the procedure by creating the Permanent Court of Arbitration at The Hague. Arbitration is also listed as a proper method of settling disputes between countries by the Covenant of the League of Nations (Article 13) and by the Charter of the United Nations (Article 33). In 1958 the International Law Commission submitted to the General Assembly its suggested Model Rules on Arbitral Procedure.

Award   A judgment in the form of an indemnity or compensation of a monetary nature handed down against a state by an international arbitral tribunal, court, or claims commission. An award can be made in favor of an individual or his government. If the award is made to a government, its distibution becomes a matter of domestic jurisdiction. *See also* ARBITRATION, p. 252; COMPROMIS, p. 255.

Significance   The granting of an award is an amicable mode of redressing grievances between states that have decided to employ legal techniques for the peaceful settlement of their dispute. The *compromis*, or preliminary arbitral agreement, establishes the general principles and specific rules by which a tribunal is guided in making an award. Under the principle of *res judicata* (the case having been decided), awards are final and binding unless reopened by the consent of the parties in a new agreement, or unless the award is voided by the tribunal's having exceeded its authority as laid down in the *compromis*.

Calvo Clause   A clause sometimes inserted by Latin American governments in public contracts with aliens. The Calvo clause requires that, in case of differences arising under the contract, the alien party will rely solely on local remedies and will not appeal to his government for diplomatic interposition on his behalf. International arbitral tribunals and mixed claims commissions have split in their decisions as to whether, under international law, the inclusion of the clause in such a contract can prevent the foreign government from entering the dispute. The clause is named after Carlos Calvo, the Argentine jurist who wrote extensively on the subject.

Significance   Supporters of the Calvo clause assert that aliens have no claim to better treatment than that accorded to nationals, and that foreign interference in such matters does violence to the principle of the sovereign equality of states. Opponents hold that, although an individual may sign such a contract, his act cannot prevent his government from insisting that other governments remain responsible for dealing with him according to the standards established by international law.

Citizen   A legal status whereby an individual has both the privileges and responsibilities of full membership in the state. The status of citizen can be acquired: (1) at birth, by *jus soli*, or citizenship by place of birth; (2) by *jus sanguinis*, or citizenship at birth determined by the allegiance of the parents; (3) by naturalization, the formal transference of allegiance. *See also* JUS SANGUINIS, p. 277; JUS SOLI, p. 277; NATURALIZATION, p. 280.

Significance   The status of citizen insures the individual the protection that his country's laws and power afford. The citizen performs certain duties, such as paying taxes and serving in the armed forces, and enjoys certain privileges, such as voting and, when abroad, calling on the services of his country's diplomatic and consular missions. The status of citizen may be lost for reasons that vary among countries. Typical reasons for loss of citizenship include extended residence abroad, serving a foreign state without permission, taking a foreign oath of allegiance, or denaturalization. An individual may have dual citizenship, depending on the laws of the countries involved, or, more seriously, may be stateless and thus unable to claim the protection of any country as a matter of right.

Codification of International Law   The systematic organization and statement of the rules of international law. Codification is necessary for the progressive development of international law because of the length of time over which rules of state conduct have been accumulating, because of the changing circumstances in which the rules are applied, and because of the differing interests and interpretations of the rules by various states. Codification has been attempted: (1) by setting forth the rules actually in force; (2) by setting forth the rules as amended to conform to present conditions and standards of justice; (3) by re-creating the entire system in accord with an ideal standard of law. *See also* INTERNATIONAL LAW, p. 266.

Significance   Major efforts at codifying international law have been undertaken at international conferences on a specialized topical basis. Important contributions were made on military and related subjects, for example, by the Hague Conferences of 1899 and 1907, and in the Geneva Convention of 1929, on such topics as occupation of territory and prisoners of war. The League of Nations Codification Conference in 1930 produced wide agreement on the subject of nationality. Other successful efforts included the Geneva Conferences on the Law of the Sea, 1958, 1960, and the Vienna Conferences on Diplomatic Privileges and Immunities in 1961 and on Consular Relations in 1963. Article 13 of the Charter of the United Nations charges the General Assembly with promoting the codification of international law, and in 1947 the Assembly created the International Law Commission to carry on studies in this field.

Compromis   A preliminary agreement by the parties to a dispute which establishes the terms under which the dispute will be arbitrated. The *compromis* specifies the jurisdictional limits of the arbitral tribunal by: (1) defining the subject of the dispute; (2) setting forth the principles that are to guide the tribunal; and (3) establishing the rules of procedure to be followed in deciding the case. Specific questions relating to its jurisdiction are decided by the tribunal under the terms of the *compromis*. An award or decision by the arbitrators may, however, be null and void if the tribunal exceeds its authority as laid down by the parties in the *compromis*. *See also* ARBITRATION, p. 252.

Significance   The decision to arbitrate implies the presence of an international dispute and the necessity of negotiating a *compromis*. By its nature, arbitration cannot take place unless a *compromis* is first established, regardless of whether the arbitration is agreed to *ad hoc* or whether it is provided for in a prior bilateral or multilateral treaty. With a dispute already in existence and the level of tension rising, the disputants may find it difficult to arrive at the required preliminary agreement. In such a case, arbitration may be facilitated by a preexisting arbitration treaty under which the fundamental procedures detailed in a *compromis* have already been settled.

Compulsory Jurisdiction The power of an international court to hear and decide certain classes of cases without the necessity of both parties agreeing in advance to accept the jurisdiction of the court in each case. The Statute of the International Court of Justice provides for compulsory jurisdiction in its "Optional Clause" (Article 36), which specifies that "The states parties to the present Statute may at any time declare that they recognize as compulsory *ipso facto* and without special agreement, in relation to any other state accepting the same obligation, the jurisdiction of the Court in all legal disputes concerning: (1) the interpretation of a treaty; (2) any question of international law; (3) the existence of any fact which, if established, would constitute a breach of an international obligation; (4) the nature or extent of the reparation to be made for the breach of an international obligation." *See also* CONNALLY AMENDMENT, p. 257; INTERNATIONAL COURT OF JUSTICE, p. 265; JURISDICTION, p. 269.

Significance Compulsory jurisdiction depends upon prior agreement and is designed to facilitate peaceful international relations by providing for advance acceptance of legal techniques for dispute settlement. The compulsory jurisdiction of the Court has been weakened, however, by reservations which states have attached to their acceptance of the "Optional Clause." Nevertheless, compulsory jurisdiction is also provided for in more than six hundred international treaties that stipulate that issues arising over their interpretation and application shall be decided by the Court. No national legal system could function effectively if its courts lacked compulsory jurisdiction, but in the international arena the concept of compulsory settlement of legal disputes before an international court runs head on into conflict with the doctrine of sovereignty. Statesmen and scholars continue to advocate voluntary acceptance of compulsory jurisdiction by all nations as the means for resolving this conflict and building a stable world legal order.

Conflict of Laws (Private International Law) Legal situations in which the laws of more than one country may be applied. Conflict-of-laws situations typically involve such subjects as torts, contracts, inheritance, acquisition and transmittal of property, nationality, domicile, and marriage and divorce. The conflict-of-laws rules of the state determine whether or not, and to what extent, effect will be given to the acts of another state.

Significance A major problem of conflict of laws involves the relationship between private international law and public international law. Some states, particularly in Continental Europe, hold conflict-of-laws rules to be a branch of international law and hence binding on all states. The Anglo-American countries treat such rules as a branch of national law. Practice indicates that, in the absence of specific treaties, the Continental view has not been fully accepted by international tribunals. Thus, international law does not generally require one state to give effect to the conflict-of-laws rules of another. Much work is being done, however, to codify rules of private international law and to bring about uniformity in national legislation on these rules.

Connally Amendment The reservation attached by the United States to its acceptance in 1946 of compulsory jurisdiction under the Optional Clause of Article 36 of the Statute of the International Court of Justice. The Connally Amendment denies the Court compulsory jurisdiction in "disputes with regard to matters which are essentially within the domestic jurisdiction of the United States of America as determined by the United States of America." The practical effect of the Amendment is to destroy the intended compulsory feature of the Court's jurisdiction since the United States is left free to determine what is a domestic matter and therefore beyond the purview of the Court. *See also* COMPULSORY JURISDICTION, p. 256; INTERNATIONAL COURT OF JUSTICE, p. 265; JURISDICTION, p. 269.

Significance The role of the International Court of Justice has been substantially reduced by the Connally Amendment's restriction of the jurisdiction of the Court in its handling of contentious cases. Many states that have accepted the optional clause followed the American example by attaching similar reservations. The impact of the Connally and other reservations is multiplied by their reciprocal application in cases involving other states that have not attached such reservations to their acceptance of the Optional Clause. The result is that in most legal disputes the parties continue to determine whether the Court has jurisdiction.

Customary Law   Rules of international conduct based on practices and usages accepted by states to be obligatory. As customary law is applied over the years, its precepts tend to become clarified and its uncertainties reduced. Often important rules of customary law are transmuted into positive law by their inclusion in treaties. Article 38 of the Statute of the International Court of Justice specifies that "International Custom, as evidence of a general practice accepted as law" is one of the sources of international law to be applied by the Court. *See also* INTERNATIONAL LAW, p. 266; POSITIVISM, p. 284.

Significance   Specific rules of customary law are difficult to ascertain with precision. By its nature, evidence of customary rules must be found in observed practices rather than in specific international enactments and agreements. Evidence of usage believed to be binding as law may be sought in instructions to diplomatic and military officers, in national legislation, and in the opinions of national and international courts. The difficulty of demonstrating the establishment of a new custom in international law, however, has led to increasing use of the law-making treaty. In addition, the emergence of many new states that played no part in the development of customary law has weakened its general applicability.

Domestic Jurisdiction   Those spheres of national life which are regulated exclusively by national law and within which the validity of international law is denied. Domestic jurisdiction is thus a concomitant of national sovereignty. Article 2 of the Charter of the United Nations provides that "Nothing contained in the present Charter shall authorize the United Nations to intervene in matters which are essentially within the domestic jurisdiction of any state or shall require the Members to submit such matters to settlement under the present Charter. . . ." *See also* CONNALLY AMENDMENT, p. 257; JURISDICTION, p. 269; UNITED NATIONS: DOMESTIC JURISDICTION CLAUSE, p. 341.

Significance   The concept of domestic jurisdiction implies that international law is not universal but is limited in its application to those subjects that have been accepted by the sovereign states which comprise the international community. In establishing boundaries between national and international jurisdiction, problems of interpretation inescapably arise. Some of the most difficult to resolve involve questions of human rights and self-determination. In the case of the United States acceptance of compulsory jurisdiction of the International Court, the practical question of who is to determine what constitutes domestic jurisdiction was resolved by the Connally Amendment in favor of national determination.

Drago Doctrine   A position opposing the use of force by states in the recovery of contract debts. The Drago Doctrine was enunciated in 1902 by the Foreign Minister of Argentina. The doctrine held that a state's defaulting on its public debt owed to aliens did not give another state the right to intervene forcibly on their behalf to collect that debt, or the right to occupy the territory of the debtor state. *See also* CALVO CLAUSE, p. 253; INTERVENTION, p. 175; MONROE DOCTRINE, p. 393.

Significance   The Drago Doctrine was occasioned by the 1902 naval blockade of Venezuela established by Britain, Germany, and Italy when Venezuela defaulted on its public debt and other claims held by nationals of those countries. The Drago Doctrine was defended by the United States as supportive of the principle of European nonintervention in the hemisphere proclaimed in the Monroe Doctrine. In 1907, the United States by treaty assumed control of the customs houses of the Dominican Republic to insure the payment of foreign debts and thus forestall European intervention. Current practice indicates that forcible intervention for such purposes by any state is legally inadmissible. The debtor state may, however, be subject to a charge of denial of justice under the standards of international law if it fails to provide local judicial and administrative remedies to the claimants. In such an event a foreign government could, however, intervene diplomatically on behalf of its citizens.

Dual Nationality   Citizenships simultaneously held in more than one country. Dual nationality can occur when an individual acquires citizenship in one country through his parents (*jus sanguinis*) and citizenship in a second country in which he is born (*jus soli*). Dual citizenship also results where a person is a citizen by birth in one country and by naturalization in another when the former does not recognize the right of the individual to renounce his allegiance.

Significance   Dual nationality becomes a problem for a person who moves between two states, each of which claims his allegiance on different grounds. He is thus subject to two sets of rights and duties, some of which may conflict. Foreign offices have been plagued by cases involving the individual's duty to perform military service in either or both countries. In the absence of specific agreements on the subject, claims are frequently resolved in favor of the state possessing *de facto* jurisdiction over the individual. A person with dual nationality is well advised to investigate his status thoroughly before moving between different jurisdictions claiming his allegiance.

Ex Aequo Et Bono   A basis for a decision by an international court on the grounds of justice and fairness. The *ex aequo et bono* concept, set forth in Article 38 of the Statute of the International Court of Justice, can be applied by the Court as the basis for arriving at a decision only if the parties so agree. It is a variation from the more usual bases for reaching decisions in the International Court by applying the rules of positive and customary international law. *See also* INTERNATIONAL COURT OF JUSTICE, p. 265.

Significance   A decision *ex aequo et bono* looks beyond specific law for justice and, in this sense, is somewhat analogous to the concept of equity found in Anglo-Saxon jurisprudence. The International Court of Justice has never been called upon to decide a case *ex aequo et bono*. The concept has been used, however, by international arbitral tribunals in resolving such disputes as the Guatemala-Honduras boundary issue in 1933, and in the settlement of the Gran Chaco conflict between Bolivia and Paraguay in 1938.

Expatriation   The act whereby an individual is released from citizenship by his government through some specific action on his part or at his own request. Actions which constitute grounds for expatriation in most countries include taking an oath of allegiance to another state, serving in foreign military services without permission, voting in foreign elections, and public renunciation of citizenship. The key to expatriation lies in a voluntary action undertaken by the individual rather than by a government. *See also* CITIZEN, p. 254; NATIONALITY, p. 279.

Significance   Persons who expatriate themselves are often unaware that they are doing so and may not understand the consequences of their actions. Unless the expatriate is assured of naturalization elsewhere, he may become a stateless person unable to obtain a residence permit, a passport, or visas to travel to other countries. In short, he could claim no protection as a matter of right from any state.

Extradition   The procedure whereby fugitives from justice found in one state are surrendered to the state where the law violations occurred. Extradition is initiated by a formal request from one state to another and is governed by the specific obligations set forth in extradition treaties between states. *See also* JURISDICTION, p. 269.

Significance   The apprehension by the authorities of one state of a fugitive found within the jurisdiction of another state without the permission of the latter constitutes a grave violation of independence and sovereignty. Mutual interest in the application of justice and the maintenance of law and order, however, have led states to cooperate in surrendering fugitives from justice. Such cooperation is based on carefully drawn agreements that establish conditions and list the specific offenses under which extradition can be demanded. Normally, political crimes are not considered to be extraditable offenses and states have often been unwilling to surrender their own citizens for trial in another state. Extradition is governed mainly by bilateral treaties, which have produced a tangled web of law that is unlikely to be simplified until states can come to agreement on more uniform rules.

Extraterritoriality   The exercise of jurisdiction by one state within the territory of another. Extraterritoriality is established by a treaty which specifies the persons, the subject matter, and the degree to which local jurisdiction will not be applied to the citizens of the treaty partner. Examples of extraterritoriality antedate the modern state system. "Capitulations" were a form of extraterritoriality which established certain privileges for Christians in countries under Muslim rule. *See also* JURISDICTION, p. 269.

Significance   Extraterritoriality was often imposed by a powerful state on a weaker state during the era of Western imperialism and colonialism. The object of extraterritoriality was to protect the citizens of the dominant state where the cultures and legal systems of the two were markedly different, as between Western countries and those of the Near and Far East. Frequently, it meant that foreigners accused of crime were tried under their own law and judges rather than the law of the place. Such treaties, normally lacking reciprocity, were bitterly resented as "unequal" limitations of sovereignty and have virtually disappeared. Extraterritoriality in a special sense, however, continues to exist in that diplomats are immune from legal process in the host country, and in connection with "status of forces" treaties that accord special rights and duties to the troops of one country stationed within the territory of another.

Genocide   The destruction of groups of human beings because of their race, religion, nationality, or ethnic background. World concern over genocide was aroused by the mass murders perpetrated by the Nazis against the Jews and other racial and national groups. The United Nations General Assembly in 1948 adopted an International Convention on the Prevention and Punishment of the Crime of Genocide, which became effective in 1951 after 20 nations had ratified it. Categories of crime recognized in the Convention include killing, causing physical or mental harm, inflicting poor conditions of life, enforced birth control, or transferring children from one group to another. Persons committing or inciting acts of genocide are liable to punishment whether they are public officials or private individuals. *See also* GENOCIDE CONVENTION, p. 348.

Significance   Genocide, recognized by the contemporary world as one of the most despicable crimes, requires international action because it may be perpetrated by a government or with its consent. The United States was a leader in drafting the Convention but the Senate refused to ratify it because of public indifference and the belief that some provisions of the Convention contravene federal law. Although the Convention establishes virtually unprecedented individual responsibility under international law for acts of genocide, no institutions for international enforcement have been established.

Government   The institutionalized process through which the internal and external aspects of state sovereignty are exercised. Many types of government exist, described by such words as democratic, authoritarian, oligarchic, dictatorial, republican, parliamentary, monarchical, presidential, unitary, and federal. Regardless of type, all governments make and enforce law, provide services for their citizens, and administer justice. The type of government is determined by the way in which legislative, executive, and judicial power is organized and distributed. No matter how it is organized, effective government, or the ability to demonstrate control over the populace, is an essential attribute of statehood under international law. *See also* STATE, p. 286.

Significance   The government of the nation-state is the most powerful instrument for social control yet devised by man, and takes precedence over other institutions for social control, such as family or church. Organized society implies the presence of rules applicable throughout the society, and it is government, exercising the rule-making power and the monopoly of force necessary to insure ultimate compliance, that prevents anarchy and makes organized social living possible. The extent of control exercised by government is dependent on the relative power of the various groups in the state, and on the extent of value consensus within the society.

Hague Peace Conferences (1899 and 1907)   The first general international conferences called to codify and develop rules and procedures related to the problems of armaments and war. The Hague Conferences, with twenty-six states participating in the first and forty-four in the second, produced conventions on the pacific settlement of international disputes, rules for the conduct of war and the treatment of prisoners, the rights and duties of neutrals, and rules regulating action to collect international debts. The conferences, however, produced no general agreement in the crucial areas of disarmament, arms limitation, and compulsory arbitration. *See also* PERMANENT COURT OF ARBITRATION, p. 283; HAGUE PEACE CONFERENCES (1899 AND 1907), p. 210.

Significance   The most notable contribution of the Hague Conferences to the cause of peace was the creation of the Permanent Court of Arbitration at the Hague. Participating states were encouraged but not bound to submit their disputes to the Court rather than resort to war. Although the conferences were concerned with the prevention of war, war was not outlawed and twelve of the fourteen final agreements related only to its regulation. The conferences are of historic importance because participation approached universality for the first time, because great and small states participated on the basis of sovereign equality, because international peacekeeping machinery was established, and because the parliamentary diplomacy which characterized the meetings set a precedent for the League of Nations and United Nations systems.

Hot Pursuit   The international legal doctrine that permits the apprehension on or over the high seas of vessels or aircraft suspected of having violated national laws within national territorial jurisdiction. Under international law, hot pursuit must be: (1) begun within the jurisdiction of the offended state; (2) engaged in only by the public vessels or aircraft of the territorial sovereign; (3) continuous until the pursued vessel is arrested; or (4) broken off when the vessel has passed into the territorial waters of another state. *See also* INNOCENT PASSAGE, p. 264; TERRITORIAL WATERS, p. 275.

Significance   Hot pursuit means that an offending vessel cannot escape the consequences of its acts merely by moving its location out into the high seas, which by law belong to no state. Should suspicions of the arresting state prove to be unfounded, it may become liable for the payment of compensation. The doctrine is justified in international law as necessary to the efficient exercise of territorial jurisdiction.

Innocent Passage   The right of foreign vessels to traverse the territorial waters of another state without capricious interference by the coastal sovereign. Innocent passage includes stopping and anchoring but only when incidental to ordinary navigation, or made necessary by *force majeure* (superior force) or by distress. *See also* TERRITORIAL WATERS, p. 275.

Significance   Passage is innocent provided it does not prejudice the peace, good order, or security of the coastal state.
Under international law, vessels in innocent passage are subject
to normal rules of transport and navigation and to the laws of the
coastal sovereign. In return, the vessels of all states are afforded
the advantage of using the most expedient route. Under these
same conditions, the 1958 Geneva Convention on the Territorial
Sea and the Contiguous Zone recognizes the right of innocent
passage for warships, although the Soviet Union and several
of its Eastern European allies entered the reservation that
foreign warships require prior authorization before passage is
permitted.

International Court of Justice (ICJ)   The principal judicial organ of the United Nations. The International Court of
Justice is the successor to the Permanent Court of International
Justice (PCIJ), which functioned from 1922 to 1946. All United
Nations members are automatically parties to the Statute of the
ICJ, and the General Assembly on recommendation of the Security Council establishes conditions under which nonmembers,
such as Switzerland, may accede to the Statute. The Court is
competent to hear any case brought to it by parties to a dispute
who accept its jurisdiction in the particular case or who have
accepted its compulsory jurisdiction under the Optional Clause.
The ICJ may also render advisory opinions on legal questions
referred to it by states, by the principal organs of the United
Nations, and by most of the specialized agencies. To reach a
decision, the Court applies: (1) treaties; (2) international customs; (3) general principles of law; and (4) judicial decisions,
and, with the consent of the parties, the teachings of qualified
international jurists. The Court with the consent of the parties
may also render a decision *ex aequo et bono* (based on justice and
fairness rather than law). Decisions are arrived at by majority
vote and cannot be appealed. The Security Council and the
General Assembly, voting separately, elect the fifteen judges for
nine-year terms, with five judges elected every three years and all
eligible for reelection. Article 9 of the Statute of the ICJ provides
that the judges should be selected on the basis of their individual
qualifications and represent the main forms of civilization and
the principal legal systems of the world. *See also* ADJUDICATION,
p. 249; ADVISORY OPINION, p. 250; COMPULSORY JURISDICTION,
p. 256; EX AEQUO ET BONO, p. 260; INTERNATIONAL LAW, p. 266.

Significance   The International Court of Justice represents the broadest effort to date to substitute the rule of law for the use of force in settling international disputes. The ICJ has heard over forty-five disputes, rendered final judgments in many, and has issued numerous advisory opinions. The Court has not, however, settled any major international disputes, largely because states appear reluctant to submit their vital interests to the finality of its decisions, and because of disagreement as to the norms to be applied. The judicial independence of the Court, although questioned on occasion in the heat of partisan controversy, has never been successfully challenged. Nevertheless, political considerations, such as whether or not a country is represented on other principal organs of the United Nations, have influenced the selection of judges. The principle of equitable geographic distribution has also been applied by the General Assembly and the Security Council even though this criterion for selection of judges is not prescribed by the Statute of the Court. Practice also reveals the continuous presence on the Court of a national of each of the five permanent members of the Security Council. Regardless of statute criteria for selection of judges, many Afro-Asian states have expressed dissatisfaction with the Court on the ground that they are inadequately represented on the bench. The International Court of Justice nonetheless is the high point of efforts by the state system to develop dispute-settlement procedures through international judicial tribunals.

International Law   The system of rules on the rights and duties of states in their mutual relations. International law is based on the concept of the sovereign equality of states and rests ultimately on agreement among them. The sources of international law include: (1) treaties or specific bilateral or multilateral agreements between the states; (2) international custom as evidenced by practice so long continued as to be considered binding; (3) general principles of law based on such ideas as justice, equity, and morality recognized by civilized nations; and (4) a subsidiary source of law found in judicial decisions and in the teachings of the recognized legal publicists of the various nations. Although international law is applied by international judicial tribunals, it is most frequently interpreted and applied by national courts. Based initially on precedents of earlier eras, international law has developed in the modern state system since the Peace of Westphalia of 1648. Hugo Grotius, author of the celebrated treatise *De Jure Belli et Pacis* (1625), is often regarded as the father of modern international law.

Significance International law provides a guide for state action and a technique for peacefully resolving disputes between states by reference to agreed norms of conduct rather than by resort to force. Because the modern state system developed first in Western Europe, international law, which assumes universal applicability, is largely a product of Western culture. Yet the community of states has more than doubled since World War II, with the vast majority of new states located in Asia and Africa— areas which had little or no part in developing existing rules of international law. Consequently, many non-Western states as well as communist countries challenge many aspects of the law in its present form. The challenges are based on cultural and ideological differences, nationalistic pride, and antipathy for rules created by former colonial masters. Thus, a major problem in establishing the rule of law among nations is the creation of a new international legal system to which all can agree. Such United Nations agencies as the Economic and Social Council, the International Law Commission, special committees created by the General Assembly, and various regional organizations are leading the way. The process involves attempts to codify existing law and, through lawmaking treaties, attempts to create new law according to the needs of a worldwide community of states.

International Law Commission (ILC) An agency created by the General Assembly in 1947 to aid it in carrying out its Charter responsibility (Article 13) to "initiate studies and make recommendations . . . encouraging the progressive development of international law and its codification." The International Law Commission consists of twenty-one experts on international law who represent the world's main legal systems and forms of civilization. Chosen on the basis of equitable geographic distribution, the commissioners serve five-year terms in their individual capacities rather than as representatives of governments. The ILC has presented a variety of reports to the General Assembly and numerous draft conventions with the recommendations that the Assembly convene international conferences to consider the drafts. When this procedure is followed, the conferences adopt law-making treaties that bind the states which ratify them. The ILC has concerned itself with such subjects as recognition, state succession, jurisdictional immunities, the high seas, territorial waters, nationality, statelessness, aliens, asylum, the law of treaties, state responsibility, and arbitral procedure. *See also* CODIFICATION OF INTERNATIONAL LAW, p. 254.

Significance The International Law Commission has made its chief contributions in the codification of law rather than in the development of a new universal system of norms. Present international law is largely the product of the older states in whose interests it was created and which are reluctant to see it undergo rapid change. Pointing to the law's Western origin, however, some of the non-Western and communist states have called for a "modernized" system in keeping with "current political realities." The ILC is unlikely to produce a new universal system until a worldwide political consensus emerges on which it can be based. While the ILC continues to make progress in codifying existing law, new law on a variety of subjects, such as road traffic, political rights of women, and freedom of information is also emerging in draft conventions from other agencies, such as the Economic and Social Council and its commissions.

International Legislation Multilateral treaties or conventions designed to codify, modify, and initiate legal rules to be followed by states in their mutual relations. International legislation can be accomplished only by a law-making treaty since states insist, as a function of sovereignty, that they can be bound only by their consent. Law-making treaties can be written by *ad hoc* conferences, by regional institutions, and by international organizations, such as the specialized agencies and the General Assembly of the United Nations. A procedure followed by the United Nations for the creation of international legislation includes: (1) a study by the International Law Commission, which results in the writing of draft articles of agreement and their submission to the General Assembly; (2) a resolution by the Assembly calling an international conference to consider the draft; (3) approval and subsequent ratification by the individual states; and (4) registration of the instrument by the Secretary-General of the United Nations. Recent illustrations of international legislation by law-making treaty include the Geneva

Conventions on the Territorial Sea and Contiguous Zone (1958) and on Fishing (1958), and the Vienna Conventions on Diplomatic Relations (1961) and Consular Relations (1963).

Significance International legislation as a concept indicates the intention to create rules for orderly relationships between states. This intent suggests an analogy with national legislation that is helpful in the study of international relations, although the legislative process in each level are not the same. There is no world legislative body comparable to a national legislature, and, in writing the United Nations Charter in 1945, proposals for conferring legislative powers on the General Assembly were overwhelmingly rejected.

Jurisdiction The right of a state or a court to speak or act with authority. Jurisdiction involves the assertion of control over persons, property, subjects, and situations in a given juridical, political, or geographic area. Under international law, jurisdiction over territory can be acquired by accretion, cession, conquest, discovery, and prescription.

Significance In a world of over one hundred and sixty independent sovereign states, questions of jurisdiction comprise a major share of the subjects of international conflict, negotiation, or adjudication. Jurisdictional conflicts between states are common in such areas as citizenship, boundaries, air space, high seas, fishing rights, territorial waters, innocent passage, and outer space.

Jurisdiction: Accretion Acquisition of title to territory created through the slow depositing of materials by rivers and seas, which vests in the mainland or riparian state. The principle of accretion—that natural additions to the original territory come under the same jurisdiction—can be traced back to Roman law through the work of Hugo Grotius. Such additions may occur on river banks or ocean shores or may take the form of islands or deltas.

Significance The accretion method of territorial acquisition may create serious political and economic questions related to territorial jurisdiction. These may involve islands raised in rivers used as international boundaries or islands or deltas in the maritime belt, which extend a state's territorial waters further out into the ocean.

Jurisdiction: Admiralty   State authority over maritime affairs. Admiralty jurisdiction is a highly technical area of jurisprudence dealt with in the municipal law of states concerned with sea-borne commerce and navigation, and their regulation. Admiralty law includes such subjects as jurisdiction over vessels, ports, seamen, and territorial waters, civil and criminal suits, liabilities of vessels and cargoes, passenger carriage, the rights of crew members, and safety regulations.

Significance   The increasing importance of maritime trade and commerce to a growing number of states has produced a vast quantity of national rules and regulations that in turn have brought recognition of the need for greater uniformity. Efforts at bringing about such uniformity of maritime law by treaty and implementing legislation have met with considerable success in such areas as sanitary regulations, salvage and assistance, collisions, safety at sea, load lines, use of maritime ports, high seas fisheries, and territorial seas. In the absence of such treaties, however, admiralty jurisdiction is determined by national laws.

Jurisdiction: Airspace   The sovereignty of a state over the airspace above its territory. Jurisdiction over the national airspace was recognized by the Chicago Convention on International Civil Aviation (1944) and is limited only by the bilateral and multilateral treaties to which a state may be a party. The Chicago conference established the International Civil Aviation Organization to implement the principles of the Convention and to develop rules for international air travel. Freedom of the air as a general principle exists only over the high seas and any other portions of the earth's surface not subject to the control of any state, such as Antarctica. Military and other state aircraft not common carriers always require special authorization before using the airspace of another state. *See also* INTERNATIONAL CIVIL AVIATION ORGANIZATION, p. 318; OUTER SPACE, p. 273.

Significance   Jurisdiction over national airspace has been a subject of increasing concern as technology has advanced the speed and volume of airborne commerce. Prior to World War I, two theories of airspace jurisdiction were expounded—freedom of the air, and national control. Demonstrations of the effectiveness of aerial surveillance and bombardment brought general acceptance of the idea of national jurisdiction. Technological developments since World War II have raised to a practical level the question of how far above its territory a nation's sovereignty extends. The launching and return to earth of rockets, missiles, satellites, and space craft are opening new areas of conjecture and negotiation in the international development of airspace law.

Jurisdiction: Avulsion   A rule of international law that determines the location of an international boundary between two states separated by a river. When a sudden shift in the location of the main channel occurs, under the avulsion rule the boundary remains in its prior location. *See also* JURISDICTION: THALWEG, p. 275.

Significance   The sudden shift of a main channel may involve a considerable amount of territory compared to the changes brought about by gradual erosion and accretion. In the absence of such a rule this could cause serious international problems, such as the Chamizal Tract Dispute between the United States and Mexico. In 1864, the Rio Grande suddenly changed its course and the question of jurisdiction over the territory between the old and the new channels was not finally resolved until 1967.

Jurisdiction: Cession   The transfer of sovereignty over territory by agreement between ceding and acquiring states. Cession may involve all or a portion of the territory of the ceding state. In the former instance, the ceding state disappears by absorption into the acquiring state. Thus, by the treaty of 1910, Korea became Japanese territory. *See also* PLEBISCITE, p. 243.

Significance   A treaty of cession legitimates the acquisition of territory by formal transfer of sovereignty, describes the territory in question, and sets forth the conditions of the transfer. The legality of a cession does not necessarily depend on the consent of the people of the ceded territory. The principle of self-determination, however, would seem to make an expression of consent desirable. Cession of territory may be voluntary, as in the Louisiana Purchase, or involuntary, as imposed by the terms of a peace treaty.

Jurisdiction: Condominium   A dependent territory governed jointly by two or more sovereigns. In a condominium the legal systems of the states exercising control operate side by side, and questions of jurisdiction are governed by an agreement between the sovereigns. Examples of joint control through condominium arrangements include the Sudan (Britain and France, 1914) and Canton Island and Enderbury Island (Britain and the United States, 1938).

Significance   In a condominium, no external sovereign has exclusive jurisdiction nor does sovereignty reside in the people of the territory. In international relations and law, the condominium as a form of territorial jurisdiction is a relatively rare phenomenon. The control exercised by Britain, France, the Soviet Union, and the United States over Germany after World War II did not constitute a condominium but was a form of military occupation.

Jurisdiction: Contiguous Zone   An area beyond the territorial waters in which the coastal state remains free to enforce compliance with its laws. The extent of the contiguous zone and the jurisdiction of the coastal state are defined in Article 24 of the Geneva Convention on the Territorial Sea and Contiguous Zone (1958) as follows: "1. In a zone of the high seas contiguous to its territorial sea, the coastal state may exercise the control necessary to: (a) Prevent infringement of its customs, fiscal, immigration, or sanitary regulations within its territory or territorial sea; (b) Punish infringement of the above regulations. . . . 2. The contiguous zone may not extend beyond twelve miles from the baseline from which the breadth of the territorial sea is measured." *See also* TERRITORIAL WATERS, p. 275.

Significance   The contiguous zone concept implies the existence of a specified area of the high seas wherein the coastal state may not claim sovereignty, but where it may nevertheless exercise jurisdiction for certain limited purposes such as the enforcement of customs laws. All states recognize that coastal states have jurisdiction over a band of territorial waters at least three miles wide. Beyond territorial waters, however, historically there has been little general agreement on the extension of national jurisdiction, although individual states have asserted various jurisdictional claims. Britain and the United States, for example, have traditionally asserted a right to extend limited jurisdiction to a zone extending twelve miles beyond their shores. The concept of the contiguous zone was finally accepted, however, in the discussions of the International Law Commission and at the Geneva Conference on the Law of the Sea and became part of international law in 1964 for those signatories that ratified the Territorial Sea Convention.

Jurisdiction: High Seas   All of the world's oceans, seas, connecting arms, bays, and gulfs that lie outside of the national territorial waters of coastal states. The high seas are open to commerce and navigation by all countries. States may extend jurisdiction to vessels flying their flags on the high seas but not to the seas themselves. *See also* ADMIRALTY, p. 270.

Significance   Under the 1958 Geneva Convention on the High Seas, "no state may validly purport to subject any part of them to its sovereignty." By international law, all states have equal rights to engage on the high seas in such activity as fishing, laying of submarine cables and pipelines, and overflight by aircraft. The exercise of the freedom of the seas by any state is, however, qualified by the general requirement that reasonable regard is due to the interests of other states in the exercise of their freedom to use the high seas.

Jurisdiction: Outer Space   International authority over the area beyond the airspace. Although no state exercises jurisdiction over outer space, the subject has become one of increasing international concern since the first earth satellite was orbited in 1957. In 1959 the United Nations established a permanent Committee on the Peaceful Uses of Outer Space. In 1961, the General Assembly unanimously proclaimed that "International law, including the Charter of the United Nations, applies to outer space and celestial bodies"; and that "Outer space and celestial bodies are free for exploration and use by all States in conformity with international law, and are not subject to national appropriation." In 1963, these principles were augmented by the Declaration of Legal Principles Governing Activities in Outer Space, which provided that: (1) space exploration and use is to be for the benefit of all mankind; (2) states conducting such activities bear international responsibility for their acts; (3) all space activity shall be guided by the principles of cooperation and mutual assistance; (4) states launching objects and personnel retain jurisdiction over them in outer space and on their return to earth wherever they may land; (5) states are liable for any damages on earth, in the airspace, or in outer space caused by objects they launch into outer space; and (6) astronauts are to be considered envoys of mankind in outer space, and in case of accident, all states are to render them every possible assistance and to return them promptly to the state of registry of their space vehicle. These principles were embodied in the Outer Space Treaty, which was adopted by the General Assembly in 1966 and entered into force for ratifying states in 1967. *See also* JURISDICTION: AIRSPACE, p. 270; OUTER SPACE TREATY, p. 217.

Significance   Outer space and airspace are recognized in international law as two distinct zones, but the demarcation between them remains unclear. Some authorities define "airspace" as the area of aerodynamic flight. Outer space is therefore beyond national sovereignty, whereas airspace is within the jurisdiction of the subjacent territorial sovereign. The principles eunciated in United Nations declarations were merely suggestive until the Outer Space Treaty was ratified in 1967. Although that Treaty sought to internationalize outer space and insure its peaceful exploration and use, military considerations of the United States and the Soviet Union have jeopardized its objectives. Effective international use of outer space hinges on the solution of earthbound conflicts.

Jurisdiction: Prescription   A method recognized in international law whereby one state, through long and uninterrupted dominion, acquires title to territory previously claimed by another state. The prior sovereign's long-term acquiescence in the exercise of jurisdiction by another state constitutes the grounds for the transference of valid title.

Significance   Prescription can create title for one state only when sovereignty over the territory previously resided in another state; in the absence of a prior sovereign, title would be acquired by discovery. Prescription implies that mere ownership is not enough to maintain title; it must be accompanied by the exercise of effective jurisdiction over the territory. International law does not specify any particular time period following which title passes to the state that has enjoyed uninterrupted use. When claims based on prescription are contested before a court or arbitral tribunal, each case is decided on its merits in line with rules of international law. The Palmas Island Arbitration (1928) between the United States and the Netherlands, for example, recognized the Dutch title on the basis of long, uninterrupted exercise of jurisdiction.

Jurisdiction: Territorial Waters   The belt of water immediately adjacent to the coast of a state over which the state exercises sovereignty. Territorial waters three miles wide are the minimum generally recognized by the states of the world. There is no generally accepted maximum width although a number of states claim twelve miles and, in individual cases, up to two hundred miles. *See also* INNOCENT PASSAGE, p. 264.

Significance   The extent of territorial waters has always been a matter of international controversy. The three-mile minimum limit was accepted by the eighteenth century as the range that could be covered effectively by cannon fire from the shore. Claims to a greater distance are usually of a political or strategic nature or are based on the location of some resource, such as fisheries or oil, over which the coastal state wishes to establish exclusive jurisdiction. Although the Geneva Conferences on the Law of the Sea (1958 and 1960) produced conventions on the high seas, the continental shelf, the conservation of fisheries, and the regime of territorial waters (rules governing their use), they failed to produce the two-thirds vote necessary to establish a uniform limit for territorial waters.

Jurisdiction: *Thalweg*   The rule of international law which determines the exact location of the boundary between two states separated by a navigable river. The *thalweg*, or "down-way," is the middle of the main channel or downstream current. *See also* JURISDICTION: AVULSION, p. 271.

Significance   Rivers may shift their course as a result of natural causes. Unless the boundary can be determined with precision, problems can arise over such matters as customs duties, tolls, jurisdiction over vessels, and fugitives from justice. The *thalweg* rule can also be applied to estuaries and bays.

Jus Civile   The early civil law of the primitive Roman city-state, which applied to citizens only. *Jus civile* may be contrasted with the *jus gentium* which applied to the diverse peoples of the Empire. *See also* JUS GENTIUM, p. 276.

Significance   The *jus civile* became one of the bases for the later development of various systems of national law. *Jus civile*, along with the *jus gentium* of the Roman legal system, provided precedents and established principles later used in the development of international law.

Jus Gentium   That body of Roman law and equity which applied to all foreigners resident in the Empire. The *jus gentium* governed relations between foreigners and between foreigners and citizens, and was based on common ideas of justice found in the laws and customs of the various peoples of the Empire. Because it was thought to be simple, reasonable, and adaptable, early jurists regarded the *jus gentium* as universal in its applicability. *See also* JUS CIVILE, p. 276; JUS NATURALE, p. 276.

Significance   The *jus gentium* of Rome can be viewed as a system of private international law which came to be associated with the *jus naturale* and with the Greek idea of a natural and, therefore, universal law. Based on these associations, the *jus gentium* has provided modern international law with many useful analogies in such fields as the occupation of territory, property rights, contracts, and treaties.

Jus Naturale   A Roman adaptation of the Greek Stoic concept of a set of principles that ought to govern the conduct of all men. The *jus naturale* or natural law is founded in the explanation of the nature of man as a rational and social being. This law of reason based on what ought to be, when coupled with the universalism of the *jus gentium*, gave Roman law the adaptability and progressiveness that enabled diverse peoples to live together in relative peace in spite of changing conditions. *See also* JUS GENTIUM, p. 276.

Significance The concept of *jus naturale*, based on reason and existing above men and states, influenced Grotius and other early founders of international law who sought to establish a system of orderly relations between states. Natural law formulations still evident in international law include such concepts as international morality, equality, justice, and reason. The natural law school of international law was gradually displaced in the eighteenth and nineteenth centuries by the advocates of legal positivism, who hold that only custom, legislation, and treaties can create rights and duties for sovereign states.

Jus Sanguinis The "law of blood," or the rule that at birth a person acquires the citizenship of his parents. *Jus sanguinis* is one of two legal rules that states follow in determining citizenship by birth. The other rule is *jus soli*, or the "law of the soil." *See also* CITIZEN, p. 254; JUS SOLI, p. 277.

Significance States that follow the rule of *jus sanguinis* establish nationality through that of the parents rather than that of the place of birth. Under this rule, for example, children born to British parents outside the jurisdiction of the United Kingdom are citizens of Great Britain even though the basic rule followed by Britain is *jus soli*. Most continental European countries follow the rule of *jus sanguinis*.

Jus Soli The "law of the soil," or the rule that a person's citizenship is derived from his place of birth. *Jus soli* is one of two legal rules that states follow in determining citizenship by birth. The other rule is *jus sanguinis*, or the "law of blood." *See also* CITIZEN, p. 254; JUS SANGUINIS, p. 277.

Significance *Jus soli* is the rule of citizenship followed by most English-speaking and Latin American countries. Children born within the jurisdiction of the United States, for example, are American citizens even if their parents are ineligible for citizenship. Children born to foreign diplomats serving in countries that follow the rule of *jus soli* are an exception to that rule.

Justiciable and Nonjusticiable Disputes A formulation that results from the assertion of the existence of two distinct categories of international disputes—legal and political. Justiciable disputes are those that lend themselves to legal settlement by arbitration or adjudication. Nonjusticiable disputes are those to which techniques of political settlement are applied by bilateral diplomacy, good offices, mediation, inquiry, or conciliation. *See also* PEACEFUL SETTLEMENT, p. 241.

Significance   Whether a dispute is or is not justiciable does not depend so much on the nature of the dispute as it does on the importance of the issues to the parties involved and their decision as to which set of settlement norms to apply, if either. The idea of peaceful settlement through arbitration experienced a considerable vogue during the opening decades of the twentieth century, as evidenced by the creation of the Permanent Court of Arbitration (1899), the Root arbitration treaties (1908), and the Taft-Knox arbitration treaties (1911). Nevertheless, the distinction between legal and political (and therefore justiciable and nonjusticiable) disputes arose because states wished to exempt from the finality of legal settlement matters touching on national independence and vital interests as interpreted by themselves. That states may not wish to settle disputes by law does not mean that there is no law applicable to the dispute.

Law of the Sea   Those international legal rules that pertain to the maritime rights and duties of the states. The law of the sea, which is the oldest branch of international law, has grown out of ancient codes based on customs related to the maritime rights and duties of merchants and ship owners. Precedents include the Rhodian Laws (ninth century), the Tabula Amalfitana (eleventh century), the Laws of Oleron (twelfth century), the Laws of Wisby (thirteenth and fourteenth centuries), and the *Consolato del Mare* (fourteenth century). Sources of the law of the sea include international custom, national legislation, treaties, and the work of international conferences on the subject. *See also* JURISDICTION: ADMIRALTY, p. 270; JURISDICTION: HIGH SEAS, p. 273.

Significance   The law of the sea is based on two fundamental principles—the freedom of all states to use the high seas without interference, and the responsibility of each state to maintain law and order on the sea. Each state exercises jurisdiction over its own ships and within its territorial waters. Vessels in the territorial waters of a foreign state remain under the jurisdiction of the state whose flag they fly unless they threaten the peace and good order of the coastal sovereign. The Geneva Conferences of 1958 and 1960 augmented the law of the sea with conventions on: (1) the definition of baselines for measuring territorial seas and contiguous zones; (2) innocent passage; (3) the recovery of food and minerals from the subsoil of the continental shelf and from the sea bed; and (4) the conservation of animal and plant sea life. A new series of Law of the Sea Conferences began in 1973 and continued on into the 1980s. Considerable agreement has evolved concerning: (1) national jurisdiction over a twelve-mile territorial sea; (2) coastal state rights over a 200-mile exclusive economic zone; and (3) transit through, over, and under straits used for international navigation. The major unresolved issues relate to the nature of control over deep-sea resource mining and other forms of exploitation of the wealth of the sea beyond the 200-mile national economic zones. These issues are tied to the extent of authority to be granted to a proposed United Nations International Seabed Authority. This Authority would govern exploration and exploitation of deep-sea resources when agreement can be reached on such key issues as voting, licensing, and collection of royalties.

Nationality   The legal relationship between an individual and a state whereby the individual claims protection from the state and the state in turn requires his allegiance and the performance of certain obligations. Nationality is acquired by birth or by naturalization, although the rules covering each method vary from country to country. The principle that an individual can be divested of his nationality is commonly accepted in the state system, and diverse methods recognized by states include denationalization, denaturalization, expatriation, and renunciation. *See also* CITIZEN, p. 254.

Significance   Nationality implies membership in a state. Conflicts over the nationality of an individual can arise between a state that follows *jus sanguinis* and another that asserts the rule of *jus soli*. Similarly, conflict can occur when a person born in a state that follows the doctrine of inalienable allegiance becomes the naturalized citizen of another state. Since individuals move between states in large numbers, such conflicts over questions of nationality affect the relations of states and are responsible for protracted efforts at codifying international law on the subject.

Naturalization The legal process whereby an individual changes his citizenship from one country to another. Details vary from country to country but normally include a formal renunciation of allegiance to one sovereign and an oath of allegiance to the new state. *See also* CITIZEN, p. 254.

Significance Naturalization is the only way in which a person who cannot claim citizenship in a state by right of birth (*jus sanguinis* or *jus soli*) can acquire citizenship in that state. Immigrants from other countries are naturalized individually. Collective naturalization can occur, however, by a treaty or legislative enactment granting citizenship to the people of a newly acquired territory. Thus, for example, the United States conferred citizenship on the people of Alaska, Florida, Hawaii, Louisiana, and Texas. Whether individual or collective, naturalization cannot be claimed as a matter of right. It is a discretionary prerogative of the granting state, which, in the absence of specific treaty commitments, is free to establish conditions.

Neutrality The legal status wherein a state takes no part in a war and which establishes certain rights and obligations vis à vis the belligerents. The rights of a neutral state recognized by belligerents include: (1) freedom from territorial violations; (2) acceptance of the fact of the neutral's impartiality; and (3) freedom from interference with its commerce except to the degree sanctioned by international law. Neutral duties include: (1) impartiality; (2) refraining from aiding any belligerent; (3) denying to belligerents the use of neutral territory; and (4) permitting belligerents to interfere with commerce to the extent specified by international law. *See also* CONTRABAND, p. 165.

Significance The concept of total war has brought into question the use of neutrality as a legal restraint on belligerents. In a total war, any commerce between a third party and a belligerent can be interpreted as aiding the enemy. When such commerce is cut off, the neutral can only acquiesce or enter the war. In cases of aggression, a policy of strict neutrality could be branded as immoral since it makes no distinction between the perpetrator and the victim of aggression. The legitimacy of neutrality is further called into question by the United Nations Charter obligation that all members oppose aggression. Nevertheless, the permanent neutrality of a few states, such as Austria and Switzerland, is recognized in international law. Legal neutrality should not be confused with political neutralism which implies non-alignment in the rivalry between the Soviet Union and the United States.

Optional Clause   A method outlined in Article 36 of the Statute of the International Court of Justice, by which states may agree in advance to accept the compulsory jurisdiction of the Court in certain circumstances. If a state accepts compulsory jurisdiction, it agrees to submit to the Court all legal disputes involving questions of treaty interpretation, international law, breaches of international obligations, and amounts of reparations to be awarded. *See also* COMPULSORY JURISDICTION, p. 256; CONNALLY AMENDMENT, p. 257.

Significance   The purpose of the Optional Clause is to overcome the inability of the Court to exercise jurisdiction over sovereign states, which otherwise could refuse to appear in court. More than fifty states have accepted compulsory jurisdiction, either unconditionally or on the condition of reciprocity by other states in similar types of cases. The United States accepted compulsory jurisdiction under the Optional Clause but reserved the right to interpret the application of compulsory jurisdiction (Connally Amendment), which had the effect of rendering its acceptance almost meaningless. The failure of the Optional Clause to achieve a satisfactory system of compulsory jurisdiction indicates that most states are not yet ready to entrust the Court with the settlement of disputes over vital issues.

Pacta Sunt Servanda   The rule of general international law that treaties are binding and should be observed. *Pacta sunt servanda* is the principle that establishes the legal basis whereby treaties constitute binding contracts between signatory states. *See also* REBUS SIC STANTIBUS, p. 284; TREATY, p. 247.

Significance   The rationale of *pacta sunt servanda* is that, in the absence of an international enforcement agency, each member of the international community has the responsibility to keep its agreements. To assume otherwise would be to question the very existence of international law in a community of sovereign states. When a treaty is violated, the offending state usually attempts to justify its act not in terms of the absence of the norm but in terms of extenuating circumstances, which, it asserts, should release it from the operation of the rule (*rebus sic stantibus*). Such attempts at self-justification constitute indirect admission of the existence and validity of *pacta sunt servanda* as a general rule of law.

Partition   A way of establishing or rearranging territorial jurisdiction by the division of territory between two or more sovereignties. Partition is a device that has often been used to resolve disputes over territorial claims. *See also* PEACEFUL SET-TLEMENT, p. 241; PLEBISCITE, p. 243.

Significance   Partition of territory is as old as the history of the nation-state. Historically Russia, Prussia and Austria had a con-tinuing interest in the partition of Poland to the point that the latter disappeared as a state until resurrected after World War I. Partition may be called for in a peace settlement and may or may not include a plebiscite, or vote, of the people involved. Follow-ing World War II, British India was partitioned between the predominantly Hindu and Muslim communities and became the states of India and Pakistan. Growing antagonism among the victorious allies after World War II led to the *de facto* partition of Germany into the Federal Republic of Germany (West Germany) and the German Democratic Republic (East Germany). In the same way Korea has become the Republic of Korea (South Korea) and the Democratic People's Republic of Korea (North Korea).

Passport   A legal document issued by a state, which iden-tifies an individual and attests to his nationality. Passports are issued to citizens who wish to travel abroad and entitle the bearer to the protection of his country's diplomatic and consular repre-sentatives. They are also requests to foreign governments to allow the bearer to travel or sojourn within their jurisdiction and to grant him lawful aid and protection. Diplomatic passports are issued to emissaries of foreign governments which identify their official status and insure their receipt of appropriate diplomatic privileges and immunities. *See also* DIPLOMAT, p. 235; VISA p. 287.

Significance   A passport is essentially a travel and identity document that attests to the bearer's claim to protection by the issuing government and provides prima facie evidence of nationality. Passports are, therefore, not only essential to legitimate foreign travelers but are also sought by those who would enter another country fraudulently. Cleverly faked passports can command a high price in black markets in many places around the world. Prior to World War I, passports were not generally required for international travel. Some countries in recent years have moved by special agreements toward discontinuing passport requirements between them, as, for example, among the members of the European Economic Community.

Permanent Court of Arbitration   A panel of internationally recognized jurists who stand ready to serve as arbitrators in any international dispute. The Permanent Court of Arbitration, with headquarters at the Hague, was established by the Convention for the Pacific Settlement of International Disputes as adopted and revised by the Hague Peace Conferences of 1899 and 1907. The panel of available arbitrators includes four jurists of recognized competence appointed by each signatory. Each party to a dispute selects two judges, only one of whom may be a national. The four arbitrators so chosen then select a fifth to serve as umpire. Thus, the Court is not a standing body but only a panel from which arbitral tribunals can be selected. The parties identify the points at issue, define the authority of the tribunal, and agree that a decision made within these limitations will be accepted as legally binding. *See also* ARBITRATION, p. 252; HAGUE PEACE CONFERENCES, p. 263.

Significance   The chief value of the Permanent Court of Arbitration lies not in the extent of its jurisdiction but in its existence prior to a dispute and in its readily available machinery. Signatories of the Convention are not, however, obligated to use the personnel and procedures of the Court. This decision is made in each case by the parties, although their actions may be governed by preexisting arbitration treaties or arbitration clauses found in other treaties. Most arbitration treaties follow the example of the Anglo-French Treaty of 1903, which required differences of a legal nature and those related to the interpretation of treaties to be referred to the Court. In most arbitration treaties, questions involving the vital interests, independence, or honor of the parties, and the interests of third parties, have usually been exempted. In United States practice, the Senate has regarded each decision to arbitrate under a general treaty as a separate treaty requiring Senate approval. The Hague Court represents an early effort at institutionalizing the peaceful settlement of disputes through the rule of law and was the forerunner to the Permanent Court of International Justice during the League of Nations era and of the International Court of Justice of the United Nations.

Positivism   The doctrine which holds that international law consists only of those rules by which states have consented to be bound. Positivism, which emphasizes the concept of state sovereignty, asserts that consent may be granted expressly in the form of a treaty, or by implication through adherence to international customary practices. *See also* CUSTOMARY LAW, p. 258; JUS NATURALE, p. 276; INTERNATIONAL LAW, p. 266; TREATY, p. 247.

Significance   Positivism is the principal method of international legal reasoning in an age that is dominated by nationalism and recognizes the nation-state as the ultimate form of human organization. A weakness of the positivist approach, according to some legal scholars, involves the validity of the concept of implied consent as an explanation for the binding force of international law. The issue concerns the question of whether a sovereign state can be bound except by formal consent. Nevertheless, positivism has contributed to understanding the nature of modern international law by emphasizing state practice rather than a priori reasoning as the source of legal norms.

Rebus Sic Stantibus   The international law doctrine that an essential change in the conditions under which a treaty was concluded frees a state from its treaty obligations. *Rebus sic stantibus* is a rationalizaton for unilateral, unauthorized denunciation of a treaty commitment. The doctrine asserts that every treaty contains an unwritten clause to the effect that substantial changes in the conditions that existed at the time the treaty was signed alter the obligations established by the treaty. *See also* PACTA SUNT SERVANDA, p. 281; TREATY, p. 247.

Significance   Stability in international relations requires that agreements should be observed (*pacta sunt servanda*). *Rebus sic stantibus*, however, might be invoked by a state if its existence were threatened by its performance of a treaty obligation. The assertion of the doctrine is of more questionable validity, on the other hand, when a state feels that its obligations are inconvenient, onerous, incompatible with a change in its status, or damaging to self-esteem. The doctrines of *pacta sunt servanda* and *rebus sic stantibus* are not necessarily incompatible in principle. The sanctity of treaties must be admitted if international relations are to be conducted on the basis of the rule of law, but at the same time treaty obligations must be kept reasonable through periodic renegotiation or adjustment lest the strict application of the law precipitate chaos and conflict.

Sanctions   Penalties meted out as consequences of illegal conduct. Sanctions in international relations involve the collective effort of the international community to force a lawbreaking state to comply with international law when diplomatic and legal techniques of dispute settlement have failed. Authority to impose sanctions was embodied in the Covenant of the League of Nations and in the Charter of the United Nations. *See also* SANCTIONS, p. 332.

Significance   In the absence of an international executive to enforce the law, the imposition of sanctions depends upon the degree of consensus in the international community and on the willingness of each member of the state system to accept a responsibility to uphold the law. To be effective in specific cases, sanctions must create more hardship for the offending state than is created for the states applying the sanctions.

Sovereignty   The supreme decision-making and decision-enforcing authority possessed by the state and by no other social institution. The doctrine of sovereignty arose in the sixteenth century as a defense of the monarch's right of complete territorial jurisdiction in opposition to the claims of lesser local princes, the Papacy, and the Holy Roman Emperor. By the end of the Thirty Years' War (1618–1648), the doctrine had become an accepted political fact, and the modern nation-state became the most important unit of political organization in the world. Sovereignty does not mean that states enjoy absolute freedom of action. State conduct is conditioned by the prescriptions and restraints of international law and by the rules of the various international organizations to which states belong, under the theory that supreme power can be modified by consent. Sovereignty also implies state equality but only in the sense of equal capacity to acquire rights and to be subjected to obligations. Sovereign states are further limited in their freedom of action by the informal restraints imposed by a state system in which varying capabilities must be harmonized with specific objectives. *See also* INTERNATIONAL LAW, p. 266; POWER, p. 17; STATE, p. 286.

Significance   The doctrine of sovereignty implies the decentralization of power in the community of states and legitimates the freedom of the individual state to make independent decisions. It has come under increasing attack by those who point to the unrestrained pursuit of national self-interest as a fundamental cause of war, and who look to a more highly centralized state system as the means for regularizing interstate relations. State sovereignty is incompatible with a centralized state system, just as independent power exercised by a feudal nobility was incompatible with absolute monarchy. Thus, as long as the doctrine of sovereignty prevails, international law will remain a relatively weak, decentralized legal order when compared with the internal legal systems of the individual members of the international community. Theoretically, integration of the world community cannot proceed beyond the confederal stage, typified by the United Nations, because adherence to the doctrine of state sovereignty requires that the ultimate power of decision must remain with the individual members of the group. Since the end of World War II, certain aspects of sovereignty have been surrendered on a regional scale with the development of such organizations as the European Economic Community. The ultimate political integration of the original six states of the community was stalled, however, by the continued vitality of sovereignty and nationalism symbolized by Charles de Gaulle's confederal concept of a "Europe of the fatherlands." Elsewhere, among the older states, nationalism and the conflict over values strengthens dedication to the doctrine of sovereignty. The independence of the newer states of the world is emphasized in the United Nations by their dedication to the concept of sovereign equality. Sovereignty is the central feature of political community at any level since, in a given area, there can be only one supreme law-making and law-enforcing authority.

State   A legal concept describing a social group that occupies a defined territory and is organized under common political institutions and an effective government. Some publicists add the qualification that the group must be willing to assume the international legal obligations of statehood. States legally come into being when they are recognized by other individual members of the international community. *See also* RECOGNITION OF STATES, p. 245; SOVEREIGNTY, p. 285.

Significance States are the primary units of the international political and legal community. States emerged out of the collapse of the feudal order in Europe, and they stand in a relationship of sovereign equality to one another. As sovereign entities, states have the right to determine their own national objectives and the techniques for their achievement. State freedom of action is conditioned, however, by the formal restraints of international law and international organization, and by the relationship between state power and the informal situational factors that characterize the international enviroment at any given time.

Statelessness The condition of an individual who is not recognized by any state as one of its nationals. Statelessness may result from dislocations caused by war or revolution, from a conflict of nationality laws, or by some act of denationalization undertaken by a government against some of its citizens. An individual act of expatriation which is not followed by the acquisition of a new allegiance would also result in statelessness. *See also* CITIZEN, p. 254; NATIONALITY, p. 279; REFUGEE, p. 188.

Significance Statelessness means that a person has no legal claim to protection from any country. In the case of political refugees, the individual may have no legal right to be where he is, nor is he likely to be able to secure a passport or the necessary visa to go elsewhere. The international and human problems of statelessness and of refugees are of particular concern to such international agencies as the General Assembly, the Economic and Social Council, the International Law Commission, and the Office of the High Commissioner for Refugees. In 1961, the General Assembly opened for signature a Convention on the Reduction of Statelessness that establishes circumstances under which a country could be required to grant nationality.

Visa An endorsement on a passport by an official of the country to be entered, authorizing admission to that state. The visa indicates that the identity and nationality of the individual have been authenticated and his reasons for entry approved. *See also* PASSPORT, p. 282.

Significance   Many governments require foreigners to secure a visa before admitting them to the country. In American practice, foreigners wishing to enter the United States must present a valid passport to an American consular officer abroad. The consul exercises final discretionary power in granting nonimmigrant visas to businessmen, tourists, students, and other visitors. Before granting an immigrant visa to aliens wishing to settle in the United States, the consul must determine that the annual quota for the alien's country has not been filled and that the individual meets other immigration requirements. Throughout the world, a trend has developed to eliminate the visa requirement.

War Crimes Trials   Trials of persons from defeated states to determine their individual, as opposed to national, guilt and punishment for criminal acts committed in the course of war or in bringing on war. The Treaty of Versailles after World War I set a precedent by providing for the trial and punishment of the German Emperor and individuals in the armed forces, although the Allies never carried out the trials. After World War II, twenty-two major German war criminals were tried at Nuremberg by the International Military Tribunal, representing Britain, France, the Soviet Union, and the United States. Charged with crimes against peace, war crimes, and crimes against humanity, twelve defendants were sentenced to death, others received jail sentences, and three were acquitted. Under the Charter of the International Military Tribunal for the Far East, major Japanese war criminals were tried in Tokyo on similar charges by judges representing the eleven countries at war with Japan.

Significance   The Nuremberg and Tokyo war crimes trials opened a new page in the development of the international law of war. Prior to World Wars I and II, customary law provided that, on the termination of war, an amnesty be granted all individual enemies for any wrongful acts connected with their military service. The ferocity of total war and the bitter hatreds engendered by ideological conflict raise a question of whether a general amnesty will ever again be granted. Juristic reaction to the Nuremberg and Tokyo trials has varied. Little criticism of the judgments regarding war crimes and crimes against humanity has been raised since customary law has long recognized the right of the victor to try individual members of enemy armed forces for violations of the international laws of war. The concept of crimes against peace, however, opens new ground. Legal questions raised relating to that charge include: (1) Can a clear distinction be properly made between aggressive war as a crime in itself and crimes committed during the course of war? (2) Did the Kellogg-Briand Pact, which made aggressive war illegal, also imply individual criminal responsibility? (3) Was the distinction between aggressive war and defensive war sufficiently clear to assess individual criminal responsibility? and (4) Could the Nuremberg court, composed of judges from only four states, be considered an international tribunal representing the world community? The United Nations has sought to legitimate the principle of individual responsibility underlying the war crimes trials by developing a code of international law on crimes against the peace and security of mankind. The General Assembly has charged the International Law Commission with preparing a draft code, but the problem of developing a generally acceptable definition of aggression has delayed the process.

10. International Organization:
The United Nations and Regional Organizations

Admission The process of accepting a state for membership in an international organization. In the United Nations, the admission of new members requires a recommendation by the Security Council followed by a two-thirds vote in the General Assembly. Any permanent member of the Council may block an application since the veto is applicable to membership questions. The Charter specifies that states desiring admission to membership: (1) be peace loving; (2) accept the obligations contained in the Charter; and (3) in the judgment of the Organization, be able and willing to carry out these obligations. International public unions, such as the specialized agencies of the United Nations, generally require a two-thirds vote of the organization to admit a new member. Regional groups such as the European Community usually require a unanimous vote to admit.

Significance The admission of new members to an international organization may influence the nature, objectives, and decision-making functions of the organization. The sizable influx of new members into the United Nations during the 1960s and 1970s resulted in an expanded role for the General Assembly, increased membership in the Security Council and the Economic and Social Council (ECOSOC) to provide wider representation, and an increased emphasis on securing the objectives of economic development, human rights, and disarmament. The major admission questions for the United Nations involve the divided state of North and South Korea and Taiwan.

The goal of universalism (admission of all states to membership) is unlikely to be realized in the United Nations until major political settlements can be reached among the great powers. In addition, Switzerland has chosen to remain outside the United Nations because the obligations of membership would violate her traditional neutrality. Other states, such as Western Samoa, have chosen for financial reasons not to apply for admission to the United Nations. The major UN membership issues of the past, however, have been resolved with recognition of the People's Republic as the legitimate government of China, and with the admission of East and West Germany and Vietnam.

Amazon Pact   A treaty aimed at coordinating the development of the Amazon river basin and protecting the region's environment through rational use of its resources. Parties to the 1978 treaty include Bolivia, Brazil, Colombia, Ecuador, Guyana, Peru, Surinam, and Venezuela. Treaty provisions include: (1) careful use of the region's water resources; (2) the right of each to develop its Amazon territory so long as it does not adversely affect other members' territories; (3) free navigation on all rivers in the region; (4) improvement of health and the building of a transportation and communication infrastructure; (5) encouragement of a common research effort; and (6) promotion of tourism. An Amazon Cooperation Council, composed of ministers from each member country, meets annually to carry out the provisions of the treaty and to develop policies and programs.

Significance   The Amazon Pact is an excellent example of how independent nations within a geographical region can, despite their different political and social systems, unite to cope with common ecological and developmental problems. Although it is not a powerful and united supranational group, its ability to elicit cooperation demonstrates that certain kinds of problems can be dealt with through interstate cooperation even though no state can be bound against its will. Its main objective—to stop a ruthless, ecologically-disastrous plundering of the resources of the Amazon basin—has not been achieved, but progress has been made. Moreover, the potential for war growing out of national competition in opening the vast area to economic exploitation has been reduced. The Amazon Pact has practical and symbolic value, and both tend to contribute to the improvement of relations among the Pact's signatories.

Amendment Process Procedures by which formal changes in the constitutions of international organizations are proposed and ratified. The League Covenant provided in Article 26 that amendments would take effect when ratified by all Council members and by a majority of the Assembly, and that any member refusing to accept such amendments would cease to be a member of the League. The United Nations Charter provides that the General Assembly may propose amendments by a two-thirds vote of its members (Article 108), or a General Conference may be called by a two-thirds vote in the Assembly and by any nine members of the Security Council to propose alterations in the Charter (Article 109). Amendments, however proposed, must be ratified through national constitutional processes by two-thirds of the United Nations members, including all of the permanent members of the Security Council, before they come into force.

Significance Although the League of Nations adopted numerous amendments to the Covenant, they had little impact on the effectiveness of that organization. In the United Nations, two amendments were ratified in 1965, one enlarging the Security Council from eleven to fifteen and changing its voting majority from seven to nine, the other enlarging the Economic and Social Council from eighteen to twenty-seven members. In 1973, ECOSOC was enlarged to fifty-four members. Like most constitutional systems, that of the United Nations has been altered more extensively by interpretation, custom, and usage than by formal amendments. Because any one of the great powers may block an amendment, extensive use of the process in the future is as unlikely as in the past.

Andean Common Market An economic group established to improve its members' bargaining power within the larger Latin American Free Trade Association (LAFTA), and to foster trade and development. Members of the Andean Group include Bolivia, Chile, Colombia, Ecuador, Peru, and Venezuela. Concerned with the slow pace of economic integration within LAFTA, these nations reached agreement to establish a common market as a means for reinvigorating LAFTA. Objectives pursued by the Andean Group include: (1) eliminating trade barriers among members by establishing a common market; (2) establishing common external tariff rates; (3) encouraging industrialization through specialization by assigning industry rights among members; (4) giving special concessions to the poorer members; and (5) extending control over multinational corporations operating within the common market. The Andean Group set up a Mixed Commission at its headquarters in Lima, Peru, that functions as the Supreme Organ, aided in its decision making by a Council and a Consulting Committee of Experts. A Development Corporation that helps finance developmental projects is also part of the institutional structure. *See also* LATIN AMERICAN FREE TRADE ASSOCIATION (LAFTA), p. 321.

Significance   The Andean Common Market was originated largely as a means to overcome the lack of progress within LAFTA. Unlike the other two major economic groups in Latin America—LAFTA and the Central American Common Market—the Andean nations reject free trade and market economics in favor of "central planning," "directed economies," and "regional cooperation" as the best approaches to achieving modernization. Virtually all tariffs have been eliminated within the common market, and a common external tariff has been constructed. Despite its difficulties, the Andean Group continues to function within LAFTA despite its conflicts with the larger, more conservative members of that group.

Arab League   An Islamic regional group formed in 1945 to coordinate the members' political activities, safeguard their independence and sovereignty, and encourage cooperation in economic, social, and cultural matters. Its members are independent Middle East and North African states. The original members, Egypt, Iraq, Jordan, Lebanon, Saudi Arabia, Syria, and Yemen, have been joined by the remaining independent Arab states. The supreme decision organ of the League is the Majlis, or Council, which meets twice each year and is composed of a representative from each member. Binding decisions can be made only by unanimous vote, as in a decision to repel aggression, but those reached by a majority "bind only those that accept them." In addition, permanent committees function under Council authority to study economic and social matters and to elicit support for joint projects and programs. A secretariat headed by a secretary-general is located at League headquarters in Cairo.

Significance   Although the Arab League has demonstrated a lack of unity and common military strength in its continuing struggle against Israel, during the 1970s and 1980s an increased membership, growing economic strength, and a rising level of shared interests reflect a desire for a broader level of cooperation. This growing compatibility is reflected in League programs that established an Arab common market and set up an Arab Development Bank, several educational institutes, an Anti-Narcotics Bureau, and an Arab Press. The League has also functioned effectively as a caucusing group at the United Nations. Yet, this growing compatibility has not overcome traditional rivalries among Arab states and the struggle for leadership within the Arab bloc. After direct negotiations between Egypt and Israel led to the signing of a peace treaty, Arab unity was shattered.

Asian and Pacific Council (ASPAC)   A regional organization established in 1966 to encourage economic, social, and cultural cooperation among members. Unlike most Asian regional organizations, ASPAC's membership includes only Asian nations: Australia, Japan, Malaysia, New Zealand, Philippines, South Korea, Taiwan, and Thailand. The initiative to establish ASPAC originated with South Korea. ASPAC conferences are held annually in major cities of member states. Between general conferences, the ambassadors of member states to Thailand meet monthly in Bangkok as a standing committee under the chairmanship of the Thai foreign minister. Thailand also provides the secretariat for the organization.

Significance   Although members of the Asian and Pacific Council are openly anticommunist in their policies and support American policy in Asia, the organization professes to be nonmilitary, nonaligned, and nonideological. Unsuccessful efforts have been made to attract India to membership. ASPAC has issued proclamations and declarations on matters of common interest, as, for example, its condemnation of nuclear testing in the Asia-Pacific area. Most programs inaugurated or under consideration by ASPAC relate to joint efforts to solve problems of economic development.

Association of Southeast Asian Nations (ASEAN)   A regional organization established in 1967 to accelerate economic growth, social progress, and cultural development in Southeast Asia. The members of the ASEAN group are Indonesia, Malaysia, Philippines, Singapore, and Thailand. The regional organization is an expanded version of the Association of Southeast Asia (ASA) established in 1961 by Malaysia, Philippines, and Thailand.

Significance The Association of Southeast Asian Nations represents an effort to develop Asian solutions to Asian problems in a cooperative arrangement consisting wholly of nations in the region. Although mainly concerned with economic and social problems, the preamble to the declaration establishing ASEAN affirmed that all foreign bases in the region are "temporary and remain only with the expressed concurrence of countries concerned. . . ." Projects undertaken by the group are aimed at improving tourism, shipping, fishing, and trade. Above all, ASEAN is a forum where discussions such as those concerning the future creation of a Pacific Community are carried on. In 1980, ASEAN and the European Community signed a Cooperation Agreement to encourage increased trade between members of both.

Atlantic Charter A joint World War II declaration of war aims made by President Franklin Roosevelt and Prime Minister Winston Churchill following their discussions at sea in August, 1941. In the Charter, the two statesmen renounced territorial aggrandizement and called for acceptance of the principles of self-determination, economic cooperation, freedom of the seas, freedom of speech and religion, freedom from fear and want, and disarmament in a secure world. *See also* ATLANTIC CHARTER, p. 39.

Significance The Atlantic Charter is regarded as the initial spark that led eventually to the establishment of the United Nations. Although no specific mention was made of a postwar general international organization, the eighth and final point of the declaration referred to a "permanent system of general security" to maintain the peace after victory. The high-minded principles enunciated in the Charter were often recalled in the postwar period by independence movement leaders in Asia and Africa in the struggle for self-government.

Atlantic Community The concept of a partnership among the states of Western Europe and North America to solve common security, economic, social, and political problems. The

Atlantic Community idea, based on a common Western cultural heritage, received added impetus from the threat of aggression from Eastern Europe. Although no regional organization includes all Atlantic Community states, the Organization for Economic Cooperation and Development (OECD) and the Council of Europe have memberships that include most of the twenty-five states in the region. Other groups that have helped to integrate the policies of the states in the region include the North Atlantic Treaty Organization (NATO), the European Community, and the European Free Trade Association (EFTA). *See also* POLITICAL COMMUNITY, p. 331.

Significance The development of the Atlantic Community idea helped to produce a *rapprochement* between former enemies of World War II and a unity of policy fostered through joint consultations on major issues. In the 1960s and 1970s, France's withdrawal from NATO, American preoccupation with the Vietnam war, and the reduced threat of aggression from Eastern Europe contributed to a weakening of Atlantic Community ties. Resurgent nationalism has slowed progress toward the original goal of an Atlantic union based on a supranational institutional framework for political decison making. Yet, in the 1980s the rationale for an Atlantic Community of shared interests that fostered the original integration movement persists.

Benelux A customs union agreement established by Belgium, Luxembourg, and the Netherlands to eliminate trade barriers, establish a single external tariff, and foster economic union among the three. The agreement, which was signed in London during World War II and entered into effect on January 1, 1948, abolished most internal tariffs and established a common external tariff. A treaty to harmonize the fiscal and monetary policies of the three by establishing an economic union came into force in 1960. Benelux countries have also agreed to negotiate and enter economic and trade treaties and arrangements as a unit, with no separate national treaties to be concluded. Benelux organization includes a Conference of Cabinet Ministers, a Council for Economic Union, an Administrative Council on Customs Duties, an Administrative Council to provide for a common foreign economic policy toward other states, and a secretariat located at Benelux headquarters in Brussels. *See also* CUSTOMS UNION, p. 116.

Significance   The full realization of economic integration objectives has not been achieved by Benelux, but much progress has been made. Increasingly, Benelux has been overshadowed by the larger framework of the European Community (EC) as the means for securing integration. At the same time, it has proved useful in combining the bargaining power of the smallest three members of the EC against that of the larger members—France, Germany, Britain, and Italy. One of the major difficulties standing in the way of the achievement of full Benelux integration objectives has been that of harmonizing domestic policies between a laissez-faire-oriented Belgian economy and the more extensive direction of economic activity by the Dutch government.

Bretton Woods Conference   The United Nations Monetary and Financial Conference that drafted the Articles of Agreement for the International Bank for Reconstruction and Development (IBRD) and the International Monetary Fund (IMF). Called at the initiative of President Franklin Roosevelt, the conference met at Bretton Woods, New Hampshire, July 1–22, 1944, with forty-four nations represented. *See also* INTERNATIONAL BANK FOR RECONSTRUCTION AND DEVELOPMENT, p. 133; INTERNATIONAL MONETARY FUND, p. 135.

Significance   The Bretton Woods Conference represented the initial attack on the problems of postwar economic reconstruction. The IBRD and IMF are part of the cooperative base for building a sound international monetary and investment system to replace the chaotic conditions fostered by the economic nationalism of the 1930s. The Bank and the Fund were established on December 27, 1945, when the necessary number of nations accepted the Articles of Agreement for each, and in November, 1947, both were brought into a specialized agency relationship with the United Nations. The Bank and the Fund represented the application of Keynesian economic principles and policies to the international economic system.

Caribbean Community and Common Market (CARICOM)
A regional economic group established by the Treaty of Chaguaramas of 1973 which set up a customs union with free trade among members and a common external tariff, and called

for the harmonization of the domestic economic policies of its members. Its basic Charter objectives include maximizing the balanced development of members, achieving the highest level of economic integration possible, developing a common bargaining position toward other regional economic groups, and fostering import protection through a Common Protective Policy aimed at encouraging local industry and agriculture. CARICOM grew out of the successful economic cooperation engendered by the Caribbean Free Trade Association (CARIFTA). CARICOM membership has included a number of Caribbean independent states, semi-independent states still "associated" with Great Britain, and several colonies. All remaining nonsovereign entities, however, are moving toward full independence. Members are divided for decision-making purposes into two categories: (1) the More Developed Countries (MDCs) which include the independent states of Barbados, the Bahamas, Guyana, Jamaica, and Trinidad; and (2) the Less Developed Countries (LDCs) which include Antigua, Belize, Dominica, Grenada, Montserrat, St. Kitts, St. Lucia, and St. Vincent. Other Caribbean states and colonies have shown interest in joining CARICOM. CARICOM functions through a Heads of Government Conference (HGC) which is its central governing body. It also uses a Common Market Council (CMC) to make recommendations to the HGC, and a Caribbean Community Secretariat serves both CARICOM and CARIFTA. Subsidiary agencies also help the organization make progress toward achieving its goals.

Significance   The Caribbean Community and Common Market has moved a long way toward realization of its basic Charter objectives. In doing so, it has served as a model for other Third World developing countries that are searching for a breakthrough approach that will show them the way to modernization. Using the European Community as a model, CARICOM continues to make steady progress toward economic and political integration, but the process is a slow one. The main problems standing in the way of a more rapid transition toward unity is the built-in conflict between the MDCs and the LDCs. As in most such groupings, members with stronger economies tend to push for freer trade whereas the weaker-economy members are reluctant to give up many governmental programs of protection for their industry and agriculture. Other threats to CARICOM's continued growth include conflicts among members over the role of foreign investment, and over whether free enterprise or socialism should provide the basic guidelines for the future.

Central American Common Market (CACM)   A regional organization that seeks to promote economic development in member states through a customs union and industrial integration scheme. Five Central American states—Costa Rica, El Salvador, Guatemala, Honduras, and Nicaragua—have ratified an Economic Integration Treaty of 1960 that, together with several protocols and supplementary agreements, provides for a significant integration of their economies. Under an Integration Industries proposal in 1958, each member would be permitted to designate certain industries that will, in each case, have exclusive unrestricted free trade access to the entire five-country market for a ten-year period. The assumption underlying the common market system is that industrialization and specialization will be encouraged by the broader market and free trade arrangement, so that foreign investment capital in sizable amounts will be attracted to the region. Common Market decisions are made by: (1) the Central American Economic Council, which consists of members' Economic Ministers and develops policies concerning the integration of their economies; (2) an Executive Council, which implements decisions made by the Economic Council; and (3) a secretariat that provides technical and administrative assistance at the Guatemala City headquarters. The Central American Bank for Economic Integration functions within the system by helping to finance the development program. *See also* ORGANIZATION OF CENTRAL AMERICAN STATES, p. 330.

Significance   The Central American Common Market eliminated virtually all customs duties and trade increased substantially during the 1960s and 1970s. The common market idea had to overcome much nationalist rivalry dating back more than a century, and the CACM represents the highest level of economic integration yet obtained in Latin America. Although it has not provided an easy shortcut to development, significant progress occurred and investment capital was increasingly attracted from the United States. However, in the 1980s several members are torn by guerrilla warfare, and political and economic differences have sapped much of CACM's strength.

Central Treaty Organization (CENTO) A regional alliance established on American initiative in 1955 to provide security in the Middle East against communist aggression and to foster economic and social cooperation among its members. CENTO was known as the Baghdad Pact until Iraq withdrew in 1959, following the revolutionary overthrow of its pro-Western government. Membership after 1959 included Britain, Iran, Pakistan, and Turkey. The United States, although never a formal member, functioned as an associate and concluded bilateral agreements with Iran, Pakistan and Turkey that committed it to take action to aid the signatories to resist a communist attack. A Council was set up to function as the Supreme Organ of the Organization, aided by four main committees (military, economic, countersubversion, and liaison) and a secretariat headed by a secretary-general was located at CENTO headquarters in Ankara. *See also* BAGHDAD PACT, p. 160.

Significance The Central Treaty Organization functioned primarily as a security alliance, and only incidentally in economic and social affairs. Combined CENTO forces carried out naval, ground, and air exercises, and actions were undertaken under CENTO auspices to control subversion in member countries. A 3000-mile military telecommunication service linking Ankara to Teheran and Karachi was developed, and numerous other communication and transportation links among member states were constructed. Yet, political differences among its members, its failure to attract Arab states to membership, and the absence of an overt threat of aggression from communist states weakened the ties among alliance members. In 1979, the Iranian Revolution and the seizure of American hostages led to a *de facto* withdrawal of Iran from the alliance, raising questions about CENTO's future.

Collective Security A concept that provides for a global security system based on the agreement of all or most states to take common action against any nation that illegally breaks the peace. To be effective, a collective security system requires agreement to defend the status quo against violent change, a definite assurance from member states that action will be undertaken against law-breaking states, and a willingness of states not directly threatened to participate in sanctions against an aggressor. Theoretically, a collective security system is based on the assumption that no state will be likely to challenge the power of the world community, but that if aggression occurs, all will honor their commitment to take police action. A collective security system should not be confused with an alliance or balance-of-power system in which states on either side are kept in check and peace is maintained by the tendency toward a power equilibrium. Only two collective security systems—the League of Nations and the United Nations—have been attempted in the modern world. In the United Nations, primary responsibility to preserve world peace is assigned to the Security Council, which may call upon all members to levy sanctions under Chapter VII of the Charter. Since adoption of the Uniting for Peace Resolution of 1950, the General Assembly may authorize collective action against an aggressor when the Council is deadlocked. Each of the five great powers (Britain, China, France, United States, and Soviet Union) may block collective action by casting a veto. *See also* SANCTIONS, p. 332; UNITED NATIONS: SECURITY COUNCIL, p. 354; UNITING FOR PEACE RESOLUTION, p. 358.

Significance   Collective security meets its most severe test when confronted by an overt or covert aggression committed in violation of community norms. The world's first peace-keeping arrangement, the League of Nations, proved unable to meet these challenges when made by great powers (Japan, Italy, Germany, and the Soviet Union), resulting in the collapse of the League security system. The United Nations in 1950 undertook the world's first collective security action involving military sanctions when it called upon members to contribute forces for action against North Korea. In 1956, the United Nations was confronted simultaneously with two collective security cases: military repression of the Hungarian revolution by the Soviet Union, and an attack by Britain, France and Israel against Egypt. Although the United Nations did not employ sanctions in either situation, it produced a moral condemnation of the Soviet action and helped to pressure the belligerents in the Middle East to stop fighting. The great-power split in the Security Council and the fear of nuclear war have been the main factors in reducing the effectiveness of the United Nations collective security system.

Commonwealth of Nations   A voluntary association of independent states that were once parts of the British Empire. Commonwealth members include almost thirty European, African, Asian, Western Hemispheric, and Oceanian countries. Queen Elizabeth is recognized as "the symbol of the free association of its independent member nations and as such the Head of the Commonwealth." Some members—India, Pakistan, Malaysia, Cyprus, and Ghana, for example—have become republics and no longer accept the British sovereign as their national head of state. The essence of the Commonwealth system is free cooperation engendered through consultations among members. No formal treaty ties or permanent institutions exist, except for a secretariat. Adherence to the Commonwealth for many years was encouraged by trade preferences and sterling bloc membership, capital and technical assistance grants by advanced members to developing states, military aid to those whose security was threatened, and common institutions and language. Consultations are carried on at many levels, with meetings of the Commonwealth Prime Ministers held whenever necessary. *See also* IMPERIAL PREFERENCES, p. 131.

Significance The Commonwealth is a unique political system in that its members freely cooperate and assist each other without specific agreements or commitments. During the First and Second World Wars, for example, Commonwealth states joined Britain in declaring war and volunteered large expeditionary forces to fight the common enemy. States granted independence from the Empire may freely opt to join or reject membership, and members are free to leave the Commonwealth at any time. Burma and the Maldive Islands, for example, chose not to associate with the Commonwealth on gaining independence, and Ireland and South Africa withdrew from the association in 1939 and 1961, respectively. Increasingly, issues within the Commonwealth have strained the ties of membership. Moreover, Britain's membership in the European Community has weakened the preferential trade system central to the unity of the system. The future viability of the Commonwealth depends on how effectively its members reconcile their economic and political differences so that the association can continue to offer channels for cooperation in solving common problems.

Concert of Europe An *ad hoc* system of consultation among the great powers developed after the Napoleonic wars. The Concert met sporadically during the nineteenth century to settle major issues that threatened to disrupt the peace. It included Austria, England, France, Prussia, and Russia, later joined by Germany and Italy, and smaller powers when they were directly involved in the matter under discussion. The concert system functioned mainly through international conferences called at the initiative of a great power that believed that the peace was threatened. The result was the establishment of great power hegemony that functioned effectively until the unity of the great powers was destroyed by a rigid polarization of its members into two rival alliances—the Triple Entente (Britain, France, and Russia) and the Triple Alliance (Germany, Austria-Hungary, and Italy).

Significance The Concert of Europe system contributed much to the stability of European politics during the nineteenth century, but the breakdown of great power unity led directly to World War I. The effectiveness of the system—so long as a common interest in maintaining peace persisted—was recognized by the framers of the League Covenant and the United Nations Charter. In each global organization, a Council dominated by the great powers was assigned special responsibilities for maintaining peace and security. The Security Council continues to function as a forum for great-power negotiation in the Concert of Europe tradition.

Confederation An association of states that seek to achieve their national objectives through common political or economic institutions. A confederation differs from a federation in that its members retain full sovereignty whereas, in a federation, political authority is constitutionally divided between a central and regional units of government. Global organizations, such as the League of Nations and the United Nations, and regional organizations, such as NATO, SEATO, the OAS, and the EC, embody the confederation principle. Decisions may be made by unanimity or majority voting, but no state can be forced to accept a majority decision.

Significance Confederation is a half-way house between independent state action and the establishment of a federal system. Advocates of world federation regard a global confederation like the United Nations as an evolutionary step toward a higher level of political integration, as occurred in the American experience. Although a confederation lacks the powers to make and enforce laws, its decision-making authority is as extensive as the consensus developed within the association.

Council of Europe   A regional quasi-parliamentary organization that encourages political, economic, and social cooperation and seeks to develop a sense of "European" unity among its members. The Council of Europe was established at London in 1949 by Belgium, Britain, Denmark, France, Ireland, Italy, Luxembourg, the Netherlands, Norway, and Sweden. Eight additional states—Austria, Cyprus, Germany (Federal Republic), Greece, Iceland, Malta, Switzerland, and Turkey—were subsequently admitted to membership. In structure, the Council consists of two chambers—a Consultative Assembly composed of delegates chosen by their national parliaments but free to speak and vote as individuals, and a Committee of Ministers representing member governments. The Consultative Assembly functions as the deliberative organ of the Council, while the Committee of Ministers has sole power to make decisions, with each government having the veto power. The Council makes recommendations to member governments and approves treaties and agreements that, when ratified by member states, constitute international legislation. Both organs are free to debate any matter except military questions. The Committee of Ministers meets monthly; the Assembly meets in spring, autumn, and winter sessions. A secretariat located at Council headquarters in Strasbourg serves both organs. *See also* EUROPEAN CONVENTION ON HUMAN RIGHTS, p. 311.

Significance   The Council of Europe at its founding represented an initial step toward an eventual union of states into a European federation. The Consultative Assembly in its early years drafted a statute for a general European Political Community consisting of a parliament, executive, and court directly responsible to the people of Europe. When the French Parliament killed the proposal for a European Defense Community in 1954, however, the Political Community idea was abandoned. About fifty conventions and agreements have been signed by the Committee of Ministers in such fields as university admissions, patents, social security, human rights, extradition, and peaceful settlement of disputes. Many have been ratified by member governments, including the European Convention on Human Rights, which permits individuals to appeal beyond their national courts for a binding decision by an international body. The Council of Europe is evolving, albeit slowly, toward the ideal that guided its architects—a united, federal Community of Europe. However, the European Parliament of the European Community has taken over consideration of many economic, political, and social issues.

Council of Mutual Economic Assistance (COMECON or CEMA) A regional organization established in 1949 under Soviet direction to integrate the economies of Eastern Europe. COMECON members include Albania (active membership ceased in 1961), Bulgaria, Czechoslovakia, East Germany, Hungary, Mongolia, Poland, Romania, and the Soviet Union. The organizational machinery of COMECON is headed by a Council that functions as the decision-making organ except on matters of basic policy, on which it is limited to making recommendations to member governments. A permanent Executive Committee implements policy decisions, more than twenty standing commissions carry out planning and operations in major commodity fields, and a secretariat headquartered in Moscow functions under the Council's direction. The economic objectives of COMECON include a politically determined specialization of production in member countries, an East European free trade area, accessibility of raw materials, and cooperation in scientific research and technology.

Significance The Council of Mutual Economic Assistance was established as a Soviet response to American economic and military programs in Western Europe and the defection of Yugoslavia from the Eastern bloc. It posited a division of labor and specialization aimed at creating an economic dependence of the satellite states on the Soviet Union. Following the death of Stalin, COMECON was given a new emphasis in Nikita Khrushchev's economic programs. During the 1960s, however, growing nationalism in Eastern Europe further weakened the basic premises of COMECON, with members such as Romania and Bulgaria refusing to abide by a specialization that accords a preferred industrial role to the Soviet Union and East Germany. Although the Common Market in Western Europe provides a model for freer trade, the natural tendency of socialist states to strive for national self-sufficiency has hampered efforts to achieve economic integration. As an example of the continuing importance of the organization, in 1979 COMECON members signed an agreement in Moscow to switch from oil to nuclear power as the main source of energy over the period from 1981 to 1990.

Danube Commission An international body that regulates and facilitates traffic on the Danube. The Danube Commission, composed of one representative from each riparian state, sets up uniform traffic regulations and carries out projects to aid navigation and commerce on this major central-European waterway. Although decisions are arrived at by a majority vote, a state may block a Commission project on its territory. The contemporary Danube Commission is the successor to two Commissions established by the Treaty of Paris in 1856 to encourage and control traffic on the Danube.

Significance   The Danube Commissions of 1856 were two of the early regional international institutions that set a pattern in functional organization and decision-making processes followed by numerous regional groups today. Since adoption of the Danube Convention of 1948, most of the responsibility for maintaining navigation on the river rests with the riparian states. The once-extensive powers exercised by the Danube Commission—to levy and collect fines, build and maintain ports and facilities, even fly its own flag—have been reduced by the chilly atmosphere of the Cold War.

Egalitarianism, Elitism, Majoritarianism   Concepts that relate to the basic nature and decision processes of international organs. The principle of egalitarianism embodies the idea of traditional equality of states under international law; since each possesses supreme power (sovereignty), all are juridically equal. Elitism, on the other hand, recognizes that great-power politics makes some states in fact "more equal" than others. Majoritarianism offers a decision-making system in keeping with the practices of democratic institutions within states.

Significance   All three principles—egalitarianism, elitism, and majoritarianism—find numerous applications within international organizations in the contemporary world. The first, for example, is applied in the General Assembly of the United Nations—as it was in the League of Nations Assembly—with each member represented and having an equal vote. The typical general conference of international public unions, such as those used by most of the specialized agencies, and the basic policy-determining organ in most regional organizations are also based on equality of representation and voting. The elitist principle—based on the historical precedents of the Concert of Europe and the League Council—finds its most notable application in the permanent membership and veto power exercised by five great powers in the United Nations Security Council. Elitism is also reflected in systems of weighted voting, such as those found in the World Bank and International Monetary Fund (member votes are determined by financial contributions), and in the European Parliament, where seats accorded members range from a maximum for Britain, France, Germany, and Italy to a minimum for Luxembourg. Majoritarianism has gained wide acceptance among international institutions in the twentieth century. Every principal organ of the United Nations, for example, may reach decisions by less than a unanimous vote.

European Atomic Energy Community (Euratom)

A regional organization established by the Treaty of Rome of 1957 that coordinates peaceful atomic research and development, provides for joint power projects, and encourages a pooling of scientific and technical information. Euratom, which became operational in 1958 at the same time that the European Economic Community (EEC) began to function, has the same membership as the European Coal and Steel Community (ECSC) and the Common Market (Belgium, Britain, Denmark, France, Germany, Greece, Ireland, Italy, Luxembourg, and the Netherlands). Decisions of Euratom are made within the common institutional framework of the European Community. *See also* EUROPEAN COMMUNITY, p. 309.

Significance The European Atomic Energy Community has established a common market for nuclear products, developed four major atomic research centers, and helped to build a number of atomic power plants on the continent. Some observers view Euratom's long-range objectives of securing cheap atomic power for Continental industry as at least equal in importance to those of the EEC's common market and ECSC's coal and steel union. Dwindling reserves of coal and the possible cutoff of oil shipments from the Middle East—as occurred during the Suez crises of 1956–57, 1967, and 1973—have accentuated anxiety over future power resources. Major research activities of Euratom are aimed at unlocking the door to the unlimited and inexpensive potentiality of atomic fusion as a power source.

European Coal and Steel Community (ECSC)   A regional organization established by the Treaty of Paris in 1952 to harmonize production policies and establish a common market for coal, iron ore, and steel. The members of the

Community—Belgium, Britain, Denmark, France, Germany, Greece, Ireland, Italy, Luxembourg, and the Netherlands— have agreed on various common domestic policies to encourage production and competitive marketing conditions. Decisions of the ECSC are made within the common organizational framework of the European Community. *See also* EUROPEAN COMMUNITY, p. 309.

Significance   The European Coal and Steel Community's original objectives included not only the creation of a vast Continental market to spur mining and production, but the fostering of a *rapprochement* between France and Germany and control over Germany's future war-making potentiality. These objectives have been generally realized. Although coal production has slumped drastically as other energy sources have replaced it, steel output has more than doubled since 1952. In a typical outside reaction to a preferential marketing system, however, the percentage of steel sales to the rest of the world has declined. Closer political ties between France and Germany during the 1960s are at least in part a result of the economic integration movement inaugurated by the ECSC arrangement. The successes of the European Community, including operations of the Common Market and of Euratom, owe much to the early achievements of ECSC.

European Community   The common political structure established to make economic decisions for the European Coal and Steel Community (ECSC), the European Economic Community (EEC), and the European Atomic Energy Community (Euratom). The European Community institutions include the Council of Ministers, the Commission, the European Parliament, and the Court of Justice. The Council and the Commission constitute a dual executive, with the former directly representing the views of the governments of the Six and the latter functioning as a supranational organ for the Community. Some decisions are made by the Council, some by the Commission, and some by the Council following proposal by the Commission. The Commission's main function is to initiate Community policy under guidelines provided by the three basic treaties or by the Council. Important decisions are given final approval by the Council. Large states (Britain, France, Germany, and Italy) have two members on the Commission whereas the small states (Belgium, Denmark, Greece, Ireland, Luxembourg, and the Netherlands) have only one. The Council makes important decisions by unanimity, but others are made by a qualified majority through a weighted voting system, and by a simple majority. The European Parliament, first created as the Common Assembly for the ECSC in 1952, serves as a deliberative body and consultative organ for the Community, and as an overseer of its actions. Although it has no power to make laws or decisions binding upon member states, it has served as a source for the initiation of new policies of economic liberalization and political unity. Delegates to the Parliament, formerly appointed by national parliaments, have been elected since 1979 by direct universal suffrage and are organized and vote on most issues as three transnational political groups—Christian Democrat, Socialist, and Liberal—rather than as national blocs. The ten-member Court of Justice, also established in 1952, functions as the common court to interpret and apply the Community treaties and to resolve disputes between Community organs and member states or within either group. Its powers to interpret and review more closely resemble those of a national supreme court than those of other international courts. Other institutions that operate within the Community framework include the European Investment Bank (EIB), which encourages balanced Community development through loans and guarantees, and almost a hundred specialized committees. In addition, the Community has working arrangements with outside countries, such as Turkey, Spain, and Portugal, and with sixty-one African, Caribbean, and Pacific states as a result of the Lomé Agreement of 1975 which established special EEC/Associated States trading arrangements. *See also* EUROPEAN ATOMIC ENERGY COMMUNITY, p. 308; EUROPEAN COAL AND STEEL COMMUNITY, p. 308; EUROPEAN ECONOMIC COMMUNITY, p. 312.

Significance The common institutions of the European Community represent the highest level of integration achieved in the contemporary state system. They are both products and participants in an integrative process which is moving Western Europe toward full political and economic union. As "European" institutions, they have helped to develop concepts of a European man, of European solutions to European problems, and the still-distant but evolving idea of a United States of Europe. But in a more immediate way they have functioned as effective decision-making bodies in resolving common economic problems in coal and steel production, marketing, general trade and commercial policies, tariff negotiations, and atomic energy development. Observers anticipate that during the 1980s membership in the European Community will be considerably expanded, with Portugal and Spain among the potential new members.

European Convention on Human Rights   A treaty, in force since 1953, that establishes international machinery for the protection of human rights in controversies arising among signatory states. The European Convention, developed under the auspices of the Council of Europe, has been accepted by fifteen states (Austria, Belgium, Britain, Cyprus, Denmark, Germany, Greece, Iceland, Ireland, Italy, Luxembourg, the Netherlands, Norway, Sweden, and Turkey). Only three Council of Europe members—France, Malta, and Switzerland—decided not to become parties to the Convention. Ten of the ratifying states further agree that appeals on human rights issues by individuals and private groups can be carried beyond their state courts to an international body. Petitions are first reviewed by a Commission on Human Rights composed of fifteen members selected from member states. If the complaint is admissible, the Commission reports its findings and recommends action to the Committee of Ministers of the Council of Europe. The Committee of Ministers, if unable to work out an amicable settlement, may decide the case by a two-thirds vote. Finally, a losing party may appeal to the European Court of Human Rights if he or she is a citizen of one of the states that has ratified an optional protocol accepting its jurisdiction. Each of the twenty members of the Council of Europe is represented on the Court whether it has accepted the protocol or not. Enforcement of Court decisions depends on voluntary compliance by affected states since no sanctions are provided by the Convention. *See also* COUNCIL OF EUROPE, p. 305; HUMAN RIGHTS, p. 316.

Significance   The European Convention on Human Rights provides for the most extensive international machinery for the protection of human rights in the history of the state system. Yet, in practice it has not served as a vigorous defender of individual liberties. Of several thousand complaints brought to the Commission, only a few have been found admissible, and the Court has considered only a handful of cases. In 1979, in a typical case, the European Court of Human Rights ruled by an 11 to 9 vote that a British court injunction prohibiting London's *Sunday Times* from publishing an article because it would prejudice a lawsuit against the manufacturer of thalidomide violated the European Convention on Human Rights. The Convention's most important impact has been in breaking new ground for international action in a field in which individuals are increasingly demanding more protection than is provided by their own governments. The European system serves as a model for other regional groups and may contribute to the building of a global system under the aegis of the United Nations.

European Economic Community (EEC)   A regional organization, established by the Treaty of Rome of 1957, which has developed a common market among its members, reached agreement on common Community and national economic policies, and set up a common external tariff wall. Among its ten member countries (Belgium, Britain, Denmark, France, Germany, Greece, Ireland, Italy, Luxembourg, and the Netherlands), goods may flow freely without tariffs or other hindrances, labor and capital are completely mobile, and many national policies relating to production and marketing have been harmonized. Agricultural products, as a result of an agreement reached in 1966, are subsidized by the Community from a common EEC fund financed equally from import levies and from contributions by member governments. Forty-six African, Caribbean, and Pacific Associated States, all former colonies of EEC members, are linked with the EEC through the Lome Convention of 1975, and other European states have established an associate relationship with the Community. Decisions of the EEC are made within the common institutional framework of the European Community. *See also* EUROPEAN COMMUNITY, p. 309.

Significance   The original objective of the European Economic Community, to establish a common market and a common external tariff among its members within twelve to fifteen years, was accomplished in ten and one-half, by July, 1968. Although the EEC helped to promote an unprecedented prosperity on the Continent, encouraged a free flow of capital and the migration of millions of workers, and vastly improved transportion and communication facilities, its most lasting contribution may be the impetus it has given to eventual political federation. Its impact, however, has not always been wholly salutary: British membership at first was vetoed by France, resulting in the establishment of the rival European Free Trade Association (EFTA); the new Franco-German relationship encouraged by the EEC partnership helped to strain Continental relations with the United States, resulting in French withdrawal from NATO; and other preferential trading systems have been established in many areas of the world, increasing trade rivalry and discrimination between blocs. EEC's future role will depend upon whether it pursues "inward-" or "outward-looking" policies, that is, whether it limits the scope of its preferential system or encourages an expanding membership aiming at a broader multilateral system.

European Free Trade Association (EFTA)   A regional organization established by the Stockholm Convention of 1959 to eliminate tariffs and other trade barriers among members and to harmonize internal production cost factors. In addition to setting up a timetable to eliminate industrial tariffs by 1970, EFTA's members (Austria, Britain, Denmark, Norway, Portugal, Sweden, and Switzerland) agreed to try to reduce trade barriers on agriculture and fish. In 1961, EFTA was joined by Finland as an associate member through the FINEFTA treaty, which provided for extension of the free trade area to Finland, a special council to resolve questions relating to Finnish membership, and the continuance of Finland's special trade arrangements with the Soviet Union. Heading EFTA's simple organizational structure is a Council of Ministers that settles disputes, reviews complaints, makes recommendations to member governments, and serves as the agency for negotiating major decisions. In addition, six standing committees make recommendations to the Council on policy questions, a secretariat functions at the Geneva headquarters, and representatives of EFTA countries to the Consultative Assembly of the Council of Europe meet informally at Strasbourg during annual sessions. EFTA's role was greatly weakened but not destroyed by the decision of two members—Britain and Denmark—to join the rival European Economic Community (EEC) in 1973. By 1977, a free trade area comprising all EEC and EFTA members was completed.

Significance   Dubbed from the outset the "Outer Seven," EFTA represented in the main an effort to secure a sound bargaining position with the "Inner Six" of the Common Market. EFTA's existence was threatened in 1973 when Britain and Denmark were admitted to membership in the European Economic Community, but EFTA was revitalized by the creation of a common free trade area. All tariffs and other barriers to trade in industrial goods among members have been abolished. Little progress, however, has been made in reducing tariffs on fish and agricultural products. EFTA's future will depend to a considerable extent on the success or failure of the larger, more powerful EEC, and on whether EFTA nations can compete effectively with EEC members.

Expulsion, Suspension, Withdrawal   Procedures by which membership or the rights of membership in an international organization are terminated or temporarily suspended. Expulsion and suspension are potential sanctions that can be applied against recalcitrant members of an international organization, and the right of withdrawal confirms the sovereignty of all members. Under the League of Nations, the Covenant provided: (1) that any member could withdraw from the organization after giving two years' notice, provided that all its obligations were fulfilled (Art. 1); (2) that a member that had violated any convenant of the League could be expelled by a unanimous vote of the Council (Art. 16); and (3) that a member that refused to accept an amendment adopted to the Covenant would terminate its membership (Art. 26). The United Nations Charter provides: (1) that the rights and privileges of membership may be suspended by the General Assembly upon Security Council recommendation when preventive or enforcement action has been taken against the member (Art. 5); (2) that a member that persistently violates Charter principles may be expelled by the General Assembly upon Security Council recommendation (Art. 6); and (3) that any member two or more years in arrears in its financial contributions may be deprived of its vote in the General Assembly. Although the Charter does not provide for withdrawal, its framers at San Francisco approved a declaration that admitted the right of withdrawal.

Significance   Three members—Germany, Italy, and Japan—withdrew from the League of Nations after committing aggressions, some of the smaller member states left for financial reasons, and the Soviet Union was expelled for its attack on Finland in 1939. In the United Nations, only one member—Indonesia—withdrew, but returned to active membership a year later in 1966. Efforts to invoke Article 19 to deprive financially delinquent members of their votes in the General Assembly in 1964 temporarily immobilized the Assembly during its nineteenth session. By 1981, not one of the three available Charter provisions to suspend rights or expel members had been invoked. Membership in the United Nations, more so than in the League, remains a coveted privilege unlikely to be taken from members or voluntarily relinquished by them.

Food and Agriculture Organization (FAO)   A specialized agency of the United Nations, originally created in May, 1943. Members agree in the Preamble to FAO's Constitution to work toward "raising levels of nutrition and standards of living . . . efficiency in the production and distribution of all food . . . bettering the conditions of rural populations, and thus contributing toward an expanding world economy. . . ." These goals are sought through: (1) collecting and distributing information; (2) recommending national and international action to improve conservation, production, processing, marketing, and food distribution; and (3) furnishing technical assistance and organizing agricultural missions. Headquarters of FAO are in Rome. See also SPECIALIZED AGENCY, p. 355.

Significance   Considerable progress has been made through FAO's efforts to raise food production, especially in underdeveloped areas. In many cases, however, population growth has reduced these gains or turned them into losses when measured on a per capita basis. Paradoxically, FAO's success in helping to avert famines and in improving nutrition has added to its long-range problem of feeding an ever-expanding world population. Many developing countries that once exported surplus food, for example, have become net importers.

Functionalism   The theory that postulates the building of a world community slowly and cumulatively through progressively expanding programs of economic and social cooperation rather than by political integration. Functionalism is based on the premise that economic and social problems tend to be worldwide in scope and, hence, a coherent attack upon them necessitates common action by members of the state system. Habits of cooperation that result from successful progress toward objectives in one field may be transferred into other areas of needed activity.

Significance Functionalism as a theory of international integration helps to explain the evolution of a consensus among nations which enables them to move to higher levels of cooperation. The ultimate consequence of the process, functionalists assert, might be a world government based on interlocking functional units. Moreover, as the base of economic and social cooperation expands, a "spin-off" effect may occur that could encourage the building of a political community per se. The functionalist theory has been used by scholars seeking to develop a comprehensive explanation for the twentieth century phenomenon of economic and social integration in the state system.

Human Rights Protection for individuals from arbitrary interference with or curtailment of life, liberty, and equal protection of the laws by government or private individuals and groups. Domestic guarantees embodied in national constitutions and laws are supplemented by international protection afforded through the actions of international organizations. Many nations also regard the safeguarding of the economic and social rights of individuals—as, for example, the right to employment, to medical protection, to leisure—to be equal in importance to the older concept of political rights. Several regional organizations also provide guarantees for human rights. *See also* EUROPEAN CONVENTION ON HUMAN RIGHTS, p. 311; GENOCIDE CONVENTION, p. 348; UNIVERSAL DECLARATION OF HUMAN RIGHTS, p. 359.

Significance International activity in the field of protecting human rights has been carried on since 1946 mainly within the United Nations framework by the General Assembly and the Economic and Social Council and their various committees and commissions. These activities have included: (1) the enunciation of principles to serve as voluntary norms for member states, as in the Universal Declaration of Human Rights; (2) the adoption of multilateral conventions that constitute enforceable guarantees within states that have ratified them, as in the United Nations covenants that outlaw genocide and slavery and protect the political rights of women; (3) providing information and assistance to national governments, as in the annual *Yearbook on Human Rights*; and (4) undertaking action against flagrant violators through Assembly condemnations and, as in the cases of South Africa and Rhodesia, the levying of an arms embargo and economic sanctions. Much controversy in the United Nations has arisen between those states that define human rights in traditional civil and political terms and those that place primary emphasis on economic and social rights. On the regional level, examples of human rights systems include the European Convention on Human Rights, authored by the Council of Europe and signed in 1950, the 1975 Helsinki Accord developed by the Conference on Security and Cooperation in Europe, and the Inter-American Convention on the Granting of Civil Rights to Women.

Inter-Governmental Maritime Consultative Organization (IMCO)   A specialized agency of the United Nations, established to further cooperation in matters relating to shipping, safety, and passenger service on the high seas. IMCO was established under a 1948 convention that came into force in 1958 after receiving sufficient ratifications. IMCO's structure includes an Assembly that meets every two years, with all members having an equal vote, a Council of sixteen members that functions as an executive body, a Maritime Safety Committee, and a secretariat at its London headquarters headed by a secretary-general. *See also* SPECIALIZED AGENCY, p. 355.

Significance   The Inter-Governmental Maritime Consultative Organization has been active in diverse fields ranging from prevention of pollution of the sea by oil to encouragement of tourism. It has sought to reduce governmental discrimination against foreign shipping and restrictive business practices carried on by shipping concerns. Numerous conventions have been hammered out by the Assemblies, convoked every two years since 1959.

International Atomic Energy Agency (IAEA)   An agency of the United Nations established in 1957 to foster cooperation among nations in developing atomic energy for peaceful purposes. The IAEA was first proposed by President Eisenhower in his Atoms for Peace proposals before the General Assembly in 1953. *See also* ATOMS FOR PEACE PLAN, p. 204.

Significance   The International Atomic Energy Agency was created to reduce the threat of war by encouraging cooperation, especially between the atomic powers and the developing states. It seeks to raise living standards in the world by developing cheap power sources and by teaching the new technology to the scientists of the underdeveloped countries. The IAEA has sponsored numerous research projects, made studies concerning health and safety standards, and furnished fissionable materials to countries for research purposes. Special safeguards have been established to prevent the use for military purposes of fissionable materials supplied by the IAEA. Founders of the Agency hoped that its operations would build the foundation for an eventual international system of control and inspection for nuclear weapons.

International Civil Aviation Organization (ICAO) A specialized agency of the United Nations established in 1947 to develop and to regulate international air transportation. The ICAO applies the principles and law incorporated in the Convention on International Civil Aviation signed at Chicago in 1944, which supersedes earlier air agreements for member states. An Assembly composed of all members, each having one vote, meets once every three years to decide general policies of the Organization. An executive Council elected by the Assembly for three-year terms meets regularly to adopt navigation standards, to arbitrate disputes among members, and to provide extensive information on air transport. Subsidiary bodies appointed by the Council study all aspects of international air transportation and make reports to the Council. Under the Chicago Convention members have reciprocal privileges to fly across each other's territories without landing and, under varying circumstances, to land and take on passengers and cargo. Headquarters of the ICAO are in Montreal. Most nations are members of ICAO. *See also* SPECIALIZED AGENCY, p. 355.

Significance The International Civil Aviation Organization has been one of the most active of the specialized agencies as a result of the expansion in world air transportation. Every international flight today depends heavily upon information, standards, facilities, and services around the globe provided through ICAO programs. The ICAO has also been a leading contributor to the United Nations Development Program by providing experts and missions as consultants to developing states and in setting up regional training centers to prepare new nations for the air age.

International Labor Organization (ILO)   A specialized agency of the United Nations, originally established in 1919 under the League of Nations to improve working conditions in member countries. The ILO functions by offering advice and providing for information exchange, by setting standards, and by mobilizing world opinion to support higher labor standards. Its main areas of concern are full employment, migration of workers, social security, workers' health, labor standards, and technical assistance for economic development. The ILO organization includes an all-member International Labor Conference and a forty-eight member Governing Body—both based on a tripartite system of national representation by one employer, one worker, and two government delegates—and an unusually active secretariat, known as the Labor Office. The Conference meets annually at the ILO's headquarters in Geneva to determine general policies and the Governing Body functions as an executive between Conferences supervising the operations of ILO committees and commissions. *See also* SPECIALIZED AGENCY, p. 355.

Significance   The International Labor Organization has encouraged progress in labor affairs in most of the more than one hundred member countries. International conventions have helped to improve labor standards simultaneously in many states that otherwise might have refused to take unilateral action since it would place them at a competitive disadvantage. Members that persistently disregard ILO labor rules and principles are placed by the organization on a special "blacklist" until they improve their standards. ILO has increasingly directed its efforts toward helping developing states to improve their labor productivity, working conditions, and general well-being of workers. ILO experts provide technical assistance to countries in Asia, Africa, and Latin America.

International Organization   A formal arrangement transcending national boundaries that provides for the establishment of institutional machinery to facilitate cooperation among members in security, economic, social, or related fields. Modern international organizations, which began to emerge more than a century ago in the Western state system, have flowered in the twentieth century—the age of international cooperation. Two types of international organizations are active—public arrangements between two or more states, and private associations of individuals or groups known as non-governmental organizations (NGO). Public international organizations include global political arrangements (the League of Nations and the United Nations), regional groups (for example, NATO, the OAS, and the Arab League), and public international unions (the Universal Postal Union and the World Health Organization). Examples of private international organizations include Rotary International, the International Confederation of Free Trade Unions, and the International Red Cross.

Significance International organizations of great variety and institutions of varying degrees of integration exist in the contemporary world. It is difficult to assess the degree to which such institutions contribute to peace, international understanding, and well-being. Critics have tended to polarize their views: one group would prefer a unilateral approach to security and greater national flexibility in economic and social affairs; the other views international organization as ineffectual and calls for a stronger union in the form of one or several federal arrangements. Supporters of international organization assert that it offers means by which states can achieve many objectives; in each case, however, the extent of cooperation necessary to produce useful results depends upon the degree of common interest among the members.

International Telecommunication Union (ITU) A specialized agency of the United Nations established to facilitate all types of telecommunications and to harmonize the actions of member states in such fields. The ITU was set up in 1932 as a successor to the International Telegraph Union, which had functioned since 1865. Organs of the ITU include a Plenipotentiary Conference that meets once every five years to decide basic policies, two Administrative Conferences (one for telegraph and telephone, the other for radio and television) that adopt regulations binding on all members, an Administrative Council to implement policies, and a secretariat, headed by a secretary-general located at ITU headquarters in Geneva. By 1982, almost all nations of the world and some colonies were members or associate members. *See also* SPECIALIZED AGENCY, p. 355.

Significance The cooperation fostered through the International Telecommunication Union makes possible a global communications network that links national and private telephone and telegraph services. World radio transmission would be chaotic without the allocation of frequencies by the ITU, and television channels may have to be similarly allocated on an orderly basis as international telecasting increases. The ITU's role highlights the necessity for functional cooperation in a technologically tight-knit world.

Latin American Free Trade Association (LAFTA) A regional organization that sought to spur the rate of economic development of member states by removing trade barriers. Ten Latin American states (Argentina, Brazil, Chile, Colombia, Ecuador, Mexico, Paraguay, Peru, Uruguay, Venezuela) agreed in the Montevideo Treaty of 1960 to liberalize their trade to achieve substantially free trade among member countries. The Treaty, however, included escape clauses, provided for renegotiation of tariff cuts that cause substantial domestic injury, and gave agriculture a preferred status. Two organs constituted the decision-making machinery for LAFTA: (1) a Conference of the Contracting Parties met annually to decide basic policies by a two-thirds voting procedure; and (2) a Standing Executive Committee implemented trade policies and treaty provisions. A small secretariat provided technical and administrative assistance. *See also* LATIN AMERICAN INTEGRATION ASSOCIATION (LAIA), p. 321.

Significance The Latin American Free Trade Association was an attempt to apply the successful European techniques of economic integration to promote economic growth in an underdeveloped region. Unlike the EEC and EFTA, LAFTA members had to negotiate periodically to make progress since no provision was made in the integration treaty for automatic, across-the-board cuts in tariffs. Weakening the LAFTA approach, also, was the competitive rather than complementary nature of their foreign trade, which consists mainly of primary commodities. In 1980, the ten LAFTA states were joined by Bolivia to create the new Latin American Integration Association (LAIA).

Latin American Integration Association (LAIA) A regional group, established by a treaty signed in Montevideo in 1980, that seeks to increase regional economic development through joint action. The Latin American Integration Association supersedes the Latin American Free Trade Association (LAFTA) which was set up by the 1960 Treaty of Montevideo. LAIA is also known by the Spanish acronym, ALADI, for *Asociación Latinoamericana de Integración*. Unlike LAFTA, it does not aim to eliminate all tariffs among its members by a specified date. Rather, LAIA wants tariff concessions to be granted individually based on the economy of each member. Under the new arrangement, the richer members are expected to grant more liberal concessions to the poorer ones. To encourage such actions, the treaty creating LAIA divides the eleven signatory states into three groups according to their level of development: (1) less developed (Bolivia, Ecuador, and Paraguay); (2) medium developed (Chile, Colombia, Peru, Uruguay, and Venezuela); and (3) more developed (Argentina, Brazil, and Mexico).

Significance   The membership of the Latin American Integration Association includes the most important countries of Latin America with three-fourths of the population south of the United States border. The creation of the new organizaton was a direct result of the failure of LAFTA to reach its goal of a regional free trade area. The decision to replace LAFTA was taken at a final meeting of that organization in 1980. LAFTA's stagnation was the result of such factors as different levels of development among members, demands by powerful groups and industries for continued protection of local products, communication and transport problems in the region, conflicting economic systems, and political and economic changes. The threefold classification system adopted by LAIA is aimed at overcoming some of these problems. Whether the new organization can surmount the difficulties that plagued LAFTA for the twenty years of its existence remains problematical.

League of Nations   A global international organization established by the victors in the First World War to preserve peace and security and to promote economic and social cooperation among its members. A covenant consisting of twenty-six articles included in the Versailles peace treaty served as the constitution for the organization. Although President Woodrow Wilson provided the leadership in developing the League and was chairman of the committee that wrote the Covenant, the United States failed to join when the Senate refused to consent to the treaty. Neutral states were invited to become original members and defeated enemy states were in time permitted to join, resulting in near universality, with the United States the only major holdout. Sixty-three countries ultimately accepted membership although the maximum number of members at any one time was fifty-eight. A Council and Assembly, resembling the Security Council and General Assembly of the United Nations, were the major organs, each requiring unanimity for reaching decisions. Subsidiary bodies aided the two major organs in carrying out their responsibilities in such fields as mandates, disarmament, and economic and social welfare. A Permanent Court of International Justice, forerunner of the present International Court of Justice, and the International Labor Organization were independent of the League but coordinated their activities with it. The heart of the League peace-keeping system called for the members to accept political or legal settlement of their disputes with sanctions to be levied by the League community against any state that went to war in violation of its covenants.

Significance   Unlike the United Nations Charter, which outlaws war, the League Covenant tried to make war illegal in most situations and sought to avoid precipitate action. Although its record in resolving many dangerous disputes and situations during the first decade was good, the League failed to act decisively when confronted with the challenge of direct aggression by Japan against China in the Manchurian crisis of 1931. In 1935, following an attack by Italy on Ethopia, the League for the first and only time levied sanctions against an aggressor but failed to deter the conquest. The Italian success encouraged further aggressions by Nazi Germany, Japan, and the Soviet Union in the 1930s, but no collective action was undertaken against them. The League, despite its failure to maintain peace, helped to settle many disputes, encouraged technical cooperation among members, and helped to improve economic and social conditions in some. The League experience also helped to develop new ideas and procedures that have proved useful in the United Nations. In 1946, the League met for a final session at Geneva and voted itself out of existence, turning its assets over to the United Nations.

League of Nations: Covenant   A multilateral treaty (Part I of the Treaty of Versailles) that created the League of Nations. The Covenant of the League resembled a national constitution in that it provided for the establishment of major organs and a decision-making system and enunciated principles to guide the actions of its members. *See also* LEAGUE OF NATIONS, p. 322.

Significance The Covenant delineated the procedures whereby the League's twofold objectives of preserving peace and security and promoting international cooperation could be achieved. The brief document of twenty-six articles and general language provided flexibility for adjusting to changing world conditions. The collapse of the League resulted not from internal constitutional weaknesses but from the failure of key member states to support its principles and the refusal of the United States to join the organization.

League of Nations: Mandates System The arrangement whereby the colonial territories of the defeated Central Powers of World War I were placed under the guardianship and tutelage of Allied nations. Each Mandatory Power was responsible to the League of Nations in the administration of its mandate. Mandated territories were classified into three groups according to their relative stages of development. Class A mandates (Arab territories formerly under Turkish dominion) were regarded as ready for independence and self-government after a minimal period of tutelage. Class B mandates (German East and West Africa) were given no promises of early independence and were to be governed as colonies with certain fundamental rights guaranteed. Class C mandates (German South-West Africa and Pacific islands) were to be governed as "integral portions of the [Mandatory Power's] territory," with no promise of eventual independence. A Permanent Mandates Commission of ten private experts was established under the Covenant to oversee the administration of the mandates and report its findings to the League Council. *See also* TRUST TERRITORY, p. 357.

Significance The mandates system, adopted at the Versailles peace conference as an alternative to annexation by the victors, established the precedent that the international community has a responsibility for the well-being of subject peoples. Several mandates—Iraq, Syria, and Lebanon—achieved independence; all other mandates except South-West Africa were placed under the trusteeship system of the United Nations in 1946. Each of these trust territories has become an independent state with the exception of the Trust Territory of the Pacific Islands (U.S. strategic trust). South-West Africa remains in a hazy legal status; the General Assembly in 1966 adopted a resolution extending its jurisdiction over South-West Africa (Namibia), but the Republic of South Africa rejected international claims.

Non-Governmental Organization (NGO)   A private international organization that serves as a mechanism for cooperation among private national groups in international affairs, especially in the economic, social, cultural, humanitarian, and technical fields. Under the United Nations Charter (Article 71), the Economic and Social Council is empowered to make suitable arrangements for consultation with NGOs on matters within its competence. NGOs are also known as transnational associations.

Significance   Non-governmental organizations have been active in international affairs for many years, some dating back over a century. Over one thousand are active in today's world, and more than three hundred have entered into arrangements as consultants for ECOSOC. Examples of NGO's include consumer and producer associations, religious groups, teacher organizations, professional legal and medical societies, and trade unions.

Nordic Council   A Scandinavian regional organization composed of elected and appointed delegates who meet as a Council to recommend common policies and programs to the governments of the member states. Established in 1952, the membership of the Nordic Council includes Denmark, Finland, Norway, Sweden, and Iceland. Delegates are chosen by their national parliaments (Iceland was accorded five, the other members sixteen each), with major political groups and opinions represented. Each state may also appoint as many governmental representatives as it wishes, but voting power is limited to the elected delegates. Ordinary sessions of the Council are held annually, but extraordinary sessions may be convoked by two members or twenty-five elected delegates. A Presidium of elected officers directs deliberations which are concerned with economic, social, cultural, legal, and transport matters.

Significance   The Nordic Council has served its members as a superparliament for deliberative purposes. One of its original objectives—to establish a Scandinavian common market—was suspended by the establishment in 1959 of the European Free Trade Association, with Denmark, Norway, and Sweden as full members and Finland as an associate. The Council has also been instrumental in eliminating the requirement of passports for Scandinavian citizens to travel in member countries, in providing for a Scandinavian labor market, and in promoting common legislation through recommendations in various fields.

North Atlantic Treaty Organization (NATO)   A regional organization established in 1949 to provide mutual security for its members in the North Atlantic area. NATO serves as the means for pursuing the security objectives established by the collective action provisions of the North Atlantic Treaty. Its fourteen members—Belgium, Britain, Canada, Denmark, Germany, Greece, Iceland, Italy, Luxembourg, the Netherlands, Norway, Portugal, Turkey, and the United States—use NATO as a framework for cooperation in military, political, economic, and social matters. The alliance is aimed chiefly at blocking the threat of Soviet military aggression in Europe by combined conventional forces and by affording Western European states the protection of the American nuclear deterrent. The complex NATO organizational structure includes: (1) the North Atlantic Council, which develops and executes basic alliance policies; (2) a military command structure built around the Supreme Headquarters Allied Powers Europe (SHAPE), the Supreme Allied Commander Europe (SACEUR), the Supreme Allied Commander Atlantic (SACLANT), the Channel Committee, and the Canada-U.S. Regional Planning Group; (3) various production and logistic organizations; (4) major Council Committees that comprise the main consultative structure within NATO; and (5) the NATO Secretariat which is headed by a secretary-general who also functions as Chairman of the Council. *See also* NORTH ATLANTIC TREATY, p. 183.

Significance   NATO has functioned as a cornerstone of the Western system of defense against the threat of communist aggression in the North Atlantic area. Its political-military framework has served as an instrument for resolving many of the issues that have arisen within the alliance, involving the reconciliation of the foreign and defense policies of fourteen independent nations. In the 1970s and 1980s, however, the alliance has been strained by a growing polycentrism, an American preoccupation with Middle East affairs, controversies over nuclear strategy and policies, and a growing sense of independence in Western Europe. In the 1960s, France withdrew her troop units from the integrated NATO command and her fleet from NATO operational control. In 1966 President Charles de Gaulle required that all NATO headquarters and facilities be withdrawn from French soil or be placed under French control. Although France continued her commitment under the North Atlantic Treaty for joint action against an aggressor, her actions effectively removed her as a member of NATO. NATO's future depends largely on how credible the Soviet threat to Western Europe appears to the West Europeans.

Organization for Economic Cooperation and Development (OECD)

A regional economic organization established in 1961 to promote economic growth and freer trade and to expand and improve Western aid to the developing countries. OECD's twenty-four members include the ten of the European Community (Belgium, Britain, Denmark, France, Germany, Greece, Ireland, Italy, Luxembourg, and the Netherlands), the members of EFTA (Austria, Norway, Portugal, Sweden, and Switzerland), Australia, Iceland, New Zealand, Finland, Spain, Turkey, Canada, the United States, and Japan. Yugoslavia has a special status with OECD. The OECD replaced the Organization for European Economic Cooperation (OEEC) established in 1948 to elicit common action among Marshall Plan recipient countries to aid their recovery from World War II. Major organs include a Council of representatives from all member countries that meets weekly, an Executive Committee of ten members elected annually by the Council, and a secretariat, headed by a secretary-general, located at its Paris headquarters. Subsidiary bodies include the Development Assistance Committee (coordinates aid programs to developing states), the Economic Policy Committee (recommends policies to encourage economic expansion), and the Trade Committee (strives to resolve trade issues).

Significance The Organization for Economic Cooperation and Development represents a major effort on the part of the advanced Western nations to harmonize their internal and foreign economic policies. Major subjects of concern for the OECD are consumer demand, output, employment, costs, prices, foreign trade, and the problem of eliciting cooperation among members to combat inflation and OPEC oil pricing. American objectives sought through the OECD framework have included opening European markets to overcome discrimination fostered by EEC and EFTA preferential trading systems, correcting the deficit in the American balance of payments, and equalizing the foreign aid burden among the industrialized states. The OECD has been most active in trying to harmonize national programs of technical and developmental assistance. It has established general policies and principles to guide member nations and holds an annual review conference in which representatives of member countries defend their programs and policies in open inquiry.

Organization of African Unity (OAU)   A regional organization established in 1963 to develop unity, end colonialism, foster economic development, and provide security for African states. OAU's membership includes fifty nations—every independent African state except South Africa. In addition, Liberation Movements associated with the OAU include: (1) the African National Congress (South Africa); (2) the Pan African Congress (South Africa); (3) *Polisario* (Spanish Sahara); and (4) SWAPO—South-West African Peoples Organization (Namibia). Its organization consists of an Assembly of Heads of State that meets annually and a secretariat located at OAU headquarters in Addis Ababa.

Significance   The broad objectives of the Organization of African Unity are commonly accepted by its members, but it has remained a loose association of sovereign states with joint pronouncements but little in the way of concerted action. Its pan-African well-springs have been sapped by internal political rivalries, ideological differences, conflicting ties with major powers, and an overriding concern with the preservation of personal power and state sovereignty. Security provisions in its Charter have not been implemented or broadened, its efforts to establish a common force to fight the South African racist regime have not succeeded, and cooperative programs to aid members in economic development have suffered from a lack of capital. Yet, a base for more extensive cooperation is being constructed. An African Development Bank has been established and setting up a common market arrangement on the continent has been discussed. In the United Nations, the OAU functions as an effective caucusing group when issues of common interest come before the General Assembly. The African bloc has played a major role in the decolonization process, in efforts to create a new international economic order, and in building international development strategies.

Organization of American States (OAS) A regional organization established by the Ninth International Conference of American States at Bogotá in 1948 to determine political, defense, economic, and social policies for the Inter-American system. Twenty-one American republics subscribed to the OAS Charter, although the Castro government of Cuba was expelled from the organization in 1962. Organs of the OAS include: (1) the Inter-American Conference, which functions as the supreme organ of the OAS, meeting every five years to consider any matter relating to the American states; (2) the Meeting of Consultation of Ministers of Foreign Affairs, which takes up pressing security and related problems when a majority of members call for a meeting; (3) the Council, which serves as the coordinating agency for the OAS and meets at its headquarters in Washington, D.C.; (4) the Pan-American Union, which functions as the secretariat for the OAS, coordinating inter-American social and economic activities and promoting the welfare of members; (5) the Specialized Organizations, which carry on cooperative programs in such fields as health, agriculture, education, and child welfare; and (6) the Specialized Conferences, which are called to encourage joint efforts to solve technical problems. In addition, special agencies, such as the Inter-American Development Bank and the Inter-American Peace Committee, function autonomously in support of general OAS objectives. The main activities carried on by the OAS relate to the peaceful settlement of disputes, common action against aggression, and economic and social collaboration among members. *See also* ALLIANCE FOR PROGRESS, p. 368; INTER-AMERICAN DEVELOPMENT BANK, p. 389; RIO TREATY, p. 190.

Significance The Organization of American States has devoted its main efforts since 1948 to dealing with the threat of communism in the hemisphere. Situations confronting the OAS have included the rise to power of the Castro government in Cuba, several international crises involving the great powers, the intervention of an OAS Peace Force in the Dominican Republic in 1965 "to prevent another Cuba," and revolutionary guerrilla warfare in several states. Conflicts of jurisdiction between the United Nations and the OAS over handling Latin American disputes have usually been won by the OAS, with the United Nations role limited to that of debate. The United States plays a dominant role in the OAS, especially in security matters, where most governments depend on it to provide the resources to meet threats of aggression, and in the field of economic development, where Latin American development programs depend heavily on United States financing. The main challenge facing the OAS is that of coping with indirect aggression and political subversion in hemispheric countries without stifling genuine political and social revolutions necessary for progress.

Organization of Central American States (ODECA)   A regional organization that fosters political, economic, and social cooperation among Central American states. Established under the terms of the 1951 Charter of San Salvador, ODECA's members are Costa Rica, El Salvador, Guatemala, Honduras, and Nicaragua. Panama has been invited to join. A new Charter was negotiated for ODECA in 1962. ODECA organs include: (1) a Conference of the Presidents of the Central American Republics that functions as the supreme body; (2) a Meeting of Ministers of Foreign Affairs that convenes every two years and serves as the principal decision-making agency, with unanimity required for all substantive decisions; and (3) the Central American Bureau, headed by a secretary-general, that functions as a general secretariat for ODECA. Members of ODECA have established the Central American Common Market (CACM) to promote economic integration. *See also* CENTRAL AMERICAN COMMON MARKET, p. 300.

Significance   The Organization of Central American States has played a substantial role in fostering the unity of the region. Numerous agencies, including the Central American Bank for Economic Integration (CABEI), a Superior University Council of Central America (CSUCA), and a Permanent Secretariat of the General Treaty on Central American Integration (SIECA), have emerged out of understandings fostered by ODECA. The evolution of political unity in Central America will depend mainly on the success of Central American states to cope with guerrilla insurrections and implement economic and social reforms.

Political Community   Any social unit or group holding common values, utilizing mutual institutions for decision making, and complying with decisions made. The level of integration within a political community is determined by the volume of social transactions carried on, the extent to which decision making is centralized, and the degree of nonviolent resolution of conflict among members of the community. A political community may take the form of: (1) a regional organization that fosters limited cooperation among members in specific areas; (2) a federal system with the central authority possessing supranational powers; or (3) a unitary community resulting from the merger of previously sovereign entities. *See also* CONSENSUS OF VALUES, p. 60.

Significance   The creation of political communities beyond the level of the national state has become commonplace in the contemporary state system. Functionalism has provided the main integrating force for the new movement; states have for pragmatic reasons joined in cooperative attacks on common economic, social, and political problems. More than thirty major regional groups have been established since World War II. The Commission of the European Community illustrates supranational organization in that it can make decisions binding on its members. Unitary communities have been created by the merger of two or more state units, as in the case of Tanganyika and Zanzibar (Tanzania) in the 1960s, and Libya and Syria in 1980.

Regionalism   The concept that nations situated in a geographical area or sharing common concerns can cooperate with each other through a limited-membership organization to meet military, political, and functional problems. Regionalism provides a middle-level approach to problem solving, between the extremes of unilateralism and universalism. The United Nations Charter encourages regionalism as complementary to the world organization's objectives and activities, but provides that all regional actions be consistent with the purposes and principles of the United Nations. Regional organizations include: (1) military-alliance systems, such as NATO, SEATO, Western European Union, and the Warsaw Treaty Organization; (2) economic arrangements, such as the European Community, the European Free Trade Association, Benelux, the Latin American Free Trade Association, the Central American Common Market, and COMECON; and (3) political groupings, such as the Organization of American States, the Council of Europe, the Commonwealth of Nations, the Arab League, and the Organization of African Unity. (*For specific regional organizations, see* Index.)

Significance The prolific growth of limited-member organizations since World War II has stemmed from a new emphasis placed on regional integration as a means for achieving national interest goals. The role of regional alliances has been the most controversial during this period, superimposing several balance of power systems upon the collective security approach of the United Nations. Observers differ as to whether military groups have added to the threat of war or contributed to the maintenance of peace and security. In pacific settlement cases, jurisdictional controversies have arisen between those supporting regional handling of the disputes and those that have sought to bring them under the aegis of the United Nations. Jurisdictional disputes arose, for example, between the OAS and the United Nations during the Cuban, Dominican, and Guatemalan crises. Functional organizations have received the most support and have been the least controversial outgrowths of regionalism, although increasing trade discrimination by rival groups could result in a stifling of freer world trade. Psychologically, individuals are more likely to give their support to limited-member groups than to a distant world organization. Regionalism may prove to be a "gradualist" approach to the building of international communities and political federations beyond the nation-state.

Sanctions Diplomatic, economic, or military punitive actions undertaken through a collective security system against an international law breaker. Under the League of Nations, each member state could determine for itself whether it would levy sanctions against a nation found in violation of the Covenant of the League. The United Nations security system provides that, when the Security Council determines that a "threat to the peace, breach of the peace, or act of aggression" exists, the Council may invoke voluntary or compulsory sanctions against the law-breaking state. The Charter specifies that the Council, assisted by the Military Staff Committee, may call upon members to undertake actions which may include "demonstrations, blockade, and other operations by air, sea, or land forces...." Nonmilitary sanctions may include "complete or partial interruption of economic relations and of rail, sea, air, postal, telegraphic, radio, and other means of communication, and the severance of diplomatic relations." Under the Uniting for Peace Resolution of 1950, the General Assembly may, by two-thirds vote, authorize members to take action against an aggressor if the Council is unable to act because of a veto. To facilitate the levying of sanctions, the Charter (Article 43) provides that member states should conclude special agreements with the Council to make available, when needed, armed forces to maintain peace and security. *See also* UNITED NATIONS: SECURITY COUNCIL, p. 354.

Significance   The Cold-War split among the great powers on the Security Council has prevented the conclusion of the special agreements by which armed forces were to have been made available to the Council and has emasculated the sanctions system envisaged by the founders of the United Nations. In 1950, however, with the Soviet delegate absent from the Council table, the Security Council was able to *recommend* that members undertake collective measures against North Korea. United Nations troops have also been used as police forces to help keep peace in the Middle East and in the Congo, but in neither case did their actions consist of levying sanctions against an aggressor. In the first application of compulsory sanctions, the Security Council in 1966 levied an economic embargo on Rhodesia, declaring its internal racial situation a threat to international peace and security. Effective military sanctions, however, await the development of consensus on the application of collective security among the great powers.

Secretariat   An international body of officials and civil servants that performs administrative, budgetary, linguistic, secretarial, and housekeeping functions for an international organization. Individuals who comprise a secretariat are recruited from member states, usually according to a formula that combines the concepts of member-state representation and personal competence. Although they retain their national citizenship, secretariat personnel are expected to perform their duties in a professional and objective manner that upholds the principles of the organization. All functioning regional organizations and public international unions, such as the Universal Postal Union, use international secretariats, but the most extensive in the number of personnel and variety of operations is that of the United Nations Secretariat. The Secretariat, with about 20,000 persons employed at the New York headquarters and in field staffs in numerous countries, functions as one of the six principal organs of the United Nations. It is headed by a Secretary-General appointed by the General Assembly by majority vote following nomination by the Security Council, with the veto power applicable. More than a score of under- and deputy-secretaries-general aid the Security-General in the performance of his duties.

Significance   Secretariats face complicated challenges in seeking to carry out their role within the structure of international organizations. Personnel standards must be maintained through recruitment based on merit, yet "geographical distribution" must assure each member state adequate representation, especially in the more important offices. Persons with diverse backgrounds, attitudes, ideologies, abilities, and languages must be integrated into a smoothly functioning bureaucracy. Professional dedication that rejects national partisanship must be cultivated so that members can support the goals and operations of the organization with independence, impartiality, and integrity. Controversies over efforts to develop these characteristics in the United Nations Secretariat have kept the Secretariat embroiled in the internal politics of the United Nations, particularly in conflicts involving the great powers. Demands for greater representation in the Secretariat, stemming from the influx of new nations into the United Nations, have also jeopardized standards of professional competence, although the Secretariat has proved to be an excellent training ground for inexperienced administrators from Asian and African countries.

Secretary-General   The chief administrative officer of an international secretariat, sometimes called director-general. Responsibilities of a secretary-general include those of preparing an agenda for major organs, compiling the budget and expending funds, providing initiative in developing new programs, supervising day-by-day operations, serving as a diplomatic go-between among the member delegations, and offering political leadership for the organization. The Secretary-General of the United Nations is chosen by the General Assembly for a five-year term following his nomination by the Security Council. In addition to the foregoing tasks, he has authority under the Charter to place matters relating to peace and security before the Security Council, and he sits in on meetings of the Assembly and three Councils to offer advice when requested. During the first thirty-six years of United Nations operations there have been five Secretaries-General: Trygve Lie (Norway), Dag Hammarskjöld (Sweden), U Thant (Burma), Kurt Waldheim (Austria), and Javier Pérez de Cuéllar (Peru).

Significance   The office of secretary-general has evolved over the period of a century, reaching its highest level of development in the United Nations. The extent of powers exercised depends not only on the nature of the organization and its constitutional framework but on the capabilities of the person holding the office and his conception of the role to be played, as well as the problems and issues that arise. U Thant and Kurt Waldheim, for example, conceived of the office as primarily concerned with administrative duties, whereas Trygve Lie and Dag Hammarskjöld additionally viewed it as a vehicle for providing executive-type leadership for the United Nations. By taking a stand in a crisis situation that has split the great powers, the Secretary-General may incur the active hostility of one bloc while strengthening his support from the other. The Korean conflict and the Congo crisis, for example, found the Secretary-General actively in support of Western objectives since in his view they tended to square with Charter principles. Soviet opposition to a political role by the Secretary-General led to their proposal for a "troika" arrangement of a presidium of three secretaries-general to replace the single official. Each of the three would possess the power to veto decisions of the Secretariat and thus block action. Lack of support among the smaller members of the United Nations resulted in the failure of the troika proposal, but the Soviets continued to insist that the Secretary-General act with restraint in the exercise of the powers of his office.

Supranationalism   Power exercised by international institutions to make majority-vote decisions that are binding upon
all member states or their citizens. Supranationalism involves a
transfer of decision-making authority in prescribed areas from
constituent units to a central body. Members must accept supranational decisions or withdraw from the system. Decisions may
be made either by representatives of member governments or by
an institution that functions as an integral unit of the international arrangement. Supranationalism in effect establishes a limited federal system with powers divided between the two levels.
See also POLITICAL COMMUNITY, p. 331.

Significance   Supranationalism is possible when states voluntarily delegate some of their sovereignty to central institutions.
Yet supranationalism has received little support in a world composed of independent, sovereign states whose leaders jealously
guard against any loss of their decision-making prerogatives.
The Commission of the European Community is a rare example
of a supranational institution that initiates policies, functions as
an executive body, and makes decisions within prescribed areas
that are binding upon member states and private groups and
individuals. The Security Council, unlike other United Nations
organs, is empowered under the Charter to make supranational
decisions in peace and security matters that are binding upon the
members. The Council has exercised this power only once, in
levying compulsory economic sanctions on Rhodesia in 1966.

Unanimity   The voting procedure in international organs
that provides that no state may be bound by a decision without
giving its consent. The rule of unanimity has generally involved
the *liberum veto* (a single member, by voting against a proposal,
can defeat it), although some organizations' constitutions provide that the dissenting state either accept the decision of a
majority or quit the organization. The principle of unanimity is a
modern adaptation of the traditional rule of international law
that a sovereign state can be bound only by those decisions to
which it consents.

Significance   The rule of unanimity has progressively given
way in international organs to decision making by simple or
extraordinary majorities. Vast differences of interests and judgments among diverse states have made the change essential for

reaching decisions in contemporary institutions, although on matters of vital interest to states' foreign policies, most international organizations retain the *liberum veto*. In the United Nations, however, none of the six principal organs provides for decision making by unanimity, although in the Security Council the Charter requires the unanimity of the five permanent members on substantive decisions.

United Nations: Caucusing Group Representatives of member states whose common interests impel them to meet regularly to determine group approaches on substantive and procedural issues arising in the General Assembly. Nine caucusing groups are active in the Assembly: the Afro-Asian, Arab, African, Benelux, Commonwealth, Latin American, Scandinavian, Soviet, and Western European and "other" (Canada, Australia, and New Zealand) states. A considerable overlap in membership exists, especially among the Afro-Asian, Arab, African, and Commonwealth states. A few states—China, Israel, South Africa, the United States, and Yugoslavia—do not caucus with any group. A caucusing group may be distinguished from a voting bloc in that members of the former are not bound to vote in the Assembly according to the caucus decision and exhibit less cohesion. The Group of Seventy-Seven (G77) functions as the largest caucusing group at the United Nations and in major international conferences. G77 became active for the first time at the first UNCTAD Conference in 1964 and has expanded from its original seventy-seven members to a current membership of over 120 Third World countries. G77 includes most of the nations of Asia, Africa, Latin America, the Caribbean, Oceania, and the Middle East which take a common stand against what they regard as neo-colonial policies of the First and Second Worlds, and in favor of development aid, human rights, and the creation of a New International Economic Order.

Significance Caucusing groups developed early as the various regions of the world began to fight for an equitable share of the elective seats in the principal United Nations organs. The emergence of many new nations and the greatly increased membership in the Assembly accelerated the process of caucusing before important votes. The first identifiable group to emerge—the Soviet bloc—is also the one having the highest percentage of solidarity in voting—over 95 percent. The Commonwealth, with members scattered about the globe, has generally recorded the lowest rate of solidarity in voting. Caucusing groups have helped to change the decision process in the Assembly from one involving individual sovereign states voting independently on issues, to one resembling a Continental parliament with its multiparty system, its fleeting coalitions, and the need for compromise among various power blocs to reach agreement on issues. The Group of Seventy-Seven meets before important sessions of the General Assembly or other organs to hammer out a common Third World position on issues under consideration.

United Nations Charter   A multilateral treaty which serves as the "constitution" for the United Nations Organization. The Charter was drawn up and signed at San Francisco on June 26, 1945, and was ratified by fifty-one original members and put into effect on October 24, 1945, since known as United Nations Day. The document consists of a preamble and 111 articles that proclaim the purposes and principles of the organization, provide for the establishment of six major organs, and enumerate the procedures and functions of each. *See also* UNITED NATIONS CONFERENCE ON INTERNATIONAL ORGANIZATION, p. 339.

Significance   The United Nations Charter represents an effort by the community of nations to establish norms of international conduct to outlaw war, provide for the peaceful settlement of international disputes, regulate armaments, govern trust territories, and encourage cooperation among nations in dealing with economic and social problems. Like the United States Constitution, the Charter has proved to be a flexible document, subject to many broad interpretations. Without this feature of adaptability, the United Nations would probably have collapsed under the impact of the Cold War.

United Nations Children's Fund (UNICEF)   An organization established by the General Assembly in 1946 to provide emergency supplies of food, medicine, and clothing to destitute children in war-ravaged countries. Originally called the United Nations International Children's Emergency Fund (UNICEF), when the General Assembly gave it permanent status its name was changed by deleting the words "International" and

"Emergency," but its well-known acronym UNICEF was retained. UNICEF has since expanded its operations to include the underdeveloped countries and has increased its activities to include sponsorship of national projects for better education, improved health, and disease control, with matching funds provided by recipient nations. Increasingly it has called upon specialized agencies, such as WHO, UNESCO, and FAO, for advice and help in carrying out its programs. Financing for its programs has come from member governments, from private contributions, from UNICEF holiday greeting card programs, and from Halloween "trick or treat" collections by children in the United States.

Significance Millions of children in Europe, Latin America, Africa, and Asia have been helped by the United Nations Children's Fund. The magnitude of the challenge facing UNICEF is underscored by the fact that two-thirds of the world's children are ill-fed and ill-housed, and suffer from lack of medical and sanitation facilities. UNICEF has placed special emphasis on administering mass health campaigns against epidemic and endemic diseases that attack children, on providing milk as a dietary staple, on caring for refugee children, and on overcoming illiteracy among the young. It has also been assigned a primary role in the United Nations Development Decade programs for encouraging a substantial rate of economic growth in the developing states.

United Nations Conference on International Organization (UNCIO) The major conference at San Francisco (April 25 to June 26, 1945) that wrote the Charter of the United Nations and approved the Statute of the International Court of Justice. The fifty participating states, together with Poland, became the fifty-one original members of the United Nations. The deliberations at San Francisco were based on the Proposals formulated by the four sponsoring governments (Britain, China, the Soviet Union, and the United States) at the Dumbarton Oaks Conference of 1944. The work of the San Francisco Conference resembled that of a constituent body drafting a constitution. It was carried on in four commissions and twelve committees, with final approval recorded at plenary conference sessions. Leadership was provided by the great powers at each stage. The Charter became effective on October 24, 1945 (since designated United

Nations Day) when a majority of signers, including the Big Five, had ratified it. Before the meeting of the First General Assembly in January, 1946, the Charter had been ratified by all fifty-one original members. *See also* DUMBARTON OAKS CONFERENCE, p. 342; YALTA AGREEMENT, p. 200.

Significance   The San Francisco Conference, which was held prior to the end of World War II, demonstrated that great-power unanimity was not impossible. The major conflicts occurred between the great powers and the middle and small states, as the latter sought unsuccessfully to challenge the dominant role that the great powers had carved out for themselves in the new organization. The threat of empty great-power chairs in the new organization was sufficient to deter the smaller powers from exploiting their voting majority. The location of the conference gave indication of an anticipated major role for Asia in the new world organization. The Charter remains the basic constitution for the United Nations, altered formally only by two amendments adopted in 1965 that increased the memberships of the Security Council and the Economic and Social Council, and one in 1973 that again expanded the latter.

United Nations: Dispute Settlement Procedures

Techniques and tools available for use by agencies of the United Nations in efforts to achieve a peaceful settlement of an international dispute. The Charter (Article 33) provides that the parties to a dispute should "first of all, seek a solution by negotiation, inquiry, mediation, conciliation, arbitration, judicial settlement, resort to regional agencies or arrangements, or other peaceful means. . . ." If these traditional pacific settlement approaches fail or are inappropriate, the dispute may be brought before the Security Council or General Assembly by a member state or by a nonmember if it agrees to accept Charter obligations relating to dispute settlement. The Secretary-General, under the Charter (Article 99), may also bring any situation that threatens peace and security to the attention of the Security Council. Initial actions by the world organization may take the form of an appeal to refrain from aggravating the situation or, if fighting has broken out, a cease-fire order may be issued. The parties to a dispute are given an opportunity to present their cases before the Council or Assembly, and such discussions may be useful to discover common ground for a settlement. "Quiet diplomacy," a blend of public and private negotiations carried on at United Nations headquarters, has proved useful in breaking deadlocks. When mediation and conciliation techniques applied in New York fail, a commission of inquiry and mediation or a United Nations representative or mediator may be appointed to go to the scene of the dispute to establish the facts and try for an on-the-spot settlement. If a great-power confrontation threatens to expand the dispute, "preventive diplomacy" in the form of a United Nations "presence" or police force to fill a power vacuum may be employed. Finally, when it is possible to secure the acceptance of both parties, the legal approaches to settlement—arbitration or adjudication—may be used to settle a dispute. *See also* PEACEFUL SETTLEMENT, p. 241.

Significance The United Nations has applied its pacifying and moderating influences to many disputes and situations over its history. Although its appeals and cease-fire "orders" under pacific settlement procedures are merely recommendations and disputants cannot be compelled to obey them, many hostilities have been arrested by the timely intervention of the United Nations. Its prestige as a global organization and its ability to marshal world opinion to pressure the disputants to accept pacific procedures have probably been more useful than if the United Nations had sought to play the role of world policeman, judge, and jury. Great-power confrontations have been avoided by filling power vacuums with a United Nations "presence," as in Lebanon in 1958 and the Congo in 1960. Bitter communal feuds over territorial jurisdiction have been moderated in Kashmir, Palestine, and Cyprus, and fighting that threatened to escalate into a major subcontinental war between India and Pakistan was stopped through United Nations efforts in 1948 and again in 1965. Two disputes—the Arab-Israeli and the Indo-Pakistani cases—have proved to be the most intractable facing the United Nations, with final settlements no closer now than they were in 1948. As a general rule, the most effective techniques employed by the United Nations have been those that have encouraged the parties to engage in bilateral negotiations. In the early 1980s, United Nations efforts to free American hostages held in Iran and to get the Soviet Union to withdraw its troops from Afghanistan were major dispute settlement challenges.

United Nations: Domestic Jurisdiction Clause The Charter limitation (Article 2) placed upon the competence of the United Nations, which provides that "nothing contained in the present Charter shall authorize the United Nations to intervene in matters which are essentially within the domestic jurisdiction of any state." Collective action to maintain international peace and security is specifically excluded from the limiting clause, but beyond this no definition is provided as to what constitutes an *international* problem (and, hence, a proper subject for United Nations consideration) and what is strictly a *national* or *domestic* question. *See also* DOMESTIC JURISDICTION, p. 258.

Significance   The domestic jurisdiction clause proclaims a political principle more than it provides a legal limitation on United Nations powers. It is, however, one of the most frequently invoked sections of the Charter. On controversial matters, members opposing United Nations action typically open their defense by claiming that consideration of the issue by the world organization is an unwarranted intrusion into their sovereign affairs. In the final analysis, questions of domestic jurisdiction are decided by United Nations organs through their voting procedures. In considering questions dealing with colonialism (e.g., Portuguese Africa) and denial of human rights (e.g., apartheid in South Africa), the General Assembly rejected assertions that these were essentially domestic matters, but the affected states refused to cooperate with the Assembly.

United Nations: Dumbarton Oaks Conference

Preliminary conversations over the nature and functions of the anticipated United Nations organization. The Dumbarton Oaks Conference met from August to October, 1944, in Washington, D.C. Delegations from the United States, Britain, and the Soviet Union joined in the first and more important phase of the talks, while China participated with Britain and the United States in the second phase. Views were exchanged, compromises secured, and a preliminary working draft of Proposals for the new world organization was hammered out. *See also* YALTA AGREEMENT, p. 200.

Significance   Agreement among the great powers concerning the nature of the contemplated world organization was reached on most issues. Those in which agreement was lacking (e.g., use of the veto power, membership, and dispute settlement procedure) were referred to higher political levels for resolution by the Big Three—Churchill, Roosevelt, and Stalin—at the Yalta Conference of 1945. The preliminary draft of the Proposals, with some alterations and additions, became the United Nations Charter following the work of the San Francisco Conference from April to June, 1945.

United Nations Economic and Social Council (ECOSOC)

A major organ of the United Nations, which functions under the authority of the General Assembly in planning and recommending economic and social programs. ECOSOC is composed of twenty-seven members elected by a two-thirds vote in the General Assembly for three-year terms, nine elected each year. Although all United Nations members are equally eligible for membership, the major powers have consistently been elected. This situation led to the enlargement of the Council by Charter amendment in 1965 from eighteen to its present twenty-seven members to give the new nations of Asia and Africa a larger voice. Major functions of ECOSOC include: (1) research and debate on economic, social, educational, cultural, and related topics; (2) drafting conventions that, if adopted by the General Assembly and ratified by member states, become international law and bind states domestically; and (3) coordinating the activities of thirteen specialized agencies. To aid it in its operations, the Council established eight functional commissions (Human Rights, International Commodity Trade, Narcotic Drugs, Population, Prevention of Discrimination and Protection of Minorities, Statistical, Status of Women, and Transport and Communications) and four regional economic commissions (Africa, Asia and the Far East, Europe, and Latin America).

Significance The Economic and Social Council has been mainly concerned with the two areas that a majority of United Nations members consider to be of primary importance—economic development and human rights. In the field of economic development, ECOSOC has played a major role in building the United Nations Development Program with its technical assistance and special fund approaches to spurring modernization in underdeveloped states. In 1966, ECOSOC was instrumental in securing the establishment of the Capital Development Fund to help finance industrialization, culminating a decade of efforts by the developing countries for a Special

United Nations Fund for Economic Development (SUNFED proposal). ECOSOC's most notable achievements in the human rights field have been the Universal Declaration of Human Rights, adopted by the General Assembly in 1948, and numerous human rights conventions to expand individual freedom.

United Nations Educational, Scientific, and Cultural Organization (UNESCO)   A specialized agency of the United Nations which promotes cooperation among members in the fields of education, science, and culture. Through recommendations to member governments and through its own activities, UNESCO has carried on exchange programs, promoted teaching and research, and has sought to advance the ideals of equal rights and educational opportunity. UNESCO machinery includes a General Conference, an Executive Board, and a Secretariat, with its headquarters in Paris. *See also* SPECIALIZED AGENCY, p. 355.

Significance   UNESCO and its projects have been the most controversial of the fifteen specialized agencies. Some critics charge that its efforts to promote better international understanding and to reduce the forces of nationalism are steps toward world government. Others assail UNESCO on the opposite ground, that it has failed to contribute effectively to the building of a world community and has done little to spread knowledge and understanding of diverse cultures. UNESCO supporters reject both criticisms and reaffirm its basic principle, as stated in the Preamble to UNESCO's Constitution, that "since wars begin in the minds of men, it is in the minds of men that the defenses of peace must be constructed."

United Nations Emergency Force (UNEF)   A special peace-supervising force established by the General Assembly during the Middle East crisis of 1956 to supervise the Israeli-Egyptian cease-fire line. UNEF included contingents from ten countries and built up to a peak of about 6000 officers and men. Principles underlying the establishment of UNEF included: (1) that it be composed of contingents from "neutral" nations; (2) that the United Nations determine the function of the force; (3) that the approval of the host country be secured (Egypt but not Israel agreed to permit UNEF to operate on its territory); (4) that the force be limited to a nonfighting, conciliation role; and (5) that the major costs be financed by a special peace-keeping operations levy on all United Nations members. UNEF functioned continuously from 1956 to 1967 when Egypt's request to withdraw UNEF was followed by a reopening of Arab-Israeli hostilities. UNEF was reinstated as UNEF II in the aftermath of the Arab-Israeli War of 1973. Its mandate ended in 1979. *See also* UNITED NATIONS: INTERNATIONAL POLICE FORCE, p. 351.

Significance The United Nations Emergency Force established a precedent for the operations of international police forces under United Nations auspices. The role of a United Nations police force, as typified by UNEF, is not, as the Charter framers had intended, one of confronting warring states with the overwhelming force of the international community. It is rather one of deploying a "United Nations presence" between the belligerents as a pacification tool, employing sophisticated diplomatic and military tactics to reduce the threat of war, and filling a power vacuum with a neutral United Nations force to avoid a great-power confrontation at the scene of a limited war. The United Nations Operation in the Congo (ONUC) and the United Nations Force in Cyprus (UNFICYP) have been conducted as peace-supervising operations based on the UNEF precedent.

United Nations: Finance The function of raising operating funds to expend on overhead costs and the broad-gauged programs carried on under the aegis of the United Nations. Almost all regular budget income comes from contributions assessed upon member states according to a formula that takes account of their national incomes, per capita incomes, and foreign exchange earnings. Each state must pay the major portion of its assessment in dollars, with the balance payable in local currencies. Assessments range from about 25 percent for the largest contributor, the United States, to the established minimum of 0.01 percent required of nearly one-half of the members. Overall operations of the organization are divided into four budgets: (1) the regular budget (general overhead and administrative operating costs); (2) the specialized agencies (WHO, UNESCO, FAO, IBRD, etc.); (3) special voluntary programs (United Nations Development Program, refugees, and UNICEF); and (4) peace-keeping operations (e.g., United Nations Emergency Force [UNEF] and United Nations Operation in the Congo [ONUC]).

Significance United Nations financial costs have increased more than fivefold since the organization began its operations in 1946. Controversies among the great powers over programs and policies and the poverty of many members have contributed to a sizable deficit that precipitated a crisis in the organization in the mid-1960s. The major budgetary conflict concerns the question of whether members that oppose specific peace-keeping operations like UNEF and ONUC can be held financially accountable to pay their share of the costs. Some supporters of the organization have proposed that member-state assessment be supplemented or replaced by independent sources of income to enable the United Nations to carry out voted programs. Some of the suggested new sources include charges levied by specialized agencies for services performed, tolls on the use of international waterways, issuance of charters for the exploitation of minerals and other resources of the seabeds of international waters and Antarctica, and charges for fishing, whaling, and sealing rights in international waters. Member states, however, have shown little interest in developing independent sources of income for the world organization that would weaken their control over its decisions.

United Nations Force in Cyprus (UNFICYP) A peace-supervising force established by the Security Council in 1964 to help end the violence between the Greek and Turkish communities on Cyprus. UNFICYP was assigned the objectives of maintaining law and order on the island, preventing a recurrence of the fighting, and preserving international peace and security. The formula for financing UNFICYP provides that costs be paid by countries supplying troops for the Force, by Cyprus, and by voluntary contributions from United Nations members. The Force includes troop units from Austria, Britain, Canada, Denmark, Finland, Ireland, and Sweden, with special civilian police units contributed by Australia, Austria, Denmark, New Zealand, and Sweden. *See also* UNITED NATIONS: INTERNATIONAL POLICE FORCE, p. 351.

Significance Although the United Nations Force in Cyprus has been successful in reducing the violence between the two communities, the United Nations has failed to find a formula for resolving the dispute. UNFICYP's mandate has regularly been renewed by the Security Council to prevent the likely resumption of civil war. Most of the contributions to support the Force have come from NATO countries that are primarily concerned with maintaining stability in the region. UNFICYP illustrates the role of an international police force under United Nations auspices—essential to the preservation of peace in the area, but unable to resolve the basic issues between the parties.

United Nations: General Assembly   One of the six principal organs of the United Nations which functions as a general conference of all member states. Each member is accorded ten delegates and one vote, and each is represented equally on all of the Assembly's seven main committees. Assembly jurisdiction extends to any world problem or internal organizational or procedural problem of the United Nations that a majority of its members wish to consider. Decisions are made by a simple majority of members present and voting except for "important questions" (defined in Article 18 of the Charter), which require a two-thirds vote. Although the Assembly cannot make binding decisions or law, it can by resolution recommend various kinds of national and international community action. Through the adoption of conventions or treaties it can play a role in the development of domestic law within states that ratify them. The Assembly annually elects a statesman of international reputation as President, and seventeen Vice-Presidents from major geographical areas of the world. A General Committee composed of the President, the Vice-Presidents, and the chairmen of the seven standing committees functions as a steering committee in planning the work of each session. Assembly powers include: (1) conciliation of international disputes; (2) recommendation of collective measures against an aggressor; (3) adoption of the organization's budget; (4) supervision of other principal organs and subsidiary bodies; (5) election of members of the three Councils and the judges of the International Court; (6) admission of new members; and (7) proposal of formal amendments to the United Nations Charter.

Significance   By an evolutionary process, the General Assembly has become the central organ of the United Nations system. This resulted in part from veto-caused deadlocks in the Security Council, which led the Assembly to assume a role in peacekeeping by adopting the Uniting for Peace Resolution of 1950. The influx of many new members into the organization also contributed to the expanding Assembly role. Mainly, however, it has been a natural evolution growing out of broad interpretations of its Charter powers, its control over the organization's purse strings, its supervisory powers over other organs, and its role as the only principal organ of the United Nations in which all members are represented. Over the first twenty-five years of Assembly activity, it has settled many disputes, helped to restore peace in several areas, adopted countless resolutions and declarations expounding norms for international conduct, helped promote economic development and freer trade, and expanded the concern for human rights in many countries. Most of all, it has served as a center for debate where disputants and aggrieved nations can air their complaints before a world forum.

United Nations: General Debate   The procedure that permits the representatives of all members of the United Nations to address the General Assembly during the opening weeks of each annual session. Often top leaders of many countries— presidents, prime ministers, monarchs—go to New York to present their nations' views on world problems during general debate. General debate usually absorbs several weeks of plenary sessions of the General Assembly each autumn.

Significance   General debate offers each member government an opportunity to unburden itself of its views on international questions. Although not really a form of debate since it consists of a series of largely unrelated speeches, it serves the purpose of raising issues, denouncing opponents, and praising friends. Typically, most speakers inveigh against the arms race, military alliances, great-power interventions, and the actions of dispute rivals or neighboring countries that displease them. During the 1970s, three demands voiced during general debate have overshadowed all others—for disarmament, for greater help in economic development, and for broader acceptance of human rights. Because general debate has become a time-consuming ritual, Assembly leaders have sought to expedite it by calling for time limits on speeches and urging self-restraint by the speechmakers.

United Nations: Genocide Convention   An international treaty that outlaws acts committed by public officials or private individuals whose intent is to destroy, in whole or in part, a national, ethnic, racial, or religious group. The International Convention on the Prevention and Punishment of the Crime of Genocide was written in an *ad hoc* committee established by ECOSOC and was adopted by the General Assembly in 1948. The Convention specifically makes it an international crime to kill, cause serious bodily or mental harm to, inflict harmful conditions upon, impose birth control on, or forcibly transfer children from any identifiable group. The Genocide Convention came into force in 1951 after the necessary twenty states had ratified it. By 1981, most nations of the world had ratified the Genocide Convention, but not the United States where the Senate has refused to act. *See also* GENOCIDE, p. 262; HUMAN RIGHTS, p. 316.

Significance   The Genocide Convention is unusual in that it recognizes and seeks to control crimes committed by individuals in violation of international norms. Although most states have ratified the Convention, it was weakened by the refusal of some—especially the United States—to accede to it because of doubts concerning its relationship to national constitutions and its effectiveness. The United States Senate has never brought the question of consent to the treaty to a formal vote. The Genocide Convention was part of the worldwide revulsion to the disclosure of Nazi atrocities during World War II.

United Nations High Commissioner for Refugees (UNHCR)   An Office established by the General Assembly in 1951 to afford temporary international protection for refugees pending permanent solutions by member states through resettlement, repatriation, or assimilation. UNHCR was set up to replace the International Refugee Organization (IRO), which had completed the major portion of the task of resettling World War II refugees. The Office of the High Commissioner receives support from the United Nations budget for administrative expenses only, with the financing of all programs dependent upon voluntary national and private contributions. Refugees receiving aid under other United Nations programs, such as the relief of Arab refugees in the Middle East and those granted the rights of nationals in the country of their residence, do not come under the High Commissioner's jurisdiction. *See also* REFUGEE, p. 188; UNITED NATIONS RELIEF AND WORKS AGENCY, p. 353.

Significance   The limited role assigned to the High Commissioner for Refugees resulted mainly from the position taken by the United States, that caring for refugees should be the responsibility of asylum states and private groups. It is estimated that there are still over one million refugees in the world who may appeal to the Office of the High Commissioner for help or protection under its operational mandate. UNHCR's main concern during the decade of the 1960s has been the refugees from Algeria, China, Tibet, Cuba, the Congo, Rwanda, and from the Portuguese African colonies. As stateless persons, such refugees can appeal only to an international organ for protection in a world in which all others seek protection by their own governments.

United Nations: Important Question   An issue placed before the General Assembly that requires a two-thirds vote to reach a decision. The Charter (Article 18) stipulates that important questions include: (1) recommendations on peace and security; (2) election of members to the three Councils; (3) admission of new members; (4) suspension of rights and privileges and expulsion of members; (5) questions relating to the operation of the trusteeship system; and (6) budgetary questions. Assembly proposals for amendments to the Charter (Article 108) also require a two-thirds vote. The determination of additional categories of important questions can be made by a simple majority of members present and voting.

Significance   The important-question rule has become more crucial as the General Assembly has expanded its membership and influence. The Cold War split, regional hostilities among the new nations, and the growth of caucusing groups have made it increasingly difficult to raise a two-thirds vote. The extension of the rule to apply to additional questions by a simple majority vote is a parliamentary tactic that may be used to defeat a measure which might otherwise be adopted. In 1961, for example, the United States succeeded in raising a majority to support a change in the designation of the issue of Chinese representation from an ordinary to an important question. In 1972, however, a majority of the General Assembly reversed that decision, resulting in the acceptance of the People's Republic as the legal representative of China.

United Nations: International Police Force   The anticipated agent for collective security enforcement action called for in the United Nations Charter plan for preserving world peace and security. Article 43 of the Charter provides that member states through prior agreements make armed forces and facilities available to the Security Council at its request. These agreements, the heart of the original peace-keeping plan, failed to materialize when the Council's Military Staff Committee was unable in 1946 to secure the agreement of the great powers concerning the size and character of their contributions. International police forces, however, have been subsequently established under United Nations auspices to function in a different capacity: as agents of pacific settlement using diplomatic and military tactics to restore peace in situations of limited war. *See also* ONUC, p. 351; UNEF, p. 344; UNFICYP, p. 346.

Significance   The failure of the Security Council to conclude agreements with member states of the United Nations means that it may only *recommend* that members undertake collective military action, as it did in the Korean conflict of 1950. The General Assembly, through the Uniting for Peace Resolution, has also acquired the power to authorize members to join in a collective police action. The new pacific settlement role for a small United Nations police force functioning as a peace-supervising body has been developed in the United Nations Emergency Force (UNEF), the United Nations Disengagement Observer Force (UNDOF) for the Middle East, the United Nations Operation in the Congo (ONUC), and the United Nations Force in Cyprus (UNFICYP). Such international police forces operate under Secretariat direction but remain responsible to their parent body, the Security Council or the General Assembly. Although they may not engage in "combat activity," they have the right to fight in self-defense. The record shows that peace-supervising forces can play a significant role in restoring and maintaining peace among small powers engaged in a limited war.

United Nations Operations in the Congo (ONUC)   A military-civilian force established in 1960 to restore peace and order in the former Belgian Congo. Secretary-General Dag Hammarskjöld organized the force (known generally by its French acronym, ONUC) under a mandate granted him by the

Security Council when it authorized action by the world organization. ONUC was built into a force of over 20,000, with military personnel furnished by twenty-nine states. In addition, the largest civilian team ever fielded by the United Nations carried out a massive countrywide technical assistance program. Over $400 million was expended between July, 1960, and June, 1964, when ONUC was disbanded. The Congo military operation contributed to a financial crisis that brought the United Nations to the verge of bankruptcy. *See also* UNITED NATIONS: FINANCE, p. 345; UNITED NATIONS: INTERNATIONAL POLICE FORCE, p. 351.

Significance   The ONUC operation was aimed at preventing great-power intervention, restoring domestic peace, rebuilding the nation's economy, and unifying the state. During its four years of operations, ONUC succeeded in preventing the Congo from becoming a great-power battleground, integrated secessionist states, and restored a measure of political and economic stability. In leading United Nations efforts to achieve a *rapprochement* among Congolese political leaders, Dag Hammerskjöld was killed in an airplane crash, and was succeeded as Secretary-General by U Thant. The United Nations Operation in the Congo is an example of the exercise of "preventive diplomacy" by which neutral forces under United Nations auspices attempt to fill a political and power vacuum to avoid a direct East-West confrontation.

United Nations Regional Commissions   Commissions established by the Economic and Social Council to foster economic cooperation within four major geographical areas of the world. Acting under authority of the Charter (Article 68), ECOSOC in 1947 established an Economic Commission for Europe (ECE) and an Economic Commission for Asia and the Far East (ECAFE), both intended to aid in fostering recovery from World War II. In 1948 ECOSOC recognized an additional role for regional commissions in promoting economic development with the establishment of an Economic Commission for Latin America (ECLA). In 1958 an Economic Commission for Africa (ECA) was founded to help the nations of that continent improve their economic lot. In each case, other states from outside the regions but having a definite interest in the areas are also members of each of the commissions. Efforts to establish a

Middle East commission have failed because of a lack of regional harmony. Headquarters for the four commissions are in Geneva, Bangkok, Santiago, and Addis Ababa.

Significance The four regional commissions have played a role in conducting research on economic and social problems, making recommendations directly to member governments, and in advising ECOSOC and specialized agencies on matters within their respective competencies. None of their activities can be carried out without the approval of the countries concerned. The regional commissions have promoted economic integration as a means of attacking underdevelopment. In Latin America, for example, ECLA was directly involved in the establishment of the Central American Common Market (CACM) in 1960, the Latin American Free Trade Association (LAFTA) in 1961, and the Latin American Integration Association in 1980.

United Nations Relief and Works Agency (UNRWA)
An organization established by the United Nations in 1949 to care for Arab refugees from the Arab-Israeli war of 1948–1949. UNRWA provides food, shelter, education and vocational training, and health services for the refugees. The major portion of the annual budget is contributed by the United States. The refugees live in temporary "refugee cities" located in Jordan, Syria, Lebanon, and in Israeli-occupied territory. The Arab-Israeli Wars of 1967 and 1973 have added to UNRWA's responsibilities by creating thousands of new refugees. *See also* REFUGEE, p. 188; UNITED NATIONS HIGH COMMISSIONER FOR REFUGEES, p. 349.

Significance Unlike most refugee organizations, the United Nations Relief and Works Agency has been unable to reduce its problem by the usual methods of resettlement, repatriation, and assimilation. The number of refugees has actually increased from the 900,000 who fled Palestine in 1948–1949 to several million three decades later, the result of a high birth rate, UNRWA care, and the Arab-Israeli Wars of 1967 and 1973. The problem remains intractable because of Israeli refusals to resettle 1948–1949 refugees and because the Arab states refuse to permit assimilation. Only a political settlement of the long-standing Arab-Israeli dispute could produce real hope that UNRWA could terminate its responsibilities.

United Nations Security Council One of the six principal organs of the United Nations. The Security Council is assigned primary responsibility by the Charter for maintaining peace and security in the world. The Council consists of five permanent members (Britain, China, France, Soviet Union, and United States) and ten (originally six) elective members that serve two-year terms. Half of the elected members are chosen each year by the General Assembly under a "gentlemen's agreement" that allots the ten elective seats to major geographical areas. Five seats are allotted to Asia and Africa, one to Eastern Europe, two to Latin America, and two to "Western European and other states." All decisions require an affirmative vote of nine members, but substantive decisions—unlike procedural ones—may be vetoed by a permanent member casting a negative vote. Nations not represented on the Council may be invited to participate in Council deliberations if they are parties to a dispute being considered. A Council member that is a party to a dispute must abstain from voting when questions concerning peaceful settlement procedures or terms are brought to a vote. Under the Charter, the Council's peace-preservation role provides for the pacific settlement of international disputes (Chapter VI of the Charter), or, following the determination that a threat to the peace, breach of the peace or act of aggression exists, it may call upon members to undertake collective action against the peace violator (Chapter VII). The office of President of the Security Council rotates monthly among the members, and the Council is considered to be in permanent session.

Significance The logic of the Charter framers' search for peace was embodied in the formula that delegated primary responsibility to the great powers functioning within the framework of the Security Council. So long as unanimity prevailed among them, no power or group of powers could effectively challenge the peace. Each permanent member was accorded a veto power so that the organization could not be used by one group of great powers against another; this would not be a police action but a Third World War. Yet, the assumption of the framers that in most cases the great powers would have common cause has not prevailed. No other organ of the United Nations has suffered a greater disparity between theory and practice. Most of the serious threats to peace since 1946 have involved great-power rivalry, direct or indirect. The Cold War, ideological hostility, disputes over admission of new members, and direct power confrontations between the Western powers and the Soviet Union have resulted in over one hundred vetoes, a primary dependence for security on regional alliances, and an expanding role for the General Assembly and the Secretariat in peace and security matters. Although the Council has dealt with many disputes successfully and has helped to stop the fighting in many areas of the world, when great-power interests have collided, the Council has been paralyzed. The increasing inability of the great powers to influence voting decisions in the General Assembly in recent years, however, has had the effect of revitalizing the Council. The Council remains a significant forum for great-power negotiation on major issues involving peace and security matters.

United Nations Specialized Agency   A functional international organization that has broad international responsibilities in the economic, social, cultural, educational, health, or related fields. Although each of the fifteen specialized agencies operates outside the general United Nations framework, each maintains a relationship with the world organization through a special agreement concluded between the agency and the Economic and Social Council. Each agency has its own budget, although the General Assembly may review it and make recommendations. The common organizational structure of the agencies includes: (1) a general conference or assembly of all members which functions as the chief policymaking organ; (2) an executive council or board that implements policies between sessions of the general conference, performing executive and supervisory functions; (3) a secretariat headed by a director or secretary-general, that performs administrative chores at the agency's headquarters. The agencies propose legislation for national enactment by members, draft treaties on matters of common concern, and carry on extensive research, publication, and informational work for the benefit of members. The specialized agencies include: the Food and Agriculture Organization (FAO); Inter-Governmental Maritime Consultative Organization (IMCO); International Bank for Reconstruction and Development (IBRD); International Civil Aviation Organization (ICAO); International Development Association (IDA); International Finance Corporation (IFC); International Labor Organization (ILO); International Monetary Fund (IMF); International Telecommunications Union (ITU); United Nations

Educational, Scientific, and Cultural Organization (UNESCO); Universal Postal Union (UPU); World Health Organization (WHO); and the World Meteorological Organization (WMO); the World Intellectual Property Organization (WIPO); and the International Fund for Agricultural Development (IFAD). Most were created during the United Nations era. (*For specific agencies, see* Index.)

Significance The decentralized pattern of functional operations provided for the specialized agencies in the Charter has permitted all to enjoy freedom of action within their fields of operations while accepting coordination and direction from the United Nations proper. In offering technical assistance to developing nations, for example, each contributes help within areas of its special competence and cooperates with other agencies through the United Nations Development Program to avoid duplication and overlap. Their efforts are part of the functional approach to peace, which postulates the building of a stable world order through cooperation in solving common economic and social problems.

United Nations: Troika Proposal A plan offered by the Soviet Union during the early 1960s to replace the one-man office of Secretary-General of the United Nations with a three-man presidium. Nikita Khrushchev coined the term with reference to a type of Russian vehicle drawn by three horses. Each of the three major world blocs—Western, Soviet, and neutralist—would be represented on the presidium and each would have the power to veto Secretariat decisions. *See also* SECRETARY-GENERAL, p. 334.

Significance The troika demand capped the sharp Soviet reaction to policies pursued by Secretary-General Dag Hammarskjöld during the United Nations operation in the Congo. Their view was that he had changed the emphasis of the office from administration to high level policymaking. The Soviet effort to change the basic nature of the Secretary-Generalship failed when the majority of United Nations members refused to accept the need for a troika arrangement.

United Nations Trusteeship Council That one of the six principal organs of the United Nations which supervises the administration of trust territories. The Council is subordinate to the General Assembly in its supervision of nonstrategic territories and to the Security Council in its supervision of strategic trusts. Membership on the Council includes: (1) all trust-administering states; (2) nonadministering permanent members of the Security Council; and (3) additional elective members, to strike a balance between trust-administering and nonadministering states. At the peak of its activity, the Council in 1968 consisted of four trust-administering states (United States, United Kingdom, Australia, and New Zealand); three permanent members of the Security Council (China, France, and Soviet Union); and one elective member. The Council carries out its responsibilities through studies and debates, makes recommendations to the General Assembly, hears petitions from trust territory representatives, requires annual and special reports, and sends visiting missions to trust territories for on-the-spot supervision. *See also* UNITED NATIONS: TRUST TERRITORY, p. 357.

Significance   The Trusteeship Council has moved a long way toward completing its task of supervising the transition of trust territories to independence. Of the eleven territories placed under trusteeship, by 1982 only one (United States-held Trust Territory of the Pacific Islands) had not achieved independence. Efforts have been made over a period of twenty-five years to bring an additional territory—South-West Africa—under the trusteeship system. Progress in the three island groups under American strategic trust—the Marshalls, the Carolines, and the Marianas—has been made with the granting of some measures of self government by the United States government.

United Nations: Trust Territory   A former League of Nations mandate or a non-self-governing territory placed under the United Nations trusteeship system. All mandates that had not achieved independence became trust territories in 1946, with the exception of South-West Africa. Only one additional territory—Italian Somaliland—was placed under trust as a consequence of World War II. Each trust territory was brought into the arrangement by a special agreement drawn up by the administering state and approved by the General Assembly. Supervision over the administration of trust territories is carried on by the Trusteeship Council, using annual reports, petitions from trust peoples, and visiting missions. *See also* MANDATES SYSTEM, p. 324; UNITED NATIONS TRUSTEESHIP COUNCIL, p. 356.

Significance   By 1982, ten of the eleven trust territories had been granted independence or united with a neighboring country on the basis of a United Nations-supervised plebiscite. These include: British Togoland (merged with Ghana, 1957); French Togoland (Togo, 1960); French Cameroons (Cameroon, 1960); Italian Somaliland (Somalia, 1960); British Cameroons (part merged with Cameroon, part with Nigeria, 1961); Tanganyika (Tanzania, 1961); Ruanda-Urundi (Burundi and Rwanda, 1962); Western Samoa (Samoa, 1962); Nauru (Nauru, 1968); and New Guinea (Papua New Guinea, 1975). The remaining territory, and its administering state, is the Trust Territory of the Pacific Islands (United States). The Pacific Islands is a strategic trust territory administered under Security Council supervision. Because these islands, captured from Japan in World War II, were considered crucial to American security, they were placed under Council jurisdiction where the veto applies. The General Assembly by numerous resolutions and declarations has tried unsuccessfully to force South Africa to place its mandate, South-West Africa, under the trusteeship system. Controversy exists over whether the people of the one remaining trust territory need years of tutelage to prepare them for self-government or should be granted independence at once. The 1960 General Assembly "Declaration on the Granting of Independence to Colonial Countries and Peoples"—often called the Anticolonial Manifesto—stipulates that "inadequacy of political, economic, social or educational preparedness should never serve as a pretext for delaying independence." The Declaration has been broadly interpreted and vigorously applied by the special Committee of Twenty-Four—created to implement the Declaration—that has become the central focus of the anticolonial movement in the United Nations.

United Nations: Uniting for Peace Resolution   An assumption of power by the General Assembly to authorize collective action against an aggressor. The Assembly's new function was made possible by the adoption of the Uniting for Peace Resolution of 1950, which gives the Assembly a backup role to the Security Council when that organ is unable to act because of a veto. Other provisions of the resolution called for summoning the Assembly into "emergency special session" within twenty-four hours in a peace and security crisis, establishment of a Peace Observation Commission and a Collective Measures Committee to aid the Assembly in such situations, and a call for a survey of resources which could be made available by members when needed.

Significance   The United States provided the initiative leading to the adoption of the Uniting for Peace Resolution in the hope that it would enable the United Nations to play a vital role in meeting future threats of communist aggression and limited war. Its adoption by the Assembly followed several months of Security Council inability to deal with the Korean conflict because of Soviet blocking tactics. The effort to turn the Assembly into an effective anti-communist instrument has been enfeebled by the great influx of new members, most of which pursue neutralist policies and refuse to permit the United Nations to be used by either side for carrying out Cold War policies. Although the Assembly retains the power which it assumed by virtue of the Resolution to authorize collective action and to meet in emergency special session following a veto in the Council, other measures provided by the Resolution have come into disuse. The Uniting for Peace Resolution has been invoked by the Assembly in its consideration of crises such as those in Hungary (1956), the Congo (1960), and the Middle East (1956, 1967, and 1973).

Universal Declaration of Human Rights   A proclamation intended to establish a "common standard of achievement for all peoples and all nations" in the observance of civil, political, economic, social, and cultural rights. Prepared by the Commission on Human Rights and the Economic and Social Council, the Universal Declaration was adopted by the General Assembly on December 10, 1948, since designated Human Rights Day. Since 1954, the General Assembly has been working on two draft covenants—one containing civil and political, the other economic, social, and cultural rights—intended to make the rights proclaimed in the Universal Declaration effective by national ratification. In addition, nations that accept the first of these covenants may also ratify an Optional Protocol to the Covenant on Civil and Political Rights by which individuals would be authorized to bring complaints to an international body. *See also* HUMAN RIGHTS, p. 316.

Significance   Although most of the rights set forth in the Universal Declaration have not yet been adopted as international legislation through the treaty ratification process, they have not remained a dead letter. Many of the new nations have been guided by the document in writing their national constitutions. In all states, the Declaration can be used as a yardstick to measure the congruity of national protection of individual rights with this international standard. In several cases, such as those of Rhodesia and South Africa, the Universal Declaration has served as a basis for condemning national constitutional systems that permit discrimination against racial, religious, social, or political groups. Within the United Nations, the Universal Declaration has established international norms that influence the making of decisions in all principal organs and subsidiary bodies.

Universal Postal Union (UPU)   A specialized agency of the United Nations for integrating national postal services. First established as the General Postal Union by the Berne Treaty of 1874, the UPU adopted its present name in 1878 and entered into an arrangement with the United Nations in 1947. The organization of the Union consists of a Congress that meets every five years, an Executive and Liaison Committee elected by each Congress, a Consultative Committee on Postal Research, and an International Bureau located at Berne that functions as a secretariat. The Universal Postal Convention is revised by each Congress; amendment proposals are circulated by the Bureau between Congresses and, following ratification by a sufficient number of members, must be acceded to by the others as a condition of retaining membership. See also SPECIALIZED AGENCY, p. 355.

Significance   The Universal Postal Union illustrates the need for international cooperation in technical fields. Before its establishment, for example, a letter with a foreign destination required special handling and the payment of postage to each country through which it passed. Rates varied widely and were often discriminatory. The UPU has overcome these shortcomings by standardizing national procedures, by establishing uniform rates, and by setting up compensatory accounts to clear balances. The success of the Union has encouraged the creation of additional international public unions in other technical fields.

Veto   A vote that forbids or blocks the making of a decision. Most international institutions operate under the principle of unanimity, which gives each member the authority to veto decisions. In the United Nations, however, the veto power is exercised only by the five permanent members of the Security Council: Britain, China, France, the United States, and the Soviet Union. On substantive questions, as distinguished from procedural ones on which the veto does not apply, decisions can be made by an affirmative vote of nine of the Council's fifteen members so long as no permanent member vetoes it by casting a negative vote. An abstention from voting by a permanent member does not constitute a veto. The Charter requires that parties to a dispute must abstain from voting when the Council considers pacific settlement procedures. Since Charter amendments must be ratified by all permanent members, failure to ratify would have the same effect as a veto. *See also* UNITED NATIONS SECURITY COUNCIL, p. 354.

Significance The veto power accorded to the five great powers by the framers of the United Nations Charter was regarded by them as central to the world organization's major role. In peace and security matters, they reasoned, great-power unanimity must prevail or the organization could be used by one group against another, resulting in a third world war rather than a community police action. The onset of the Cold War resulted in a schism between the great powers and the casting of over one hundred vetoes by the Soviet Union, mainly to block Western-sponsored states from membership. Although the United States insisted in 1945 on retaining the veto power, it had no need to use it until the decade of the 1970s. Vetos have declined in number in recent years because the great powers have recognized that a veto in the Council merely transfers the issue to the Assembly, where none exists. Numerous proposals to moderate or eliminate the veto in Council decision making, however, have lacked the support of the great powers.

Warsaw Treaty Organization (WTO) A regional military group of Eastern European communist states established to implement the Treaty of Friendship, Cooperation, and Mutual Assistance concluded in Warsaw in 1955. Membership in the Warsaw Treaty Organization includes all communist states of East Europe except Yugoslavia and Albania—Bulgaria, Czechoslovakia, East Germany, Hungary, Poland, Romania, and the Soviet Union. The WTO supplements a series of bilateral mutual aid pacts between the Soviet Union and several communist states concluded between 1943 and 1948. Decisions of the organization are made by a Political Consultative Committee that meets only sporadically, when called by the Soviets, although the Treaty calls for meetings to be held twice annually. Each member nation is represented on the Committee by a high government or party delegate. A military Unified Command anticipated by the Treaty has never been established, and the position of Commander-in-Chief has regularly been filled by Soviet marshals. Subsidiary organs, including a secretariat and a permanent subcommittee to coordinate members' foreign policies, have been set up by the Political Committee. Membership in WTO imposes a responsibility to contribute immediate military assistance to a victim of an armed attack and to consult at once on joint measures to meet the aggression. *See also* WARSAW PACT, p. 199.

Significance The Warsaw Treaty Organization represents a Communist-bloc response to the formation of NATO and, more particularly, to the 1954 Paris Accords by which West Germany was accepted as a NATO member. As a military alliance, the WTO helped to restore some semblance of equilibrium to the East-West balance following German rearmament. Yet, growing polycentrism in East Europe during the 1970s and 1980s has weakened it by preventing development of its full structure and anticipated role as a unified military group. Albania, for example, refused to participate after 1962 and withdrew from the organization in 1968, and Communist China, once a permanent observer, has ended its affiliation. Dissatisfaction of other members with Soviet domination of the alliance has sapped its unity, and the decreasing fear of war along with growing trade relations between East and West Europe have weakened its role. Its main function appears to be that of a forum for the formal ratification of Soviet foreign policy initiatives. In 1968, WTO forces invaded Czechoslovakia to reverse the trend toward liberalization within that member state. This was the last collective military action by WTO forces.

Western European Union (WEU) A regional alliance established in 1955 to defend Western Europe from attack, to control German rearmament, and to cooperate with NATO in the defense of the Atlantic Community. WEU was an expansion of the Brussels Pact to link up that earlier pact's members (Belgium, Britain, France, Luxembourg, and the Netherlands) with two former enemy states (Germany and Italy). The structure of the alliance includes: (1) a Council of the seven Foreign Ministers that may be called into session by any member to consult on threats to the security of Western Europe; (2) an Assembly that meets in Strasbourg and consists of delegations of WEU nations to the Council of Europe's Consultative Assembly; and (3) a secretariat that services the two major organs and the special bodies created to achieve alliance goals.

Significance The emergence of the Western European Union from the Brussels Treaty Organization in 1955 signified belief that existing Soviet power constituted a greater threat to the security of Western Europe than a future German resurgence. WEU has functioned mainly within the larger NATO framework, serving as an agency to develop common policies, and as a vehicle to urge their consideration by NATO. Most economic and social activities once carried on by WEU have been transferred to other regional groups, and its initial objective of controlling German rearmament has been relaxed.

World Government A concept of a global political entity that would insure peace and security through a supreme authority established over the state system. Most advocates of world government envisage the establishment of a federation having a central authority vested with specifically delegated powers, while the residue of governmental powers would remain with the constituent units. A world law directly applicable and enforceable upon individuals would emanate from the central government. The most active organization promoting the idea of world government is the United World Federalists. *See also* WORLD GOVERNMENT, p. 16.

Significance Proponents of world government are split between those who believe that the establishment of a world federal system should be given highest priority, and those who regard the evolutionary development of a world community based on common values and objectives as a necessary antecedent to the political structure. The American experience with federalism is often cited by advocates of world government as a precedent that should be emulated on the global level. The practical question of how to obtain a consensus among 160 diverse states on the establishment of a "higher authority" that would abolish their sovereignty in the most critical areas has never been satisfactorily answered. Several disarmament proposals advanced by the great powers would, if put into effect, provide for a limited form of world government to insure that the agreement would be kept through inspection and enforcement by an international agency.

World Health Organization (WHO)   A specialized agency of the United Nations established in 1948 with the basic purpose of "the attainment by all peoples of the highest possible level of health." WHO carries on some of its programs through advisory services which combat various maladies and aid in the development of national health administrations. Other programs are administered through central WHO facilities and include international health conventions and the publication of health statistics. WHO machinery includes an annual World Health Assembly, an Executive Board, and a Secretariat that functions under WHO's Director-General at the Geneva headquarters. *See also* SPECIALIZED AGENCY, p. 355.

Significance   The record of WHO has been outstanding, particularly in its effort to control endemic and epidemic diseases like malaria and smallpox, and in its promotion of maternal and child welfare. Malaria-control programs have been carried out in over twenty countries. WHO has assisted a number of countries in developing their health services and in expanding the number of trained health and medical technicians. WHO also aids the victims of natural disasters.

World Meteorological Organization (WMO)   A specialized agency of the United Nations established in 1947 to facilitate worldwide cooperation in weather observation and reporting and to encourage research and training in meteorology. The WMO succeeded the 1878 International Meteorological Organization composed of national directors of weather services. The new organization has states rather than individuals as members, including most states in 1982. The organization of WMO consists of a World Meteorological Congress that meets every four years with all members represented and each having one vote. An eighteen-member Executive Committee meets annually and functions as an executive body to implement WMO policies. A secretariat headed by a secretary-general services the

Geneva headquarters, which functions as an administrative, research, and information center. *See also* SPECIALIZED AGENCY, p. 355.

Significance   The role of the World Meteorological Organization has grown in response to the expanding needs for reliable weather data to provide safety and comfort for the millions who use air and water transportation facilities. The WMO has supported the development and use of space satellites for increasing reliability in weather prediction. The growing vulnerability of large urban populations to the destructive forces of nature will increase the need for international cooperation in the field of meteorology.

11. American Foreign Policy

Agency for International Development (AID)   A semi-autonomous agency that operates as a component of the International Development Cooperation Agency (IDCA), established in 1979. Created in 1961 by the Act for International Development, AID now reports to the Director of IDCA and administers economic and technical foreign assistance, coordinating military aid programs, and directing the economic aspects of the Food for Peace program. Differences between the Secretary of State and the Director of IDCA over aid policy are resolved by the President. *See also* FOOD FOR PEACE, p. 384; FOREIGN AID, p. 125 and p. 384; TECHNICAL ASSISTANCE, p. 149.

Significance   Since the days of the Marshall Plan, establishing the proper relationship between foreign aid programs and the Department of State has been a problem. Organization has fluctuated between departmental control of economic foreign policy on the one hand and departmental freedom from the overseas operational functions of such policy on the other. In the same vein, the optimum administrative relationship between economic and military assistance programs has been a matter of continual concern. AID's new role under the IDCA is a compromise which emphasizes long-range development plans, agency operational responsibility, and the coordination of the various aid projects within individual countries. By creating the IDCA as an independent agency, but having its Director report to the Secretary of State, administrative experts believe they finally resolved the problem of where to locate the AID. In its operations, the IDCA and Treasury Department work closely with the United Nations, the Organization of American States, the World Bank Group, the International Monetary Fund, and the regional development banks in support of modernization goals.

367

Alliance for Progress   Originally, a ten-year development program for Latin America suggested by President John F. Kennedy and established in 1961 at Punta del Este, Uruguay, by all the American republics except Cuba. The Alliance for Progress plan provided for a massive effort to meet the region's desperate need for modernization by means of mutual assistance and self-help. The United States anticipated a flow of public and private capital of approximately $20 billion over the life of the program, mainly from private investors in the capital-surplus countries outside the region. Participants in the program recognized, however, that the Latin American countries would ultimately have to provide four times that amount to meet the program's goal. The program called for regional planning by the Inter-American Economic and Social Council and the Inter-American Development Board, economic cooperation and integration, export price stabilization, land and tax reform, industrialization, and improved health care and educational opportunity. *See also* FOREIGN AID, p. 384; ORGANIZATION OF AMERICAN STATES, p. 329.

Significance   The Alliance for Progress program, launched so dramatically, languished amidst bickering and recrimination. This may be explained in part by the dimensions of a task that called for a controlled socioeconomic revolution of continental proportions. In the United States, opposition came from opponents of foreign aid, while in Latin America the established order has been slow to bring about the reforms required to insure the demise of the status quo. Meanwhile, throughout the area the high rate of population growth intensifies the need for economic, social, and political modernization. The United States has continued to provide modest levels of assistance within the general philosophy of the program.

Bipartisanship   Interparty unity in dealing with major problems of United States foreign policy. Bipartisanship is based on the idea of collaboration between the two major parties in the Congress, and between the President and the leaders of the opposition. The assumption underlying bipartisanship is that, in times of grave national peril, partisan politics should stop at the water's edge so that a united front can be presented to the outside world.

Significance   Bipartisanship was particularly successful during World War II and in the immediate postwar period of intense Cold War rivalry. The American constitutional system with its separation of powers and checks and balances generates conflict between the executive and the legislature that could paralyze foreign policymaking in the absence of bipartisan unity. Ultimately, a democracy must make a choice between party-developed alternative courses of action with a loyal opposition functioning, or a more unified but less democratic consensual approach to dealing with foreign policy issues.

Bricker Amendment A proposed amendment to the United States Constitution, introduced in Congress by Senator John Bricker of Ohio in 1953 and in 1954. The proposed Bricker amendment was designed to strengthen the role of Congress in treaty making, limit the President's power to conclude executive agreements, and insure the primacy of the Constitution over the provisions of any treaty. The proposal was killed when it failed by one vote to secure the necessary two-thirds majority in the Senate. *See also* MISSOURI CASE, p. 392.

Significance The Bricker amendment was one episode in the history of legislative-executive rivalry over control of American foreign relations. Supporters of the amendment were motivated by a fear that the President might do by treaty that which would be unconstitutional by statute, as had occurred in the famous case of *Missouri v. Holland* in 1920. The amendment also reflected dissatisfaction with the wartime executive agreements concluded at Yalta and Potsdam in 1945, and apprehension over the internal effect of United Nations actions, such as implementing the Universal Declaration of Human Rights. The net effect of the proposed amendment would have been to reverse the historic trend toward strong executive leadership in foreign affairs.

Central Intelligence Agency (CIA) The principal federal agency for the accumulation and evaluation of data gathered by all the units of the national intelligence community. The CIA, created by the National Security Act of 1947, is responsible to the National Security Council (NSC) and to the President. Though not a member of the NSC by law, the civilian Director of the CIA usually attends NSC meetings by presidential invitation. In addition to serving as the central receiving and interpreting agency, the CIA also gathers intelligence data and carries on covert operations. *See also* INTELLIGENCE, p. 174; NATIONAL SECURITY COUNCIL, p. 394.

Significance   The Central Intelligence Agency functions as the principal instrument of the United States government for conducting clandestine operations in foreign countries. Its operations and evaluations in the intelligence field appear to have an important impact on foreign policy decisions made at the highest levels. Revelations of the extent of its *sub rosa* penetrations of other domestic and foreign programs, both public and private, have stirred political controversy over questions of control. A central issue involves the question of the ultimate effectiveness of White House and State Department control over foreign policy if the gatherer of data also plays a substantial role as a diplomatic actor.

Civilian Control   An American constitutional principle, based on British traditions, that ultimate control of the military must be vested in civilian leaders to insure the maintenance of democracy. Civilian control is established by the Constitution, which makes the civilian President commander in chief and gives Congress the power to raise and maintain the armed services, make military law, and declare war. Statutory amplification of the principle of civilian control has required that the Secretary of Defense as well as the Secretaries of the Army, Navy, and Air Force Departments must also be civilians. The Second Amendment to the Constitution buttresses the principle by forbidding the quartering of troops in private homes without consent, and the Third Amendment insures the right of the people to keep and bear arms.

Significance   The principle of civilian control has taken on added importance for the United States and for the world as a result of the post-World War II arms race. Military leaders, by offering solutions to military problems, are increasingly influential in determining broader questions of foreign policy. In addition, the bewildering sophistication of military technology forces the Congress to turn for advice on military appropriations to the military services for whose control they are responsible.

Congress   The national legislature of the United States, composed of the Senate and the House of Representatives. The principle of state equality entitles each of the fifty states to two senators who serve six-year terms, with one third of the senators elected every two years. Membership in the House of Representatives is based on population and all 435 members face the electorate every two years. The foreign relations role of the Congress comprises: (1) its general legislative power in such matters as creating or eliminating agencies and in establishing or changing trade and immigration policy; (2) the executive powers of the Senate in approving treaties and confirming appointments; (3) control over appropriations; (4) power to conduct investigations, particularly in relation to the functioning of old law and the need for new law. Congress is also related indirectly to foreign affairs through: (1) resolutions indicating the "sense of the Congress"; (2) speeches, travels, and other activities of individual members; and (3) political party activity, which can either diminish or increase the distance between the White House and Capitol Hill.

Significance   The main functions of the Congress in foreign affairs fall within the broad framework of the separation of powers and checks and balances established by the Founding Fathers. These principles were intended to insure that action by one branch of government in the legitimate exercise of its powers would face some form of validating activity in another branch before it could become final. Thus, for example, though the President is responsible for the conduct of foreign policy, necessary funds must be voted by the Congress, with appropriations bills starting in the House; and the President cannot take final action on treaties or appointments until he has secured Senate approval. Increasingly, however, the Congress serves a policy-validating rather than a policymaking function. The complex nature of foreign affairs and the American leadership role in the world require constant presidential attention, initiative, and flexibility that Congress as a deliberative body cannot supply.

Congress: Confirmation of Appointments   The function of the national legislature to approve or disapprove nominations made by the President to fill vacancies in executive and judicial positions. The power to confirm appointments is delegated to the Senate by Article II, Section 2, of the Constitution of the United States and is accomplished by a simple majority vote. Confirmation applies only to political appointments—positions not filled by Civil Service procedures or some other formal merit system. *See also* PRESIDENT: APPOINTMENT POWER, p. 396.

Significance Under the American system of checks and balances, the making of appointments is an executive act shared by the Senate. This insures that the filling of diplomatic and policymaking positions in the Department of State and other executive agencies will be subject to legislative scrutiny. The President usually seeks to determine in advance by informal consultation with key senators the acceptability of his candidate for the appointment. Nominees for ambassadorial posts and for high positions in the Department of State are usually questioned by the Senate Foreign Relations Committee, the body that makes confirmation recommendations to the full Senate. Presidential appointments in the field of foreign affairs are rarely denied by the Senate.

Congress: Declaration of War A joint resolution adopted by Congress and signed by the President informing the international community that the nation intends to pursue or defend its interests by military action. Technically, the Congress could pass a declaration of war resolution against the wishes of the President; in such a case he would have the option of the veto. Except for the War of 1812, every declaration of war by the United States has come at presidential request. Termination of a state of war is also accomplished by joint resolution or treaty. *See also* DECLARATION OF WAR, p. 167; PRESIDENT: COMMANDER IN CHIEF, p. 399; WAR POWERS ACT OF 1973, p. 406.

Significance The declaration of war as a constitutionally discretionary prerogative of Congress may be of little practical importance since war may be forced by the aggressive acts of other states. Moreover, the President as director of the nation's foreign affairs may present Congress with a situation leaving no real alternative. Indeed within the limits of the War Powers Act of 1973 the President, as commander in chief, can order the armed forces into combat situations in the absence of a formal declaration of war, as in Korea and Vietnam. Experience in World Wars I and II, however, indicates that the declaration of war is important for another reason. When the country is formally in a state of war, Congress appears more willing to grant and the courts appear more reluctant to question the validity of the delegation of vast quasi-legislative powers to the President for the duration. This means that the President, because of the nature of modern war, will be empowered to virtually reorganize the life of the entire nation for the successful prosecution of the war effort so long as he does not overtly and flagrantly violate the provisions of the Constitution. The declaration of war also has domestic and international legal consequences in that it fixes the date at which rights and liabilities related to the state of war come into force.

Congress: House Foreign Affairs Committee

The standing committee of the House of Representatives that has primary responsibility in the field of foreign affairs. The detailed work of the Foreign Affairs Committee is assigned to standing subcommittees whose members develop expertness by their continued involvement with particular geographic and problem areas. The power of the committee in foreign affairs derives from the general legislative power of the House, the power to conduct investigations, and the role of the House in appropriating the funds necessary for all foreign policy activities. Thus, the committee plays an important role in determining the administrative organization, policy orientation, and budget for such bodies as the Agency for International Development, the United States Information Agency, and the Department of State.

Significance Once considered a minor committee, the role of the House Foreign Affairs Committee has increased with United States involvement in world affairs. The committee keeps abreast of international developments through the participation of its members in study missions abroad, subcommittee hearings, participation in international and domestic conferences, and by committee representation on the United States delegation to the United Nations General Assembly. Although the Senate Committee on Foreign Relations historically has dominated congressional involvement with foreign policy, the House Foreign Affairs Committee has increasingly insisted upon a substantive role related to the constitutional powers of the House.

Congress: Joint Resolution

A legislative act similar to a statute. A joint resolution, like a bill, must pass in identical form by simple majorities in both houses of Congress and be signed by the President to become law. When this device is used by the Congress to propose amendments to the Constitution, the President's signature is not necessary. Joint resolutions are labeled "HJ Res" and "SJ Res" to distinguish them from bills.

Significance   Joint resolutions are frequently used in foreign policy matters to declare or terminate a state of war, to approve an action by the President, or to attempt a foreign policy initiative. In certain circumstances, a joint resolution by both houses may be substituted for treaty action by the Senate, with the consequent substitution of simple majority votes in both houses for the two-thirds vote required in the Senate. The annexations of Texas and Hawaii were accomplished by this means.

Congress: Legislative Powers   The statute-making authority of the national legislature. Article I, Section 1, of the Constitution provides that "All legislative powers herein granted shall be vested in a Congress of the United States, which shall consist of a Senate and House of Representatives," and these powers are detailed in Article I, Section 8. Through its legislative power, the Congress establishes the need for, creates, empowers, diminishes, and eliminates the agencies of the executive branch through which the President conducts foreign policy. Thus, until Congress provides the machinery of government and operating funds, the President is restricted in his conduct of foreign policy to those few powers given him in the Constitution. *See also* PRESIDENT: CHIEF LEGISLATOR, p. 398.

Significance   The importance of the legislative powers of Congress in the conduct of American foreign policy is derived from the system of separated powers of government that requires the cooperation of at least two branches if the national government is to operate effectively. As a consequence, subjects of international concern yet unknown will come within the purview of the Congress since American foreign policy depends on statutory implementation.

Congress: Power of the Purse   The authority of Congress to control government finances both in terms of revenue and of expenditures. The power of the purse exercised by Congress includes the "power to lay and collect taxes, duties, imposts, and excises, to pay the debts and provide for the common defense and general welfare of the United States. . . ." (Art. I, Sec. 8), and the restriction that "No money shall be drawn from the Treasury but in consequence of appropriations made by law. . . ." (Art. I,

Sec. 9). Before a new program can enter into force, it must pass through both chambers of Congress twice, first as a policy matter to authorize the program, and second to appropriate the necessary funds. Under the first function, bills are considered by the House Foreign Affairs Committee and the Senate Foreign Relations Committee, whereas the second concerns the Appropriations Committees of the two houses. Once an appropriation has been made, its expenditure by the executive branch is audited by the General Accounting Office, which was created by Congress to insure that such expenditures come within the limits set by congressional appropriations.

Significance   The historic power of the purse is the principal vehicle by which Congress may exert control over the foreign policy process. It is virtually impossible for the President to implement foreign policy without the expenditure of funds. The extent to which Congress uses this power to influence foreign policy depends in large measure on the political relationship between the individuals in the White House and the leaders on Capitol Hill. Once the President commits the nation to a course of action, however, the power of the Congress to check him by denying funds is weakened by a fear that the national interest would suffer.

Congress: Senate Foreign Relations Committee   A standing committee of the Senate that serves as the principal agent of the Senate in the field of United States foreign policy. The Foreign Relations Committee functions largely through standing subcommittees patterned on and coordinated with the geographic and topical divisions of the Department of State. The committee's authority derives from the Senate's general legislative and investigatory powers which are similar to those exercised by the House of Representatives. As a result of the system of checks and balances, however, the Senate has certain powers not given to the House, such as a share in the executive branch's treaty- and appointment-making powers. Article II, Section 2, of the Constitution gives the President power "by and with the advice and consent of the Senate, to make treaties, provided two-thirds of the Senators present concur; and he shall nominate, and, by and with the advice and consent of the Senate, shall appoint ambassadors, and other public ministers and consuls. . . ." The Senate usually accepts the recommendations of its Foreign Relations Committee in these and other foreign policy matters.

Significance   The role of the Senate Foreign Relations Committee has expanded with American involvement in world affairs. Its close liaison with the State Department in the development of policy was demonstrated in the negotiations of the United Nations Charter and the North Atlantic Treaty. Presidents frequently consult with the committee's chairman and ranking minority leader and other influential members. Perhaps the most dramatic illustration of the committee's power to check the executive involved its role in the rejection of the Treaty of Versailles and the League of Nations by the Senate.

Congress: Treaty Power   The participation of the Senate in the executive act of treaty making. The President negotiates treaties, but under the constitutional system of checks and balances he cannot ratify them until the Senate by a two-thirds majority of those present and voting gives its consent. Under its treaty power the Senate may: (1) consent to ratification; (2) refuse consent; (3) consent to ratification after specified amendments have been made; and (4) consent to ratification with specific reservations. In no case, however, is the President legally required to ratify following Senate action. Although the Senate Foreign Relations Committee is the principal focus of the treaty power in Congress, other committees in the Senate and the House also become involved, depending on the treaty's subject matter. The House of Representatives, for example, has no treaty power per se; however, it has assumed an active role through its Appropriations Committee's insistence on a substantive review of treaty provisions before recommending the funds necessary to implement the treaty. *See also* PRESIDENT: TREATY POWER, p. 401.

Significance   The roles played by the Senate and the House in the treaty process indicate that the ratification stage in treaty making is often as crucial as the original negotiations. The powers constitutionally fixed in the Senate make it possible for a small bloc of senators representing states inhabited by a minority of the population to negate the wishes of the majority. The treaty process in Congress is typically slow and cumbersome, exacting a price in executive time and tempers by duplicate hearings, by amendments and reservations, and by the ultimate ability of the Senate to frustrate the executive will. The President will not automatically be checked, but he can never ignore the fact that he may be. Although most treaties submitted by the President to the Senate are duly approved, some have been voted down and others killed through Senate inaction. Important treaties that have failed to secure Senate consent, for example, cover such diverse subjects as the League of Nations Covenant (1919), the Charter of the International Trade Organization (1948), and the Genocide Convention (1949).

Congress: War Powers   The congressional powers expressed in or implied from the Constitution or inherent in the duty to provide for the common defense. The war powers include the authority of the Congress to tax, spend, raise and maintain the military services, enact military law, establish rules governing captures, and supervise the state militias. Beyond this, the elastic clause of Article I, Section 8, permits Congress to take any action that may be deemed necessary and proper to carry out its delegated powers. *See also* PRESIDENT: COMMANDER IN CHIEF, p. 399; WAR POWERS ACT OF 1973, p. 406.

Significance   In time of war and with the acquiescence of the courts and the people, Congress has been inclined to delegate to the President quasi-legislative authority in the form of "emergency war powers" that virtually enable him to mobilize the entire life of the nation behind the war effort. These vast delegations of war powers are temporary, for the duration of the emergency. Under international law, the power to wage war is an attribute of national sovereignty irrespective of domestic law on the subject. The Constitution, as domestic law, specifies that this sovereign war power is to be activated internally by congressional declaration. Despite the constitutional requirement, the power of Congress to declare war is of limited significance. In the War Powers Act of 1973, Congress sought to limit the president's historic power to commit American troops to action abroad without a declaration of war. Nevertheless, when the President as commander in chief commits the armed forces to combat, it is politically unlikely that Congress would deny them supplies and equipment in the absence of a formal declaration.

Containment   The basic Cold War United States foreign policy and its theoretical assumptions, aimed at halting Soviet expansion. The containment theory started with the assumption that Soviet foreign policy was most likely motivated by the imperatives of a dictatorship modified by communist ideology and Russian historicism. This formulation is associated primarily with George F. Kennan, chief of the Policy Planning Staff of the Department of State in 1947. The containment theory was implemented by a two-phase policy which dates from the Greek-Turkish aid program in 1947. Phase I, enunciated in the Truman Doctrine, called for halting any further geographical advances by the Soviet Union. It involved drawing a geopolitical "shatter zone" from Norway through Central and Southeast Europe and from the Middle East to South and East Asia. With the containment line thus drawn, Phase II called for building "situations of strength" through countervailing American power along this perimeter, and for the United States to react at a time, place, and manner of its own choosing to any Soviet effort to break the ring. The policy was intended to frustrate achievement of Soviet foreign and domestic objectives and thus to intensify the internal pressures and dissatisfactions held to be inherent in the dictatorship. Soviet leaders were to be brought to the realization that, while Soviet interests could not be gained by violence, disorder, and subversion, some of them might be achieved by accommodation through peaceful diplomacy. *See also* TRUMAN DOCTRINE, p. 404.

Significance   The containment policy implied action based on a well-developed, long-term, realistic theory of foreign policy rather than on a collection of abstract, idealistic principles that had been developed historically as guides to American foreign policy. Containment, as postulated by Kennan, called for cool nerves, a sense of timing, and a delicate touch. The Soviets were not to be backed into a corner where they might feel forced to turn and fight. They were always to be permitted room to maneuver and save face. The ultimate purpose of containment was not war, but accommodation. Containment produced a military stalemate that has been followed by lessening of tension and a measure of accommodation. The containment doctrine was also extended to include Chinese expansion in Asia.

Cultural Exchange   Programs aimed at fostering understanding and improving relations between the people of the

United States and the peoples of other countries. Although a Division of Cultural Relations was established in the State Department in 1938, the Fulbright Act of 1946 marks the beginning of an intensified program of cultural relations, largely administered today by the Bureau of Educational and Cultural Affairs. The Fulbright Act permits the use of foreign currencies and credits, obtained from the sale of surplus United States property abroad, to finance study by Americans in foreign universities, and helps foreign students to attend American universities. In addition to student and professorial exchanges under the Fulbright program, the Smith-Mundt Act of 1948 and later programs have made possible the exchange of scientists, businessmen, and governmental and professional leaders. *See also* CULTURAL EXCHANGE, p. 61.

Significance   The Fulbright and other cultural exchange programs have been favored since 1946 by executive and congressional leaders of both parties over other programs for influencing foreign attitudes toward the United States. Supporters of cultural exchange recognize students and teachers as important political elites, particularly in the developing countries. They believe that common educational backgrounds may facilitate good future relationships with the United States by establishing wider paths of communication across national cultural lines. Cultural exchange programs also reflect American faith in the efficacy of individual contacts to promote long-range acceptance of American perceptions of the nature of the international community.

Department of Defense   The executive department responsible for the military security of the United States. The Department of Defense, created in 1947, directs, supervises, and coordinates the Army, Navy, and Air Force Departments. These military departments, under civilian secretaries, are subordinate to a single civilian Secretary of Defense, who is a member of the President's Cabinet. The military chiefs of staff of each service advise their civilian secretaries, and, together with the Chief of Staff to the Secretary of Defense, comprise the Joint Chiefs of Staff, the highest military advisory body in the nation. The Secretary of Defense also receives advice from the Armed Forces Policy Council, which consists of the service secretaries, the Joint Chiefs, and the Director of Defense Research and Engineering. The Secretary of Defense and the Chairman of the Joint Chiefs of Staff serve as top-level advisers to the President on military and defense policies and are members of the National Security Council. *See also* JOINT CHIEFS OF STAFF, p. 391; NATIONAL SECURITY COUNCIL, p. 394.

Significance   The Department of Defense is responsible for national military policy, civil defense, maintenance and operation of the armed forces, coordination of military programs with over forty allied countries, maintenance of overseas bases, research, and development. With over one million civilian employees, the department accounts for almost half of the federal government's civilian personnel and at times for more than one-half of the entire national budget. Because national security is a fundamental goal of foreign policy, it is often difficult to distinguish between foreign and military policy. Although a unified defense establishment was a primary objective in the creation of the Defense Department, interservice rivalries continue, often with congressional encouragement. The Defense Reorganization Act of 1958, for example, enabled each military service to establish individual contact with the Congress, permitted no changes to be made regarding the Marine Corps or the National Guard except by congressional consent, and denied the President power to merge the armed services or to create a military general staff system. Each branch remains relatively autonomous, stands guard over its traditional role, competes vigorously for its share of the military budget, and seeks control over new weapons systems.

Department of State   The primary staff arm of the President in all matters dealing with foreign relations. Since its creation in 1789, the department, under the direction of the Secretary of State: (1) advises the President; (2) initiates and implements foreign policy; (3) administers those foreign programs assigned to it by Congress; (4) examines domestic policy in terms of its international impact; (5) provides for coordination among the increasing number of governmental agencies whose activities affect foreign relations; and (6) promotes good relations between the United States and the nations of the world. The pyramidal structure of the department is organized by levels; in descending order these include: (1) the Office of the Secretary, which includes the Under Secretaries; (2) Assistant Secretaries in charge of functional bureaus, such as Economic

Affairs, or of geographic bureaus, such as European Affairs; and (3) field missions of various types, mainly diplomatic, staffed largely by Foreign Service Officers. Several semiautonomous agencies, such as the Peace Corps and the Agency for International Development, also come under the policy guidance of the Department and the International Development Cooperation Agency (IDCA). *See also* SECRETARY OF STATE, p. 402.

Significance The State Department, as one of the oldest federal agencies, carries on a proud, elite tradition. Because it is mainly concerned with external affairs, a sympathetic reciprocal identification between the department and the American public has been difficult to establish and maintain. "Democratization" in recruitment policies and "professionalization" in the sense of career service have, however, improved this relationship in recent years. The department's freedom of action to develop policy is conditioned by the nature of the American system, in which the President has ultimate responsibility in the field of foreign affairs. Consequently, the role of the department depends in large measure on the relationship between the President and the person he selects as his Secretary of State.

Dollar Diplomacy Active use of the power of a state against other countries to promote the private foreign investment interests of its citizens. Dollar diplomacy is associated primarily with United States foreign policy toward Latin American countries during the administrations of Theodore Roosevelt, William Howard Taft, and Woodrow Wilson. The policy was based on the idea that American investment abroad would benefit the region as well as the investor, and that constructive investment required political stability in an area of chronic instability. The policy called for United States military intervention whenever necessary to insure stability and to prevent foreign intervention, particularly in the vicinity of the Panama Canal.

Significance Dollar diplomacy involved various forms of intervention, including the use of armed force and the establishment of financial protectorates in Cuba, the Dominican Republic, Haiti, and Nicaragua. The policy led to charges of "Yankee imperialism" and economic imperialism and produced lasting suspicion and ill will toward the "colossus of the north." The animosities thus engendered continue to affect relations between the United States and Latin America despite the Good Neighbor efforts begun in the Hoover Administration and pressed forward by all presidents since Franklin Roosevelt. The growing multilateral cooperation efforts evidenced by the Organization of American States and the Alliance for Progress have not ended the concern with intervention exhibited by Latin American states in such episodes as the Guatemalan crisis (1954), the Cuban Bay of Pigs invasion attempt (1961), and the initial unilateral intervention by the United States in the Dominican crisis (1965).

Executive Agreement   An international agreement concluded between heads of state. In the United States, executive agreements are not subject to the formal treaty process, which requires Senate consent to ratification by the President. The categories of executive agreements include: (1) Agreements designed to execute the stipulations of a treaty already approved. Hundreds of agreements, for example, were required to carry out the North Atlantic Treaty, the cornerstone of United States policy in Europe in the post-World War II period. (2) Agreements made by the President under a prior grant of authority from Congress. Under the Reciprocal Trade Act of 1934 and the Trade Expansion Act of 1962, the President was delegated authority to negotiate reciprocal tariff reductions with foreign governments. The Lend-Lease agreements of World War II were also of this type. (3) Agreements made with subsequent congressional approval. In 1940, before American entry into World War II, President Franklin Roosevelt traded Prime Minister Winston Churchill fifty over-age American destroyers for leases on British territories for several airbase sites in an arc stretching from Newfoundland to South America. Congress could have repudiated the agreement but gave its tacit approval when it appropriated the funds to construct the bases. (4) Agreements made by the President based solely on his power as commander in chief and his general authority over the nation's foreign relations. Examples include the Rush-Bagot Agreement of 1817 whereby Britain and the United States limited naval forces on the Great Lakes and the Yalta and Potsdam Agreements of 1945 on the conditions for terminating World War II. The principal legal distinction between treaties and executive agreements is that agreements cannot change existing domestic law but must operate within it. Treaties, on the other hand, are part of the supreme law of the land under Article VI of the Constitution and can supersede earlier statutes or treaties. Although the Constitution does not mention executive agreements, they have been in use since the first one was concluded on the subject of reciprocal mail delivery in 1792 during the Washington administration. In recent years, the number of executive agreements has far outstripped the number of treaties. One treaty or trade statute, however, may require the negotiation of any number of agreements to carry it out. Hence, it is of questionable value to compare the frequency of executive agreements with treaties without a subject-matter analysis in each instance.

Significance Public criticism of executive agreements is frequently based on the assumption that the President intends to circumvent the Senate's power to check the President in his conduct of foreign affairs. The charge may or may not be true in the few agreements that can be made without congressional participation. In an international emergency involving national security, however, when publicity might not be in the public interest and might provoke crises, agreements made on the sole authority of the President have the advantages of speed and secrecy. The existence of this alternative to the treaty process for reaching international accord may also contribute to Senate acceptance of some treaties. The Case Act of 1972 requires the President to report all agreements to Congress within sixty days.

Executive Office of the President A group of staff agencies directly responsible to the President, created to advise and aid him in carrying out his wide range of executive duties. Agencies within the Executive Office have varied since its creation by executive order under the Reorganization Act of 1939. The Office currently includes the White House Office, Intelligence Oversight Board, Office of Management and Budget, Domestic Policy Staff, National Security Council, Energy Resources Council, Office of Science and Technology Policy, Council of Economic Advisers, Office of the Special Representative for Trade Negotiations, Council on International Economic Policy, Council on Environmental Quality, and the Council on Wage and Price Stability as its major components.

Significance The Executive Office, originally established to aid the President in domestic matters, now reflects the President's equal or greater concern with foreign policy and related matters. Prior to its creation, the President was dependent on the major operating agencies for reports, recommendations, projections, and daily assistance. Today, the Executive Office has institutionalized the presidency. This presidential "team" numbers approximately 2000 people who aid the President in establishing and implementing broad policies ranging across the spectrum of the executive branch.

Food for Peace Program   The disposition of surplus American agricultural products to improve United States foreign relations and to increase consumption of such commodities abroad. The Food for Peace program (also called Food for Freedom) was established by Public Law 480 in 1954. *See also* FOREIGN AID, pp. 125 and 384.

Significance   The Food for Peace Program recognizes that the population explosion has made food supply a matter of increasing importance in international politics. Under the program, agricultural products in excess of usual marketings are sold through regular trade channels for local currencies. The local currency thus acquired is used by the United States government to expand international trade, encourage economic development, buy strategic materials, pay foreign obligations, promote educational and cultural exchanges, build collective strength, and foster American foreign policy. The act also empowers the President to furnish emergency assistance in famine and other extraordinary relief situations. Such assistance may be granted to any nation friendly to the United States, or to friendly but needy populations without regard to the friendliness of their government.

Foreign Aid   Military, economic, and social assistance offered by the United States to foreign countries. The names of the programs and the geographic foci have varied since World War II with the problems involved and the nature of American national interest. Several trends, however, can be noted. First, from 1948 to 1952, foreign aid was concentrated in massive economic assistance to Western Europe in the Marshall Plan. From 1952 to 1959, the emphasis of foreign aid became predominantly military with the advent of the Korean War and a policy of resisting Soviet and Chinese expansionism. Since 1959 the mix of economic and military foreign aid has been determined by United States national interest and local problems in various regions of the world. The second trend has been the gradual geographic shift of foreign aid from Western Europe to the developing nations of the Third World. The emphasis in aid programs as a result of public and congressional criticism has also shifted from outright grants to long-term, low-interest loans. Finally, as more systematic criteria for the provision of assistance have developed, a greater degree of selectivity has been evident in the awarding of American foreign aid. *See also* FOREIGN AID, pp. 125 and 384.

Significance   The vast economic power of the United States is a political fact of international life; and foreign aid programs, as instruments of American foreign policy, have been vehicles for the expression of that power. Foreign aid can and has been used for a number of reasons, some selfish, some humanitarian, some short-sighted and opportunistic, some long-range and visionary. From the start, a core objective appears to have been to gain time to frustrate the forces leading to violent change and establish a world order based on peaceful international processes. After many years of involvement, however, American executive, legislative, and public support for foreign aid has waned. Although the per capita income gap between rich and poor countries has widened since 1949, the portion of the national budget of the United States allocated to foreign aid has shrunk.

Foreign Service   The diplomatic and consular establishment of the United States. Created by the Rogers Act of 1924 and augmented by the Foreign Service Act of 1946, as amended, the career Foreign Service is entered by passing a nation-wide competitive examination and advancement is based on a merit system. Personnel are divided into five broad categories: (1) Chief of Mission (CM), either a senior career officer or a political appointee who serves as an ambassador or as head of a special mission, such as to the United Nations; (2) Foreign Service Officer (FSO), the standard title for the various grades of career diplomatic and consular officers who form the core of the service; (3) Foreign Service Reserve Officer (FSR), a technical expert or specialist, such as a commercial attaché, who may serve for nonconsecutive periods of up to five years at the discretion of the Secretary of State; (4) Foreign Service Staff (FSS), which includes diplomatic couriers, executive secretaries, and embassy administrative staff involved in such matters as disbursing, budget, and telecommunications filing; (5) Foreign Service Local Employees (FSL), several thousand noncitizens employed at Foreign Service posts around the world to perform duties ranging from translation to custodial services. *See also* DIPLOMAT, p. 235.

Significance   The United States Foreign Service, under the control of the Department of State, is charged with conducting the day to day relations between the United States and the other countries of the world. Functions of the Foreign Service include: (1) execution of American foreign policy objectives; (2) protection of American citizens and interests abroad; (3) collection and interpretation of information; (4) negotiation; and (5) staffing delegations to multilateral and regional organizations, such as the United Nations and the Organization of American States.

Foreign Service Examination   Written, oral, and physical examinations that constitute the basis for appointment to the career Foreign Service. The Board of Examiners for the Foreign Service determines the nature, scope, and date of the written examination and selects the panels of officers who will conduct the oral examination of those who pass the written. Physical requirements are similar to those for entering into military service. Upon successful completion of the first three hurdles, passage of the language requirement may be deferred and a provisional appointment to the Foreign Service may be made.

Significance   Appointment to the service by means of a nationwide competitive examination is intended to insure a high level of preparation and background among applicants. This together with the career concept is designed to provide the nation with high quality diplomatic representation in keeping with its status as a great power.

Foreign Service Institute   A division of the Department of State that trains Foreign Service and State Department personnel in the various fields of international relations, administrative operations, management, supervision, and foreign languages.

Significance   The Foreign Service Institute offers Foreign Service officers and other federal personnel thorough indoctrination concerning their overseas responsibilities before receiving their foreign assignments. Some observers have urged that the institute be expanded into a Foreign Service Academy with a four-year curriculum to train diplomats in the same way that the military services prepare their officers.

Foreign Service Officer (FSO)   A United States career diplomatic officer. Foreign Service Officers usually enter the Foreign Service in Class 8 through competitive examination. Promotion by merit goes through Class 1 up to career minister and ultimately career ambassador.

Significance   The FSO is the skilled professional and the backbone of the Foreign Service. During his career, the Foreign Service Officer can expect to serve anywhere in the world. He will probably learn two foreign languages, become expert in one geographical area, and perform a range of duties involving political, economic, intelligence, commercial, informational, and consular activities. The personnel of the Foreign Service have been integrated with the diplomatic backup personnel in the State Department so that each serves in domestic and foreign posts.

Good Neighbor Policy   A United States policy toward Latin America intended to overcome the fear and suspicion evidenced by such terms as "Yankee imperialism" and "colossus of the north." In his inaugural address in 1933, President Franklin Roosevelt spoke of the "good neighbor who resolutely respects himself, and because he does so, respects the rights of others...." For the first third of the century, United States policies characterized by dollar diplomacy, military intervention, unilateralism, and a generally paternalistic attitude engendered much resentment in Latin America. The Good Neighbor Policy was an about-face and embodied the idea that United States-Latin American relations should be conducted on the basis of sovereign equality and mutual cooperation.

Significance   Under the Good Neighbor Policy, a nonintervention treaty was signed at Montevideo in 1933. In 1934 the

Platt Amendment limiting Cuban sovereignty was abrogated and United States troops were withdrawn from Haiti. The good relations that prevailed during World War II resulted in mutual security treaties in 1945 and 1947 and a vast array of cooperative enterprises under the aegis of the Organization of American States (OAS). It should be recognized, nevertheless, that the enormous power of the northern partner, its occasional support of unpopular regimes, and unilateral acts like the Bay of Pigs fiasco in 1961 and military intervention in the Dominican Republic in 1965, all continue to limit the credibility of the policy for many Latin Americans.

Implied Power   A power possessed by the United States government by inference from a specific power delegated to it in the Constitution. Thus the power to create an air force may properly be exercised by implication from the power to raise and maintain an army and navy even though manned flight and intercontinental ballistic missiles did not exist at the time the Constitution was written. The concept was authoritatively set forth by the Supreme Court in *McCulloch v. Maryland* (4 Wheaton 316 [1819]). *See also* CONGRESS: LEGISLATIVE POWERS, p. 374.

Significance   The implied-powers doctrine has enabled the United States to function effectively in the field of foreign as well as domestic policy without a vast proliferation of amendments to the Constitution. A strong national government would be impossible if its powers were limited exclusively to those enumerated in the Constitution. A loose construction of the Constitution, however, through the vehicle of the "necessary and proper" clause of Article I, Section 8, has enabled the national government to adapt itself to contemporary conditions.

Inherent Powers   Powers exercised by the United States government that are neither enumerated nor implied in the Constitution. The inherent powers are derived from the nature of the United States as a sovereign state and, by definition, the equal of all other such states in the international community. Under this doctrine, the United States government can do those things which any national government must do, such as making treaties and acquiring territory. *See also* CURTISS-WRIGHT CASE, p. 405; PRESIDENT: CHIEF OF FOREIGN POLICY, p. 399.

Significance　　The inherent-powers doctrine has given the United States government, operating under the limitations of a constitutional system, the flexibility to meet the challenges that arise from the interaction of the nation with more than 160 other states. In domestic affairs, the Supreme Court has held in *Youngstown Sheet and Tube Co. v. Sawyer* (343 U.S. 579 [1952]) that the powers of the national government must be traced from a specific grant or be reasonably implied from such a grant. In international affairs, the Court has held that the doctrine of the sovereign equality of states provides the necessity and the authority to act even though the Constitution may be silent. Although the national government cannot do anything forbidden by the Constitution, the limits of its inherent powers beyond this point are unspecified.

Inter-American Development Bank (IDB)　　An international banking institution created by the Organization of American States (OAS) in 1959 to accelerate regional economic and social development in Latin America. Originally capitalized at $1 billion, the total resources of the Bank now stand at about $15 billion. Members include most Latin American countries, plus Austria, Belgium, Britain, Canada, Denmark, France, Israel, Japan, the Netherlands, Spain, Switzerland, West Germany, Yugoslavia, and the United States, the largest contributor. Funds come from member subscriptions and from the sale of Bank bonds. As in the International Monetary Fund (IMF), voting is weighted according to each member's contribution. Loans are normally repayable in hard currency. However, a Fund for Special Operations (FSO) makes possible some soft currency loans for non-self-liquidating projects repayable in the debtor's currency. *See also* CAPITAL, p. 107; INTERNATIONAL MONETARY FUND, p. 135; REGIONAL DEVELOPMENT BANKS, p. 145.

Significance　　The Inter-American Development Bank promotes public and private investment by: (1) making developmental capital available; (2) aiding members to establish policies for more effective resource utilization; (3) providing assistance to members in the planning and programming of development projects. Latin American states have welcomed non-regional membership in the Bank because it adds to the resources of the Bank and because it tends to dilute the dominance of the United States. Over one thousand Latin American development projects have been financed through the IDB.

International Communication Agency (ICA)   The official overseas propaganda organization of the United States government. Created in 1978 under the Presidential Reorganization Plan, the ICA carries out functions previously performed by the United States Information Agency and the State Department's Bureau of Educational and Cultural Affairs. The ICA is closely associated with the State Department and ICA personnel are attached to overseas diplomatic missions. *See also* IDEOLOGICAL WARFARE, p. 74; PROPAGANDA, p. 76.

Significance   ICA's activities are aimed at foreign publics and elites to explain and build support for United States foreign policy and to foster an image of American society as being complex, pluralistic, tolerant, and democratic. The message is disseminated through books, periodicals, film, TV programs, and exhibits. Perhaps its most widely known activity is the Voice of America (VOA) broadcasts received in many languages all over the globe. ICA also administers exchange programs involving artists, musicians, dramatists, scholars, educators, students, and athletes.

Interest Group   An association of persons who share a particular value orientation and who seek government support for the promotion or protection of those values. Interest groups operate through lobbying activities directed toward agencies of government, usually by paid professionals. They also operate by propaganda activities directed toward the general public to build popular support for their particular value or values. The number and diversity of interest groups is astronomical. Some of the most prominent involve the concerns of: (1) business, labor, and agriculture; (2) ethnic, national, patriotic, religious, and veterans groups; and, (3) consumer and environmental advocates.

Significance   Interest groups, unlike political parties, are not interested in operating the entire government. They are minorities that seek to influence or control policy and those who make and implement policy. Some, like the United States Chamber of Commerce, operate continuously. Others, like the National Rifle Association, become highly active only when a particular value seems threatened. In modern pluralist societies, interest or pressure groups can be viewed as a normal part of the political process.

Isolationism   A doctrine which views the national interest of the United States as best served by withdrawing the country from the political entanglements of the international community. Proponents of isolationism base their arguments on the concept of the geographical, ideological, and cultural separateness of the United States. This attitude was particularly prevalent in the United States in the period between the First and Second World Wars.

Significance   During the nineteenth and early twentieth centuries, the United States practiced varying degrees of noninvolvement in international politics but was never actually isolated. The United States has never implemented the principle of noninvolvement in Pacific or Far Eastern affairs to the extent that it did so in Europe. The application of the doctrine vis à vis Europe helps to explain American efforts at neutrality in the early stages of World Wars I and II. The technological developments of the mid-twentieth century, particularly the splitting of the atom, raise questions about the relevance of the doctrine.

Joint Chiefs of Staff   A top-level military staff agency in the Department of Defense responsible for all matters related to military strategy. The Joint Chiefs of Staff, composed of the Chiefs of Staff of the Army and Air Force, the Chief of Naval Operations, the Commandant of the Marine Corps, and the Chief of Staff to the Secretary of Defense, was created by the National Security Acts of 1947 and 1949. A second staff agency, the Armed Forces Policy Council, composed of the civilian and military heads of the Departments of the Army, Navy, and Air Force, advises the Secretary of Defense on broader policy questions. *See also* DEPARTMENT OF DEFENSE, p. 379.

Significance   The Joint Chiefs of Staff function as the highest military advisory body available to the President and the Secretary of Defense. Although intended to present a unified military point of view, the Joint Chiefs also reflect the views of their individual services. In spite of the creation of a single Department of Defense, the diversity of advice offered by the Joint Chiefs demonstrates that the integration of the armed services envisioned by the National Security Acts has not been fully accomplished. Consequently, the institution of the Joint Chiefs of Staff has not been free from the criticism that traditional interservice rivalries, traditional budget procedures, and traditional thinking that insists on a division of labor among the separate services have made it difficult to secure clear strategic guidance.

Marshall Plan　　A program of massive American assistance to rebuild the European economies ravaged by World War II. Proposed by Secretary of State George C. Marshall in 1947, Congress adopted the plan under the title of the European Recovery Program. Between 1948 and 1952, the United States provided $15 billion in grants and loans to sixteen (seventeen when West Germany was included) West European countries. With the encouragement of the United States, the participants formed the Organization for European Economic Cooperation (OEEC) to work cooperatively for economic recovery on a regional rather than strictly national basis. The Soviet Union and the countries of East Europe, though invited, chose not to participate. *See also* FOREIGN AID, pp. 125 and 384.

Significance　　The Marshall Plan provided the catalyst which enabled European experience and enterprise to raise the economies of all the countries involved above prewar levels by 1951. As a result the Soviet Union was denied the opportunities for exploitation inherent in economic dislocation and in social and political unrest. The cooperative relationships fostered in the OEEC became a precedent for subsequent efforts at European economic integration leading to creation of the European Community, with American encouragement.

Missouri v. Holland (252 U.S. 416 [1920]　　A leading case in which the United States Supreme Court answered affirmatively the question of whether the national government, acting through the treaty power, could establish jurisdiction in areas otherwise reserved to the states. In *Missouri v. Holland*, the Supreme Court upheld the constitutionality of a federal statute implementing a treaty with Great Britain for the regulation and protection of migratory birds flying between Canada and the United States. Previously, in the absence of the treaty, similar legislation had been found by the lower federal courts to be an unconstitutional exercise of national power. *See also* BRICKER AMENDMENT, p. 369; PRESIDENT: TREATY POWER, p. 401.

Significance   The decision in *Missouri v. Holland*, while not destroying the federal principle, enables the national government to accomplish by treaty objectives that might be unconstitutional in statute form. No treaty has ever been declared unconstitutional. Treaties, however, are part of the supreme law of the land under Article VI of the Constitution and may be made only on appropriate subjects affecting international relations. The *Missouri* case gave rise to a fear among opponents of strong national power that the treaty power might be used to subvert the Constitution. This opposition culminated in the unsuccessful effort in the 1950s to secure passage of the Bricker Amendment that would have seriously weakened the treaty-making powers of the President and Senate. The amendment would have restricted national authority by permitting treaties to become effective only through legislation that would be valid in the absence of the treaty.

Monroe Doctrine   A basic principle of United States foreign policy, opposing foreign intervention in the Western Hemisphere. The Monroe Doctrine, which began as a unilateral policy statement by President James Monroe in his State of the Union message to Congress in 1823, also stated a reciprocal United States intention, since abandoned, to refrain from interfering in the internal affairs of Europe. The statement was occasioned by concern that, with the end of the Napoleonic Wars, the Holy Alliance might assist in the reestablishment of the Spanish colonial empire through the subjugation of the newly independent Latin American republics.

Significance   The Monroe Doctrine has provided the basic guidelines of United States policy in the Western Hemisphere for a century and a half. Following the Congress of Vienna of 1815, British sea power established the *Pax Britannica*, which indirectly supported the Monroe Doctrine because of parallel British and American interests in the Western Hemisphere. By the end of the century American military power was sufficient to back its own doctrine, which, through interventions, unilateral corollaries, and restatements, increasingly offended the Latin Americans. Beginning with the Good Neighbor Policy in 1933, however, the doctrine has gone through a process of multilateralization that has produced political unity in the form of the OAS and a common security policy against foreign intervention embodied in the Rio Treaty. Consensus, however, is lacking on the question of whether and how the Monroe Doctrine should be applied to such problems as the establishment of a communist government in Cuba, subversive activities elsewhere in Latin America, and United States intervention in domestic revolutions.

National Security Council (NSC) A staff agency in the Executive Office created by the National Security Act of 1947 to advise the President on the integration of domestic, foreign, and military policies related to national security. The National Security Council's statutory members include the President, the Vice President, the Secretaries of State and Defense. Also present are the Chairman of the Joint Chiefs of Staff and the Director of the Central Intelligence Agency, which operates under the direction of the Council. The President invites other officials, such as the Director of Management and Budget or the Secretary of the Treasury, when he deems their presence to be desirable. The President's National Security Adviser heads NSC. *See also* CEN-TRAL INTELLIGENCE AGENCY, p. 369; JOINT CHIEFS OF STAFF, p. 391.

Significance The National Security Council was designed to function as the highest-level advisory agency available to the President on national security affairs. The President, however, has ultimate constitutional authority in defense matters and decides whether and in what circumstances to use its services. The Council does not decide strategies, nor does it have active responsibility for policy implementation. It studies major defense problems and makes recommendations. Since its establishment, the degree of reliance on the Council has varied with the styles of the presidents.

Peace Corps A program through which American volunteers work in other countries for world peace through development and cultural relations. The Peace Corps was intially created by executive order by President John Kennedy in March, 1961, and established by statute in September of that year. The act states that the program is designed to aid developing countries upon request "in meeting their needs for trained man power, and to promote a better understanding of the American people . . . and of other peoples on the part of the American people." *See also* CULTURAL EXCHANGE, p. 378; FOREIGN AID, pp. 125 and 384.

Significance   The Peace Corps represented a new emphasis in the field of foreign assistance by providing human resources to aid nations in their process of modernization. Since its inception, thousands of Americans have served on a voluntary basis, usually for two-year periods, at the grass roots level in over forty-six countries. The volunteers receive a period of training in the United States before going abroad to live and work alongside the people they serve. The small salary received indicates that most volunteers are motivated by a desire to help and by a spirit of adventure. Approximately half of the volunteers are teachers and the other half engage in agricultural, health, public works, and community development projects. The attitude of the receiving countries is indicated by the fact that their requests for volunteers exceed the supply.

Point Four Program   A program designed to foster economic development and modernization by making available to the recipient countries American technical knowledge and skills. The Point Four Program resulted from an appeal to Congress to provide foreign technical assistance. The program received its name because it was the fourth major point in President Harry Truman's inaugural address delivered on January 20, 1949. The President advocated the maintenance of peace and freedom by means of "a bold new program for making the benefits of our scientific advances and industrial progress available for the improvement and growth of underdeveloped areas." Implementation was provided in 1950 by the Act for International Development. *See also* FOREIGN AID, pp. 125 and 384.

Significance   The Point Four Program was popular in the United States for several reasons. There was confidence in the quality of American knowledge and skills, and such a program was comparatively inexpensive. Forty-five million dollars was appropriated the first year. The economy of the program, however, explains the limited success of Point Four. At the time, there was a failure to realize that there had to be some input of capital to complement the developing country's newly acquired technical competence if the program was to produce the intended results. Point Four was the first of many assistance programs that have since been provided by the United States, other advanced countries, and the United Nations to aid developing countries in the process of modernization.

President   The central figure in the American system of government. The President is the nation's chief executive, the commander in chief of its armed forces, and represents the nation to the rest of the world. The power of the President in foreign affairs is based on the Constitution, statutes, custom and tradition, judicial interpretations, party leadership, and public support. Each of these sources of power has been developed and applied by the men who have filled the position. The dimensions of the office of President are best understood in terms of his roles as chief diplomat, chief of foreign policy, chief legislator, and commander in chief, and in terms of his appointment, recognition, and treaty powers.

Significance   In the field of foreign affairs the powers arising from the President's combined roles as head of state and head of government, together with the strength of the nation he leads, make the American chief executive the most powerful in the world. The President in his many roles serves as the chief architect in developing foreign policy and as the nation's exclusive spokesman in international relations. The lives of nations and peoples in many areas of the world are affected by the American people's choice of the person to occupy the White House.

President: Appointment Power   Authority to nominate individuals who will serve in government positions. The appointment power (usually an executive function) in the United States is modified by the system of checks and balances. Article II, Section 2, of the Constitution provides that the President "shall nominate, and, by and with the advice and consent of the Senate, shall appoint ambassadors, other public ministers and consuls. . . ." The appointment power of the President and his Secretary of State has been augmented by statute under the same constitutional clause that states that "the Congress may by law vest the appointment of such inferior officers, as they think proper, in the President alone . . . or in the heads of departments." The President is also empowered to fill vacancies in ambassadorial, ministerial, or consular posts if any occur while the Senate is in recess. If upon the reconvening of the Senate the interim appointment is not confirmed for any reason, the appointee's temporary commission expires at the end of that session. Thus the President's power of appointment is derived directly from the Constitution and augmented by congressional legislation. See also CONGRESS: CONFIRMATION OF APPOINTMENTS, p. 371.

Significance   Since the President is ultimately responsible for the conduct of American foreign policy, his appointees must be persons who, he is confident, will scrupulously and skillfully implement his policies. Consequently, in nominating ambassadors and other diplomats, the President has wide discretion and is rarely checked by the Senate's refusal to confirm the appointment. The President is not required to select high-level diplomatic appointees from among the career Foreign Service Officers, and a number of political appointments occur in every administration. The number of career diplomats nominated, however, ranges between 50 and 75 percent. On a more informal basis, the President can also send a personal emissary on a diplomatic mission without the advice or consent of the Senate. The President has power to remove diplomatic officers at any time since executive and administrative officials serve at his pleasure.

President: Chief Diplomat   The role of the chief executive as the nation's highest-level negotiator with foreign powers. The President as chief diplomat is the official medium through which the government of the United States communicates with foreign countries. The President's powers are derived directly and by implication from Article II of the Constitution. Thus he can send and receive ambassadors, grant or withhold recognition, sever diplomatic relations, negotiate treaties, and, through his power as commander in chief, focus the military power of the nation in support of his foreign policy. In the formulation and implementation of foreign policy, the President depends most heavily on the Secretaries of State and Defense and on the executive departments that they head. See also DIPLOMACY, p. 234; NEGOTIATION, p. 240; SUMMIT DIPLOMACY, p. 246.

Significance   The primacy of the President as chief diplomat has been recognized since the early days of the Republic. The Supreme Court, in *United States v. Curtiss-Wright Export Corp.*, held that "the President alone has the power to speak or listen as a representative of the nation." Direct negotiation at the presidential level was carried on by Woodrow Wilson in World War I and by Franklin D. Roosevelt in World War II. In the post-World War II period, summit diplomacy with other heads of government has become the most dramatic manifestation of the President's role as chief diplomat, a role enhanced by such developments as the 1963 "hot-line" agreement establishing a direct communications link between the White House and the Kremlin. Richard Nixon's reopening of relations with the People's Republic of China and Jimmy Carter's Camp David peace talks with Egypt and Israel during the 1970s further illustrate the presidential diplomatic role.

President: Chief Legislator   A concept which emphasizes the importance of the President's role in the legislative process. The President's legislative powers are based on Article I, Section 7, and Article II, Section 3, of the Constitution, which enable him: (1) to exercise a legislative veto; (2) to adjourn the Congress under unusual circumstances; (3) to call special sessions of the Congress; and (4) to call matters to the attention of the Congress and to recommend legislation in special messages. In his efforts to guide national policy, the President also uses equally important but less formal devices. The power and prestige of the office are exerted through his position as party leader, his control of patronage, his personal persuasiveness, and his careful attention to public relations in building public support for his leadership. *See also* CONGRESS: LEGISLATIVE POWERS, p. 374.

Significance   The President's role as chief legislator is as vital in foreign as in domestic affairs because most foreign policy requires legislative support and implementation. Most legislation affecting foreign relations is first drafted in the executive branch and then introduced by legislators friendly to the administration. Whether the item is the annual foreign aid bill, a request for a new agency like the Peace Corps, or a plan for the reorganization of the armed services, it is assured of careful congressional scrutiny when it is known to be an "administration measure" and part of "the President's program."

President: Chief of Foreign Policy   The role of the chief executive as the nation's highest policymaker in the field of foreign affairs. As chief of foreign policy, the President is ultimately responsible for the security and well-being of the nation. His responsibilities derive from his constitutional roles as chief executive officer and commander in chief, which require him to formulate, develop support for, and carry out foreign policies calculated to maximize the national interests of the United States. The President's leadership function is exercised largely through the Secretary and Department of State, although he can exert foreign policy leadership in a variety of other ways. These include the drafting of legislation, messages to Congress, personal diplomacy, public addresses, press conferences, and press releases. The Monroe Doctrine, for example, was contained in a State of the Union message, and the Point Four Program was first enunciated in President Harry Truman's inaugural address. Public statements by cabinet and other executive officials and by persons known to speak with the authority of the President constitute an informal channel through which the President can reach the peoples and governments of the world. *See also* CURTISS-WRIGHT CASE, p. 405.

Significance   The framers of the American system could hardly have anticipated the development of the presidency into a position of individual world leadership. Although the foreign policy involvement of some presidents has been minimal, others have so directly immersed themselves in foreign policy matters that they functioned, in effect, as their own Secretaries of State. The degree of personal involvement is a matter of individual choice. The primacy of office as the nation's highest official level for developing and implementing foreign policy, however, is grounded in the Constitution and has been clearly set forth by the Supreme Court.

President: Commander in Chief   The role of the chief executive as director of the nation's armed forces. Under Article II, Section 2, of the Constitution the President is designated commander in chief of all United States armed forces and of the state militias when they have been called into federal service. *See also* WAR POWERS ACT OF 1973, p. 406.

Significance   The President as commander in chief exercises the vast war powers affecting the security of the United States and many other nations. Since the President is the nation's highest elected official, his legal authority over the military implements the American democratic principle of civilian control. In wartime the President can coordinate and direct military operations and such related activities as arranging an exchange of prisoners and negotiating an armistice. In peacetime his disposition of forces and his ability to order armed intervention to protect American interests can profoundly affect foreign policy and the state of international relations. He can commit forces to hostilities commenced by foreign governments, as President Harry Truman did in Korea in 1950. Although the President cannot declare a state of war, he can act in ways that leave Congress little alternative, as when President Franklin Roosevelt ordered naval forces to protect convoys of war supplies bound for Britain early in World War II before the United States was actually at war with Germany. This freedom of action has been modified in some degree by the War Powers Act of 1973.

President: Recognition   Recognition indicates willingness to establish normal diplomatic relations with another state or government. The President's plenary power of recognition is derived by implication from his power to send and receive ambassadors (Art. II, Sec. 2), and is used at his discretion. *See also* RECOGNITION OF GOVERNMENTS, p. 244.

Significance   Recognition is a most important step for a great economic and military power like the United States since it can facilitate or hamper the success of a new state or government in its international relations. It may also promote or impede good relations between the United States and interested parties. American Presidents have followed no single line of policy on recognition. At times it has been held to be purely a legal act not necessarily implying approval, and at other times it has been considered primarily a political act with the definite implication of approval. In 1914, during the Mexican Revolution, Woodrow Wilson's refusal to recognize the Huerta regime because he considered it to be illegitimate led to the collapse of that government. In 1933, Franklin D. Roosevelt recognized the government of the Soviet Union after it had been in power since 1917. Harry Truman recognized the state of Israel within hours of its creation in 1948. No President was willing to recognize the government of the People's Republic of China from 1949 to 1979, yet most of the communist regimes of the states of Eastern Europe were recognized. The President alone has the legal power to grant or to withhold recognition, but the effects of his decision are of profound political importance at home and abroad. He can be expected to weigh legislative, executive, and public opinion against his own concept of the national interest before he exercises his exclusive authority.

President: Treaty Power Treaties are negotiated under the President's direction as the nation's chief diplomat and chief of foreign policy. The treaty power is set forth in Article II, Section 2, of the Constitution. Under the system of checks and balances, the President can negotiate but cannot ratify a treaty until the Senate has given its consent in the form of a two-thirds vote of approval. Courses of action open to the President in connection with the Senate's role in the treaty process include these possibilities: (1) normally, he will submit the treaty to the Senate and then ratify it after the Senate has consented; (2) if the Senate is hostile, the President may refuse to submit a treaty and let it die rather than suffer a defeat; (3) under similar conditions, the treaty can be withdrawn from the Senate before a vote has been taken; and (4) if the Senate has approved a treaty with Senate amendments and if the President deems renegotiation inappropriate, he may refuse to ratify. The technical steps in the entire treaty process are negotiation, signature, ratification, exchange of ratifications, publication, proclamation, and execution. *See also* CONGRESS: TREATY POWER, p. 376.

Significance The President is properly charged with initiating treaties because of the incomparable resources available to him in the executive branch and because it is through him that foreign governments conduct their relations with the United States. The Congress, however, by joint or concurrent resolution can attempt to induce the President to negotiate a treaty. On the other hand, since President Woodrow Wilson's experience with the Treaty of Versailles in the Senate, Presidents have tried to involve the Senate in the treaty process in the early stages. Certain senators, for example, were appointed to the United States delegation to the San Francisco Conference and participated in the negotiation of the United Nations Charter. Key senators, especially members of the Foreign Relations Committee, are likely to be kept informed during the progress of negotiations so that Senate attitudes can be taken into account before submission of the completed document for Senate approval. Depending on the subject matter, the President as chief negotiator also may use the alternative of the executive agreement should the Senate prove intractable.

Reciprocal Trade Agreements Act of 1934　An act which empowered the President on the basis of reciprocity with other countries to raise or lower tariffs up to 50 percent of the existing rates. The Reciprocal Trade Act provided for the most-favored-nation principle, which permitted the best trade concessions negotiated with any participating state to be granted automatically to all states that included the most-favored-nation clause in their trade agreements. Revisions of the act permitted further percentage reductions in the remaining tariff rates, but protectionists secured the inclusion of peril-point and escape-clause procedures. The peril point is that tariff level at which foreign competition might threaten or injure the domestic producer, in which case the Tariff Commission would so inform the President and the Congress. By use of the escape-clause procedure, the President could raise the tariff rate to restore protection for the affected industry. *See also* ESCAPE CLAUSE, p. 120; MOST-FAVORED-NATION CLAUSE, p. 140; TARIFF, p. 148; UNITED STATES INTERNATIONAL TRADE COMMISSION, p. 405.

Significance　The Reciprocal Trade Agreements Act was a break in the rampant worldwide economic nationalism of the early days of the Great Depression. It resulted in the negotiation of reciprocal tariff reductions by executive agreements with forty-three countries. The act with its eleven extensions is sometimes referred to as the Hull Reciprocal Trade Agreements Program after Cordell Hull, Secretary of State during the crucial pre-World War II period when international trade policy began to shift toward emphasizing trade expansion. The act was finally superseded by the Trade Expansion Act of 1962, which broadened the powers of the President and in particular strengthened the trade position of the United States vis à vis the European Common Market.

Secretary of State　Head of the Department of State and chief adviser to the President on foreign policy, for which, however, the President is ultimately and completely responsible. The office of secretary was established in 1789 with the creation of the department. The position is political in nature and is filled by the personal choice of the President. As with any other high level position, the appointment is subject to senatorial confirmation, but since final responsibility for foreign affairs vests in the President, the Senate is hardly likely to refuse confirmation. As a political appointee, the secretary has no fixed term but serves at the pleasure of the President. The importance of the post can be inferred from the facts that the secretary ranks first among cabinet officers, and first among the nonelective officials in line of presidential succession. See also DEPARTMENT OF STATE, p. 380.

Significance   The importance of the office of Secretary of State has increased in the same ratio as United States participation in international affairs. The secretary personally and through his department seeks to establish specific national interests and to formulate programs calculated to achieve them by suggesting the particular combination of negotiation, propaganda, economic power, and military force to be applied. The degree to which the secretary is free to act as a decision maker depends on the relationship between himself and the President. Some Presidents like Woodrow Wilson and Franklin Roosevelt have, in effect, been their own secretaries of state. Others, like Dwight Eisenhower and Gerald Ford have at times permitted their secretaries a virtually free hand in ordering the affairs of the Republic among the nations of the world.

Trilateral Commission   A private interest group organized to promote understanding and cooperation among Japan, the United States and Western Europe, hence the title. The association was founded in 1973 by David Rockefeller, President of the Chase Manhattan Bank, which is among the largest in the world. The approximately 275 members are drawn from business, labor, academia, and politics. Its annual budget of over $1 million comes from foundations, corporate gifts, individual donations, and investments. A thirty-five member executive committee guides affairs in the interim between the closed annual meetings of the Commission. The three regional executive committees headquartered in New York, Paris, and Tokyo have the additional responsibility of nominating new members. The United States has approximately seventy-six members. In the United States, members who join the executive branch of the government are obliged to resign from the Commission, although some have rejoined after leaving office. The Commission makes studies, issues reports, and serves as meeting ground for the exchange of views among high level influential persons from these three most highly industrialized areas of the world. See also INTEREST GROUP, p. 390.

Significance   Most interest groups confine their activities to fairly narrow segments of foreign, domestic, and economic policy. A few, such as the Council on Foreign Relations, the League of Women Voters, and the Trilateral Commission concern themselves with political, economic, and military issues of global proportions. The prominence of the Commission increased in the late 1970s and early 1980s when one of its members, Jimmy Carter, occupied the White House. Carter developed an appreciation of international affairs through the Commission and its Executive Director, Zbigniew Brzezinski, a Columbia University professor. In all, Carter appointed about seventeen Commission members to high level government posts. In addition to Vice President Walter Mondale, these included Secretary of State Cyrus Vance, Secretary of the Treasury Michael Blumenthal, Secretary of Defense Harold Brown, United Nations Ambassador Andrew Young, and National Security Adviser Zbigniew Brzezinski. The impact on policy of the views of private interest groups outside the formal structure of the government has always been a subject of study by political scientists and students of politics.

Truman Doctrine   The first post-World War II statement of the United States policy to aid countries that requested help against Soviet expansion or subversion. The Truman Doctrine began with a dramatic address to a joint session of Congress on March 12, 1947, in which President Harry Truman declared that "it must be the policy of the United States to support free people who are resisting subjection by armed minorities or outside pressures." At the President's request, Congress appropriated $400 million to help Greece resist Communist-led attacks against the government and to bolster Turkey against Soviet pressure, particularly in the area of the Dardanelles. The United States thereby assumed a commitment in the eastern Mediterranean which the British, for economic reasons, felt compelled to relinquish. See also AGENCY FOR INTERNATIONAL DEVELOPMENT, p. 367; CONTAINMENT, p. 376; FOREIGN AID, p. 384.

Significance   The Truman Doctrine as an open commitment of United States economic and military power in peacetime represents a break with American foreign policy tradition and marks the start of the containment policy. The Truman Doctrine was also the first of the series of economic and military aid programs that apparently have become a permanent feature of American foreign policy. The enunciation of the Truman Doctrine demonstrates how the President can commit the nation to a course of action in foreign policy that Congress is virtually powerless to oppose.

United States International Trade Commission   An independent agency created in 1974 to serve as a continuing observer of the foreign trade position of the United States. The International Trade Commission's main responsibility concerns the impact of imports on American producers. Six commissioners, three from each of the two major political parties, are appointed by the President with the consent of the Senate for six-year terms.

Significance   The International Trade Commission investigates and reports on matters affecting foreign trade at the request of the President, the Congress, the House Committee on Ways and Means, and the Senate Committee on Finance. It replaced the Tariff Commission that had functioned since 1916. The Commission also serves as the agency to provide information to the President which he may use to activate the perilpoint and escape clause procedures of the Reciprocal Trade Agreements Act of 1934, the Trade Expansion Act of 1962, and subsequent tariff legislation.

United States v. Curtiss-Wright Export Corp. (299 U.S. 304 [1936])   A leading constitutional law case that recognized the inherent power of the federal government to control the foreign relations of the nation. The case involved the constitutionality of a broad grant of power by the Congress to the President under which the latter embargoed shipment of war supplies to Bolivia and Paraguay in the Gran Chaco War. The Supreme Court recognized the "exclusive power of the President as the sole organ of the Federal Government in the field of international relations. . . ." *See also* INHERENT POWERS, p. 388; PRESIDENT: CHIEF OF FOREIGN POLICY, p. 399.

Significance   The *Curtiss-Wright* case established the principle that, whereas the internal powers of the national government are restricted to those delegated by or implied from the Constitution, its external powers are more broadly based. In the field of international relations, the United States as a sovereign state possesses all the powers inherent in its sovereign nature. To hold otherwise, the Court noted, would render the United States inferior in comparison to other sovereign states. Justice Sutherland concluded for the Court that, even if the Constitution were silent on the subject, such power "would be vested in the national government as a necessary concomitant of nationality." Hence, in foreign affairs any restrictions on the power of the President to act for the nation must be specified in appropriate provisions of the Constitution. The *Curtiss-Wright* doctrine has greatly facilitated the conduct of American foreign relations under the American constitutional system.

War Powers Act of 1973   An act to limit the war making power of the president. The president is required to secure congressional authorization for any troop commitment to action within sixty days. An additional thirty days may be approved without a declaration of war if Congress agrees that the safety of the forces involved requires it. After ninety days Congress can, by concurrent resolution, require the withdrawal of American forces. This decision is not subject to presidential veto. *See also* PRESIDENT: COMMANDER IN CHIEF, p. 399.

Significance   The act does not affect the President's power to commit troops to action following a congressional declaration of war. It is designed to curb undeclared wars based solely on the President's authority as chief executive and commander in chief by bringing the Congress back into the decision making on the use of armed force by the United States. The act is a reaction to the growth of presidential power in general, and, more specifically, to the heavy and unpopular United States involvement in the undeclared wars in Korea and Vietnam. The War Powers Act gives the Congress the *legal* power to participate in decision making in this area but it will be a *political* determination as to whether or not Congress will use the power to restrain the President in actions relative to national security.

12. National Political Systems

Britain: Cabinet   The group of politicians at the center of the Government of Britain. Varying in size from sixteen to twenty-three, the Cabinet is chosen by the Prime Minister, usually from leading members of the majority party in the House of Commons. Two or three members of the House of Lords are usually included. A typical Cabinet includes the Chancellor of the Exchequer (Treasury), the Foreign and Commonwealth Secretary, the Home Secretary, and Secretaries of State for the Environment, Trade, Industry, Energy, Defence, Education and Science, and other major departments. The official Opposition in Parliament now forms a shadow Cabinet to lead its challenge to government policies and practices.

Significance   The posts of Prime Minister and Cabinet Minister are recognized in statutes, but the keys to their power are found in convention and political realities. The Cabinet determines policy in relation to Parliament, usually for the majority party, and in the public arena. It also controls the rest of the government, the central administration, and, through the Chancellor of the Exchequer, government finances. Unlike the American system where executive power and responsibility are focussed in one office and one person, the British Cabinet system assumes the unity and collective responsibility of the ruling group—though it has been difficult to sustain the appearance of unity in recent decades. Although the British cabinet system provides for a plural executive body and collective responsibility, the Prime Minister is considered *primus inter pares*, first among equals.

407

Britain: Cabinet Government A system based on a fusion of executive and legislative powers in the hands of a cabinet operating in conjunction with the principle of ultimate parliamentary supremacy. Usually selected from among the leaders of the majority party, the Cabinet has collective responsibility for: (1) establishing and implementing domestic and foreign policy; (2) coordinating the operations of government agencies; (3) dealing with emergency situations; and (4) maintaining long-range policy objectives. Cabinet-approved measures are introduced and defended in the House of Commons by the appropriate minister. Passage is usually expected because the Cabinet leads the party which controls the House. Since any division within the Cabinet is seized upon by the Opposition, Cabinet unity and collective responsibility for all decisions constitute traditional doctrines of the system, though actual behavior is now more individual. Defeat in Commons on an issue of confidence would require the resignation of the entire Cabinet. In this event, the Monarch might request the Leader of the Opposition or other leading statesman to form a new government, or, more likely, the Prime Minister would ask the Monarch to dissolve Parliament. In the latter case, a general election would decide whether the Prime Minister's party was returned to power or a new political majority appeared.

Significance The ultimate power of the House of Commons to bring down the Government is to some extent offset by the power of the Government to force a dissolution of the Commons. While the threat of a new election exists as a theoretical possibility, a more satisfactory explanation for government dominance of Parliament is party discipline and loyalty. No government in this century has been brought down by defections among its own party members in Commons. The changes that have occurred have resulted when the party in power has been defeated in a general election. General elections must be held every five years unless called sooner by a Prime Minister seeking to renew his or her party's mandate to govern. The distinguishing feature of cabinet government in the British parliamentary system is that responsibility for the initiation and administration of policy lies with the Prime Minister and the Cabinet chosen from the Parliament and accountable to it. This system insures against the kind of deadlock between executive and legislature that can occur in the American system when the two branches are controlled by different parties.

Britain: Conservative Party   One of the major parties in British politics. Traditionally the party of the aristocracy and middle class, the Conservatives are descended from the old Tories and are sometimes called by that name. The party has always attracted votes from all sectors of the electorate. The party operates under a Leader who exercises extensive personal control over its affairs. The Leader sets party policy, appoints top officials, chooses the shadow cabinet when his party is in opposition, and is not dependent on annual re-election by the parliamentary party to retain his office. Outside Parliament, the party operates through a hierarchy of institutions that include: (1) local constituency associations; (2) the National Union and its Annual Conference; (3) the Central Council; (4) the Executive Committee; and, at the apex of party structure, (5) the Leader. Inside Parliament, the Leader also exercises power over the parliamentary party (all Conservative MPs) as long as he maintains their confidence and no effective rival emerges. *See also* BRITAIN: PARTY SYSTEM, p. 416.

Significance   Compared with other parties, the Conservative party was traditionally more pragmatic and eclectic in its philosophy and practice. This outlook was much changed under the leadership of Margaret Thatcher. Its deep sense of history leads it to preserve what it considers best from British political traditions. This ancient defender of the monarchy and the church functions in the second half of the twentieth century as the main champion of business and farm interests. With some exceptions, the Conservative party has dominated British elections in this century.

Britain: Constitution   That set of fundamental principles which organize the distribution and use of power, set forth the basic organs of government and their operation, and establish the relationship between the individual and the state. In Britain, the Constitution includes: (1) historic documents which have shaped the system, such as the Magna Charta (1215), the Petition of Right (1628), the Bill of Rights (1689), the Act of Settlement (1701), various Reform Acts, and the Parliament Act of 1911; (2) statutes of fundamental importance, such as those which determine the suffrage; (3) judicial decisions which interpret and clarify the principles of the Constitution, especially those based on the common law (in Britain there is no judicial review in the

American sense because of the supremacy of Parliament); and (4) customs or conventions of the Constitution. The latter are neither written nor enforceable in the courts; yet they are precedents of such importance as to be binding in the public mind. One such precedent is that a Cabinet minister may have to resign when he disagrees publicly with government policy. *See also* CONSTITUTION, p. 427.

Significance   All democracies have constitutions in the sense of possessing the basic instruments described above which establish and maintain the particular system. The common distinction made between the United States and British Constitutions as written and unwritten is therefore a superficial comparison. In the British system, it is of fundamental importance that the ultimate guardian of the Constitution is a supreme Parliament which has the power to change constitutional provisions in the same manner as any other law. Consequently, in Britain there is no judicial review in the American sense. The British constitutional system has been evolving over many centuries and serves as a prototype for democratic societies in many countries.

Britain: Crown   The legal and symbolic unity of the executive in British government. It is composed of the Monarch, the Cabinet, the Ministers, and the Civil Service. The powers of the Crown are composed of the remaining portions of the royal prerogative and statutory grants by the Parliament. The Crown formulates and executes national policy, issues executive orders and administrative directions, manages public property, and conducts foreign relations. The authority of the Crown is used for major executive actions, for the appointment of judges and other notable officers of state, the declaration of war, and the issuance of pardons and reprieves.

Significance   The person of the Monarch symbolizes the political power of the Crown. The power is actually wielded by the Cabinet under the leadership of the Prime Minister. Decisions and orders technically come from the Monarch. Actually, the Monarch never acts to set in motion the powers of the Crown except upon the advice of his or her ministers.

Britain: Foreign Secretary   A leading member of the Cabinet responsible for the formulation and conduct of foreign policy. The Foreign Secretary defends the government's policy in the House of Commons or Lords by participating in debate and, in the Commons, by responding to the probing attacks and searching analysis of the Question Hour. He also administers the Foreign Office, meets with foreign diplomats, and at times represents his country at a variety of international meetings. The Foreign Secretary is assisted by two Ministers of State, two Parliamentary Under-Secretaries of State (all Members of Parliament), and by a Permanent Under-Secretary of State who is the highest ranking career civil servant in the Foreign Service.

Significance   The Foreign Secretary is typically a man of considerable political stature. He is responsible to the Cabinet, Parliament, and to the Prime Minister. The degree of freedom of action he enjoys varies with the individual in terms of his relationship with the Prime Minister, his public stature, and his political influence in his party. It is always possible, however, for the Prime Minister to assume control and direction of foreign policy at any time. Continuity in British foreign policy is provided by consultation between the Foreign Secretary and the permanent Foreign Service. The latter is responsible for advice and caution, but not for making policy. The office of Foreign Secretary is a high level proving ground in the ascent of British party leaders toward the Prime Ministership, and in post-World War II years, Eden, Macmillan, Home, and Callaghan have held the Foreign Secretaryship before becoming Prime Minister.

Britain: Governor-General   The personal representative of the Monarch with comparable duties in Britain's remaining colonies and in those Commonwealth countries which have not become republics. The Monarch seeks advice of local ministers before appointing a Governor-General.

Significance   The Governor-General is a visual symbol of unity in the Commonwealth and Empire. Formerly, distinguished Britons were appointed to this position. Today, depending on the unit's level of political development, the Governor-General is likely to be selected among local notables. The Governor-General is not an agent of the British Cabinet in Commonwealth countries which have attained independence, but exercises the royal prerogatives on the advice of the local government.

Britain: House of Commons   The lower and more powerful of the two Houses of Parliament. The House of Commons meets more frequently for longer periods and considers a wider and more complex range of topics than the House of Lords. Commons is a representative body and members are elected by universal suffrage from constituencies established by nonpolitical, permanent boundary commissions. Minimum age to vote is eighteen and to sit in Commons is twenty-one. The 635 Members of Parliament (MPs) are chosen from Wales, Scotland, Northern Ireland, and England, with most elected from England. MPs are chosen by general election after dissolution of Parliament or at a by-election when vacancies occur.

Significance   Though several minor parties are represented, the House of Commons is the focus for the contest between the majority party, which establishes the government, and the loyal Opposition, with its shadow cabinet. The House of Commons transacts the nation's financial business, considers legislation, mainly that proposed by the Government, scrutinizes executive and administrative activity, and provides the criticism of the Government essential to the maintenance of democracy.

Britain: House of Lords   The upper but less powerful of the two Houses of Parliament and the world's oldest legislative assembly. Lords is descended from the ancient *Curia Regis* or King's Court, nobles summoned by the sovereign to provide him with "aids" (taxes) when the expenses of the kingdom outran his private resources. Later, when representatives of cities, towns, and countries were summoned, the House of Commons began to evolve. Thus representation in Parliament came to be based in one chamber on "name" (title), and, in the other, on election. Peers (lords) are created by the Monarch on the advice of the Prime Minister. The major legislative role of the nine-hundred-member House of Lords involves reviewing legislation passed in Commons, approving it, or returning it for revision. The Lords may reduce the workload of the Commons by originating noncontroversial legislation. Since the Parliamentary Act of 1911, the House of Lords cannot reject a money bill. The Parliamentary Act of 1949 permits a bill to become law over the opposition of the House of Lords if it has been passed by two successive sessions of the House of Commons and if one year has elapsed since the second reading. The House of Lords, the highest judicial tribunal in the nation, does not possess the United States Supreme Court's power to review the constitutionality of legislation because of parliamentary supremacy and the fusion of powers. However, the eminent Law Lords who actually sit when the House acts in this capacity change the character of the body from that of a political and legislative assembly to that of a court.

Significance   The House of Lords complements but no longer rivals the political power of the Commons. Removed from the heat of partisan politics, it serves as a useful forum for calm deliberation and responsible discussion. Through its powers to delay legislation, it can restrain precipitate action by the Commons. By the system of elevating to life peerages persons from many fields, the nation can benefit from their continued service. Yet, diminished interest among hereditary peers is demonstrated by a reduced regular attendance of approximately one hundred members. Consequently, critics have called for its elimination as an anachronism. Nevertheless, the strong British attachment to tradition and the preservation of historic institutions militates against its early demise.

Britain: Labour Party   One of the major parties in British politics. A complex amalgam of trade unions, socialist and other professional groups, cooperative societies, and local constituency parties, the Labour party was formed in 1900 and named in 1906. Broad policy consideration takes place at the annual party Conference. Between Conferences, the National Executive Committee conducts party affairs and directs the party headquarters. A rival focus of power is found in the parliamentary Labour party (all Labour MPs). When Labour is in opposition, the parliamentary party elects the shadow cabinet. As Prime Minister, the Leader has such individual power and influence that in practice he has sometimes resisted the wishes expressed at the annual Conference. Liaison is usually maintained by the Cabinet with the parliamentary party and the party at large. *See also* BRITAIN: PARTY SYSTEM, p. 416.

Significance   Although Labour party membership is found across the spectrum of the electorate, most of the members and financial support come from the trade unions. However, the most dedicated workers for "the cause" are Labour ideologues found mainly in the local constituency parties, and animosities sometimes develop between them and the trade unionists. Labour has a stronger ideological articulation than the Conservatives or the major American parties. Also, by comparison, more of its members are likely to feel a stronger attachment to their party as an institution than to individual party leaders. Its frequent failure to win general elections may be explained by its dedication to broad, programmatically directed social change in a tradition-imbued nation. The party suffered a considerable loss of membership between the mid-1960s and the early 1980s.

Britain: Liberal Party   An important party in British politics. The Liberals, descended from the Whig party, were once one of the two major parties. Their decline has resulted from the rise of Labour, the liberalization of Conservative positions, internal disunity, and the lack of a broad socioeconomic base. The Liberals have run approximately one hundred candidates in recent general elections. They also continue to receive a substantial number of votes, but these are spread so evenly that, given the single-member constituency system, the size of their popular vote is not reflected in the size of their parliamentary party. Party organization is roughly analogous to that of the major parties. See also BRITAIN: PARTY SYSTEM, p. 416.

Significance   The contemporary tactic of the Liberal party is to win sufficient seats in the Commons to hold a balance of power between the major parties. Third-party policies, however, are often absorbed into the programs of the major parties, and the Liberals have seen their potential support drained to the right and the left by the Conservatives and Labour. Nevertheless, many Liberals continue to work for a centrist revival of the party.

Britain: Monarch   The hereditary chief of state of the United Kingdom and British Empire, and the symbol of Commonwealth unity. Prior to the establishment of the ultimate authority of Parliament, the king ruled by the power of the royal prerogative. With the Glorious Revolution of 1688, the primacy of parliamentary statutes was recognized, and today's constitutional monarchy is based on statutes and conventions. The remaining prerogatives are exercised on the advice of the Cabinet and include appointing the Prime Minister, dismissing the government, dissolving Parliament, creating peers, and granting patronage, honors, and mercy. *See also* MONARCHY, p. 452.

Significance Elizabeth II is Queen of the United Kingdom and of the remaining Empire and, individually, Queen of each former possession that has not become a republic. As Head of the Commonwealth, the Queen is recognized as the symbol of the free association of a worldwide, heterogeneous group of nations. The British Monarch provides the nation with unity, cohesion, and continuity, dignifies the governmental process, and, as head of the Church of England, is expected to set the moral tone of British society. The Monarch reigns but the Prime Minister and the Cabinet rule. Yet, through "the right to be consulted, the right to encourage, and the right to warn," the British Monarch, because of a life of nonpartisan devotion to the affairs of state, may exercise a degree of influence that is difficult to measure or to ignore.

Britain: Parliament The two-chamber (House of Commons, House of Lords) legislative assembly that is the focus for political power in Britain. The British Parliament, legally supreme, is actually the vehicle for formalizing government policies. The Cabinet, through its control of the majority party, uses the power of Parliament to establish such policies. *See also* PARLIAMENTARY GOVERNMENT, p. 453.

Significance Victory in a general election gives the winning party the right to use the power of the Parliament to enact its program. The rise of party government in Britain has changed the nature of the Parliament from that of a genuinely deliberative body to one that legitimates decisions made elsewhere in the system. Nevertheless, this "mother of parliaments" has become a model for most of the world's democratic governments. The British Parliament may be contrasted with the American Congress, which is but one of three co-equal branches of government.

Britain: Party Government The decisive role of the majority party in the political decision-making process. In the British system, the party that wins a majority at the polls has the right to form the government. The Prime Minister and the Cabinet as majority party leaders wield the powers of the Parliament to implement their programs. They can continue so long as the government retains the confidence of Parliament.

Significance   Party government in Britain has been based on an essentially two-party system in which the Conservative and Labour parties, by advocating varying public policies, have offered the electorate a choice of alternatives. Although Parliament remains legally supreme, its role has been diminished by a dependence upon the Cabinet as the source for the initiation and determination of policy. Contrasted with the American party system, the British parties are characterized by centralized organization, a degree of ideological unity, and party whip discipline. Hence, leadership is usually assured of an automatic majority in Parliament on government-sponsored measures.

Britain: Party System   The British have had for many years a two-party system composed of the Labour and Conservative parties. Other parties like the Liberals, the Social Democrats, the Welsh and Scottish Nationalists, and the Communists exist, however, and contest elections. The tendency to regroup around a two-party norm was demonstrated in the early twentieth century when Labour took the place of the Liberals as a major party. Growing independence among voters began in the 1960s, with a lower proportion of the electorate professing loyalty to major parties.

Significance   Contrasted with the American party system, British parties are typified by a high degree of centralization with leadership, organization, and monetary support supplied from the top levels of the national organization. The relatively small size of the country, the homogeneity of the people, and dependence on the central organization make possible a high degree of party discipline. Disciplined party voting in Parliament makes it relatively easier for the electorate to fix responsibility for program failure and success than is the case in the American party system.

Britain: Prime Minister (PM)   The head of government in Britain. In the British system, the Prime Minister's title has meant chief adviser to the Crown. Given the two-party system, it is virtually automatic for the Monarch to select as Prime Minister the leader of the majority party in the Commons. The Prime Minister forms a government by selecting the members of the Cabinet, and can reshuffle, remove, or call upon them to resign. The PM selects the heads of the non-Cabinet ministries and other departments and agencies. As "first among equals" in the Cabinet, the Prime Minister is responsible for framing and coordinating policy and for introducing and passing legislation. As head of government, the PM is charged with administering the affairs of the nation and with serving as its chief representative in international relations. In 1979, Margaret Thatcher, leader of the Conservative party, became the first woman Prime Minister in British history.

Significance The powers of the Prime Minister are not drawn from specific constitutional or statutory provisions. They are derived from the nature of the system as it has evolved, which serves to insure that they will be employed responsibly. The Prime Minister, unlike the American President, has no fixed term but can remain in office as long as he or she can command the confidence of their party in the House of Commons, and the support of the public as expressed in general elections at least every five years.

Britain: Role of Opposition The function of the principal minority party in the British political system. Her Majesty's loyal Opposition subjects government programs to constant questioning and scrutiny. It places on the party in power the constant requirement to lead, to explain its policies, to justify its actions, and to remain responsive to the wishes of the public. It is in fact an alternative government. The role of the opposition is recognized also by the granting of a state salary to the Leader of the Opposition and his Deputy.

Significance The role of the opposition is crucial to the nature of British parliamentary democracy. This highly organized adversary system of alternative governments depends upon discipline, loyalty, and support of the leadership within each parliamentary party. The party in Opposition endeavors to keep its criticism responsible since it looks to the day when positions in the Commons will be reversed. Unlike the American system where the opposition party in Congress is often able to kill executive proposals or force compromises, in Britain the opposition normally has only the power to criticize, to delay legislation, and to offer the electorate an alternative in preparation for future election campaigns.

Britain: Royal Commission   A nonpartisan ad hoc committee appointed by the government to study a major problem of public interest. A royal commission is assigned a task usually so complex and controversial as to require more time and effort than a regular parliamentary committee could devote to it. The commission is composed of members of Parliament, experts, and private citizens, with a well-known public figure as chairman and a civil servant from the appropriate ministry as secretary. The commission, which can function as long as necessary, operates by holding hearings, taking testimony, consulting experts, gathering data, and sifting evidence. The final report usually contains recommendations for executive and legislative action. Dissenting members of a commission are free to issue one or more minority reports.

Significance   Royal commissions have an enviable reputation because of the completeness and impartiality of their work. Although the government is not bound by a report, policy is usually affected because commission findings influence members of Parliament and inform and educate the general public. In recent years royal commissions have studied such matters as social-welfare problems, the press, trade, and the distribution of wealth.

Britain: Social Democratic/Liberal Alliance   An agreement in Britain in 1981 between the new Social Democratic party and the Liberal party. Its principal feature was an electoral pact whereby the two parties were not to rival each other in Parliamentary or local elections and were to give mutual support in campaigns. Both parties have advocated change in the British electoral system to a form of proportional representation in which all parties would be represented in Parliament in proportion to their voting strength in the electorate. *See also* BRITAIN: PARTY SYSTEM, p. 416.

Significance   The Alliance has increased the credibility of the emergence of a strong center group in British politics for the first time in many decades. The Alliance hopes to build its strength from disillusioned members of both the Labour and the Conservative parties and from among the increasing number of British independents.

Britain: Social Democratic Party (SDP)   A new British political party started in 1981 by a small group of high level defectors from the Labour party. The immediate cause of the split lay in constitutional changes within the Labour party which were designed to strengthen party control over the Parliamentary members. The *raison d'être* for the new party can be found in the widening gulf between the policies of the Labourites and the Conservatives. *See also* BRITAIN: PARTY SYSTEM, p. 416.

Significance   The Social Democratic Party aims at the political center, rejecting the more radical policies of the Labour Party. It supports such policies as continued British membership in NATO, the European Community, and other international bodies. At home it favors retention of a mixed economy and decentralizaton of government. The new party is experiencing a rapid rise in popularity.

Caudillismo   The principle of personal or "boss-type" political rule in Latin American politics. The *caudillo* depends on the personal loyalty of his followers. Founded in the feudal systems of Spain and Portugal, *caudillismo* serves as a substitute for formal institutions of government from the local to the national level. *See also* DICTATORSHIP, p. 428; PERSONALISMO, p. 454.

Significance   Latin American politics have traditionally tended to focus on individual loyalties rather than on issues. Thus, the "boss" can control affairs from a presidential office as did Juan Peron in Argentina, or from behind the scenes as was the case with Fulgencio Batista in Cuba from 1933 to 1940. *Caudillismo* may retain the trappings of republicanism, but, at its worst, more closely resembles absolute monarchy or dictatorship.

China (PRC): Central Committee   Under the CCP Constitution of 1977, this is the vehicle through which the decisions of the party directorate are tested and transmitted. According to the rules of the Chinese Communist Party (CCP), the Central Committee is "the highest leading body of party organization . . .

when the National Party Congress is not in session." During these intervals, it is charged with directing the entire work of the party. The approximately 201 full members plus 132 candidate members of the Central Committee are formally elected by the National Party Congress. The Central Committee meets once or twice annually for a few weeks at a time. The sessions are closed to outside scrutiny and brief communiqués simply announce topics discussed and politics or programs adopted. *See also* SOVIET UNION: CENTRAL COMMITTEE, p. 456.

Significance   Although lack of precise knowledge makes it difficult to appraise the role of the Central Committee, certain cautious observations can be made. A significant portion of the committee's voting membership is made up of members of the Politburo. Like that of the Soviet Union, the Politburo of the CCP is the top decision-making body in the country. Thus the highly disciplined Central Committee could serve to legitimate and transmit directives from the Politburo. The secrecy of its meetings and the representative nature of the membership could also serve the leadership as an effective arena in which to iron out difficulties, test opinions, and gauge the effectiveness of policies and administration. The various subagencies of the Central Committee together with the position of alternate member have provided centralized proving grounds where rising leaders can be subjected to constant surveillance and evaluation.

China (PRC): Chinese Communist Party (CCP)   The largest Communist party in the world, with a colossal membership (in excess of thirty-five million). This highly disciplined, monolithic party is the vehicle by which its leaders manipulate the world's largest population, for the most part illiterate. It makes all significant decisions and is organized to insure their execution. Its doctrines bind both member and nonmember. It fills every significant office in the country and it permits no organized opposition. Standards of initiation and indoctrination are strict, but standards of selection of new party members have varied with the military, technical, intellectual, or peasant leadership needs in a given period. The principal organs of the central apparatus of the party start with the National Party Congress whose thirty-five hundred members are a vehicle for the enunciation of policy determined at higher levels. The Central Committee of 201 members and 132 alternates brings together all major leaders for formal discussion, approval and promulgation of policy. The Politburo of about thirty members exercises the powers of the Central Committee between sessions. The highest level of authority is found in the Politburo's Standing Committee, whose five to nine or so members are the most powerful leaders in the party. *See also* CENTRAL COMMITTEE, p. 419; NATIONAL PARTY CONGRESS, p. 423; POLITBURO, p. 424.

Significance   The CCP is the source of all power in the PRC. It alone establishes political, economic, and social policy. The structure is pyramidal with power nominally located at the base. Actually, the party, and through it the country, is controlled from the top by the Politburo and its apex, the Standing Committee. Since the party and the government interlock and since the state is organized on a unitary basis, all phases of Chinese life come under the purview of a relatively few officials at the top of the party. The rationalization for such control can be found in the phrase "democratic centralism."

China (PRC): Communes   Primary units of Chinese Communist social organization designed to maximize production through a reorganization of work and living patterns. Communes were established to replace traditional units of local administration for the purpose of integrating industrial, agricultural, commercial, cultural, military, and police functions. Private and cooperative property and equipment were to be communalized, and all labor from housekeeping through local agricultural and industrial production and management was to be carried on as a function of the collectivity. Work was to be performed by variously named production teams patterned in echelons like a military organization (squad, company, battalion, regiment, and so on).

Significance   Complete integrative communalization of Chinese society, which began in 1958, was revised between 1961 and 1964 because of the alienation and growing frustration of the workers through overorganization, and because of a decline in the level of production. Urban communes at the street and neighborhood level never attained the acceptance gained for rural communes. In order to raise production levels to those of the pre-commune period, the regime was forced to take into account local conditions and prejudices. De-emphasis of the communal pattern of organization appears to be an admission that although the state has power to establish collectivist policies based on communist theory, it lacks the capacity to exert absolute managerial control over Chinese society. Nevertheless, communes continue to exist as administrative and production units.

China (PRC): Cultural Revolution

The name given by the followers of Mao Tse-tung to their chaotic struggle in the mid-1960s against revisionism and betrayal of the revolutionary cause. The Cultural Revolution, according to Maoists, was a mass proletarian movement against either a Western or Soviet type of capitalist restoration and materialism. Constant struggle was held to be necessary because capitalist resistance increases as its end draws near.

Significance In the Cultural Revolution, the real power struggle is not between communism and capitalism but between the old revolutionaries and the succeeding generation of bureaucrats and technocrats. This struggle pits the spirit of revolution against the imperatives of nation building. The struggle between the two contending forces has so split Chinese society that the old leaders could not depend on the loyalty of party, state, and military bureaucracies and turned to the mob in the form of the Red Guard to reassert their leadership. The ultimate goal of communism—the changing of human nature to create "the new Communist man"—provided the inspiration for the Cultural Revolution.

China (PRC): Maoism

One of the two major contending philosophies that divided the leaders of the Communist party in the People's Republic of China. Maoism insisted on the primacy of ideological purity and the attainment of revolutionary goals over technological expertness and material well-being. To reassert their control, the Maoists appealed to the idealism of high school and college-age youth to save the soul of China from "capitalists" and "revisionists" of the types found in the West and the Soviet Union, who would destroy the revolution as defined by Chairman Mao before his death in 1976. *See also* COMMUNIST DOCTRINE: MAOISM, p. 45.

Significance Maoism feared the control of Chinese society passing from the old revolutionary elite to a new generation of nation builders—bureaucratic managers and industrial and agricultural technicians. The desperation of the ideological purists was seen in their virtual deification of Mao and his ideas that were collected in the booklet entitled *Quotations from Chairman Mao Tse-tung*. The attacks of the youthful Red Guard on Mao's opponents by public humiliation, burning, pillage, violence, and disorder generated reprisals and brought some sections of the country close to rebellion and civil war.

China (PRC): National Party Congress   The "rubber stamp" institution that represents the rank-and-file party members. The supreme authority of the CCP is nominally located in the National Party Congress. As in the USSR's All-Union Congress, the twelve to fifteen hundred delegates to the National Party Congress are chosen indirectly through a series of municipal, county, and provincial party congresses. In China, the delegates, once chosen, serve for five years. Under all party constitutions including that of 1977, the Central Committee has been given the power to cancel meetings of the National Party Congress because of "extraordinary circumstances." The Committee also has power to postpone meetings of its parent body. Thus, it can free itself of immediate responsibility to the Congress and to the party rank and file. The National Party Congress hears party leaders expound previously determined policy, passes previously prepared resolutions, and elects Central Committee members previously selected at the Politburo level. *See also* SOVIET UNION: ALL-UNION PARTY CONGRESS, p. 455.

Significance   In the organization of its major agencies, the CCP is clearly based on the earlier Russian model. On paper, all agencies in the hierarchy are ultimately responsible to the National Party Congress at the base of the pyramid. In practice, the keys to power are held at the top, in the Politburo and its Standing Committee, and, under the principle of democratic centralism, all other party institutions serve to legitimate, transmit, execute, and publicize policies and directives handed down from above.

China (PRC): National People's Congress (NPC)   The policy-validating legislature of the People's Republic of China. The PRC Constitution labels the Congress "the highest organ of state authority in the People's Republic" and "the only legislative authority in the country." Election is by secret ballot after "democratic consultation" through a series of people's congresses beginning at the local level and ultimately reaching the national level. The voters are presented with a single list of candidates prepared in secret by the local party officials. The only choice occurs when the local party runs more candidates than there are seats at stake. Each year about thirty-five hundred delegates, chosen for five year terms, meet in Peiping for several days to endorse the policies of the party leaders. The NPC also elects its Standing Committee, a body analogous to the Presidium of the Supreme Soviet, to function between congresses. The Chairman of the Standing Committee is also elected by the NPC and serves as titular head of state. *See also* SOVIET UNION: SUPREME SOVIET, p. 464.

Significance The National People's Congress illustrates the differences between appearances and realities in the Chinese system. Although the Congress is the "highest organ of state authority," behind-the-scenes control by the party machinery relegates the Congress to a policy validating role. In addition, election of the NPC Chairman and the Standing Committee are more a procedure for validating previous selections by higher authorities than they are elections in the Western sense. However, the NPC may bring to the large and heterogeneous Chinese society a sense of unity, contact with the higher officials of the country, and feelings of continuity and purpose.

China (PRC): Politburo The chief decision making body in the Chinese Communist Party (CCP) and nation. It is composed of about thirty members. Here issues are settled and policy is sent on to the hand-picked Central Committee for legitimation and transmittal to the appropriate action groups in the party or government, or both. The Politburo is functionally organized parallel to the government ministries. Thus the party and the government interlock and the party controls the government. *See also* SOVIET UNION: POLITBURO, p. 461.

Significance The nexus of power in the Politburo is in its Standing Committee of five to nine members. The Standing Committee is the absolute, top ruling clique in the PRC. Not enough is known of the detailed workings of the Standing Committee, the Politburo, or the Central Committee to predict the form or direction that future changes in leadership will take. Nominally, the Central Committee elects the Politburo and its Standing Committee. Actually, the Standing Committee is the "apex of apexes" and controls the entire central organization of the CCP.

China (PRC): Red Guard   A largely unorganized, undisciplined, militant mob of young people and students of college and high school age, incited by Maoists in the government and party in the mid-1960s to search out and destroy bourgeois values and institutions in Chinese society. The Red Guard thus functioned as the instrument of Mao Tse-tung's "great proletarian Cultural Revolution." The Guard physically assaulted individuals and humiliated public leaders in addition to destroying ancient Chinese art treasures and denouncing "high living standards, Hong Kong fashions, and bureaucratic behavior."

Significance   The Red Guard appears to have served a dual function. It was used to coerce those intellectuals, economists, engineers, and military men more concerned with nation building than with revolutionary zeal. It may also have been intended to produce replacements for the aging revolutionary veterans of the "Long March" by providing younger leaders with revolutionary experience, giving them a future claim to power. The excesses of rival Red Guard factions and their supporters and attackers in the People's Liberation Army brought much of the party apparatus and some government institutions to a halt at times between 1966 and 1968.

China (PRC): State Council   The highest executive decision-making body of the state apparatus, comparable to the Council of Ministers in the Soviet Union. The chairman of the State Council is the premier of the PRC. The members of the State Council include various vice premiers, thirty ministers or more, and the heads of various state commissions and bureaus, and a secretary-general, all named by the Premier and confirmed by the National People's Congress. The State Council meets monthly and is the center of state executive and administrative activity. It also has a standing committee or inner cabinet that meets more frequently and is analogous to the Presidium of the Council of Ministers in the Soviet system. Members of this inner group include the Premier, vice-premiers, and the secretary-general of the Council. *See also* SOVIET UNION: COUNCIL OF MINISTERS, p. 459.

Significance   The State Council administers the affairs of the nation in accord with policy laid down by the party. Lack of final decision-making authority in the council is mitigated by a high degree of cross-membership between the State Council standing committee and the Party's Politburo. In authority, membership, and function, the State Council resembles the Council of Ministers in the Soviet Union.

Coalition Government   A government in which several minority parties form the Cabinet when no single party can command a majority. The leader of the strongest party tries to secure agreement from enough smaller parties so that their combined strength will constitute a majority in the legislature. The price of agreement may include promises to pursue, modify, or abandon certain policies and programs, and cabinet or other posts for all parties in the coalition. Coalition government is most likely when a nation lacks broad social consensus, parties have strong ideological orientations, diverse minority groups feel they cannot entrust their interests to major parties beyond their control, and the electoral system is based on a form of proportional representation. *See also* MULTIPARTY SYSTEM, p. 452; PARLIAMENTARY GOVERNMENT, p. 453.

Significance   Coalition government is inherently more unstable than governments controlled by a single majority party. It requires compromise across lines of party doctrine, and each participant must decide how far compromise can be carried without violating basic party principles. A multiparty government also makes the task of the electorate in fixing responsibility more difficult. In a two-party system, coalitions or governments of national unity may also be formed during a war or other national emergency when partisanship must temporarily be put aside. In coalitions as in alliances, the least-willing partner controls the level of cooperation. Although it is unusual, a majority party may coalesce with one or several minor parties to strengthen its parliamentary position.

Constituency   A voting district or geographical unit represented in a legislature, or the people so represented. The individual voter is called a constituent. Under a single-member district system, a constituency sends one representative to the legislature; under systems of proportional representation, several representatives are elected from each constituency.

Significance   The constituency is the base of representative government. Given the mobility of modern society, one of the continuing problems of democratic representative government is drawing and maintaining constituency or district lines so that each area is roughly equal in population.

Constitution   A state's organic or fundamental law, which prescribes the basic organs of government and their operations, the distribution and use of power, and the relationship between the individual and the state. No constitution is completely written or unwritten. In the United States, the written document has been amplified by statute, court interpretation, custom, and usage. Where no specific document exists, as in Britain, historic acts of state, basic statutes, judicial interpretation, and custom and convention serve similar functions. In all cases, the function of constitutions is to establish the norms by which the system operates. *See also* BRITAIN: CONSTITUTION, p. 409; FRANCE: CONSTITUTION, p. 430; GERMANY: BONN CONSTITUTION, p. 439; SOVIET UNION: CONSTITUTION, p. 458.

Significance   Constitutions may range in complexity and content from the rigid document of the German Weimar Republic to the flexible Constitution of the United States. An extremely rigid, detailed constitution is usually symptomatic of a minimal degree of consensus regarding the ends and means of government. Because of the difficulty encountered in the amending process to keep such constitutions abreast of changing social, economic, and political conditions, they tend to be short-lived. In a consensual society, the constitution can be confined to basic principles and adapted to changing conditions by means of statutory and judicial interpretation rather than by formal amendment. In communist states and right-wing dictatorships, constitutions are used by the regime to provide legitimacy and perpetuate their rule rather than to limit the powers of government.

Constitutional Dictatorship   A system in which the executive is empowered to rule by decree, usually for a specified period of time. The scope of the dictator's power is set forth in the instrument that establishes the dictatorship. Constitutional dictatorship usually results from a national crisis and is rationalized as necessary to the ultimate preservation of the democratic constitutional order threatened by the emergency. *See also* DIC-TATORSHIP, p. 428.

Significance   Constitutional dictatorship is characterized by the delegation of legislative power to the executive, curtailment of economic and political rights, and, at times, by martial rule and the abridgment of civil liberties. The temporary suspension of the normal functioning of representative government in democratic countries is triggered by such things as war, rebellion, and economic depression. General Charles de Gaulle, for example, was given temporary authority to rule by decree when the regular French government proved incapable of dealing with the crises brought on by the Algerian war for independence.

Dictatorship   Arbitrary rule by an individual or junta not constitutionally responsible to the people or their elected representatives. Changes in government can come about only by death, revolution, *coup d'etat*, war, or voluntary surrender of power. Characteristics of contemporary dictatorships usually include: (1) a veneer of democratic jargon and institutions; (2) an ideological rationalization; (3) elimination of active opposition; (4) control of the military; (5) an aggressive foreign policy; (6) a charismatic leader who personifies the state; (7) subordination of the individual to the state; (8) control of the mass media of communication; and (9) a single party which supports the leader, controls the administration of the state, and transmits government policy to the citizenry. *See also* CONSTITUTIONAL DICTATORSHIP, p. 428; FASCISM, p. 69.

Significance   Dictatorship results from a variety of political, economic, and social factors. These may include frustration with existing institutions, the broad appeal of a sweeping plan to deal with the situation, and the seizure of power by constitutional or extra-constitutional means. Dictatorship can be civilian in nature supported by the armed forces, as in the case of Nazi Germany, or it can be carried on by the military as in pre-World War II Japan or in a number of African states. Totalitarianism, the ultimate degree of dictatorship, implies control over every facet of individual and public life, as in Hitler's Germany. The ultimate problem faced by every dictatorship is that of succession since, by its nature, the system does not provide for the peaceful transfer of power.

Federal Government   A political system in which power is constitutionally divided between the central government and the nation's constituent subdivisions (provinces, states, regions, etc.). Each of the two sets of governments exercises authority directly on the people; neither owes its powers to a grant of authority from the other, but to a constitution that is superior to both. When a conflict occurs between the national government and a subdivisional government, and each is acting properly within its jurisdictional limits, the case is resolved in favor of the national government as the ultimate focus of sovereignty. To resolve the dispute in favor of the constituent unit would be to convert the system into a confederation of sovereign states. States with federal governments include Australia, Canada, Mexico, Switzerland, the United States, and West Germany. *See also* SOVIET UNION: FEDERAL SYSTEM, p. 460; UNITARY GOVERNMENT, p. 464.

Significance   Federal government stands between the concentration of power in a single, national government, and the diffusion of power in a confederation of sovereign states. Where it has been adopted it has normally been designed to accommodate a variety of peoples, cultures, languages, and traditions in a single large state. Federalism is one of the most sophisticated systems of government ever devised because of the dual requirement of organizing national unity on common purposes while preserving local diversity in the same society. Success requires that the value consensus that holds the federal system together must be stronger than the diversity of local values which tend to pull it apart. Yet those who emphasize local values must have confidence, demonstrated in practice, that the central government will respect them. The necessity of balancing unity and diversity makes a federal system difficult to operate effectively, with the result that it has never enjoyed the widespread popularity of unitary government.

France: Cabinet   The ministers constitutionally charged with determination and direction of national policy, execution of the laws, operation of the government, and responsibility for national defense in the Fifth French Republic. The President of the Republic selects the Premier (prime minister), who in turn suggests the ministerial appointments to be made by the President. The government thus created is technically responsible to the National Assembly. Under Articles 49 and 50 of the Constitution, however, the power of the legislature to control the life of the government through votes of confidence or censure is seriously restricted. *See also* BRITAIN: CABINET GOVERNMENT, p. 408.

Significance   The Cabinet in the Fifth Republic operates in conjunction with a constitutionally powerful and independent presidential office. Thus a key to understanding French parliamentary democracy is the superior-inferior relationship between the President and the Premier. Contrary to tradition in France and other parliamentary systems, members of parliament who become Cabinet ministers are required to resign their seats in the legislature. The Cabinet has been largely divorced from concern with political parties and the politics of parliamentary strategy by the appointment to ministerial positions of increasing numbers of nonparliamentarians—administrators, civil servants, and "technicians." In large measure, the policy-making function has been transferred to the President of the Republic and the Cabinet has become an instrument for interministerial coordination and policy implementation. Substantive discussion and broad-ranging policy debate no longer occur in the Cabinet under the Premier. Such activities take place only when they meet as the Council of Ministers, with the President of the Republic in the chair directing and actively participating in the proceedings. Even if the National Assembly should become seriously disaffected, the presidential weapons of dissolution, referendum, and rule by emergency powers could still be used in defense of the government in office.

France: Constitution   The fundamental law of the Fifth French Republic. The constitution places great power in the office of the President and, through an emergency procedure, enables him to rule by decree. The President chooses the Premier, who in turn advises the President on Cabinet appointments. The system differs from traditional Cabinet government in that Cabinet ministers cannot serve in Parliament. Details on selection, composition, and organization of Parliament, the judiciary, and administrative agencies were left to be filled in by organic laws and later statutes. The constitution also established the Community to replace the French Union of the Fourth Republic. *See also* CONSTITUTION, p. 427.

Significance   The constitution does not create a traditional republic in which the representatives of the people exercise power in the name of, and are legally responsible to, the people. Power is concentrated in the hands of the President, who is not so much the agent of a sovereign people as he is the steward of the historic French state. The constitution was originally shaped to the figure of Charles de Gaulle who from 1958 to 1969 molded it through organic laws provided for in the document, an easy amendment process, and through interpretation.

France: Constitutional Council   A review body established as a guardian of the constitution of the Fifth French Republic. The direct antecedent of the Council was the Constitutional Committee of the Fourth Republic, which was to resolve jurisdictional disputes between the two houses of the legislature. The main function of the present Council is to resolve similar difficulties between the executive and the legislature. The constitution also requires that the Council be consulted on the constitutionality of organic laws and on the standing rules of both houses. The President of the Republic must consult the Council on procedures to be followed when he wishes to initiate emergency powers that permit him to rule by decree. The Council supervises referenda and elections and resolves election disputes. The presidents of the two houses, the President of the Republic, and the Premier each have the option of referring ordinary legislation to the Council for review prior to final enactment. The Constitutional Council is composed of nine justices who serve nine-year non-renewable terms, and all former Presidents of the Republic, who are *ex officio* members for life. The presiding officer is appointed by the head of state.

Significance   The Constitutional Council has been ineffectual in that its decisions have proved to be advisory rather than binding. On occasion, it tried unsuccessfully to restrict the activities of General de Gaulle, who used his prestige to go over its head and secure a mandate directly from the people by referendum. The result has been that France has no effective institutional check on the exercise of executive power similar to that wielded by the judiciary in the United States and the Parliament in Britain.

France: Council of State   An institution of almost two hundred members that stands at the apex of the French system of public administration. Administrative functions of the Council of State cover finance, interior, public works, and social affairs. Its judicial function deals with cases arising out of the impact of administrative law on the rights of individual citizens. In its legislative role, the Council advises the Cabinet on the legality and consequences of legislation, and puts bills into final form. Like the Constitutional Council, the Council of State was designed to aid in keeping executive powers, particularly emergency powers, within constitutional bounds. The Council of State also has a role in settling jurisdictional disputes between the legislature and executive. When the law in question predates the Constitution of the Fifth Republic, the Council of State determines jurisdiction between the executive and legislature, but disputes arising under laws passed under the present constitution are referred to the Constitutional Council.

Significance   The Council of State is a typically French institution dating from the Napoleonic era, and is without direct parallel in either the United States or Britain. It is the court of last resort in cases involving administrative law, which in France, unlike Britain and the United States, is an entirely separate body of law administered and applied by a separate system of courts. As a trusted mechanism of administrative management, the work of the Council resembles some of the functions carried on by the United States Office of Management and Budget (OMB) and the British Treasury.

France: Economic and Social Council   A national consultative body created by the Constitution to advise the Government on economic and social programs. The Economic and Social Council is a deliberative body of more than two hundred civil servants, representatives of various interest groups, and persons of economic, social, and cultural prominence in French national life. Its members are appointed in part by the government and in part by the groups represented. The Council lacks power to initiate legislation but may be called upon by the Government for its opinion on government bills, ordinances, and decrees, or on parliamentary bills submitted to it. Its advice, for example, has been sought in connection with the national economic "Plan" by which various sectors of the economy have been stimulated by public funds.

Significance   The Economic and Social Council stands at the top of the French system of advisory bodies designed to aid the work of the government, various ministries, and the Parliament. The Council has developed on the one hand out of French acceptance of the concept of governmental responsibility for economic and social well-being, and on the other hand, out of the necessity for building support for government programs by a broadly based consultative process. Although the Economic and Social Council resembles similar institutions of the Third and Fourth Republics, its purpose is to serve the government rather than the Parliament.

France: Gaullism   The political philosophy of Charles de Gaulle and its impact on French national life since World War II. The essence of Gaullism is the idea of national interest above self-interest, as interpreted by de Gaulle. He altered the emphasis in French politics by downgrading traditionally organized party politics and making the presidency the dominant feature of the government. He shaped the concept of an effective national administration run by an apolitical technocracy motivated by his idea of "the reality of an objective national interest." He insisted upon an almost selfless loyalty from his subordinates and earned deep and lasting opposition from those who challenged the philosophy of his regime. Though he demonstrated a readiness to crush obstruction, he had also shown a dedication to French constitutionalism, if not to every letter of the constitution. Through dramatic public appearances and masterful domination of the mass media he sought to convey an awesome impression of the President of France standing alone above politics, as the symbol of sovereignty and the guarantor of national independence and integrity.

Significance   The history of the Fifth Republic until 1969 was dominated by the personality of Charles de Gaulle. From a condition of external weakness and internal disarray he achieved the restoration of France's international prestige and national pride. The present style of French government seems to represent a lasting change in governmental technique and is not the mirror and vehicle of one man. The problem of succession was resolved in 1969 when Georges Pompidou was elected President but the impact of Gaullism on French politics is still evident in the 1980s.

France: Minister of Foreign Affairs   The Cabinet official charged with the development and execution of French foreign policy. The Foreign Minister is appointed by the President at the suggestion of the Prime Minister and is removable by the President. The President determines the extent of the role to be played by the Foreign Minister. The Foreign Minister advises the President and participates in the deliberations of the Council of Ministers.

Significance   The traditional office of Foreign Minister in French government has been modified by the impact of Gaullism. No longer filled by a political figure in his own right, the post of Foreign Minister has come to resemble that of the American Secretary of State. Because of the shift toward presidential government in France, the primacy of the chief executive in the determination of foreign policy is unlikely to be challenged successfully by the Parliament.

France: National Assembly   The lower but dominant house of the bicameral Parliament. All 490 members of the National Assembly are elected as a unit for five-year terms from single-member voting districts under a two-ballot system. To be elected on the first ballot, a candidate must receive a majority that includes at least 25 percent of the eligible voters. Otherwise, a second balloting occurs one week later and the candidate receiving a plurality is declared elected. Candidates post a deposit which is forfeited unless they poll 5 percent of the vote. If this figure is met, the deposit is refunded and the state provides additional funds toward campaign expenses. Deputies must be at least twenty-three years of age, must have completed their military service, and must have been French citizens for at least ten years. Parliament meets for a three-month spring session and for two and one half months in the fall.

Significance　　The role of the National Assembly in the Fifth Republic has been drastically circumscribed by the division of the crucial rule-making power between the executive and the legislature. Conflicts of jurisdiction are settled by the Constitutional Council or by the executive, which also determines the legislative order of business. The procedure for parliamentary censure of the government has also been modified so that the Assembly can theoretically bring down a government but in fact is powerless to create a new one. This function now belongs to the President of the Republic, acting through his personally selected Premier. Despite the inroads of executive power into areas of former legislative prerogative, the system remains fundamentally parliamentary in nature, though possessing features of the American concept of separation of powers.

France: Parliament　　The bicameral legislature of the Fifth Republic. The lower house, the National Assembly, consists of 490 members, and the Senate, or upper house, has 283. Parliament sits in two regular sessions each year up to a legal maximum of 170 days. Special sessions are called by the Premier or the National Assembly. Each house is run by a bureau of parliamentary officials and is presided over by a president. The numerous standing committees that had characterized previous French systems have been reduced in each chamber to six committees of unwieldy large membership. Attendance at sessions of Parliament is obligatory but irregular even though absence is punishable by forfeiture of pay. The executive controls the work of Parliament; but members of the government are forbidden to occupy a seat in the legislature. While the forms of parliamentary government have been preserved, the substance has been diluted. For example, it is open to question whether Parliament's legal power to bring down a government by censure exists in fact. *See also* PARLIAMENTARY GOVERNMENT, p. 453.

Significance　　Parliamentary government in the classic sense does not exist in the Fifth Republic. Instead, a form of presidential government has been established (in line with de Gaulle's concepts of administrative efficiency) under the leadership of the President of the Republic as arbiter and oracle of the national interest. Although the system lacks the advantage of executive-legislative unity that typifies parliamentary systems, de Gaulle's forceful presidential leadership often overcame the deadlocks that characterize the separation of powers. Whether de Gaulle's successors can assert comparable leadership in their relations with Parliament will determine the future role of the French Parliament.

France: Party System   Politics in France historically has been organized on a multiparty basis with no one party capable of winning a majority. Governments have traditionally been coalitions, a form which reached a high point of instability during the period of the Fourth Republic. A few parties are nationwide. Many parties, however, are sectional, and many voters tend to group around individual leaders. Indeed, party loyalty and unity are not highly valued by most Frenchmen, who tend to be independent and individualistic. Party identification for election purposes bears little resemblance to the parliamentary parties. Individual members of Parliament exhibit considerable freedom in attaching themselves to leaders or parliamentary groups in the National Assembly since only parties or groups of thirty or more are entitled to be represented on committees. After these groups are formed, the attempt is made to seat them from Left to Right around the chamber according to their ideological identification in the political spectrum. Major exceptions to this highly individualized approach to politics and parliamentary government have been the Communists and the Socialists. *See also* MULTIPARTY SYSTEM, p. 452.

Significance   Under the Fifth Republic, the power of political parties to win control of the mechanisms of the state has been diminished as broad constitutional powers have been granted to the executive. If the contemporary system prevails, French politics may shift in emphasis from the traditional party struggle to an executive-legislative contest between the government and its opposition. The French multiparty system is distinguished from the British and American two-party systems not so much by the number of parties as by the inability of the system to produce an effective loyal opposition.

France: Premier   The constitutional head of government in the Fifth Republic. The President of the Republic, as chief of state, appoints the Premier, who in turn proposes to the President the individuals to be appointed to the Cabinet. The Premier and other Cabinet ministers have no fixed term of office. The

President has power to remove ministers from office, although the Constitution makes no mention of the removal of the Premier. The prime criterion for the premiership is the individual's acceptability to the President and, only secondarily, acquiescence by the National Assembly. The Premier is officially charged with the operation of the government, the execution of the law, and the responsibility for national defense. The Constitution is, however, vague concerning the specific functions of the Premier and his Cabinet. Consequently, the personalities of the President and Premier, as well as the nature of the relationship between them, are likely to define the Premier's role.

Significance In the Third and Fourth Republics, the Premier was not only a well-known political figure but a leader in the National Assembly. In contrast, in the Fifth Republic the executive power belongs to the President. Success in retaining the office has required the Premier to be intensely loyal to the President almost to the point of selflessness. He must try to preserve the support of the Assembly, yet be willing to stand between the President and the Parliament by accepting responsibility for the policies and decisions of the President. Only when the premiership is so interpreted can the President present his image of standing alone and aloof, above politics, the arbiter and custodian of an objective national interest.

France: President The chief of state of the Fifth Republic. Under the Constitution of 1958, the President of France was elected for a seven-year term by an indirect method involving an electoral college of some 80,000 electors. The bulk of the electors consisted of mayors and other representatives of the smaller communes throughout the country, with some representatives from the Parliament and the overseas territories. De Gaulle changed this method in October, 1962, when he won popular approval on a referendum calling for the direct popular election of the President.

Significance The President exercises all the traditional powers attributed to French executives as well as new powers that break with tradition. The latter include the President's power: (1) to name the premier without any requirement of National Assembly approval; (2) to negotiate treaties and issue pardons; (3) to send messages to Parliament and require Parliament to reconsider bills; (4) to rule on the holding of a referendum; (5) to request opinions from the Constitutional Council, a body whose function is somewhat analogous to the American practice of judicial review; (6) to dissolve the Parliament and to rule by emergency powers after nominal consultation with the Premier, the presidents of both houses, and the Constitutional Council. Indeed, in times of national peril he can do almost anything he deems necessary to preserve the state, its constitution, and its international agreements. The only restriction in such circumstances is his conscience and the provision that the National Assembly must remain in session.

France: Senate The upper house or second chamber of the bicameral French Parliament. One third of the 283 senators are elected every three years for nine-year terms. Senators must be at least thirty-five years old. They are elected indirectly by electoral colleges in the various departments. Densely populated areas elect senators by a list system. Smaller departments (administrative districts) with four or less senators use the two-ballot method, by which candidates receiving a majority on the first ballot are elected. Remaining seats are filled the same day by plurality voting on a second ballot. The indirect method of election, designed as a counterfoil to direct popular election of the Assembly, produces a rural rather than an urban political orientation in the Senate. Election success is also more dependent on party loyalty, reputation, and personal connections than in election to the Assembly. The Senate is technically equal in power with the Assembly and, in theory, neither can override the other. In practice, however, an impasse between the houses throws the initiative to the government. If the executive decides to do nothing, the bill is killed by being shuttled back and forth between the two houses. Alternatively, if the government wants the bill enacted, it can manipulate a conference committee procedure which forces reconsideration in both houses on terms established by the government. If necessary, it can maneuver an Assembly vote that overrides the Senate. Unlike the Assembly, the Senate has no power to bring down a government. The President of the Senate may temporarily exercise the duties of the President of the Republic when a vacancy occurs.

Significance The role of the Senate, prestigious in the Third Republic, has been more drastically reduced in favor of the executive than has the role of the Assembly. Senate powers are confined mainly to delaying action and to suggesting alternatives.

Germany (Federal Republic): Bonn Constitution   The Basic Law of the Federal Republic of Germany. In 1948, the Western occupation powers, concerned with the reconstruction of the German economy and its role in European recovery, agreed to self-government for West Germany. The Bonn constitution was drafted by a Parliamentary Council called by the Allied military governors and the minister presidents of the eleven German states in the American, British, and French occupation zones. The sixty-five delegates chosen by the states were apportioned among the Christian Democratic, Social Democratic, Free Democratic, Centrist, German, and Communist parties according to party strength. Representatives from Berlin were also invited. The Basic Law was approved by the allies and ratified by the states in 1949. The document shows strong influences from the post-World War I, pre-Hitler Constitution of the Weimar Republic. At Allied insistence, however, the highly organized, detailed, and lengthy document created a federal system rather than the centralized government desired by the delegates. Its main features include a bicameral legislature with the major legislative power located in the Bundestag or lower house, a strong chancellorship (prime minister), and a weak presidency. The capital was established at Bonn until the expected reunification of the divided state would make possible a return to Berlin. *See also* CONSTITUTION, p. 427.

Significance   The Bonn constitution was officially called the Basic Law to avoid acceptance of a permanently divided Germany. The preamble indicates that the Parliamentary Council in 1948 considered itself the representative of all Germans within postwar boundaries, including those in the Soviet zone (later the Democratic Republic of Germany), in establishing a West German Federal Republic so as "to give a new order to political life for a transitional period." The document also states: "This Basic Law shall become invalid on the day when a constitution adopted in a new decision by the German people comes into force." References to the provisional nature of Federal institutions have become increasingly rare, with the GDR recognized by the Federal Republic and other Western states.

Germany (Federal Republic): Bundesrat (Federal Council) The upper chamber of the West German parliament. The Bundesrat is composed of forty-one voting members and four nonvoting members from Berlin. Each German state (*Land*) appoints a delegation composed of state officials. Representation is weighted but is not fully proportional to population. Each state has a minimum of three delegates, those with a population over 2 million have four, and those over 6 million receive five. Delegations are bound by the instructions of their state governments and their votes are cast *en bloc*. The political situation at the local governmental level is reflected in the Bundesrat at the national level in that the party process in the states produces the cabinets and coalitions which instruct the delegations to the upper house. Standing committees of the Bundesrat must scrutinize all government bills for their possible effects on the *Länder* before the government submits them to the Bundestag (lower house). This serves as a check on the central government in the German federal system. The Bundesrat can only delay final passage of ordinary legislation by the Bundestag. On financial measures and constitutional amendments, its power is equal to that of the lower house in that passage requires a two-thirds majority in each chamber.

Significance In accord with German governmental tradition, the constituent units represented in the Bundesrat are responsible for the execution of national law. Consequently, the *Länder* administrations coordinate national law making and local execution. The Bundesrat also operates to prevent national legislation from infringing on local interests. The price paid for this check on national authority by an essentially bureaucratic body is a loss of some freedom of action by the more democratic Bundestag. The Bundesrat resembles the United States Senate in that both represent the constituent parts of a federal union. The Bundesrat, however, represents state government whereas the Senate represents the people of the states.

Germany (Federal Republic): Bundestag (Federal Diet) The lower and legislatively more powerful chamber of the bicameral West German parliament. The Bundestag is composed of approximately five hundred voting members apportioned on the basis of population among the states of the federal union. There are also about twenty representatives from Berlin, who participate in virtually all legislative activity except voting in plenary sessions. In each voting district approximately half of the seats are filled by direct election and the rest by a system of proportional representation. The Basic Law specifies that candidates must be at least twenty-five years old, that they are to be chosen in "universal, direct, free, equal and secret elections," that they represent the entire people, and that they cannot be "bound by orders and instructions and are subject only to their own conscience." The chamber is arranged in the French manner of a political spectrum from Left to Right and is dominated by moderate parties, particularly the Christian Democratic Union and the Social Democratic party. The life of a Bundestag is four years unless the Chancellor demands and fails to receive a vote of confidence. In that event the national President, on the proposal of the Chancellor, can dissolve the chamber so that a general election can establish the basis for creating a new government. Although floor debate may be more significant than in the United States, detailed legislative activity and necessary compromise is worked out in several dozen standing committees. Membership ranges between fifteen and thirty, and the party groups (*Fraktionen*) in the Bundestag are represented on the committees in proportion to their strength in that house. The work of the chamber is largely organized and controlled by a twenty-man steering committee, the Council of Elders, composed of the chamber president and vice presidents and the leaders of the parliamentary party groups. The Council advises the presiding officer, proposes the calendar, chooses committee chairmen, and allots time for debate. Its function is somewhat analogous to that of the Rules Committee in the U.S. House of Representatives. Once the house has elected the Chancellor, its power to control him is strictly limited. Ultimately he can be brought down, but only by a procedure called the "constructive vote." That is, when the Bundestag votes to request the national President to dismiss the Chancellor, it must simultaneously elect his successor so as to avoid the dangers of executive instability and recurrent Cabinet crises.

Significance   The structure of the West German Bundestag, carefully set forth in the Basic Law, reflects experience gained from the operation of the British, French, and American systems and draws heavily on German governmental tradition. Thus far it appears that the Bundestag may well be the vehicle for the development of genuine parliamentary democracy in Germany.

At the same time, the creation of what also appears to be the most powerful chancellorship in any parliamentary system, and a highly centralized bureaucracy, indicates that traditional authoritarianism in government has not passed out of German life altogether.

Germany (Federal Republic): Cabinet   The institution that together with the Chancellor constitutes the government of the Federal Republic. The Cabinet is composed of approximately twenty ministers, most of them selected by the Chancellor from his own party. The remaining appointments are the result of hard bargaining between the Chancellor and the leaders of other parties when their support is required to form a coalition. The Cabinet meets in frequent formal executive sessions and the agenda is not publicized. Meetings are attended by ministers, State Secretaries (the highest level civil servant in each ministry whose role corresponds to that of the British Permanent Secretary), the head of the Office of the Federal President, the Chancellor's personal aide, the head of the Press and Information Office, the Secretary of the Cabinet, and any experts invited to a particular meeting. Only ministers vote and a quorum of one-half of the ministers is necessary to do business. The Chancellor conducts Cabinet meetings according to established rules for formalizing government policies and for considering the problems of the individual ministries. Ministers may introduce bills in the Bundestag and about three-fourths of all legislation originates in the ministries. Although ministers are expected to support government policies in public, some have not always done so, and a few have suffered public rebuke by the Chancellor. The Chancellor and most ministers are elected members of the Bundestag and are subject to questioning by members of that house.

Significance   The Cabinet system has developed from German governmental tradition in which a strong Chancellor directed the activities of a group of high level civil servants in line with policies laid down by the monarch. Without a king or strong president, most of the executive power now resides in the Chancellor. Depending on his political strength and personality, the Cabinet makes policy as a collegial body or is called upon to give formal consent to the Chancellor's decisions. In either case, it is not in the German tradition for a dissenting minister to resign. Ministers are not responsible to the Bundestag since only the

Chancellor stands between the Cabinet and the Bundestag, with the result that German Cabinets are remarkably stable. Responsible government in the British sense, however, does not exist in the German system since the German preference for strong executive leadership allows the Chancellor and Cabinet to operate more independently of the legislative body.

Germany (Federal Republic): Chancellor The chief executive officer in the West German federal parliamentary system. The Chancellor is formally elected without debate, usually by a new Bundestag after a general election. He is nominated by the Federal President after the latter has negotiated his selection with the various parties. If he receives an absolute majority on the first ballot, he is appointed by the President. If not, the Bundestag has fourteen days to elect a Chancellor of its own choosing, but if no one receives a majority, a third balloting takes place without delay and with only a plurality required. When the third balloting fails to produce a majority, the President has seven days to choose between appointing the successful plurality candidate to the chancellorship or dissolving the Bundestag for a new election. In the absence of a general election, a new Chancellor can come to office through the constitutionally established "positive" no-confidence procedure by which the Bundestag can force the dismissal of a Chancellor only by electing his successor. Unless dismissed, the Chancellor serves for the four-year life of the Bundestag. The Chancellor forms his Cabinet from his own party if it is the majority, or by negotiation with other parties if a coalition government is necessary. The Basic Law makes the Chancellor individually responsible for the determination of the general policy of his government and for the general direction of the work of individual ministries in line with that policy. The Chancellor, his deputy, or an appropriate minister must sign all laws before the President's signature can give them effect, a requirement that has raised the constitutional question of the right to veto. Only the Chancellor has the legal authority to bring about the dismissal of a minister.

Significance The executive powers of the West German Chancellor, from the perspective of his relationship to the President, the Cabinet, and the parliament, surpass those of most prime ministers, particularly those of his French and Italian counterparts. The framers of the Basic Law sought to avoid the extremes of, on the one hand, a strong presidential office and, on the other, the instability of a multiparty system which would subject a minister to the cross-pressures of loyalty to Cabinet policies and responsiveness to the demands of his party. Their solution was a strong chancellorship. Although the Chancellor cannot claim a popular mandate and is constitutionally responsible to the Bundestag, his tenure is relatively secure, given the German preference for strong personalities in individual leadership roles. The dimensions of the office of Chancellor have been shaped in large measure by its first post-World War II occupant, Konrad Adenauer, who filled the post from 1949 to 1963.

Germany (Federal Republic): Parliament   The bicameral legislature of the West German Federal Republic. The Bundestag (lower house), composed of 496 deputies plus 22 nonvoting deputies from Berlin, represents all of the people of the Republic, and is the more powerful of the two chambers. The Bundesrat (upper house), composed of forty-one delegates from the ten states of the Federal Republic and four nonvoting delegates from Berlin, has a qualified legislative veto and is the guardian of state interests. The Cabinet reports to the Bundestag which, though it cannot dismiss a minister, can bring about the overthrow of the Chancellor by electing his successor. Both houses make extensive use of committees in the legislative process with committee membership based on party strength in the lower house. The committees exercise less control over bills than in the United States but by the same token more actual legislative work is done during floor debate than is the case in the American Congress. Legislation usually follows this course: (1) from the ministry where the bill is written (2) to the Cabinet, (3) which submits it first to the Bundesrat, for initial evaluation, (4) then to the Bundestag for action, and (5) thence back to the Bundesrat for final consideration. *See also* CABINET, p. 442; CHANCELLOR, p. 443; BUNDESRAT, p. 440; BUNDESTAG, p. 440.

Significance   German government continues traditional domination by the executive, with the result that the German parliament has never had the power and prestige enjoyed by parliaments in other Western countries. In addition, the slow development of the parliamentary institution was completely arrested during the Nazi period. These conditions serve to intensify in Germany the general trend of modern government, in which the traditional law-making function of legislatures is being over-shadowed by the role of supervising and controlling the executive. Whether, under the Bonn constitution with its strong chancellorship, the parliament can effectively control the executive without the instability that characterized the Weimar period remains to be tested.

Germany (Federal Republic): Party System   A multiparty system trending toward bipartyism. The party system emerged with allied permission during the post-World War II occupation period. Except for the subsequent banning of neo-Nazi and Communist parties, the system remains fundamentally the same under the Basic Law of the Federal Republic. Strict electoral laws have curtailed the proliferation of parties that characterized the Weimar experience. The ten parties that competed for power at the end of the occupation period have largely coalesced into two major and one minor party in the Bundestag; the Christian Democratic Union (CDU), the Social Democratic party (SDP), and the Free Democratic party (FDP). The CDU is supported in its slightly right-of-center position by middle-class business interests and by industrial and agricultural workers. As its name implies, the CDU represents a religious approach to politics, but it is not a clerical party. The Free Democratic party is also of the center-right, but unlike the CDU it rejects a role for religion in politics. The SDP, the second of the two major parties, has survived in Germany since its creation during the Empire period. Support for its left-of-center position comes mainly from the ranks of industrial workers, and its program resembles that of the British Labour party. Splinter groups exist on the extreme Left and Right, but have failed to win seats in the Bundestag because the law requires a party to poll 5 percent of the national vote or show a majority in a voting district to be represented. *See also* MULTIPARTY SYSTEM, p. 452.

Significance   The trend toward a two-party system in Germany has progressed to the point where the CDU and SDP dominate, although other parties continue to exist. To this break with German tradition can be added a decreasing emphasis on party doctrine and growing citizen interest and participation in party politics. At the same time, the German party system still emphasizes the traditional role of strong leadership and lacks the widespread popular political initiative associated with democratic representative government. Although German governments since 1949 have been coalitions, they have been notably stable.

Germany (Federal Republic): President   The formal head of state, who symbolizes national unity but wields little power. The President is elected indirectly by a Federal Convention called by the President of the Bundestag. Consisting of more than one thousand electors, the Federal Convention is made up of the members of the Bundestag and an equal number of delegates chosen proportionally by each state (*Land*) legislature. The convention proceeds without debate and, if no candidate receives a majority on the first two ballots, the person receiving a plurality of the votes on a third ballot is declared elected. The term of office is five years and the law permits reelection to one additional consecutive term. Any German citizen is eligible for the presidency if he has reached forty years of age and is qualified to vote for the Bundestag. The President exercises the normal functions of a chief of state in form but not in fact. New laws and other state papers that require his signature must be countersigned by the Chancellor or an appropriate minister. The President's appointments, foreign relations functions, and other ostensibly discretionary acts are decided for him elsewhere in the executive structure.

Significance   The Basic Law reflects the German penchant for strong executive leadership, but executive power is focused in the chancellorship rather than the presidency. Since the President is chosen indirectly, he cannot claim a popular mandate as a basis for challenging the leadership of the Chancellor. In this way, the framers of the Basic Law attempted to avoid the problems inherent in bifurcated top-level executive leadership. None of the Presidents, Theodor Heuss, Heinrich Leubke, or Karl Carstens, has asserted sufficient individual initiative to force a decision on important constitutional questions as, for example, whether the President can refuse to appoint a minister chosen by the Chancellor.

Italy: Council of Ministers (Cabinet)   The government in the Italian parliamentary system. The Council of Ministers is usually a coalition government since no party is strong enough to command a majority in the Parliament. The President consults with political leaders to discover which parties will cooperate in a coalition. He then nominates a chairman of the Council of Ministers (Prime Minister) who in turn suggests the other ministerial nominations to be made by the President. The Cabinet thus formed is responsible to the Parliament, and the Prime Minister has ten days in which to obtain votes of confidence in his government from both the Chamber of Deputies and the Senate. A government ends when it resigns voluntarily, when Parliament is dissolved by the President for a general election, or when a specific motion of no confidence is sustained by either chamber. About twenty ministries are established by statute, but any number of ministers without portfolio can also be nominated for Cabinet posts. Most Cabinet ministers are members of Parliament although this is not a legal requirement.

Significance Italian cabinets have been unstable, rarely lasting more than one year. There has, nevertheless, been greater governmental continuity than recurring cabinet crises indicate. Many ministers, particularly from the Christian Democratic party, have served in various posts in successive governments. Individual ministers in the coalition are responsible to their parties in spite of the constitutional requirement that ministers share collective responsibility for the acts of the government. Although the Cabinet is legally responsible to the Parliament, it is politically accountable to the various party organizations that make up the coalition. These groups are more likely to order the resignation of their party members from the government than the Parliament is likely to vote censure. Similarly, the coalition nature of Italian governments and the factional nature of political parties explain why party executives as well as the Cabinet are regularly concerned with questions of broad national policy.

Italy: Parliament The bicameral legislature of the Italian democratic republic created in 1948. By direct universal election, citizens over eighteen choose the Chamber of Deputies while those over twenty-five elect senators as well. Each member of the Chamber of Deputies (lower house) represents 80,000 people or a major fraction thereof, must be nineteen years of age, and serves a five-year term. Senators are elected in each of the twenty regions of the country; each represents 200,000 people or a major fraction thereof, must be at least forty years old, and serves a five-year term. As in the French and West German multiparty systems, Italian legislators are organized into parliamentary party groups, which are the basis for membership on legislative standing committees. The committee structure roughly parallels the pattern of government ministries. Bills are introduced by the government, by members of either house, or by initiative; they must pass both houses to become law. Committees in either house can also pass a bill unless one-tenth of the committee membership requires that the bill go to the full house. In cases of disagreement between the houses legislation is shuttled between them until a consensus is reached or until Parliament is dissolved. In addition to its normal legislative functions, Parliament also elects the President of Italy and one-third of the members of both the Constitutional Court and the High Judicial Council. *See also* PARLIAMENTARY GOVERNMENT, p. 453.

Significance   In Italy, unlike Britain, Parliament does not enjoy a high degree of prestige. This is explained by: public apathy; its failure to provide leadership, control the bureaucracy, and implement the Constitution; the tendency to legislate by committee and to vote in secret; and the lack of parliamentary initiative, party discipline, and a loyal opposition. There are about twelve parties represented in the Parliament with the Christian Democrats and the Communists being the largest. In the classical parliamentary sense, the President of the Council of Ministers (Prime Minister) and the members of the Council of Ministers (Cabinet) are responsible to the legislature, and the government must resign if it fails to maintain the confidence of either house. Since 1948, governments have fallen with remarkable frequency but without substantial change of direction or program.

Italy: Party System   The continental European type of weak, unstable multiparty system. The governing majority in the Italian party system consists of a ruling centrist party and coalition that support the established constitutional order. The system lacks an effective alternative because the forces on the far Left and Right oppose the existing constitutional order. Hence, the center party or parties continue in office with only minor variations in the composition of the government. The Christian Democratic (Catholic) party has ruled alone or in coalition with minor centrist parties since 1945. The Christian Democratic party is so large, however, that internal factionalism has limited its ability to provide programmatic leadership. The Communist party, the largest in any non-communist country, is the second-largest mass party in Italy. It is an anti-constitutional party composed both of ideological militants and a mass of persons disaffected by the present system because of poverty, corruption, unemployment, and lack of social progress. The Italian Socialist party, founded in the late nineteenth century, is the smallest of the nation's three mass parties. No longer allied with the Communists, the Socialists continue to draw their major support from the radical proletarian Left, particularly from those voters alienated by communist regimentation of the personal lives of party members and fear of Soviet domination of party policy. The Socialists also have their splinter groups, such as the Social Democrats. Minor national parties range from the South Tyrolian Party (SVP) on the extreme Right to the Proletarian Democrats (DP) on the extreme Left.

Significance   Prior to the creation of the republic under the 1947 constitution, Italy had never had an organized system of representative political parties. Single parties like the Socialists and Communists had existed under the monarchy along with other groups, factions, and personal cliques that ranged across the political spectrum. Prior to the fall of Fascism, however, Italy had little experience with the democratic process or with party organization. The contemporary party system offers no democratic alternative to centrist coalition government. There is no loyal opposition that, by its readiness to assume office, forces the government to provide leadership responsive to popular will. The result is a system characterized by continuing instability, with approximately 46 percent of the popular vote cast for the parties on the Right and Left largely as a demonstration of alienation and protest.

Italy: President of the Council of Ministers (Prime Minister)   The head of government in the Italian republic.

As first among equals, the Prime Minister (or Premier) is responsible for the direction and coordination of government policy. He is appointed by the President of the Republic, who, because of the coalition nature of Italian governments, must first gain acceptance for the nominee from the various party leaders. The Prime Minister then selects the members of his government who are also appointed by the President of the Republic. Because the government is constitutionally responsible to Parliament, the Prime Minister must, within ten days, obtain a vote of confidence in each house. Either house can subsequently force the resignation of the Prime Minister and his Cabinet by a vote of no confidence. In theory, the Prime Minister is the leader and spokesman of the parliamentary majority. Whether he is in fact depends on his ability to maintain cohesion within the coalition. *See also* BRITAIN: PRIME MINISTER, p. 416; FRANCE: PREMIER, p. 436.

Significance In political power and leadership potential, the Cabinet post of President of the Council of Ministers falls between that of the British Prime Minister and that of the French Premier. The President of the Council typically heads an unstable coalition government. He cannot therefore exert the same control over his Cabinet as a British Prime Minister who is the acknowledged leader of the majority party in the House of Commons. Contrasted with the French Premier, the Italian Prime Minister leads in the formation of his government's program and is not overshadowed by the power of the President of the Republic. The President of the Council stands at the center of the process of policy formation, legislation, and administration. But, because an Italian government rarely lasts longer than a year, no Prime Minister has been able to frame long-term programs to solve the nation's most serious problems.

Italy: President of the Republic The head of state of the Italian republic which in form is a classical unitary parliamentary state. Presumably above the vicissitudes of partisan politics, the President symbolizes national unity. He is elected indirectly for a seven-year term by a joint session of the Senate and Chamber of Deputies. The parliamentarians are joined on this occasion by three delegates from each of the twenty constituent regions. A two-thirds majority is required, but if no one is elected after two secret ballots, a simple majority on the third ballot is sufficient. The broad constitutional powers granted to the President include: (1) naming the President of the Council of Ministers, five senators for life, and five members of the Constitutional Court; (2) casting a suspensive veto to force Parliament to reconsider a measure it has already passed; (3) authorizing the submission of government bills to Parliament; and (4) dissolving Parliament, calling special sessions, elections, and referenda. The President also ratifies treaties; promulgates statutes, executive orders, and regulations; grants amnesties, pardons, and reprieves; formally declares war; bestows honors; and appoints certain ministers on the suggestion of the Prime Minister. *See also* FRANCE: PRESIDENT, p. 437; GERMANY: PRESIDENT, p. 446.

Significance   The Italian President is more than a figurehead and symbol of unity, but Italians disagree over his political role. Although parliamentary supremacy exists in principle and presidential acts must be countersigned by a minister, yet the scope of the constitutional term *presidential act* is not clear. Presidents have exercised personal political initiative by writing their own speeches, expressing their views on affairs of state, arranging their official visits to other countries, insisting on the modification of legislation, and influencing the selection of ministers. Because of the weak party system and recurring Cabinet crises, presidents have enjoyed room for maneuver in developing the powers of the office. But the Italian President can claim no popular mandate and speaks only for himself. Whatever prestige attaches to the presidency has been contributed by the personal reputations of the men who have held the office.

Latifundia System (*Latifundismo*)   A Latin American pattern of land tenure based on huge landed estates owned by local gentry, absentee landlords, and domestic or foreign corporations. The latifundia system, developed by the ancient Romans, was transplanted first to the Iberian Peninsula and thence to the Americas.

Significance   In Latin America, agriculture provides the principal income for two-thirds of the population. Since colonial times, the latifundia system has concentrated land ownership in very few hands with large numbers of workers living in conditions resembling peonage. Since agricultural labor is the principal type of employment, political power has been based largely on control of land. Problems of land tenure are closely associated with the slow pace of political, economic, and social modernization in much of Latin America. Mass frustration resulting from the political elite's failure to break up and redistribute the large estates contributes to the threat of revolution throughout the region.

List System   An electoral system based on proportional representation and used in a number of European countries. Each party presents its list of candidates for the seats to be filled. The party determines the order of names on its list and seats are filled starting with the top of the list. The voter chooses between lists, and is thus voting for a party rather than an individual. Each party wins the number of seats equated with its fraction of the total popular vote. *See also* FRANCE: PARTY SYSTEM, p. 436.

Significance   The list system is simple to operate. It adds to the power of party leaders by restricting the self-expression of individual candidates and fosters party discipline. It also prevents ticket splitting by the voters, whose freedom of choice is thus restricted and the process depersonalized. Variations of the list system allow the voter to establish the rank order of the candidates within a particular list.

Monarchy   Hereditary or constitutional rule by a king, emperor, or other royal person.

Significance   Monarchs once held absolute sovereign powers, but the spread of democracy and republicanism have all but ended this system of government. Stable monarchies of the constitutional variety are found in such democratically oriented systems as those of Britain, Norway, Sweden, and Denmark. A few of a more personal nature still exist in the Near East and Southeast Asia, but their days appear to be numbered.

Multiparty System   A representative democratic system in which more than two parties compete for power. The multiparty system usually requires the formation of a coalition to construct the majority necessary for establishment of a government. It is typical of European parliamentary systems. *See also* FRANCE: PARTY SYSTEM, p. 436; GERMANY: PARTY SYSTEM, p. 445; ITALY: PARTY SYSTEM, p. 448.

Significance   Proportional representation is usually associated with a multiparty system. The impulse to form minor parties is strong since a minority party can usually count on winning some seats in the legislature even though unable to form or participate in a government. By contrast, the single-member district system of representation in which the "winner takes all," is more typical of two-party systems. One of the strengths of a multiparty system is that it offers the electorate a wider choice of alternatives. Yet, the price exacted may be one of instability. To form a government in a multiparty system, compromise usually occurs among parties after an election. In a two-party system, compromise takes place within each major party and precedes the election.

One-Party System   A system of government in which there is only a single party. *See also* CHINA: COMMUNIST PARTY, p. 420; SOVIET UNION: COMMUNIST PARTY, p. 457.

Significance   One-party systems are alien to the Western democratic tradition because they violate the requirement of presenting the voter with alternatives. Experience with totalitarian and authoritarian forms, like those of Nazi Germany and the Soviet Union, has confirmed this sentiment. Yet, a variant may be developing, particularly in some of the newer states of Africa, which admits broad participation and some element of choice on an intraparty basis.

Parliamentary Government   A system in which legislative and executive powers are fused. Parliamentary government does not require the separate election of the head of government, as in the American system, where powers are separated. The leadership of the majority in the legislature forms the Cabinet, which exercises executive power. Leadership of the majority party or parties in the cabinet virtually guarantees the passage of government-sponsored legislation. This form of government operates with either a two-party or a multiparty system, such as those found in Britain and in Western Europe. *See also* BRITAIN: PARLIAMENT, p. 415; FRANCE: PARLIAMENT, p. 435; ITALY: PARLIAMENT, p. 447.

Significance   Parliamentary government in its various forms and adaptations is the most widely used pattern of government in the world. In its classic mold, parliamentary government is based on the ability of the legislature to grant or withhold its confidence in the executive, thus forcing the government to resign or to dissolve the legislature. The issue is usually submitted to the people in a national election. The system insures against protracted disagreement between the two branches.

Personalismo   The Latin American political phenomenon of personalizing political power. Traditionally, many Latin American political parties could be described as bands of loyal followers clustered around, and serving as a vehicle for the expression of, a dominant and colorful personality. *See also* CAUDILLISMO, p. 419.

Significance   Although *personalismo* is still a force in the political life of Latin America, more programmatic and issue-oriented parties are appearing, especially in the more developed areas.

Proportional Representation   An electoral system in which the seats in a legislative body are distributed to political parties in proportion to the size of each party's popular vote. Forms of proportional representation range from simple to complex, but all are based on voting districts with plural representation. *See also* LIST SYSTEM, p. 452; MULTIPARTY SYSTEM, p. 452.

Significance   Proportional representation affords an opportunity for the direct expression of a wide range of social, economic, religious, ethnic, and political ideas and, therefore, is associated with a multiparty rather than a two-party system. Various forms of proportional representation are used in national elections in Europe, and a few American states employ it to fill state and local offices. Proportional representation is an alternative to the "winner takes all" feature of the single-member district system in which the winning candidate represents all of the people in his constituency.

Representative Government   A democratic system that enables electors to express their wishes on the formation and implementation of public policy through their chosen representatives. *See also* REPUBLIC, p. 455.

Significance   Representative government exists in states that are federal or unitary, parliamentary or presidential, republican or monarchical. The key to representative systems lies in the electorate's delegation of its sovereign authority to periodically chosen and legally responsible officials. Authoritarian regimes often exhibit a façade of representative government by holding elections and seating legislatures, but they are not representative because they are not accountable to the electorate for their actions. The complex nature of modern society has added another dimension to the traditional concept of representation through elections—citizen interests represented through political parties, interest groups, the mass media, technical experts, and lobbyists.

Republic   A state in which the government consists of elected representatives. Republicanism may be contrasted with the right of personal rule in a monarchy or oligarchy. The representatives act in the name of and are legally responsible to the electorate. This means that: (1) they cannot hold office except by election or through appointment by an elected official; (2) their term in office can be extended only by reelection or reappointment; and (3) they can be required to answer in a court of law for any illegal acts. *See also* REPRESENTATIVE GOVERNMENT, p. 454.

Significance   Although monarchy was once the universal form of government, since the American and French Revolutions most of the states of the world have been organized as republics. The key to republicanism is the legitimating process of elections.

Soviet Union: All-Union Party Congress   The Communist party organ to which all others in the party hierarchy are constitutionally responsible. The All-Union Congress is supposed to meet at least every three years. Delegates are chosen indirectly, by party conferences ranging from the city or local district level to the national level. The Congress is charged with deciding party rules, making party program revisions, establishing party policy lines, selecting the Central Committee membership, and hearing reports from that body. The Congress is composed of approximately five thousand delegates, with each representing an average of 3200 party members or candidate members.

Significance   Resembling in structure and function a Western party convention, the All-Union Party Congress is mainly an elite gathering of government officials and local and national party leaders. Under the communist doctrine of "democratic centralism," it functions to formalize the policies and actions of top party leaders rather than as the party's highest decision-making body. Although the Congress theoretically has the power to hold party leaders accountable, the only criticism of the leadership occurred in 1956 and 1966 and was directed at former leaders, Josef Stalin and Nikita Khrushchev.

Soviet Union: Central Committee   The Communist party organ responsible for directing all party activity between All-Union Congresses. The Central Committee names the members of the Politburo and the Secretariat, the two most powerful decision-making bodies of the party in the Soviet Union. It is composed of 288 members and 139 candidate members. Nominally elected by the Party Congress, the Committee members are actually chosen in advance by party leaders.

Significance   The Central Committee exercises a minimal degree of continuing direction of party affairs. Too large to be an effective decision-making body, it can only announce policies formulated elsewhere. It can play a decisive role, however, in the outcome of a power struggle when the real leaders in the Politburo are divided. It was in the Central Committee in 1957 that Nikita Khrushchev established himself as leader, and here that he was deposed by Leonid Brezhnev in 1964. The fact that the real locus of power is the Politburo is demonstrated by the major change in Central Committee membership that has accompanied each change in Politburo leadership.

Soviet Union: Collective Farm   A huge farm created by pooling individual peasant holdings to work the land in common. Collectivization was forced upon the Russian peasants at great human and material cost during the 1920s and 1930s by Josef Stalin. Collective farms may include as many as a thousand families and several villages. Experimentation to discover the most effective system of farm management has varied from the local soviet and county level up through the provincial and republic level, with policy direction supplied from the national level. *See also* STATE FARM, p. 463.

Significance   The collectivization of agriculture to permit mechanization and economies of scale was considered by Soviet planners to be essential to support industrial development. The Communist party also sought to develop in the agricultural sector of the economy the communal spirit through which the industrial sector was brought under party control. Although the party has had considerable success in politicizing the peasantry and in increasing agricultural productivity, major problems have always been the peasants' desire for individuality and freedom of choice, and the desire to own land. The importance of those desires has been recognized by permitting the individual peasant to participate in the work of local farm councils and by granting him the use of a small plot of land for his own purposes over and above his required labor on the collective farm. However, the quality of life in agriculture remains substantially below that in industry.

Soviet Union: Communist Party (CPSU)   The ruling institution in the Soviet state. The CPSU pervades every facet of life in the Soviet Union and serves as the vehicle for control from the top. Education for life in Marxist-Leninist society begins early and progresses by age groups through indoctrination and recruitment organizations—the Little Octobrists, the Young Pioneers, and the Young Communist League. Membership through succeeding organizational levels is highly selective; only about six percent of the population have achieved full party membership. At the base of the CPSU structure, the All-Union Party Congress represents the rank-and-file party members but is too large and meets too infrequently to exercise real power. It formally elects the Central Committee to direct party activities between congresses. The Central Committee meets twice a year and is also too large to be an effective, continuing decision-making body. It nominally elects the members of the Politburo, who have been selected in advance by the party leaders. The Politburo tops the party organization on the national level. It is the supreme policymaking body in the country and consists of sixteen members and six candidate members. All party activities are coordinated through the Secretariat. *See also* ALL-UNION PARTY CONGRESS, p. 455; CENTRAL COMMITTEE, p. 456; POLITBURO, p. 461; SECRETARIAT, p. 462.

Significance   The Communist Party of the Soviet Union is not a political party in the Western sense. It does not compete in elections with other parties to win the right to control state machinery within limits established by a constitution. It was not created to function within an established order but to create a new order by making a revolution and seizing power; the organizational requirements for achieving this purpose still characterize the party. They include elitism, secrecy, iron discipline, and selfless devotion to "the cause"—the on-going revolution as set forth by the leadership. The CPSU speaks for the proletariat, expounds socialism, prevents the development of internal factions and external opposition groups, and defines good and evil. Exercising a monopoly of truth, the party is the vehicle whereby the leaders are to remake human society along Marxist-Leninist lines by creating "the new Soviet man."

Soviet Union: Constitution   The formal plan of government in the Union of Soviet Socialist Republics. The constitution establishes a government with features that resemble many found in Western states. The system is federal and representative in nature with a bicameral national legislature (Supreme Soviet) elected by secret ballot on the basis of universal, direct, and equal suffrage. A Presidium performs many of the duties of the Supreme Soviet between legislative sessions. A Council of Ministers exercises executive and administrative functions and, in so far as it is technically responsible to the Supreme Soviet and its Presidium, resembles the French and British Cabinets. The Soviet model varies from Western constitutional theory in that it recognizes the ultimate power not of the people but of the Communist party. The four constitutions of the Soviet Union were adopted in 1918, 1924, 1936 and 1977. *See also* CONSTITUTION, p. 427.

Significance   The Soviet Constitution does not function as an instrument for the prevention of the arbitrary use of power. The ultimate validity of law in the Soviet Union is found in the requirements of the continuing socialist revolution as interpreted by the leaders of the party, who are, therefore, above the formal restrictions of law. The party and the Council of Ministers often ignore the constitution and issue decrees with the force of law. The Supreme Soviet, which has the constitutional amending power, then adjusts the constitution *post hoc* to legitimate such acts. Enactments by the Supreme Soviet are by definition constitutional, and the party elite controls the Supreme Soviet. The

Western constitutional concept of the rule of law rather than of men is not relevant to the Soviet system or Russian governmental tradition.

Soviet Union: Council of Ministers   The highest executive and administrative organ of state power under the constitution. The Council of Ministers is composed of fifty or more members appointed by the Supreme Soviet in accordance with the wishes of party leaders. The Chairman, or Premier, is a high-ranking party member with a seat on the party's Politburo. Most of the individual members administer one of the large government departments. The Council thus resembles the Cabinet in the Western democracies. It is concerned with such usual items as the national budget, foreign affairs, national security, internal order, industry, and agriculture.

Significance   Technically, the Council of Ministers is responsible to the Supreme Soviet. Actually, since the Supreme Soviet sessions are brief, the Council of Ministers drafts legislation and provides the parent body with policy guidance. The Chairman of the Council constitutes a high-level bridge between the policymaking functions of the party Politburo and the policy-executing role of the government administrative apparatus. The limits within which the Council of Ministers is free to act are set by the party and by the degree of specificity with which the Politburo spells out its directives. Some of the ministries, such as foreign affairs, defense, or education, are found in any system of government. A large number of Soviet ministries reflect the state's extensive involvement in promoting planned economic growth. Problems in achieving this objective are reflected in the frequent reorganizations of the Council of Ministers.

Soviet Union: Cult of the Individual   A charge directed by party leaders at individuals who have departed from the Marxist-Leninist principle of collective leadership to establish personal rule through self-deification and totalitarian tactics. The concept of the "cult of the individual" or "cult of personality" was used by Nikita Khrushchev in a speech to the Twentieth Party Congress in 1956 to castigate the totalitarian dictatorship and autocratic rule of Josef Stalin, who had died in 1953. Specifically, he charged Stalin with ignoring the Politburo and the Central Committee and with arbitrary rule that resulted in the purging and death of thousands of party members. Subsequently, Khrushchev was himself charged with indulging in the cult of personality and was removed from power.

Significance   The downgrading of Stalin by men who had worked with him destroyed the idea of the infallibility of the Soviet Communist Party and its leaders. It produced consternation at home and in the once blindly obedient Communist parties in other countries, precipitating an international ideological crisis. The crumbling of Soviet control of the monolithic worldwide communist movement has been amplified by the increased economic strength of non-communist countries (making them less prone to revolution), by a growing nationalism within the Communist bloc, and by the nuclear stalemate. As a result, the Kremlin leaders have asserted a theoretical revision of Leninism which admits of various roads to socialism and holds that war with capitalist countries is not inevitable. The enunciation of the "cult of the individual" doctrine and the defamation of Stalin has led to a schism in the world communist movement and a contest for leadership between the Soviet Union and the People's Republic of China.

Soviet Union: Federal System   The division of power between the Soviet state and its fifteen union republics. The constituent units of the Soviet federal system are: The Russian Soviet Federated Socialist Republic; Ukrainian Soviet Socialist Republic; Byelorussian SSR; Uzbek SSR; Kazakh SSR; Georgian SSR; Azerbaijan SSR; Lithuanian SSR; Moldavian SSR; Latvian SSR; Kirghiz SSR; Tadjik SSR; Armenian SSR; Turkmen SSR; and the Estonian SSR. As understood in the West, federalism implies a formal division of power between the nation and its constituent parts that each is powerless to alter without the participation and consent of the other. In this sense, the Soviet Union is not a federation since observed practice indicates complete centralized authority in the national party and government.

Significance   Although the Soviet Union is a federal state in form but not in substance, the federal pattern serves party purposes in other ways. It recognizes the heterogeneity of the Soviet people in their cultures, languages, religions, ethnic origins, and historical traditions and manifests their desires to maintain separate national identities in spite of intensive efforts at Russification. Further evidence of the recognition of heterogeneity is seen in the creation of the Soviet of Nationalities as the upper house of the national legislature. The federal formula by which the attempt is made to accommodate both unity and diversity specifies that cultures can be national in form provided they are proletarian (Communist) in content. In this sense the Soviet Union is a federation, but its federalism has little to do with the division of decision-making power within the state.

Soviet Union: Politburo   The focus of supreme decision-making power in the Communist party and the Soviet state. Called the Presidium of the Central Committee after 1952, the older name, Politburo, was reinstituted at the Twenty-third Party Congress in 1966. The Politburo is composed of sixteen members and six candidate members.

Significance   The Politburo functions as a self-perpetuating group of national administrators and party leaders. Election by the Central Committee is ordinarily a formality, but when a power struggle develops within the Politburo, it may be resolved by the Central Committee. The Chairman of the Politburo is also the General Secretary of the party and controls the party apparatus. In the Politburo, policy can be debated freely in secret sessions, but once a decision is reached, a united front is presented to the world, and the party and government agencies carry it out.

Soviet Union: Presidium of the Council of Ministers
An executive committee or "inner cabinet" of the Council of Ministers that functions as the top-level decision-making body in the government apparatus. The Presidium is usually composed of the Chairman of the Council, two First Vice Chairmen, and several Vice Chairmen. The Chairman is the head of government, or Premier, of the Soviet Union. The First Vice Chairmen divide the supervision of administrative agencies at the highest level. At the next level, each of the Vice Chairmen supervises a cluster of related ministries.

Significance   The Presidium at the head of the Council of Ministers is the organ through which the directives of the Politburo are passed on by the Central Committee to the government. It is also the route by which the detailed information necessary for decision making moves up from the government bureaus through the party apparatus to the Politburo. Heads of individual ministries are professionally trained career bureaucrats. Members of the Presidium, however, usually rise through the party hierarchy and link the government and the party.

Soviet Union: Presidium of the Supreme Soviet   A

legislative-executive committee that directs the activities of the Supreme Soviet and exercises many functions of the parent body between sessions. The thirty-odd members of the Presidium are elected by a joint session of both houses of the Supreme Soviet. It is composed of a Chairman, one Vice Chairman from each of the union republics, a Secretary, and about twenty ordinary members. The Chairman, sometimes called the President, acts as the head of state for the Soviet Union. Under the constitution, the Presidium can convene the Supreme Soviet, issue decrees, interpret national laws, conduct nationwide referenda, void acts of the Council of Ministers when they do not conform to law, issue decorations, honors, and pardons, appoint and remove officers of the military high command, order mobilization, appoint and receive ambassadors, and proclaim martial law. Between sessions of the Supreme Soviet, the Presidium can appoint and dismiss ministers on the recommendation of the Chairman of the Council of Ministers, declare war in case of attack, and order the implementation of mutual defense treaties in cases of aggression.

Significance   Many of the functions of the Presidium of the Supreme Soviet resemble those of a cabinet in a Western democratic system. In fact, however, it is the party's Politburo that makes the significant decisions in the Soviet Union. All governmental institutions, including the Presidium, are vehicles for execution of party policies. The Presidium supplies the government with the essential quality of legitimacy between legislative sessions and demonstrates to the Soviet people the application of the principle of collective leadership.

Soviet Union: Secretariat of the Central Committee

The chief administrative organ of the Communist party. The

Secretariat exercises decision-making power second only to that of the Politburo, and drafts plans and policy proposals for that body. It is headed by a General Secretary (previously First Secretary) and about ten Secretaries. These men are leaders of the party with extensive cross-membership in the Politburo. Nominally elected by the Central Committee, they are in fact chosen by top party leaders. Their supervision of every phase of Soviet life is carried on through administrative staffs or sections that, in organization, resemble the ministries of a government. The Central Apparatus, which services the upper echelon of party agencies, is a proving ground for younger party members likely to rise to positions of prominence.

Significance　　The Secretariat supplies the continuity and expertise on which successful administration depends. Through hierarchically organized staff work, control over more than two hundred thousand full-time party officials is centered in the office of General Secretary. By exploiting this office with its powers of patronage, Josef Stalin and Nikita Khrushchev became the masters of the entire nation.

Soviet Union: State Farm　　A large-scale farm owned and operated by the state through the Ministry of Agriculture. State farm labor is hired for wages and farm managers are appointed by the state as in any large industrial enterprise. Many state farms began as experiment stations and demonstration units on public lands. Others have developed out of the "virgin lands" projects, which have taken labor from the cities to open unsettled territory to agriculture. State farms have also absorbed some collective farms and produce specialized crops such as cotton or, on the edges of industrial areas, potatoes and vegetables. *See also* COLLECTIVE FARM, p. 456.

Significance　　State farms are looked upon by party leaders as ideologically desirable because they advance the principle of complete collectivization and central direction established early in the industrial sector. Collective farms—the second major form of agricultural organization in the Soviet Union—are a compromise between state ownership and the peasant desire for individual holdings. Publicly owned state farms, however, can be run as agricultural factories through the application of industrial patterns of organization. State farms represent another effort by the Communist party to solve the long-standing problem of providing an increasingly industrial society with more adequate levels of agricultural support by collectivized methods.

Soviet Union: Supreme Soviet   The bicameral national legislature. The constitution describes the Supreme Soviet as the highest organ of state power and assigns it authority to make laws and adopt constitutional amendments. The Soviet of Nationalities, the upper chamber, with approximately 750 deputies, represents the various administrative units of the nation, such as the constituent republics, autonomous republics, autonomous regions, and national districts. Each of approximately 767 delegates to the lower house, the Soviet of the Union, represents a district of approximately 300,000 people. In contrast to the All-Union Party Congress, each delegate is directly elected by the people of the unit involved. Many delegates are administrators in the party, government, and military services. There is also a heavy percentage of manual workers and peasants and a scattering of notables in the arts, sciences, and letters. The jurisdiction of both houses is essentially equal. The Supreme Soviet meets every six to eight months in brief sessions and, therefore, cannot be considered a deliberative body in the Western sense. It appoints the Council of Ministers, the working executive of the government apparatus, and elects its own Presidium where policy decisions can be made in the long intervals between sessions of the Supreme Soviet. The Chairman of the Presidium of the Supreme Soviet acts as the head of state.

Significance   The Supreme Soviet's central position in the governmental structure creates an image of parliamentary democracy. This image distorts reality because no opposition, in the Western sense, is permitted to function within the system. Moreover, the Supreme Soviet is a law-validating rather than a law-making body. It is here that decisions made by the leadership in party and governmental executive organs are formally adopted. Election to the Supreme Soviet is often a recognition of service rendered to the party and Soviet society.

Unitary Government   A political system in which all power is centralized in the national government. In a unitary system, the subnational units of government are created by the central authority, which grants them whatever powers they exercise. In any modern state, local government is necessary, if only for administrative efficiency, but in the unitary pattern of organization the local units exist legally at the pleasure of the central government. Most of the governments of the world are unitary systems. *See also* FEDERAL GOVERNMENT, p. 429.

Significance   The unitary system of government has the advantage of simplicity when compared to a federal system. Power and responsibility exist in a single straight line between the people and the national government. This creates uniformity in law and administration and duplication of effort can be avoided. Unitary government, conversely, tends to develop large national bureaucracies and to reduce local self-reliance by transmitting problems to the national capital for solution.

INDEX

Cross-references to dictionary entries are located in the text at the end of each definition paragraph. Entries containing English and foreign-language equivalencies are indexed under each term. Page references in BOLD type indicate dictionary entries. For individual countries, consult *Guide to Countries* on p. xiii.

467

Notes

Notes

Notes

Notes

Notes

Notes

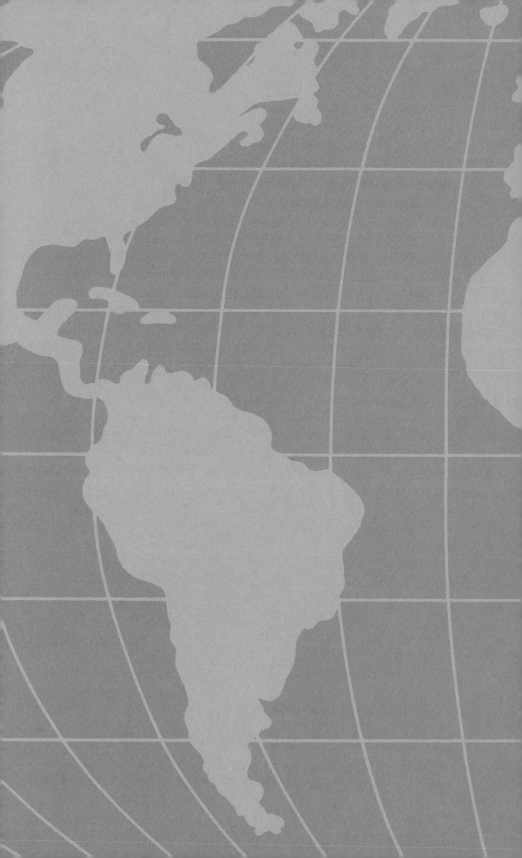